CW00449924

THE MAJOR LANGUAGES OF EASTERN EUROPE

THE MAJOR LANGUAGES Edited by Bernard Comrie

The Major Languages of Western Europe

The Major Languages of Eastern Europe

The Major Languages of East and South-East Asia

The Major Languages of South Asia, The Middle East and Africa

THE MAJOR LANGUAGES OF EASTERN EUROPE

EDITED BY
BERNARD COMRIE

London

First published as part of
The World's Major Languages in 1987 by
Croom Helm Ltd

Reprinted with revisions and additional material in 1990 by
Routledge
11 New Fetter Lane, London EC4P 4EE

© 1987 and 1990 Selection, introduction and editorial matter Bernard Comrie, chapter 1 Philip Baldi, chapter 2 Bernard Comrie, chapter 3 Bernard Comrie, chapter 4 Gerald Stone, chapter 5 David Short, chapter 6 Greville Corbett, chapter 7 Brian D. Joseph, chapter 8 Robert Austerlitz, chapter 9 Daniel Abondolo, chapter 10 Michael Branch, chapter 11 Jaklin Kornfilt.

All rights reserved. No part of this book may be reprinted or reproduced or utilized in any form or by any electronic, mechanical or other means, now known or hereafter invented, including photocopying and recording, or in any information storage or retrieval system, without permission in writing from the publishers.

British Library Cataloguing in Publication Data
Available on request

 ISBN 0–415–05771–X

Typeset in 10 on 12pt Times by Computype, Middlesex
Printed and bound in Great Britain by Mackays of Chatham

Contents

Preface

The text of this book has been extracted from that of *The World's Major Languages* (Routledge, 1987). The aim of that book was to make available information on some fifty of the world's major languages and language families, in a form that would be accessible and interesting both to the layman with a general interest in language and to the linguist eager to find out about languages outside his or her speciality. Not all of those interested in major languages of the world, however, have an interest that includes all parts of the world, and it therefore seemed advisable to publish portions of the original text in a series of paperbacks — *The Major Languages*. Readers interested in only one part of the world now have access to discussion of those languages without having to acquire the whole volume.

Perhaps the most controversial problem that I had to face in the original volume was the choice of languages to be included. My main criterion was admittedly, a very subjective one: what languages did I think the reader would expect to find included? In answering this question I was, of course, guided by more objective criteria, such as the number of speakers of individual languages, whether they are official languages of independent states, whether they are widely used in more than one country, whether they are the bearers of long-standing literary traditions. These criteria often conflict — thus Latin, though long since deprived of native speakers, was included because of its immense cultural importance — and I bear full responsibility, as editor, for the final choice.

The notion of 'major language' is obviously primarily a social character- isation, and the fact that a language was not included implies no denigra- tion of its importance as a language in its own right: every human language is a manifestation of our species' linguistic faculty and any human language may provide an important contribution to our understanding of language as a general phenomenon. In the recent development of general linguistics, important contributions have come from the Australian Aboriginal lan- guages Walbiri (Warlpiri) and Dyirbal (Jirrbal). Other editors might well have come up with different selections of languages, or have used somewhat different criteria. When linguists learned in 1970 that the last speaker of Kamassian, a Uralic language originally spoken in Siberia, had kept her language alive for decades in her prayers — God being the only other speaker of her language — they may well have wondered whether, for this person, *the* world's major language was not Kamassian.

Contributors were presented with early versions of my own chapters on Slavonic languages and Russian as models for their contributions, but I felt it inappropriate to lay down strict guidelines as to how each individual chapter should be written, although I did ask authors to include at least some material on both the structure of their language and its social background. The main criterion that I asked contributors to follow was: tell the reader what you consider to be the most interesting facts about your language. This necessarily meant that different chapters highlight different phenomena, e.g. the chapter on English the role of English as a world language, the chapter on Arabic the writing system, the chapter on Turkish the grammatical system. But I believe that this variety lent strength to the original volume, since within the space limitations of what is quite a sizable book it would have been impossible to do justice in a more comprehensive and homogeneous way to each of over 50 languages and language families.

The criterion for dividing the contents of the original volume among the four new books has been my assessment of likely common and divergent interests: if the reader is interested in language X, then which of the other major languages of the world is he or she likely to be most interested in? In part, my decisions have been governed by consideration of genetic relatedness (for instance, all Romance languages, including Rumanian, are included in *The Major Languages of Western Europe*), in part by consideration of areal interests (so that *The Major Languages of The Middle East, South Asia and Africa* includes the Indo-Iranian languages, along with other languages of the Middle East and South Asia). Inevitably, some difficulties arose in working out the division, especially given the desire not to have too much overlap among volumes, since a reader might want to acquire more than one of the paperback volumes. In fact, the only overlap among the volumes is in the Introduction, substantial parts of which are the same for all volumes, and in the fact that the chapter on Indo-European languages is included in both of the European volumes (given that most of the languages of both western and eastern Europe are Indo-European).

Editorial support in the preparation of my work on the original volume was provided by the Division of Humanities of the University of Southern California, through the research fund of the Andrew W. Mellon Professorship, which I held during 1983–4, and by the Max Planck Institute for Psycholinguistics (Nijmegen, The Netherlands), where I was a visiting research worker in the summer of 1984. I am particularly grateful to

Jonathan Price for his continuing willingness to consult with me on all details of the preparation of the text.

Bernard Comrie
Los Angeles

Abbreviations

abilit.	abilitative	conj.	conjunction
abl.	ablative	conjug.	conjugation
abstr.	abstract	conjv.	conjunctive
acc.	accusative	cont.	contemplated
acr.	actor	cop.	copula
act.	active	cp	class prefix
act.n.	action nominal	crs.	currently relevant state
adj.	adjective	Cz.	Czech
adv.	adverb	Da.	Danish
Alb.	Albanian	dat.	dative
Am.	American	dbl.	double
anim.	animate	decl.	declension
aor.	aorist	def.	definite
Ar.	Arabic	dent.	dental
Arm.	Armenian	deriv. morph.	derivational morpheme
art.	article	de-v.	deverbal
Ashk.	Ashkenazi(c)	dir.	direct
asp.	aspirated	disj.	disjunctive
AT	actor-trigger	Dor.	Doric
athem.	athematic	drc.	directional
aux.	auxiliary	DT	dative-trigger
Av.	Avestan	du.	dual
ben.	beneficiary	dur.	durative
BH	Biblical Hebrew	d.v.	dynamic verb
BN	B-Norwegian	E.	Eastern
Boh.	Bohemian	Eng.	English
BP	Brazilian Portuguese	ENHG	Early New High German
Br.	British		
BT	beneficiary-trigger	EP	European Portuguese
c.	common	erg.	ergative
Cast.	Castilian	ex.	existential-possessive
Cat.	Catalan	f.	feminine
caus.	causative	fact.	factive
cc	class concord	foc.	focus
Cent.	Central	Fr.	French
cl.	class(ifier)	fut.	future
clit.	clitic	g.	gender
comp.	comparative	gen.	genitive

ger.	gerund(ive)	neg.	negative
Gk.	Greek	NHG	New High German
Gmc.	Germanic	nm.	nominal
Go.	Gothic	NN	N-Norwegian
gr.	grade	nom.	nominative
GR	Gallo-Romance	noms.	nominalisation
gutt.	guttural	NP	New Persian
H	High	nt.	neuter
Hier. Hitt.	Hieroglyphic Hittite	Nw.	Norwegian
Hitt.	Hittite	O.	Oscan
hon.	honorific	OArm.	Old Armenian
IE	Indo-European	obj.	object
imper.	imperative	obl.	oblique
imperf.	imperfect(ive)	OBs.	Old Burmese
inanim.	inanimate	Oc.	Occitan
incl.	inclusive	OCS	Old Church Slavonic
indef.	indefinite	OE	Old English
indic.	indicative	OFr.	Old French
indir.	indirect	OFri.	Old Frisian
infin.	infinitive	OHG	Old High German
inst.	instrumental	OIc.	Old Icelandic
intr.	intransitive	OIr.	Old Irish
inv.	inversion particle	OIran.	Old Iranian
irr.	irrational	OLat.	Old Latin
It.	Italian	OLith.	Old Lithuanian
IT	instrument-trigger	ON	Old Norse
i.v.	intransitive verb	OP	Old Persian
L	Low	opt.	optative
lab.	labial	OPtg.	Old Portuguese
Lat.	Latin	orig.	original(ly)
Latv.	Latvian	OS	Old Saxon
LG	Low German	OV	object–verb
lig.	ligature	p.	person
lingu.	lingual	pal.	palatal
lit.	literally	part.	participle
Lith.	Lithuanian	pass.	passive
loc.	locative	pat.	patient
m.	masculine	PDr.	Proto-Dravidian
MBs.	Modern Burmese	perf.	perfect(ive)
ME	Middle English	pers.	person
med.	medio-passive	PGmc.	Proto-Germanic
MH	Middle Hebrew	PIE	Proto-Indo-European
MHG	Middle High German	PIt.	Proto-Italic
mid.	middle	Pkt.	Prakrit
MidFr.	Middle French	pl.	plural
ModE	Modern English	Po.	Polish
ModFr.	Modern French	pos.	position
MoH	Modern Hebrew	poss.	possessive
Mor.	Moravian	prep.	preposition
MP	Middle Persian	prepl.	prepositional
n.	noun	pres.	present
necess.	necessitative	pret.	preterit

prim.	primary	st.	standard
prog.	progressive	su.	subject
pron.	pronoun	subj.	subjunctive
PT	patient-trigger	sup.	superlative
Ptg.	Portuguese	s.v.	stative verb
Q	question	SVO	subject–verb–object
rat.	rational	Sw.	Swedish
recip.	reciprocal	tap.	tense/aspect pronoun
refl. pron.	reflexive pronoun	tg.	trigger
rel.	relative	them.	thematic
rep.	reported	Tk.	Turkish
res.	result	Toch.	Tocharian
Ru.	Runic	top.	topic
Rum.	Rumanian	tr.	transitive
Rus.	Russian	transg.	transgressive
Sard.	Sardinian	t.v.	transitive verb
SCr.	Serbo-Croat	U.	Umbrian
sec.	secondary	v.	verb
Seph.	Sephardi(c)	v.n.	verbal noun
sg.	singular	vd.	voiced
S-J	Sino-Japanese	Ved.	Vedic
Skt.	Sanskrit	VL	Vulgar Latin
Slk.	Slovak	vls.	voiceless
SOV	subject–object–verb	VO	verb–object
Sp.	Spanish	voc.	vocative
spec.	species	VSO	verb–subject–object

* The asterisk is used in discussion of historical reconstructions to indicate a reconstructed (non-attested) form. In synchronic discussions, it is used to indicate an ungrammatical item; (*X) means that inclusion of X makes the item ungrammatical; *(X) means that omission of X makes the item ungrammatical.

INTRODUCTION

Bernard Comrie

1 Preliminary Notions

How many languages are there in the world? What language(s) do they speak in India? What languages have the most speakers? What languages were spoken in Australia, or in California before European immigration? When did Latin stop being spoken, and when did French start being spoken? How did English become such an important world language? These and other similar questions are often asked by the interested layman. One aim of this volume — taking the Introduction and the individual chapters together — is to provide answers to these and related questions, or in certain cases to show why the questions cannot be answered as they stand. The chapters concentrate on an individual language or group of languages, and in this Introduction I want rather to present a linking essay which will provide a background against which the individual chapters can be appreciated.

After discussing some preliminary notions in this section, section 2 of the Introduction provides a rapid survey of the languages spoken in the world today, concentrating on those not treated in the subsequent chapters, so that the reader can gain an overall impression of the extent of linguistic diversity that characterises the world in which we live. Since the notion of 'major language' is primarily a social notion — languages become major (such as English), or stop being major (such as Sumerian) not because of their grammatical structure, but because of social factors — section 3 discusses

1

some important sociolinguistic notions, in particular concerning the social interaction of languages.

1.1 How Many Languages?

Linguists are typically very hesitant to answer the first question posed above, namely: how many languages are spoken in the world today? Probably the best that one can say, with any hope of not being contradicted, is that at a very conservative estimate some 4,000 languages are spoken today. Laymen are often surprised that the figure should be so high, but I would emphasise that this is a conservative estimate. But why is it that linguists are not able to give a more accurate figure? There are several different reasons conspiring to prevent them from doing so, and these will be outlined below.

One is that many parts of the world are insufficiently studied from a linguistic viewpoint, so that we simply do not know precisely what languages are spoken there. Our knowledge of the linguistic situation in remote parts of the world has improved dramatically in recent years — New Guinea, for instance, has changed from being almost a blank linguistic map to the stage where most (though still not all) of the languages can be pinpointed with accuracy: since perhaps as many as one fifth of the world's languages are spoken in New Guinea, this has radically changed any estimate of the total number of languages. But there are still some areas where uncertainty remains, so that even the most detailed recent index of the world's languages, Voegelin and Voegelin (1977), lists several languages with accompanying question marks, or queries whether one listed language might in fact be the same as some other language but under a different name.

A second problem is that it is difficult or impossible in many cases to decide whether two related speech varieties should be considered different languages or merely different dialects of the same language. With the languages of Europe, there are in general established traditions of whether two speech varieties should be considered different languages or merely dialect variants, but these decisions have often been made more on political and social grounds rather than strictly linguistic grounds.

One criterion that is often advanced as a purely linguistic criterion is mutal intelligibility: if two speech varieties are mutually intelligible, they are different dialects of the same language, but if they are mutually unintelligible, they are different languages. But if applied to the languages of Europe, this criterion would radically alter our assessment of what the different languages of Europe are: the most northern dialects and the most southern dialects (in the traditional sense) of German are mutually unintelligible, while dialects of German spoken close to the Dutch border are mutually intelligible with dialects of Dutch spoken just across the border. In fact, our criterion for whether a dialect is Dutch or German relates in large measure to social factors — is the dialect spoken in an area where Dutch is the standard language or where German is the standard language? By the same criterion, the three nuclear Scandinavian languages (in the traditional sense), Danish, Norwegian and Swedish, would turn out to be dialects of one language, given their mutual intelligibility. While this criterion is often applied to non-European languages (so that nowadays linguists often talk of the Chinese languages rather than the Chinese dialects, given the mutual unintelligibility of, for instance, Mandarin and Cantonese), it seems unfair that it should not be applied consistently to European languages as well.

While native speakers of English are often surprised that there should be problems in delimiting languages from dialects — since present-day dialects of English are in general mutually intelligible (at least with some familiarisation), and even the language most closely related genetically to English, Frisian, is mutually unintelligible with English — the native speaker of English would be hard put to interpret a sentence in Tok Pisin, the English-based pidgin of much of Papua New Guinea, like *sapos ol i karamapim bokis bilong yumi, orait bai yumi paitim as bilong ol* 'if they cover our box, then we'll spank them', although each word, except perhaps *i*, is of English origin ('suppose all ?he cover-up-him box belong you-me, all-right by you-me fight-him arse belong all').

In some cases, the intelligibility criterion actually leads to contradictory results, namely when we have a dialect chain, i.e. a string of dialects such that adjacent dialects are readily mutually intelligible, but dialects from the far ends of the chain are not mutually intelligible. A good illustration of this is the Dutch-German dialect complex. One could start from the far south of the German-speaking area and move to the far west of the Dutch-speaking area without encountering any sharp boundary across which mutual intelligibility is broken; but the two end points of this chain are speech varieties so different from one another that there is no mutual intelligibility possible. If one takes a simplified dialect chain A – B – C, where A and B are mutually intelligible, as are B and C, but A and C are mutually unintelligible, then one arrives at the contradictory result that A and B are dialects of the same language, B and C are dialects of the same language, but A and C are different languages. There is in fact no way of resolving this contradiction if we maintain the traditional strict difference between language and dialects, and what such examples show is that this is not an all-or-nothing distinction, but rather a continuum. In this sense, it is impossible to answer the question how many languages are spoken in the world.

A further problem with the mutual intelligibility criterion is that mutual intelligibility itself is a matter of degree rather than a clearcut opposition between intelligibility and unintelligibility. If mutual intelligibility were to mean 100 per cent mutual intelligibility of all utterances, then perhaps no two speech varieties would be classified as mere dialect variants; for instance, although speakers of British and American English can understand most of one another's speech, there are areas where intelligibility is likely to be minimal unless one speaker happens to have learned the linguistic forms used by the other, as with car (or auto) terms like British *boot, bonnet, mudguard* and their American equivalents *trunk, hood, fender*. Conversely, although speakers of different Slavonic languages are often unable to make full sense of a text in another Slavonic language, they can usually make good sense of parts of the text, because of the high percentage of shared vocabulary and forms.

Two further factors enter into the degree of mutual intelligibility between two speech varieties. One is that intelligibility can rise rapidly with increased familiarisation: those who remember the first introduction of American films into Britain often recall that they were initially considered difficult to understand, but increased exposure to American English has virtually removed this problem. Speakers of different dialects of Arabic often experience difficulty in understanding each other at first meeting, but soon adjust to the major differences between their respective dialects, and Egyptian Arabic, as the most widely diffused modern Arabic dialect, has rapidly gained in intelligibility throughout the Arab world. This can lead to 'one-way intelligibility', as when speakers of, say, Tunisian Arabic are more likely to understand Egyptian Arabic than vice versa, because Tunisian Arabic speakers are more often exposed to Egyptian Arabic than vice versa. The second factor is that intelligibility is to a certain extent a social and psychological phenomenon: it is easier to understand when you want to understand. A good example of this is the conflicting assessments different speakers of the same Slavonic language will often give about the intelligibility of some other Slavonic language, correlating in large measure with whether or not they feel well-disposed to speakers of the other language.

The same problems as exist in delimiting dialects from languages arise, incidentally, on the historical plane too, where the question arises: at what point has a language changed sufficiently to be considered a different language? Again, traditional answers are often contradictory: Latin is considered to have died out, although its descendants, the Romance languages, live on, so at some time Latin must have changed sufficiently to be deemed no longer the same language, but a qualitatively different language. On the other hand, Greek is referred to in the same way throughout its attested history (which is longer than that of Latin and the Romance languages combined), with merely the addition of different adjectives to identify different stages of its development (e.g. Ancient Greek, Byzantine Greek, Modern Greek). In the case of the history of the English language, there is even conflicting terminology: the oldest attested stages of English can be referred to either as Old English (which suggests an earlier stage of Modern English) or as Anglo-Saxon (which suggests a different language that is the ancestor of English, perhaps justifiably so given the mutual unintelligibility of Old and Modern English).

A further reason why it is difficult to assess the number of languages spoken in the world today is that many languages are on the verge of extinction. While it has probably been the case throughout mankind's history that languages have died out, the historically recent expansion of European population to the Americas and Australia has resulted in a greatly accelerated rate of language death among the indigenous languages of these areas. Perusal of Voegelin and Voegelin (1977) will show a number of languages as 'possibly extinct' or 'possibly still spoken', plus an even greater number of languages with only a handful of speakers — usually of advanced age — so that a language may well be dying out somewhere in the world as I am writing these words. When a language dies, this is sometimes an abrupt process, such as the death of a fluent speaker who happened to have outlived all other speakers of the language; more typically, however, the community's facility with the language decreases, as more and more functions are taken over by some other language, so that what they speak, in terms of the original language of the community, is only a part of that language. Many linguists working on Australian Aboriginal languages have been forced, in some cases, to do what has come to be called 'salvage linguistics', i.e. to elicit portions of a language from someone who has neither spoken nor heard the language for decades and has perhaps only a vague recollection of what the language was like.

1.2 Language Families and Genetic Classification

One of the basic organisational principles of this volume, both in section 2 of the Introduction and in the arrangement of the individual chapters, is the organisation of languages into language families. It is therefore important that some insight should be provided into what it means to say that two languages belong to the same language family (or equivalently: are genetically related).

It is probably intuitively clear to anyone who knows a few languages that some languages are closer to one another than are others. For instance, English and German are closer to one another than either is to Russian, while Russian and Polish are closer to one another than either is to English. This notion of similarity can be made more precise, as is done for instance in the chapter on the Indo-European languages below, but for the moment the relatively informal notion will suffice. Starting in the late eighteenth century, a specific hypothesis was proposed to account for such similarities, a hypothesis which still forms the foundation of research into the history and relatedness of languages. This hypothesis is that where languages share some set of features in common, these features are to be attributed to their common ancestor. Let us take some examples from English and German.

In English and German we find a number of basic vocabulary items that have the same or almost the same form, e.g. English *man* and German *Mann*. Likewise, we find a number of bound morphemes (prefixes and suffixes) that have the same or almost the same form, such as the genitive suffix, as in English *man's* and German *Mann(e)s*. Although English and

German are now clearly different languages, we may hypothesise that at an earlier period in history they had a common ancestor, in which the word for 'man' was something like *man* and the genitive suffix was something like -*s*. Thus English and German belong to the same language family, which is the same as saying that they share a common ancestor. We can readily add other languages to this family, since a word like *man* and a genitive suffix like -*s* are also found in Dutch, Frisian, and the Scandinavian languages. The family to which these languages belong has been given the name Germanic, and the ancestor language is Proto-Germanic. It should be emphasised that the proto-language is not an attested language — although if written records had gone back far enough, we might well have had attestations of this language — but its postulation is the most plausible hypothesis explaining the remarkable similarities among the various Germanic languages.

Although not so obvious, similarities can be found among the Germanic languages and a number of other languages spoken in Europe and spreading across northern India as far as Bangladesh. These other languages share fewer similarities with the Germanic languages than individual Germanic languages do with one another, so that they are more remotely related. The overall language family to which all these languages belong is the Indo-European family, with its reconstructed ancestor language Proto-Indo-European. As is discussed in more detail in the chapter on Indo-European languages, the Indo-European family contains a number of branches (i.e. smaller language families, or subfamilies), such as Slavonic (including Russian and Polish), Iranian (including Persian and Pashto), and Celtic (including Irish and Welsh). The overall structure is therefore hierarchical: the most distant ancestor is Proto-Indo-European. At an intermediate point in the family tree, and therefore at a later period of history, we have such languages as Proto-Germanic and Proto-Celtic, which are descendants of Proto-Indo-European but ancestors of languages spoken today. Still later in history, we find the individual languages as they are spoken today or attested in recent history, such as English or German as descendants of Proto-Germanic and Irish and Welsh as descendants of Proto-Celtic. One typical property of language change that is represented accurately by this family-tree model is that, as time goes by, languages descending from a common ancestor tend to become less and less similar. For instance, Old English and Old High German (the ancestor of Modern German) were much closer to one another than are the modern languages — they may even have been mutually intelligible, at least to a large extent.

Although the family-tree model of language relatedness is an important foundation of all current work in historical and comparative linguistics, it is not without its problems, both in practice and in principle. Some of these will now be discussed.

We noted above that with the passage of time, genetically related languages will grow less and less similar. This follows from the fact that, once two languages have split off as separate languages from a common ancestor, each will innovate its own changes, different from changes that take place in the other language, so that the cumulative effect will be increasing divergence. With the passage of enough time, the divergence may come to be so great that it is no longer possible to tell, other than by directly examining the history, that the two languages do in fact come from a common ancestor. The best established language families, such as Indo-European or Sino-Tibetan, are those where the passage of time has not been long enough to erase the obvious traces of genetic relatedness. (For language families that have a long written tradition, one can of course make use of earlier stages of the language, which contain more evidence of genetic relatedness). In addition, there are many hypothesised language families for which the evidence is not sufficient to convince all, or even the majority, of scholars. For instance, the Turkic language family is a well-established language family, as is each of the Uralic, Mongolian and Tungusic families. What is controversial, however, is whether or not these individual families are related as members of an even larger family. The possibility of an Altaic family, comprising Turkic, Mongolian, and Tungusic, is rather widely accepted, and some scholars would advocate increasing the size of this family by adding some or all of Uralic, Korean and Japanese.

The attitudes of different linguists to problems of this kind have been characterised as an opposition between 'splitters' (who require the firmest evidence before they are prepared to acknowledge genetic relatedness) and 'clumpers' (who are ready to assign languages to the same family on the basis of quite restricted similarities). I should, incidentally, declare my own splitter bias, lest any of my own views that creep in be interpreted as generally accepted dogma. The most extreme clumper position would, of course, be to maintain that all languages of the world are genetically related, although there are less radical positions that are somewhat more widely accepted, such as the following list of sixteen stocks, where a stock is simply the highest hierarchical level of genetic relatedness (just as a language family has branches, so families would group together to form stocks): Dravidian, Eurasiatic (including, inter alia, Uralic and Altaic), Indo-European, Nilo-Saharan, Niger-Kordofanian, Afroasiatic, Khoisan, Amerind (all indigenous languages of the Americas except Eskimo-Aleut and Na-Dene), Na-Dene, Austric (including Austro-Asiatic, Tai and Austronesian), Indo-Pacific (including all Papuan languages and Tasmanian), Australian, Sino-Tibetan, Ibero-Caucasian (including Basque and Caucasian), Ket, Burushaski – this schema still operates, incidentally, with two language isolates (Ket and Burushaski), i.e. languages not related to any other language, and retains a number of established language families as distinct (Dravidian, Indo-European, Nilo-Saharan, Niger-Kordofanian, Afro-asiatic, Khoisan, Australian, and Sino-Tibetan). In the survey of the distribution of languages of the world in section 2, I have basically retained my own splitter position, although for areas of great linguistic diversity and great controversy surrounding genetic relations (such as New Guinea and South America) I have simply refrained from detailed discussion.

While no linguist would doubt that some similarities among languages are due to genetic relatedness, there are several other possibilities for the explanation of any particular similarity, and before assuming genetic relatedness one must be able to exclude, at least with some degree of plausibility, these other possibilities. Unfortunately, in a great many cases it is not possible to reach a firm and convincing decision. Let us now examine some of the explanations other than genetic relatedness.

First, two languages may happen purely by chance to have some feature in common. For instance, the word for 'dog' in Mbabaram, an Australian Aboriginal language, happens to be *dog*. This Mbabaram word is not, incidentally, a borrowing from English, but is the regular development in Mbabaram of a Proto-Australian form something like **gudaga* (it is usual to prefix reconstructed forms with an asterisk). If anyone were tempted to assume on this basis, however, that English and Mbabaram are genetically related, examination of the rest of Mbabaram vocabulary and grammar would soon quash the genetic relatedness hypothesis, since there is otherwise minimal similarity between the two languages. In comparing English and German, by contrast, there are many similarities at all levels of linguistic analysis. Even sticking to vocabulary, the correspondence *man*: *Mann* can be matched by *wife* : *Weib*, *father* : *Vater*, *mother* : *Mutter*, *son* : *Sohn*, *daughter* : *Tochter*, etc. Given that other languages have radically different words for these concepts (e.g. Japanese *titi* 'father', *haha* 'mother', *musuko* 'son', *musume* 'daugher'), it clearly can not be merely the result of chance that English and German have so many similar items. But if the number of similar items in two languages is small, it may be difficult or impossible to distinguish between chance similarity and distant genetic relatedness.

Certain features shared by two languages might turn out to be manifestations of language universals, i.e. of features that are common to all languages or are inherently likely to occur in any language. Most discussions of language universals require a fair amount of theoretical linguistic background, but for present purposes I will take a simple, if not particularly profound, example. In many languages across the world, the syllable *ma* or its reduplicated form *mama* or some other similar form is the word for 'mother'. The initial syllable *ma* enters into the Proto-Indo-European word for 'mother' which has given English *mother*, Spanish *madre*, Russian *mat´*, Sanskrit *mātā*. In Mandarin Chinese, the equivalent word is *mā*, while in Wiyaw (Harui) (Papua New Guinea) it is *mam*. Once again, examination of other features of Indo-European languages, Chinese and Wiyaw would soon ' dispel any possibility of assigning Chinese or Wiyaw to the Indo-European language family. Presumably the frequency across languages of the syllable *ma* in the word for 'mother' simply reflects the fact that this is typically one of the first syllables that babies articulate clearly, and is therefore interpreted by adults as the word for 'mother'. (In the South Caucasian language Georgian, incidentally, *mama* means 'father' — and 'mother' is *deda* — so that there are other ways of interpreting baby's first utterance.)

Somewhat similar to universals are patterns whereby certain linguistic features frequently cooccur in the same language, i.e. where the presence of one feature seems to require or at least to foster the presence of some other feature. For instance, the study of word order universals by Greenberg (1963) showed that if a language has verb-final word order (i.e. if 'the man saw the woman' is expressed literally as 'the man the woman saw'), then it is highly probable that it will also have postpositions rather than prepositions (i.e. 'in the house' will be expressed as 'the house in') and that it will have genitives before the noun (i.e. the pattern 'cat's house' rather than 'house of cat'). Thus, if we find two languages that happen to share the features: verb-final word order, postpositions, prenominal genitives, then the cooccurrence of these features is not evidence for genetic relatedness. Many earlier attempts at establishing wide-ranging genetic relationships suffer precisely from failure to take this property of typological patterns into account. Thus the fact that Turkic languages, Mongolian languages, Tungusic languages, Korean and Japanese share all of these features is not evidence for their genetic relatedness (although there may, of course, be other similarities, not connected with recurrent typological patterns, that do establish genetic relatedness). If one were to accept just these features as evidence for an Altaic language family, then the family would have to be extended to include a variety of other languages with the same word order properties, such as the Dravidian languages of southern India and Quechua, spoken in South America.

Finally, two languages might share some feature in common because one of them has borrowed it from the other (or because they have both borrowed it from some third language). English, for instance, borrowed a huge number of words from French during the Middle Ages, to such an extent that an uncritical examination of English vocabulary might well lead to the conclusion that English is a Romance language, rather than a Germanic language. The term 'borrow', as used here, is the accepted linguistic term, although the terminology is rather strange, since 'borrow' suggests a relatively superficial acquisition, one which is moreover temporary. Linguistic borrowings may run quite deep, and there is of course no implication that they will ever be repaid. Among English loans from French, for instance, there are many basic vocabulary items, such as *very* (replacing the native Germanic *sore*, as in the biblical *sore afraid*). Examples from other languages show even more deep-seated loans: the Semitic language Amharic — the dominant and official language of Ethiopia — for instance, has lost the typical Semitic word order patterns, in which the verb precedes its object and adjectives and genitives follow their noun, in favour of the order where the verb follows its object and adjectives and genitives precede their noun; Amharic is in close contact with Cushitic languages, and Cushitic languages typically have the order object-verb, adjective/genitive-noun, so that Amharic has in fact borrowed these word orders from neighbouring Cushitic languages.

It seems that whenever two languages come into close contact, they will borrow features from one another. In some cases the contact can be so intense among the languages in a given area that they come to share a significant number of common features, setting this area off from adjacent languages, even languages that may happen to be more closely related genetically to languages within the area. The languages in an area of this kind are often said to belong to a sprachbund (German for 'language league'), and perhaps the most famous example of a sprachbund is the Balkan sprachbund, whose members (Modern Greek, Albanian, Bulgarian (with Macedonian), Rumanian) share a number of striking features not shared by closely related languages like Ancient Greek, other Slavonic languages (Bulgarian is Slavonic), or other Romance languages (Rumanian is Romance). The most striking of these features is loss of the infinitive, so that instead of 'give me to drink' one says 'give me that I drink' (Modern Greek *ðos mu na pjo*, Albanian *a-më të pi*, Bulgarian *daj mi da pija*, Rumanian *dă-mi să beau*; in all four languages the subject of the subordinate clause is encoded in the inflection of the verb).

Since we happen to know a lot about the history of the Balkan languages, linguists were not deceived by these similarities into assigning a closer genetic relatedness to the Balkan languages than in fact holds (all are ultimately members of the Indo-European family, though from different branches). In other parts of the world, however, there is the danger of mistaking areal phenomena for evidence of genetic relatedness. In South-East Asia, for instance, many languages share very similar phonological and morphological patterns: in Chinese, Thai and Vietnamese words are typically monosyllabic, there is effectively no morphology (i.e. words do not change after the manner of English *dog*, *dogs* or *love*, *loves*, *loved*), syllable structure is very simple (only a few single consonants are permitted word-finally, while syllable-initially consonant clusters are either disallowed or highly restricted), and there is a phonemic tone (thus Mandarin Chinese *mā*, with a high level tone, means 'mother', while *mǎ*, with a falling-rising tone, means 'horse'), and moreover there are a number of shared lexical items. For these reasons, it was for a long time believed that Thai and Vietnamese were related genetically to Chinese, as members of the Sino-Tibetan family. More recently, however, it has been established that these similarities are not the result of common ancestry, and Thai and Vietnamese are now generally acknowledged not to be genetically related to Chinese. The similarities are the results of areal contact. The shared vocabulary items are primarily the result of intensive Chinese cultural influence, especially on

Vietnamese. The tones and simple syllable structures can often be shown to be the result of relatively recent developments, and indeed in one language that is incontrovertibly related to Chinese, namely Classical Tibetan, one finds complex consonant clusters but no phonemic tone, i.e. the similarities noted above are neither necessary nor sufficient conditions for genetic relatedness.

In practice, the most difficult task in establishing genetic relatedness is to distinguish between genuine cognates (i.e. forms going back to a common ancestor) and those that are the result of borrowing. It would therefore be helpful if one could distinguish between those features of a language that are borrowable and those that are not. Unfortunately, it seems that there is no feature that can absolutely be excluded from borrowing. Basic vocabulary can be borrowed, so that for instance Japanese has borrowed the whole set of numerals from Chinese, and even English borrowed its current set of third person plural pronouns (*they*, *them*, *their*) from Scandinavian. Bound morphemes can be borrowed: a good example is the agent suffix *-er* in English, with close cognates in other Germanic languages; this is ultimately a loan from the Latin agentive suffix *-ārius*, which has however become so entrenched in English that it is a productive morphological device applicable in principle to any verb to derive a corresponding agentive noun.

At one period in the recent history of comparative linguistics, it was believed that a certain basic vocabulary list could be isolated, constant across languages and cultures, such that the words on this list would be replaced at a constant rate. Thus, if one assumes that the retention rate is around 86 per cent per millennium, this means that if a single language splits into two descendant languages, then after 1,000 years each language would retain about 86 per cent of the words in the list from the ancestor language, i.e. the two descendants would then share just over 70 per cent of the words in the list. In some parts of the world, groupings based on this 'glottochronological' method still form the basis of the only available detailed and comprehensive attempt at establishing genetic relations. It must be emphasised that the number of clear counter-examples to the glottochronological method, i.e. instances where independent evidence contradicts the predictions of this approach, is so great that no reliance can be placed on its results.

It is, however, true that there are significant differences in the ease with which different features of a language can be borrowed. The thing that seems most easily borrowable is cultural vocabulary, and indeed it is quite normal for a community borrowing some concept (or artifact) from another community to borrow the foreign name along with the object. Another set of features that seem rather easily borrowable are general typological features, such as word order: in addition to the Amharic example cited above, one might note the fact that many Austronesian languages spoken in New Guinea have adopted the word order where the object is placed before the verb, whereas almost all other Austronesian languages place the object after the verb; this change occurred under the influence of Papuan languages, almost all of which are verb-final. Basic vocabulary comes next. And last of all one finds bound morphology. But even though it is difficult to borrow bound morphology, it is not impossible, so in arguments over genetic relatedness one cannot exclude *a priori* the possibility that even affixes may have been borrowed.

2 Languages of Eastern Europe

Europe, taken here in the traditional cultural sense rather than in the current geographical sense of 'the land mass west of the Urals', is the almost exclusive preserve of the Indo-European family. This family covers not only almost the whole of Europe, but also extends through Armenia (in the Caucasus), Iran and Afghanistan into Soviet Central Asia (Tadzhikistan), with the easternmost outpost of this strand the Iranian language Sarikoli, spoken just inside China. Another strand spreads from Afghanistan across Pakistan, northern India and southern Nepal, to end with Bengali in eastern India and Bangladesh; an off-shoot from northern India, Sinhalese, is spoken in Sri Lanka, and the language of the Maldives is the closely related Maldivian.

In addition, the great population shifts that resulted from the voyages of exploration starting at the end of the fifteenth century have carried Indo-European languages to many distant lands. The dominant languages of the Americas are now Indo-European (English, Spanish, Portuguese, French), as is the dominant language of Australia and New Zealand (English). While in some countries these languages are spoken by populations descended primarily from European settlers, there are also instances where a variety of the European language is spoken by a population of a different origin, perhaps the best known example being the creolised forms of European languages (especially English, French and Portuguese) spoken by the descendants of African slaves in the Caribbean. It should be noted that these population shifts have not led exclusively to the spread of European languages, since many languages of India, both Indo-European and Dravidian, have also extended as a by-product, being spoken now by communities in the Caribbean area, in East Africa and in the South Pacific (especially Fiji).

Much of eastern Europe is covered by one branch of Indo-European, namely Slavonic, though a number of other Indo-European branches and languages occupy more limited territories. The Baltic languages, forming a branch of Indo-European closely related to Slavic, are spoken in Lithuania and Latvia. Rumanian is an outlier of the predominantly southwestern European Romance group of languages. Finally Greek, in its various historical and geographical variants, forms a separate branch of Indo-European (the branch sometimes being referred to as Hellenic).

Some other languages of Europe belong to the Uralic family. These include Hungarian, Finnish, Estonian and Lappish, to which can be added a number of smaller languages closely related to Finnish or Estonian. Other members of the Uralic family are spoken on the Volga and in northern Eurasia on both sides of the Urals, stretching as far as southern Siberia.

Turkish straddles eastern Europe and Asia, being spoken both in the Balkans and in Asia Minor. It belongs to the Turkic family, which is spoken in Turkey, parts of the Caucasus, some areas on the Volga, most of Soviet Central Asia (and stretching down into northwestern Iran), and large parts of southern Siberia. Turkic is perhaps to be joined in a single family (Altaic) with the Mongolian and Tungusic families, spoken in Mongolia, northern China and the eastern USSR.

3 The Social Interaction of Languages

As was indicated in the Preface, the notion of 'major language' is defined in social terms, so it is now time to look somewhat more consistently at some notions relating to the social side of language, in particular the social interaction of languages. Whether a language is a major language or not has nothing to do with its structure or with its genetic affiliation, and the fact that so many of the world's major languages are Indo-European is a mere accident of history.

First, we may look in more detail at the criteria that serve to define a language as being major. One of the most obvious criteria is the number of speakers, and certainly in making my choice of languages to be given individual chapters in this volume number of speakers was one of my main criteria. However, number of speakers is equally clearly not the sole criterion.

An interesting comparison to make here is between Chinese (or even more specifically, Mandarin) and English. Mandarin has far more native speakers than English, yet still English is generally considered a more useful language in the world at large than is Mandarin, as seen in the much larger number of people studying English as a second language than studying Mandarin as a second language. One of the reasons for this is that English is an international language, understood by a large number of people in many different parts of the world; Mandarin, by contrast, is by and large confined to China, and even taking all Chinese dialects (or languages) together, the extension of Chinese goes little beyond China and overseas Chinese communities. English is not only the native language of sizable populations in different parts of the world (especially the British Isles, North America, Australia and New Zealand) but is also spoken as a second language in even more countries, as is discussed in more detail in the chapter on English. English happens also to be the language of some of the technologically most advanced countries (in particular of the USA), so that English is the basic medium for access to current technological developments. Thus factors other than mere number of speakers are relevant in determining the social importance of a language.

Indeed, some of the languages given individual chapters in this volume have relatively few native speakers. Some of them are important not so much by virtue of the number of native speakers but rather because of the extent to which they are used as a lingua franca, as a second language among people who do not share a common first language. Good examples here are Swahili and Malay. Swahili is the native language of a relatively small population, primarily on the coast of East Africa, but its use as a lingua franca has spread through much of East Africa (especially Kenya and Tanzania), and even stretches into parts of Zaire. Malay too is the native language of relatively few people in western Malaysia and an even smaller number in Indonesia, but its adoption as the lingua franca and official language of both countries has raised the combined first and second language speakers to well over a hundred million. In many instances, in my choice of languages I have been guided by this factor rather than by raw statistics. Among the Philippine languages, for instance, Cebuano has more native speakers than Tagalog, but I selected Tagalog because it is both the national language of the Philippines and used as a linga franca across much of the country. Among the Indonesian languages, Javanese has more native speakers than Malay and is also the bearer of an old culture, but in terms of the current social situation Malay is clearly the dominant language of this branch of Austronesian. A number of other Indo-Aryan languages would surely have qualified for inclusion in terms of number of speakers, such as Marathi, Rajasthani, Panjabi, Gujarati, but they have not been assigned individual chapters because in social terms the major languages of the northern part of South Asia are clearly Hindi-Urdu and Bengali.

Another important criterion is the cultural importance of a language, in terms of the age and influence of its cultural heritage. An example in point is provided by the Dravidian languages, where Telugu actually has more speakers than Tamil; Tamil, however, is the more ancient literary language, and for this reason my choice rested with Tamil. I am aware that many of these decisions are in part subjective, and in part dangerous: as I emphasised in the Preface, the thing furthest from my mind is to intend any slight to speakers of languages that are not considered major in the contents of this volume.

Certain languages are major even despite the absence of native speakers, as with Latin and Sanskrit. Latin has provided a major contribution to all European languages, as can be seen most superficially in the extent to which words of Latin origin are used in European languages. Even those languages that have tried to avoid the appearance of Latinity by creating their own vocabulary have often fallen back on Latin models: German *Gewissen* 'conscience', for instance, contains the prefix *ge-*, meaning 'with', the stem *wiss-*, meaning 'know', and the suffix *-en* to form an abstract noun — an exact copy of the Latin *con-sci-entia*; borrowings that follow the structure rather than the form in this way are known as calques or loan translations. Sanskrit has played a similar role in relation to the languages of India, including Hindi. Hebrew is included not because of the number of its speakers — as noted in the chapter on Hebrew, this has never been large — but because of the contribution of Hebrew and its culture to European and Middle Eastern society.

A language can thus have influence beyond the areas where it is the native or second language. A good example to illustrate this is Arabic. Arabic loans form a large part of the vocabulary of many languages spoken by Islamic peoples, even of languages that are genetically only distantly related to Arabic (e.g. Hausa) or that are genetically totally unrelated (e.g. Turkish, Persian and Urdu). The influence of Arabic can also be seen in the adoption of the Arabic writing system by many Islamic peoples. Similarly, Chinese loan words form an important part of the vocabulary of some East Asian languages, in particular Vietnamese, Japanese and Korean; the use of written Chinese characters has also spread to Japan and Korea, and in earlier times also to Vietnam.

It is important to note also that the status of a language as a major language is far from immutable. Indeed, as we go back into history we find many significant changes. For instance, the possibility of characterising English as the world's major language is an innovation of the twentieth century. One of the most important shifts in the distribution of major languages resulted from the expansion of European languages, especially English, Spanish, Portuguese, and to a lesser extent French as a result of the colonisation of the Americas: English, Spanish and Portuguese all now have far more native speakers in the New World than in Britain, Spain or Portugal. Indeed, in the Middle Ages one would hardly have imagined that English, confined to an island off the coast of Europe, would have become a major international language.

In medieval Europe, Latin was clearly the major language, since, despite the lack of native speakers, it was the lingua franca of those who needed to communicate across linguistic boundaries. Yet the rise of Latin to such preeminence — which includes the fact that Latin and its descendants have ousted virtually all other languages from southwestern Europe — could hardly have been foreseen from its inauspicious beginnings confined to the area around Rome. Equally spectacular has been the spread of Arabic, in the wake of Islamic religious zeal, from being confined to the Arabian peninsula to being the dominant language of the Middle East and North Africa.

In addition to languages that have become major languages, there are equally languages that have lost this status. The earliest records from Mesopotamia, often considered the cradle of civilisation, are in two languages: Sumerian and Akkadian (the latter the language of the Assyrian and Babylonian empires); Akkadian belongs to the Semitic branch of Afroasiatic, while Sumerian is as far as we can tell unrelated to any other known language. Even at the time of attested Sumerian inscriptions, the language was probably already approaching extinction, and it continued to be used in deference to tradition (as with Latin in medieval Europe). The dominant language of the period was to become Akkadian, but in the intervening period this too has died out, leaving no direct descendants. Gone too is Ancient Egyptian, the language of the Pharaohs. The linguistic picture of the Mediterranean and Middle East in the year nought was very different from that which we observe today.

Social factors and social attitudes can even bring about apparent reversals in the family-tree model of language relatedness. At the time of the earliest texts from Germany, two distinct Germanic languages are recognised: Old Saxon and Old High German. Old Saxon is the ancestor of the modern Low German (Plattdeutsch) dialects, while Old High German is the ancestor of the modern High German dialects and of the standard language. Because of social changes — such as the decline of the Hanseatic League, the economic mainstay of northern Germany — High German gained social ascendancy over Low German. Since the standard language, based on High German, is now recognised as the standard in both northern and southern Germany, both Low and High German dialects are now considered dialects of a single German language, and the social relations between a given Low German dialect and standard German are in practice no different from those between any High German dialect and standard German.

One of the most interesting developments to have arisen from language contact is the development of pidgin and creole languages. A pidgin language arises from a very practical situation: speakers of different languages need to communicate with one another to carry out some practical task, but do not speak any language in common and moreover do not have the opportunity to learn each other's languages properly. What arises in such a situation is, initially, an unstable pidgin, or jargon, with highly variable structure — considerably simplified relative to the native languages of the people involved in its creation — and just enough vocabulary to permit practical tasks to be carried out reasonably successfully. The clearest examples of the development of such pidgins arose from European colonisation, in particular from the Atlantic slave trade and from indenturing labourers in the South Pacific. These pidgins take most of their vocabulary from the colonising language, although their structures are often very different from those of the colonising language.

At a later stage, the jargon may expand, particularly when its usefulness as a lingua franca is recognised among the speakers of non-European origin, leading to a stabilised pidgin, such as Tok Pisin, the major lingua franca of Papua New Guinea. This expansion is on several planes: the range of functions is expanded, since the pidgin is no longer restricted to uses of language essential to practical tasks; the vocabulary is expanded as a result of this greater range of functions, new words often being created internally to the pidgin rather than borrowed from some other language (as with Tok Pisin *maus gras* 'moustache', literally 'mouth grass'); the structure becomes stabilised, i.e. the language has a well defined grammar.

Throughout all of this development, the pidgin has no native speakers. The next possible stage (or this may take place even before stabilisation) is for the pidgin to 'acquire native speakers'. For instance, if native speakers of different languages marry and have the pidgin as their only common language, then this will be the language of their household and will become the first language of their children. Once a pidgin has acquired native speakers, it is referred to as a creole. The native languages of many inhabitants of the Caribbean islands are creoles, for instance the English-based creole of Jamaica, the French-based creole of Haiti, and the Spanish-and/or Portuguese-based creole Papiamentu (Papiamento) of the Netherlands Antilles (Aruba, Bonaire and Curaçao). At an even later stage, social improvements and education may bring the creole back into close contact with the European language that originally contributed much of its vocabulary. In this situation, the two languages may interact and the creole, or some of its varieties, may start approaching the standard language. This gives rise to the so-called post-creole continuum, in which one finds a continuous scale of varieties of speech from forms close to the original creole (basilect) through intermediate forms (mesolect) up to a slightly regionally coloured version of the standard language. Jamaican English is a good example of a post-creole continuum.

No pidgin or creole language has succeeded in gaining sufficient status or number of speakers to become one of the world's major languages, but pidgin and creole languages provide important insights into the processes that arise from natural language contact. And while it would probably be an exaggeration to consider any of the word's major languages a creole, it is not unlikely that some of the processes that go to create a pidgin or a creole have been active in the history of some of these languages — witness, for instance, the morphological simplification that has attended the development from Old English to Modern English, or from Latin to the modern Romance languages.

A few centuries ago, as we saw above, it would have been difficult to predict the present-day distribution of major languages in the world. It is equally impossible to predict the future. In terms of number of native speakers, it is clear that a major shift is underway in favour of non-European languages: the rate of population increase is much higher outside Europe than in Europe, and while some European languages draw some benefit from this (such as Spanish and Portuguese in Latin America), the main beneficiaries are the indigenous languages of southern Asia and Africa. It might well be that a later version of this volume would include fewer of the European languages that are restricted to a single country, and devote more space to non-European languages. Another factor is the increase in the range of functions of many non-European languages: during the colonial period European languages (primarily English and French) were used for most official purposes and also for education in much of Asia and Africa, but the winning of independence has meant that many countries have turned more to their own languages, using these as official language and medium of education. The extent to which this will lead to increase in their status as major languages is difficult to predict — at present, access to the frontiers of scholarship and technology is still primarily through European languages, especially English; but one should not forget that the use of English, French and German as vehicles for science was gained only through a prolonged struggle against what then seemed the obvious language for such writing: Latin. (The process may go back indefinitely: Cicero was criticised for writing philosophical treatises in Latin by those who thought he should have used Greek.) But at least I hope to have shown the reader that the social interaction of languages is a dynamic process, one that is moreover exciting to follow.

Bibliography

The most comprehensive and up-to-date index of the world's languages, with genetic classification, is Grimes (1988), which supersedes Voegelin and Voegelin (1977). A recent valuable work on genetic classification of the world's languages is Ruhlen (1987).

References

Greenberg, J. H. 1963. 'Some Universals of Grammar with Particular Reference to the Order of Meaningful Elements', in J. H. Greenberg (ed.), *Universals of Language* (MIT Press, Cambridge, Mass.), pp. 73–112
Grimes, B. F. (ed.). 1988. *Ethnologue: Languages of the World* (11th edition) (Summer Institute of Linguistics, Dallas)
Ruhlen, M. 1987. *A Guide to the World's Languages, Volume 1: Classification* (Stanford University Press, Stanford)
Voegelin, C. F. and F. M. 1977. *Classification and Index of the World's Languages* (Elsevier, New York)

1 INDO-EUROPEAN LANGUAGES

Philip Baldi

1   Introduction

By the term *Indo-European* we are referring to a family of languages which by about 1000 BC were spoken over a large part of Europe and parts of southwestern and southern Asia. Indo-European is essentially a geographical term: it refers to the easternmost (India) and westernmost (Europe) expansion of the family at the time it was proven to be a linguistic group by scholars of the eighteenth and nineteenth centuries (the term was first used in 1813). Of course modern expansion and migrations which have taken Indo-European languages to Africa, Hawaii, Australia and elsewhere around the world now suggest another name for the family, but the term *Indo-European* (German *Indogermanisch*) is now well rooted in the scholarly tradition.

Claiming that a language is a member of a linguistic family is quite different from establishing such an assertion using proven methods and principles of scientific analysis. During the approximately two centuries in which the interrelationships among the Indo-European languages have been systematically studied, techniques to confirm or deny genetic affiliations between languages have been developed with great success. Chief among these methods is the comparative method, which takes shared features among languages as its data and provides procedures for establishing proto-forms. The comparative method is surely not the only available approach, nor is it by any means foolproof. Indeed, other methods of reconstruction, especially the method of internal reconstruction and the method of typological inference, work together with the comparative method to achieve reliable results. But since space is limited and the focus of this chapter is Indo-European and not methods of reconstruction, we will restrict ourselves here to a brief review of the comparative method using only data from Indo-European languages.

When we claim that two or more languages are genetically related, we are at the same time claiming that they share common ancestry. And if we make such a claim about common ancestry, then our methods should provide us with a means of recovering the ancestral system, attested or not. The initial

Table 1.1: Some Basic Indo-European Terms

A. NUMERALS	*one*	*two*	*three*	*four*
Skt.	éka-	dvá, dváu	tráya-	catvára-
Gk.	oînos 'acc'	dú(w)o	treîs	téttares, téssares
Lat.	ūnus	duo	trēs	quattuor
Hitt.		dā-	*trijaš (gen.)	
Toch. A		wu	tre	śtwar
B		we	trai	ś(t)wãr
OIr.	oïn, õen	dãu, dõ	trī	ceth(a)ir
Go.	ains	twai	þreis	fidwõr
OCS	inŭ	dŭva	trĭje	četyre
Lith.	víenas	dù	trỹs	keturì
Arm.		erku	erek'	č'ork'
Alb.	një	dü	tre, tri	katër

B. ANIMAL NAMES	*mouse*	*wolf*	*cow*		*sheep*
Skt.	múṣ-	vŕ̥ka-	gó-		ávi-
Gk.	mûs	lúkos	boûs		ó(w)is
Lat.	mūs	lupus	bõs		ovis
Hitt.					
Toch. A			ko		
B			kau		
OIr.		olc 'evil'	bō		õi
Go.	mūs	wulfs	OIc. kỹr	OHG	ouwi
OCS	myšĭ	vlŭkŭ	gumŭno	'threshing floor'	ovĭca
Lith.		vi̇̃lkas	Latv. gùovs	Lith.	avìs
Arm.	mukn		kov		hoviw 'shepherd'
Alb.	mī	ulk			

C. BODY PARTS	*foot*	*heart*	*eye*	*tongue*
Skt.	pád-		ákṣi-	jihvá
Gk.	poús (gen. podós)	kardíā	ópsomai 'I will see'	
Lat.	pēs (gen. pedis)	cor (gen. cordis)	oculus	lingua
Hitt.	pat-	kard-		
Toch. A	pe		ak	käntu
B	pai		ek	kantwo
OIr.	īs 'below'	cride	enech	teng
Go.	fōtus	haírtō	augō	tuggō
OCS	pěšĭ 'on foot'	srĭdĭce	oko	językŭ
Lith.	pãdas 'sole'	širdìs	akìs	liežùvis
Arm.	otn	sirt	akn	lezu
Alb.	(për)posh 'under'		sü	

D. KINSHIP TERMS	*mother*	*father*	*sister*	*brother*
Skt.	mātár-	pitár-	svásar-	bhrátar- 'member of a
Gk. (Dor.)	mátēr	patér	éor (voc.) (Dor.)	phrátēr < brotherhood'
Lat.	mãter	pater	soror	fráter
Hitt.				
Toch. A	mācar	pācar		pracar
B	mācer	pācer		procer
OIr.	māthir	athir	siur	brāth(a)ir
OIc.	mõðir　Go.	fadar	swistar	brōþar
OCS	mati		sestra	bratrŭ, bratŭ
Lith.	mótė 'woman'		sesuõ	brólis
Arm.	mayr	hayr	k'oyr	ełbayr
Alb.	motrë			

	five	*six*	*seven*	*eight*	*nine*
	páñca	ṣáṭ-	saptá-	aṣṭá(u)	náva-
	pénte, pémpe	héks	heptá	oktố	enné(w)a
Hier. <	quīnque	sex	septem	octō	novem
Hitt.	paⁿta		šipta-		
	pën	säk	ṣpät	okät	ñu
	piś	ṣkas	ṣuk(t)	okt	ñu
	côic	sē	secht	ocht	noï
	fimf	saíhs	sibun	ahtau	niun
	pçtī	šestī	sedmī	osmī	devçtī
	penkì	šešì	septynì	aštuonì	devynì
	hing	vec'	evt'n	ut'	inn
	pesë	gjashtë	shtatë	tetë	nëntë

	pig	*dog*	*horse*
	sūkará-	śván-	áśva-
	hûs	kúōn	híppos
	sūs	canis	equus
		ku	yuk
	suwo	ku	yakwe
		cū	ech
	swein	hunds OE	eoh
	svinija		
Latv.	suvēns, sivēns Lith.	šuõ (OLith.)	ešvà, ašvà, 'mare'
	'young pig'	šun	
	thi		

Table 1.1 continued over.

Table 1.1 cont'd:

E. GENERAL TERMS	full	race, kind	month	die, death
Skt.	pūrṇá-	jána-	más-	mṛtá-
Gk.	plḗrēs	génos	mḗn	ámbrotos 'immortal'
Lat.	plēnus	genus	mēnsis	mortuus
Hitt.				merta
Toch. A			mañ	
B			meñc	
OIr.	lān	gein 'birth'	mī	marb
Go.	fulls	kuni	mēna, mēnōþs	maúrþr
OCS	plŭnŭ		měsęcĭ	mĭrǫ, mrěti
Lith.	pìlnas		ménuo	miȓti
Arm.	li	cin 'birth'	amis	
Alb.	plot		muai	

demonstration of relatedness is the easy part; establishing well-motivated intermediate and ancestral forms is quite another matter. Among the difficulties are: which features in which of the languages being compared are older? which are innovations? which are borrowed? how many shared similarities are enough to prove relatedness conclusively, and how are they weighted for significance? what assumptions do we make about the relative importance of lexical, morphological, syntactic and phonological characteristics, and about directions of language change?

All of these questions come into play in any reconstruction effort, leaving us with the following assumption: if two or more languages share a feature which is unlikely to have arisen by accident, borrowing or as the result of some typological tendency or language universal, then it is assumed to have arisen only once and to have been transmitted to the two or more languages from a common source. The more such features are discovered and securely identified, the closer the relationship.

In determining genetic relationship and reconstructing proto-forms using the comparative method, we usually start with vocabulary. Table 1.1 contains a number of words from various Indo-European languages which will demonstrate a common core of lexical items too large and too basic to be explained either by accident or borrowing. A list of possible cognates which is likely to produce a maximum number of common inheritance items, known as the basic vocabulary list, provides many of the words we might investigate, such as basic kinship terms, pronouns, basic body parts, lower numerals and others. From these and other data we seek to establish sets of equations known as correspondences, which are statements that in a given environment X phoneme of one language will correspond to Y phoneme of another language *consistently* and *systematically* if the two languages are descended from a common ancestor.

In order to illustrate the comparative method we will briefly and selectively choose a few items from tables 1.1 and 1.2, restricting our data to fairly clear cases.

old		vomit
sána- hénos senex	'last year's'	vámiti eméō vomō
sen sineigs	OIc.	vāma 'sickness'
sēnas hin		vémti

	mouse		mother		nine
Skt.	múṣ-		mātár-		náva
Gk.	mūs	(Dor.)	mátēr		enné(w)a
Lat.	mūs		māter		novem
Go.	mūs	OIc.	mōðir	Go.	niun

	dead	dog	race, kind
Skt.	mr̥tá-	śván-	jána-
Gk.	ámbrotos 'immortal'	kúōn	génos
Lat.	mortuus	canis	genus
Go.	maúrþr 'murder'	hunds	kuni

	'I am'		vomit		old
Skt.	ásmi		vámiti		sána-
Gk.	eimí		eméō		hénos 'last year's'
Lat.	sum		vomō		senex
Go.	im	OIc.	vāma 'sickness'	Go.	sineigs

We will first look only at the nasals *m* and *n*. Lined up for the comparative method they look like this:

	mouse	mother	nine	dead	dog	race, kind	I am	vomit	old
Skt.	m-	m-	-n-	-m-	-n	-n-	-m-	-m-	-n-
Gk.	m-	m-	-nn-	-m(b)-	-n	-n-	-m-	-m-	-n-
Lat.	m-	m-	-n-	-m-	-n-	-n-	-m	-m-	-n-
Gmc.	m-	m-	-n-	-m-	-n-	-n-	-m	-m-	-n-

Before we begin reconstructing we must be sure that we are comparing the appropriate segments. It is clear that this is the case in 'mouse', 'mother', 'dog', 'race, kind', 'I am', 'vomit' and 'old', but less clear in 'nine' and 'dead'. What of the double *n* in Gk. *enné(w)a*? A closer look reveals that *en-* is a prefix; thus, the first *n* is outside the equation. Similarly with *ámbrotos* 'immortal': the *á-* is a prefix meaning 'not' (=Lat. *in-*, Go. *un-*, etc.), and the *b* results from a rule of Greek in which the sequence *-mr-* results in *-mbr-*, with epenthetic *b* (cf. Lat. *camera* > Fr. *chambre*). So the *m*'s do indeed

Table 1.2: Inflectional Regularities in Indo-European Languages

A. Examples of Verb Inflection

	I am	*he, she is*
Skt.	ásmi	ásti
Gk.	eimí	estí
Lat.	sum	est
Hitt.	ešmi	ešzi
Toch. A		
B		ste
OIr.	am	is
Go.	im	ist
OCS	jesmŭ	jestŭ
OLith.	esmì	ēsti
Arm.	em	ē
Alb.	jam	është

B. Examples of Noun Inflection

tooth

	Skt.	Gk.	Lat.	Go.	Lith.
Sg.					
nom.	dán	odón	dēns	*tunþus	dantìs
gen.	datás	odóntos	dentis	*tunþáus	dantiēs
dat.	daté	odónti	dentī	tunþáu	dañčiui
acc.	dántam	odónta	dentem	tunþu	dañtį
abl.	datás		dente		
loc.	datí				dantyjè
inst.	datá				dantimì
voc.	dan	odón	dēns	*tunþu	dantiē
Pl.					
nom.	dántas	odóntes	dentēs	*tunþjus	dañtys
gen.	datám	odóntōn	dentium	tunþiwē	dantŭ
dat.	dadbhyás	odoūsi	dentibus	tunþum	dantìms
acc.	datás	odóntas	dentēs	tunþuns	dantìs
abl.	dadbhyás		dentibus		
loc.	datsú				dantysè
inst.	dadbhís				dantimìs
voc.	dántas	odóntes	dentēs	*tunþjus	dañtys

C. Examples of Pronoun Inflection

I, me

	Skt.	Gk.	Lat.	Hitt.	Go.	OCS
nom.	ahám	egő	ego	uk	ik	azŭ
gen.	máma(me)	emoū(mou)	meī	ammēl	meina	mene
dat.	máhyam(me)	emoí(moi)	mihī	ammuk	mis	mĭně(mi)
acc.	mắm(mā)	emé(me)	mē(d)	ammuk	mik	mene(mę)
abl.	mat		mē(d)	ammēdaz		
loc.	máyi			ammuk		mĭně
inst.	máyā					mŭnojǫ

C. Examples of Pronoun Inflection – *continued*
   you (sg.)

	Skt.	Gk.	Lat.	Hitt.	Go.	OCS
nom.	tvám	sú	tū	zik	þu	ty
gen.	táva(te)	soú(sou)	tuī, tīs	tuēl	þeina	tebe
dat.	túbhyam(te)	soí(soi)	tibī	tuk	þus	tebě(ti)
acc.	tvám(tvā)	sé(se)	tē(d)	tuk	þuk	tebe(tę)
abl.	tvát		tē(d)	tuēdaz		
loc.	tváyi			tuk		tebě
inst.	tváyā					tobojǫ

Note: Forms in parentheses are enclitic variants.

align, leaving us with a consistent set of *m* and *n* correspondences:

m : m : m : m   n : n : n : n

These alignments represent the horizontal or comparative dimension. Next we 'triangulate' the segments, adding the vertical, or historical dimension:

m : m : m : m   n : n : n : n

Finally, after checking all the relevant data and investigating their distributional patterns, we make a hypothesis concerning the proto-sound. In these two cases there is only one reasonable solution, namely *$*m$ and *$*n$:

*m   *n
m : m : m : m   n : n : n : n

At this stage of the analysis we are claiming that $*m >$ (develops into) *m* and $*n > n$ in the various daughter languages.

Neat correspondences such as these are more the exception than the rule in historical-comparative linguistics. It is far more common to find sets in which only a few of the members have identical segments. But the method of comparative reconstruction, when supplemented with sufficient information about the internal structure of the languages in question, can still yield replicable results. Consider the following data from table 1.1, supplemented by some additional material:

	six	old	race, kind (gen. case)	be
Skt.	ṣáṭ	sána-	jánasas	ástu 'let him be!'
Gk.	héks	hénos 'last year's'	géneos (génous)	éō (ō̃) 'I might be'
Lat.	sex	senex	generis	erō 'I will be'
Go.	saíhs	sineigs	(OCS slovese 'word')	ist 'he/she is'

We are concentrating here on the correspondences which include *s*, *h*, and *r*. In 'six' and 'old' we have the set *s* : *h* : *s* : *s* initially (cf. also 'seven' and 'pig'). In final position we find Ø : *s* : *s* : *s* in 'six' and 'old' (cf. also 'one', 'three', 'mouse' and 'wolf', among others). And in medial position we have *s* : Ø : *r* : *s* in 'race, kind' (gen.) and 'be'. What is or are the proto-sound(s)?

A brief look at the languages in question takes us straight to *s for all three correspondences. *s > *h* in Greek initially (weakens), and disappears completely medially, yielding a phonetically common pattern of *s* > *h* > Ø (cf. Avestan, Spanish). Final Ø in the Sanskrit examples is only the result of citing the Sanskrit words in their root forms; the full nominative forms (as in the other languages) would contain *s* as well (e.g. *jánas*, *sánas*, etc.). And the medial Latin *r* is the result of rhotacism, whereby Latin consistently converts intervocalic *s* to *r* (cf. *es*- 'be', *erō* 'I will be'; (nom.) *flōs* 'flower' (gen.) *flōris*).

From these few, admittedly simplified examples we see that the comparative method, when supplemented by adequate information about the internal structure of the languages in question and by a consideration of all the relevant data, can produce consistent and reliable reconstructions of ancestral forms. It is with such methods that Proto-Indo-European has been reconstructed.

2   The Languages of the Indo-European Family

The Indo-European languages are classified into eleven major groups (ten if Baltic and Slavonic are considered together as Balto-Slavonic). Some of these groups have many members, while some others have only one. Of the eleven major groups, nine have modern spoken representatives while two, Anatolian and Tocharian, are extinct.

2.1   Indo-Iranian

The Indo-Iranian group has two main subdivisions, Indo-Aryan (Indic) and Iranian. The similarities between the two subdivisions are so consistent that there is no question about the status of Indo-Iranian intermediate between Proto-Indo-European and the Indic and Iranian subgroups. The Indo-Aryan migrations into the Indian area took place some time in the second millennium BC.

2.1.1   Indo-Aryan (or Indic)

(See Chapter 1 of *The Major Languages of The Middle East, South Asia and Africa*, edited by Bernard Comrie (Routledge, 1990).)

2.1.2 Iranian
(See Chapter 5 of the same book.)

2.2 Hellenic

2.3 Italic
(See p. 170ff. of *The Major Languages of Western Europe*, edited by Bernard Comrie (Routledge, 1990).)

2.4 Anatolian
The Anatolian languages were unknown to modern scholars until archaeological excavations during the first part of this century in Boğazköy, Turkey, yielded texts which were written primarily in Hittite, the principal language of the Anatolian group. The texts, which date from approximately the seventeenth to the thirteenth centuries BC, were written in cuneiform script and contained not only Hittite, but Akkadian and Assyrian as well. Decipherment proceeded quickly and it was claimed by B. Hrozný in 1915 that the Hittite in the texts was an Indo-European language. It was later shown that Hittite contained a large number of archaic features not found in other Indo-European languages, which resulted in revised reconstructions of the proto-language. Now totally extinct, the Anatolian group contains, in addition to Hittite, Luwian, Palaic, Lydian and Lycian, the last three surviving only in fragments.

2.5 Tocharian
Around the turn of this century a large amount of material written in an unknown language was discovered in the Chinese Turkestan (Tarim Basin) region of Central Asia. The language represented in these texts is now known as Tocharian, and is unquestionably of the Indo-European group. The documents are chiefly of a religious nature, but also contain commercial documents, caravan passes and medical and magical texts. There are two dialects of Tocharian: Tocharian A, also known as East Tocharian or Turfan, and Tocharian B, also known as West Tocharian or Kuchean. The texts found in Chinese Turkestan are all from the period AD 500 to 1000, so this language has not played the same role as other twentieth-century discoveries like Hittite and Mycenaean Greek in the shaping of reconstructed Proto-Indo-European.

2.6 Celtic
The Celtic languages are largely unknown until the modern period, though it is clear from inscriptional information and place and river names that Celtic languages were once spread over a fairly wide section of Europe in the pre-Christian era. The Celtic languages are commonly classified into two groups: the Goidelic or Gaelic group, made up of Irish, Scots Gaelic and the extinct

Manx, and the Brythonic or Brittanic group, made up of Welsh, Breton and the extinct Cornish. The oldest records of Celtic are some sepulchral inscriptions from the fourth century AD, and Old Irish manuscripts which date from the late seventh to early eighth century AD.

Many specialists believe that the Celtic and Italic languages have a remote relationship intermediate between the disintegration of Proto-Indo-European and the establishment of the separate Celtic and Italic groups. The 'Italo-Celtic' topic recurs periodically in Indo-European studies.

2.7 Germanic
(See p. 58ff. of *The Major Languages of Western Europe*.)

2.8 Slavonic
(See p. 56ff.)

2.9 Baltic
This highly conservative group of Indo-European languages has played a significant role in Indo-European studies. Despite the fact that the oldest useful recorded material from Baltic dates from the mid-fourteenth century AD, Baltic has preserved many archaic features, especially in morphology, which scholars believe existed in Proto-Indo-European.

Only two Baltic languages are spoken today, Lithuanian and Latvian (or Lettish). Many others are now extinct, including Semigallian, Selonian, Curonian, Yotvingian and Old Prussian. Old Prussian is the most important of these; it became extinct in the early eighteenth century, but provides us with our oldest written documentation of the Baltic group.

The Baltic languages are considered by many specialists to be in a special relationship with the Slavonic languages. Those who follow such a scheme posit a stage intermediate between Proto-Indo-European and Baltic and Slavonic called Balto-Slavonic.

2.10 Armenian
Spoken now predominantly in Soviet Armenia, Armenian was probably established as a language by the sixth century BC. The first records of the language are from the fifth century AD, and it shows considerable influence from Greek, Arabic, Syriac and especially Persian. In fact, so extreme is the foreign influence on Armenian that it was at first thought to be a radical dialect of Persian rather than a language in its own right. Written in an alphabet developed in the fifth century, the language is quite conservative in many of its structural features, especially inflectional morphology and, by some recent accounts, consonantal phonology.

2.11 Albanian
The remote history of Albanian is unknown, and although there are

references to Albanians by Greek historians in the first century AD, we have no record of the language until the fifteenth century. Much influenced by neighbouring languages, Albanian has proven to be of marginal value in the reconstruction of Proto-Indo-European. There are two principal dialects of Albanian: Gheg, spoken in the north and in Yugoslavia, and Tosk, spoken in southern Albania and various colonies in Greece and Italy.

In addition to these eleven major groups, there remain a number of 'minor' Indo-European languages which are known only in fragments, glosses, inscriptions and other unpredictable sources. Though there is some dispute about the Indo-European character of some of these languages, scholars generally agree on the following as Indo-European: Ligurian (Mediterranean region), Lepontic (possibly affiliated with Celtic), Sicel (possibly affiliated with Italic), Raetic, Thraco-Phrygian (frequently connected with Armenian and Albanian), Illyrian (especially prevalent along the Dalmatian coast), Messapic (with uncertain Italic or Albanian connections), and Venetic (probably connected with Italic). None of these languages exists in sufficient material detail to be of systematic value in the reconstruction of Proto-Indo-European.

3 The Structure of Proto-Indo-European

There have been many attempts to reconstruct Proto-Indo-European from the evidence of the daughter languages. The discoveries of Hittite, Tocharian and Mycenaean Greek in this century have modified the data base of Indo-European studies, so it is not surprising that there have been frequent changes in views on Proto-Indo-European. Also, there have been a refinement of technique and an expansion of knowledge about language structure and language change which have modified views of the proto-language. In this section we will briefly review past and present thinking on Proto-Indo-European phonology, and we will then discuss commonly held positions on the morphological and syntactic structure of the proto-language.

3.1 Phonology

3.1.1 Segmental Phonology
The first systematic attempt to reconstruct the sound system of Proto-Indo-European was by A. Schleicher in the first edition of his *Compendium der vergleichenden Grammatik der indogermanischen Sprachen* in 1861. Using the sound correspondences worked out by his predecessors, Schleicher proposed the consonant system as in table 1.3 (from the 1876 ed., p. 10). Schleicher's vowel system was based primarily on the pattern found in Sanskrit whereby 'basic vowels' are modified by strengthening processes

Table 1.3: Schleicher's Reconstructed System

	unaspirated vls.	vd.	aspirated vd.	spirants vls.	vd.	nasals vd.	r vd.
gutt.	k	g	gh				
pal.					j		
lingu.							r
dent.	t	d	dh	s		n	
lab.	p	b	bh		v	m	

which the Indian grammarians called *guṇa* 'secondary quality' and *vṛddhi* 'growth, increment'. By these processes a basic three-vowel system is changed by the prefixation of *a* as follows (1876:11):

Basic Vowel	*First Increment*	*Second Increment*
a	a + a → aa	a + aa → āa
i	a + i → ai	a + ai → āi
u	a + u → au	a + au → āu

This system is not identical to the Sanskrit system; it is, however, patterned on it.

Schleicher's system soon gave way to the model proposed by the Neogrammarians, a group of younger scholars centred at Leipzig who had quite different views about Proto-Indo-European, and about language change generally, from their predecessors. The Neogrammarian system is embodied in the classic work of K. Brugmann, as in table 1.4 (1903:52).

Brugmann's system is much more elaborate than Schleicher's in almost every respect: there are more occlusives, more fricatives, diphthongs, etc. But probably the most significant difference is in the vowel system. Brugmann proposes a six short, five long vowel system which is much more like that of Greek or Latin than that of Sanskrit. This change was brought about by the discovery that a change had taken place whereby Sanskrit collapsed PIE *ĕ, *ŏ, *ă into ă (cf. Lat. *sequor*, Gk. *hépomai*, Skt. *sáce* 'I follow' (*e*); Lat. *ovis*, Gk. *óis*, Skt. *ávi-* 'sheep' (*o*); Lat. *ager*, Gk. *agrós*, Skt. *ájra-* 'field, plain' (*a*)). From this it could be seen that Sanskrit was not to be considered closest to the proto-language in all respects.

The Neogrammarian system, which in modified form still finds adherents today, was put to the test by the theories of Saussure and the findings of Kuryłowicz and others. Based on the irregular behaviour of certain sounds in the daughter languages, Saussure proposed that Proto-Indo-European had contained sounds of uncertain phonetic value which he called 'coefficients sonantiques'. According to Saussure, these sounds were lost in the daughter languages but not before they left traces of their former presence on the sounds which had surrounded them. For example, there is no regular explanation for the difference in vowel length between the two

Table 1.4: Brugmann's Reconstructed System

Consonants

Occlusives:	p	ph	b	bh	(labial)			
	t	th	d	dh	(dental)			
	k̂	k̂h	ĝ	ĝh	(palatal)			
	q	qh	g	gh	(velar)			
	qᵘ	qᵘh	gᵘ	gᵘh	(labio-velar)			
Fricatives:	s	sh	z	zh	þ	þh	ð	ðh	(j)
Nasals:	m	n	ñ	ŋ				
Liquids:	r	l						
Semi-vowels:	i̯	u̯						

Vowels (Brugmann 1903:67, 89, 122-38)

A.	Vowels:	e	o	a	i	u	ə	
		ē	ō	ā	ī	ū		
B.	Diphthongs:	ei̯	oi̯	ai̯	əi̯		eu̯	ou̯	au̯	əu̯
		ēi̯	ōi̯	āi̯			ēu̯	ōu̯	āu̯
C.	Syllabic Liquids and Nasals:	l̥	r̥	m̥	n̥	n̥̂	ŋ̥	
		l̥̄	r̥̄	m̥̄	n̥̄	n̥̄̂	ŋ̥̄	

forms of Gk. *hístāmi* 'I stand' and *stătos* 'stood'. Saussure theorised that originally the root had been *steA (A = a coefficient sonantique). The A had coloured the *e* to *a* and had lengthened it to *ā* in *hístāmi* before disappearing. The major changes ascribed to the action of these sounds include changing *e* to *o*, *e* to *a* and lengthening preceding vowels.

This new theory, based on abstract principles, was put to use to explain a wide range of phonological and morphological phenomena in various Indo-European languages. It came to be called the 'laryngeal theory', since it is thought that these sounds may have had a laryngeal articulation. Proposals were made to explain facts of Indo-European root structure, ablaut relations (see section 3.2.2) and other problems. Many proposals concerning the exact number of laryngeals, and their effects, were made. Some scholars worked with one, others with as many as ten or twelve. It remained an unverifiable theory until 1927, when Kuryłowicz demonstrated that Hittite preserved laryngeal-like sounds (written as *ḫ* or *ḫḫ*) precisely in those positions where Saussure had theorised they had existed in Proto-Indo-European. Some examples: Hitt. *ḫanti* 'front': Lat. *ante*; Hitt. *ḫarkiš-* 'white': Gk. *argés*; Hitt. *palḫiš* 'broad': Lat. *plānus*; Hitt. *meḫur* 'time': Go. *mēl*; Hitt. *u̯aḫanzi* 'they turn': Skt. *vāya-* 'weaving'; Hitt. *newaḫḫ-* 'renew': Lat. *novāre*.

The empirical confirmation that Hittite provided for Saussure's theories led to a complete reworking of the Proto-Indo-European sound system. We may take the system proposed by W. Lehmann as representative of these developments as in table 1.5 (1952:99):

Table 1.5: Lehmann's Reconstructed System

Obstruents:	p	t	k	kʷ	
	b	d	g	gʷ	
	bʰ	dʰ	gʰ	gʷʰ	
		s			
Resonants:	m	n			
	w	r	l	y	
Vowels:		e	a	o	e
	i·	e·	a·	o·	u·
Laryngeals:			x	γ	h ?

There are many differences between Lehmann's system and that of Brugmann. Note in particular the postulation of only one fricative, *s*, the lack of phonemic palatals, diphthongs, voiceless aspirates and shwa. These were all given alternative analyses, partly based on the four laryngeals which Lehmann assumed.

Recent criticisms of the Lehmann system (and others of its generation) centre on the typological naturalness of the overall system. While faithful to the comparative method, such a system seems to be in conflict with known patterns of phonological structure in attested languages. One problem lies in

Table 1.6: Szemerényi's Reconstructed System

Obstruents:	p	pʰ	b	bʰ				
	t	tʰ	d	dʰ				
	(k'	k'ʰ	g'	g'ʰ?)				
	k	kʰ	g	gʰ				
	kʷ	kʷʰ	gʷ	gʷʰ				
	s	h						
Resonanants:	y	w						
	m	n						
	l							
	r							
Syllabic Liquids and Nasals:	n̥	m̥		ŋ̥	m̥̄			
	l̥	r̥		l̥̄	r̥̄			
Vowels and Diphthongs:								
i		u	ī		ū		ei oi	eu ou
e ə o			ē	ō			ai	au
a			ā					

One to three laryngeals

the presence of the voiced aspirate stops without a corresponding series of voiceless aspirates. A principle of typological inference stipulates that the presence of a marked member of a correlative pair implies the presence of the unmarked member of that pair. Thus $bh \supset ph$. And as T. Gamkrelidze puts it (1981:591): 'Reconstructed systems should be characterized by the same regularities which are found in any historical system.'

Partly in response to such objections (which had been voiced earlier by both Jakobson and Martinet), O. Szemerényi proposed the system in table 1.6 (1980:142). Pursuing the dicta of typological structure and dependency, many scholars have recently begun a new approach to Indo-European sound structure. The focus of the new work has been the obstruent system of Proto-Indo-European, which has long presented problems to Indo-European scholars. Chief among the problems are the following:

(a) The traditional system without voiceless aspirates is in violation of certain markedness principles. But the solution of Szemerényi (and the Neogrammarians) to have a voiceless aspirated series only begs the question, since only one language (Sanskrit) has the four-way distinction of voiced/voiceless, aspirated/unaspirated. Thus the elaborate Proto-Indo-European system seems to rely far too heavily on Sanskrit, and is unjustified for the other groups.

(b) There has always been a problem with *b. It is extremely rare, and those few examples which point to *b (e.g. Lith. *dubùs*, Go. *diups* 'deep') are by no means secure.

(c) There are complicated restrictions on the cooccurrence of obstruents in Proto-Indo-European roots (called 'morpheme' or 'root structure' conditions) which are only imperfectly handled with traditional reconstructions. They are that a root cannot begin and end with a plain voiced stop, and a root cannot begin with a plain voiceless stop and end with a voiced aspirate, or vice versa.

(d) Plain voiced stops as traditionally reconstructed almost never occur in reconstructed inflectional affixes, in which Proto-Indo-European was rich. This is a distributional irregularity which canot be explained under the traditionally reconstructed system.

(e) It has long been a curiosity to Indo-European scholars that both Germanic and Armenian underwent similar obstruent shifts (the Germanic one came to be celebrated as 'Grimm's Law', and forms the backbone of much pre- and post-Neogrammarian thinking on sound change):

'Grimm's Law' and the Armenian Consonant Shift

PIE					Gmc.					Arm.			
*p	t	k	k^w	>	f	þ	h	h^w		h(w)	th	s	kh
*b	d	g	g^w	>	p	t	k	k^w/k		p	t	c	k
*bh	dh	gh	gh^w	>	b	d	g	g^w/g		b	d	z(j)	g

In the new reconstruction of the obstruent system, the pattern in the occlusives is based on a three-way distinction of voiceless stops/voiced aspirates/glottalised stops (see Hopper 1981, Gamkrelidze 1981, Gamkrelidze and Ivanov 1984). The traditional plain voiced stops are now interpreted as glottalised stops (ejectives).

Typologically Reconstructed Obstruents

	I Glottalised	II Voiced Aspirates/ Voiced Stops	III Voiceless Aspirates/ Voiceless Stops
Labial	(p')	b^h/b	p^h/p
Dental	t'	d^h/d	t^h/t
Velar	k'	g^h/g	k^h/k
Labio-velar	k'^w	g^{wh}/g^w	k^{wh}/k^w

The allophonic distribution of these segments has been a matter of some debate, and indeed each Indo-European language seems to have generalised one allophone or another, or split allophones, according to differing circumstances.

This new system provides phonetically natural solutions to the five problems posed above:

(a) The system with the three-way distinction above violates no naturalness condition or typological universal. In fact, it is a system found in modern Armenian dialects. Under this view, Indo-Iranian is an innovator, not a relic area.

(b) The near absence of *b now finds a simple solution. In systems employing glottalised stops, the labial member is the most marked. Thus this gap, unexplained by traditional views, is no longer anomalous.

(c) The complicated morpheme structure restrictions turn out to be fairly simple: two glottalised stops cannot occur in the same root; furthermore, root sounds must agree in voicing value.

(d) The absence of plain voiced stops in inflections turns out to be an absence of glottalics in the new reconstruction. Such a situation is typologically characteristic of highly marked phonemes such as glottalised sounds (Hopper 1981:135).

(e) Under the new system the parallel Germanic and Armenian consonant 'shifts' turn out to reflect archaisms rather than innovations. All the other groups have undergone fairly regular phonological changes which can be efficiently derived from the system just outlined.

As Bomhard has insightfully pointed out (1984), we must recognise different periods in the development of the various Indo-European groups.

Thus any attempt to arrive at an airtight, uniform reconstruction of Proto-Indo-European fails to recognise the unevenness of the records and the fact that some of the languages undoubtedly split off from Proto-Indo-European long before others did. This is especially true with Hittite, whose extreme archaism suggests that if it is not a 'sister' of Proto-Indo-European, it is at least a daughter that split off from Proto-Indo-European long before the latter started to disintegrate. It is for these reasons that Proto-Indo-European phonology continues to be a matter of debate.

3.1.2 Ablaut

In the oldest stages of Proto-Indo-European, verbs and probably nouns as well were differentiated in their various classes by a modification of the root-vowel rather than by the addition of suffixes to invariant bases, which we find predominating in later stages of the language. This type of vowel modification or alternation is known as 'ablaut' or 'vowel gradation'.

Vowel gradation patterns were based on the interplay of both vowel quality (qualitative ablaut) and vowel quantity or length (quantitative ablaut). The main alternations were between the basic root-vowel, usually *e*, called the 'normal grade', alternating with *o* ('*o*-grade'), zero (Ø) ('zero-grade') and lengthening plus change (lengthened *ō*-grade). In what follows I will treat the two ablaut types separately, though it should be emphasised that this is one system, not two. They are separated here because the daughter languages typically generalised either the qualitative or quantitative system, or eliminated ablaut altogether.

Qualitative Ablaut
The primary qualitative relations were based on the vowels *e* ~ *o* ~ Ø (*ei* ~ *oi* ~ *i*; *er* ~ *or* ~ *r̥*; *en* ~ *on* ~ *n̥*, etc.). Different forms of a morpheme were represented by different ablaut grades. This system is rather well

	e-grade		*o-grade*		Ø-*grade*	
Gk.	pét-omai	'I fly'	pot-é	'flight'	e-pt-ómēn	'I flew'
Gk.	ékh-ō	'I have'	ókhos	'carriage'	é-skh-on	'I had'
Lat.	sed-eō	'I sit'	sol-ium (<*sod-ium)	'throne'		
Lat.	reg-ō	'I rule'	rog-us(?)	'funeral-pyre'		
Lat.	teg-ō	'I cover'	toga	'a covering'		
Gk.	leíp-ō	'I leave'	lé-loip-a	'I left'	é-lip-on	'I left'
Lat.	fīdō (<*feidō)	'I trust'	foedus	'agreement'	fidēs	'trust'
Gk.	peíth-ō	'I persuade'	pé-poith-a	'I trust'	é-pith-on	'I persuaded'
Gk.	dérk-omai	'I see'	dé-dork-a	'I saw'	é-drak-on	'I saw'
Gk.	pénth-os	'grief'	pé-ponth-a	'I suffered'	é-path-on	'I suffered'

represented in Greek, but is recoverable in nearly every Indo-European language to one degree or another. (Note: $e \sim o \sim \emptyset$ alternation is not the only series, nor does this account consider the many interactions between vowel length and quality.)

Quantitative Ablaut

Quantitative ablaut patterns are based on the alternations of 'normal', 'lengthened', and 'reduced' varieties of a vowel, e.g. $o : \bar{o} : \emptyset; e : \bar{e} : \emptyset; a : \bar{a} :$ $\emptyset$. While represented vestigially in a wide number of Indo-European languages, (cf. Lat. *pēs*, gen. *pedis* 'foot'; *vōx* 'voice, *vocō* 'I call'; Gk. *patḗr*, *patrós* (gen.), *patéra* (acc.) 'father'), the quantitative system is most systematically represented in Sanskrit. This is the system which the Indian grammarians described in terms of *guṇa* and *vṛddhi* increments (though in a different order). Quantitive vowel alternation, in conjunction with the qualitative type, provided an important means of morphological marking in Proto-Indo-European, providing a basis for distinguishing different grammatical representations of a morpheme.

Normal Grade (=guṇa)	Lengthened Grade (=vṛddhi)	Reduced Grade
pát-ati 'he falls'	*pāt*-áyati 'he causes to fall'	pa*pt*-imá 'we fell'
kar-tṛ̣- 'doer'	*kār*-yá 'business'	*kṛ̥*-tá- 'done'
deś-á- (*e < ai*) 'region'	*daiś*-ika- (*ai < āi*) 'local'	*díś*- 'region, direction'

3.1.3 Accent

Because of the widely different accentual patterns found in the daughter languages, reconstructing the accent of Proto-Indo-European is a hazardous undertaking. Developments in all the descendant groups except for Sanskrit and Greek seem to be innovative, thus forcing us to rely heavily on our interpretations of accent in these two languages.

The best accounts of Proto-Indo-European accent suggest that it was a pitch accent system. Every word (except clitics, which were unaccented) had one and only one accented syllable which received high pitch accent. The accent was 'free' in that it could fall on any syllable in a word, its specific position being conditioned by morphological considerations; accent was one means of marking grammatical categories in Proto-Indo-European. (For a parallel, cf. Eng. *rébel* (n.): *rebél* (v.); *cónflict* (n.): *conflíct* (v.).)

For example, some noun cases are typically accented on the inflections, while others are accented on the root for 'foot'. Here we see that the nominative and accusative cases, the so-called 'strong cases', have root accent, while the genitive and dative (and instrumental) have inflectional accent, indicating that accent is interacting with case markers to indicate grammatical function.

Root/Inflectional Accent (Nouns)

	Gk.	Skt.
nom.	poús	pất
acc.	póda	pắdam
gen.	podós	padás (gen./abl.)
dat.	podí	padé
		padí (loc.)

Similarly, some verbal forms are accented on roots, some on inflections:

Root/Inflectional Accent (Verbs)

	Pres.	Perf.	Perf. Pl.	Part.
Skt. 'turn'	vártāmi	vavárta	vavŗtimá	vŗtanáḥ
OE 'become'	weorþe	wearþ	wurdon	worden

The original nature of the Sanskrit accent in the various morphological categories is confirmed by the evidence of Germanic, which, though it has root-initial accent throughout, treated certain obstruent forms differently (þ, ð (d)) depending on whether the accent originally preceded (þ) or followed (ð (d)) the sound in question (Verner's Law). For further evidence, cf. the following forms for 'point out, show':

Skt. didéśa (1st sg. perf.):   OE tāh OHG zeh (<*dedóika)
      didiśimá (1st pl. perf.):   tigon zigum (<*dedikmé)

3.2 Morphology
As we mentioned in the preceding discussion, the unevenness of historical records and huge chronological gaps among many of the languages (e.g. 3,000 years between Hittite and Lithuanian) pose special problems for the reconstruction of phonology. These same problems exist in the reconstruction of morphology, perhaps even more dramatically because of the much larger inventory of morphological elements. Many of the older, well-documented languages, especially Latin, Greek and Sanskrit, have very complex morphologies: they have well-developed case systems in nouns, adjectives and pronouns; they have finely marked gender and number categories with fixed concord relations. In the verb they have elaborate systems of tense, voice, mood and aspect, as well as number markers and even gender concord in some forms, all marked with complex morphological formatives.

Many Indo-European languages reflect this complex morphology to one degree or another: Baltic, Slavonic, Celtic, Armenian and, in part, Tocharian, in addition to Latin, Greek and Sanskrit. But many of the other languages of which we have adequate records show much less morphological complexity, with fewer formal categories and distinctions; and it is not only the modern ones. Hittite, Germanic, Tocharian (in part) and Albanian do not agree with the other groups in morphological complexity.

What does the analyst do? Traditionally, scholars have reconstructed the largest composite system which the data allow. Thus reconstructed Proto-Indo-European has assumed all the features of the attested languages. When a particular language shows a given feature, this is evidence for the prior existence of that feature. And when a given language does not show that feature, it is assumed that the feature has been lost, or that it has merged with another feature in that language. This preference for over-differentiated proto-systems reflects a methodological bias on the part of linguists (and not only Indo-Europeanists) to postulate rules of loss or deletion from full forms rather than to assume rules of accretion or addition from impoverished forms. In short, it is easier to assume a specific something and make it disappear than it is to assume nothing and specify when it develops into a specific something.

The fact is that the highly complex morphological systems of Sanskrit, Greek, Latin, Baltic and Slavonic must have come from somewhere! There is no justifiable reason to assume that Proto-Indo-European emerged full-blown with no history of its own. We must keep this in mind as we proceed.

3.2.1 Nominal and Pronominal Morphology

Traditionally, Proto-Indo-European is considered to be an inflecting language which uses case markers to indicate grammatical relations between nominal elements and other words in a sentence, and to indicate gender and number agreement between words in phrases. Of all the Indo-European languages, Sanskrit has the most detailed nominal morphology. It has eight cases (nominative, vocative, accusative, genitive, ablative, dative, locative and instrumental), three genders (masculine, feminine and neuter), and three numbers (singular, plural and dual). No other Indo-European language has such detailed nominal morphology: Old Church Slavonic, Lithuanian and (by some accounts) Old Armenian have seven cases, and Latin has six. But Greek, Old Irish and Albanian have only five; Germanic has only four, and Hittite may have had as few as four. In gender categories most of the groups have the three mentioned above, but Hittite and a few others have no such system, nor is there any reason to believe they ever did. The same is true with number: Sanskrit, Greek and Old Irish, for example, show the three-way singular/plural/dual distinction, and there are apparent relics of it in Latin and Hittite. Do we assume that it was lost in those groups which do not show it, or do we assume that it never developed in those languages?

This is not the place to debate the history of Indo-European noun inflection or the philosophy of reconstruction. So, following Shields (1981) we will give a brief chronological overview of what *might* have been the developmental stages in the prehistory of Proto-Indo-European. In this way one might be able to imagine how various languages might have broken off from the main stock during the formation of Proto-Indo-European. We must not think of Proto-Indo-European as a single monolithic entity, uniform and dialect-free, which existed at a certain time in a single place before it began to disintegrate. Rather, we must recognise that this language was itself the product of millennia of development. As Ivanov puts it (1965:51):

> Within the limits of the case systems of the Indo-European languages it is possible to distinguish chronological layers of various epochs beginning with the pre-inflectional in certain forms of the locative and in compound words ... right up to the historical period when the case systems were being formed ... Between these two extreme points one must assume a whole series of intermediate points. (Quoted from Schmalstieg 1980:46.)

Shields postulates the following five stages in the development of Proto-Indo-European:

Stage I. In this, the formative period of the language, Proto-Indo-European might have been an isolating language, like Chinese, in which words were monosyllabic roots and there was no complex morphology. At this point there was probably no distinction between nouns and verbs, and no agreement or concord. The lack of agreement or concord in compounds like Gk. *akrópolis* (not **akrápolis*) 'high or upper city' and *logopoiós* (not **logompoiós*) 'prose-writer' attests to this stage. Gender was based on a distinction between animate, inanimate and natural agents.

Stage II. During this period Proto-Indo-European became an ergative system, i.e. one in which the subject of a transitive verb is in a different case from the subject of an intransitive verb, and in which the object of a transitive verb is in the same case as the subject of an intransitive verb (in English it would be something like *I* (subject) *see* (trans.) *her* (object), but *her* (subject) *falls* (intrans.)). Evidence for this stage comes from noun inflection patterns in different gender categories in various languages, as well as occasional irregular subject patterns in some languages in which oblique cases serve as subjects. At this time there were only two cases, the agent case in *$\emptyset$* or *r*, and the absolutive case in *N*. Through the development of a concord relationship between verbal suffixes and noun suffixes, Proto-Indo-European starts to develop into a nominative/accusative language.

Stage III. The oblique cases start to develop, primarily from the fusion of adverbs and particles onto noun stems. Nominative and vocative functions become generalised, and gender distinctions start to develop. As the ergative marker develops into a generalised subject marker, the language changes into a nominative/accusative type, where the subjects of transitive and intransitive verbs are the same (cf. Eng. *He sees Bill*: *He falls*).

Stage IV. Dative, instrumental, locative and genitive/ablative functions start to emerge as separate entities. The dual number starts to develop, and the gender distinction (found in Hittite) based on the animate/inanimate distinction first appears. Gender and number agreement within phrases as well as concord between nouns and verbs becomes fixed. This is now close to traditionally reconstructed Proto-Indo-European.

Stage V. This is a period of highly accelerated dialect division, and the beginning of the disintegration of Proto-Indo-European. New endings and formal markers develop within various groups, with formal and functional differentiations of case forms. The feminine gender emerges.

The preceding summary, based on Shields's 1981 speculations, provides us with a brief but provocative account of the prehistory of Proto-Indo-European. We will now proceed to a discussion of the traditional system as reconstructed in the nineteenth and twentieth centuries. This system represents one, surely very late, stage of Proto-Indo-European from which some, but not all of the daughter languages descended. In this context it has validity as the most probable system based on the comparative method.

Proto-Indo-European nouns and adjectives were inflected in three genders, three numbers and eight cases. Through a comparison of the various languages we arrive at the following reconstruction of case endings (Szemerényi 1980:146):

Reconstructed Case Endings

	Sg.	Pl.	Du.
Nom.	-s, -∅	-es	
Voc.	-∅	-es	-e, -ī/-i
Acc.	-m/-m̥	-ns/-n̥s	
Gen.	-es/-os/-s	-om/-ōm	-ous? -ōs?
Abl.	-es/-os/-s; -ed/-od	-bh(y)os, -mos	-bhyō, -mō
Dat.	-ei	-bh(y)os, -mos	-bhyō, -mō
Loc.	-i	-su	-ou
Inst.	-e/-o, -bhi/-mi	-bhis/-mis, -ōis	-bhyō, -mō

These endings represent a composite set of possibilities for the Proto-Indo-European noun; no single form reflects them all. The structure of the noun was based on the following scheme: a *root*, which carried the basic lexical meaning, plus a *stem*, which marked morphological class, plus an *ending*, which carried grammatical information based on syntactic function. Thus a word like Lat. nom. sg. m. *lupus* (OLat. *lupos*) 'wolf' would be *lup + o + s*. Generally we recognise consonantal and vocalic stem nouns. Some examples of consonantal stems are **ped* 'foot' (Skt. *pád-*, Gk. (gen.) *podós*, Lat. (gen.) *pedis*); **edont-/*dont-/*dent-* 'tooth' (Skt. *dánt-*, Gk. (gen.) *odóntos*, Lat. (gen.) *dentis*); **ĝhom-* 'man' (Lat. *homo*, Go. *guma*); **māter* 'mother' (Skt. *mātár-*, Gk. *mḗtēr*, Lat. *māter*); **gonos/*genos-* 'race' (Skt.

(gen.) *jánasas*, Gk. (gen.) *géneos* (< *génesos), Lat. (gen.) *generis* (< *genesis)).

To illustrate some of the vocalic stems we may cite the *i*-stem form **egnis/* *ognis 'fire' (Skt. *agní-*, Lat. *ignis*) or *potis 'master' (Skt. *páti-*, Gk. *pósis*, Lat. *potis*); an *-eu-* diphthongal stem like **dyeu-* 'sky, light' (Skt. nom. *dyāús*, Gk. *Zeús*, Lat. *diēs*, *-diūs*); and finally the *o*-stem *wḷkʷos 'wolf ' (Skt. *vṛka-*, Gk. *lúkos*, Lat. *lupus*).

The Proto-Indo-European adjective followed the same declensional pattern as the noun. Adjectives were inflected for gender, number and case, in agreement with the nouns which they modified. Some adjectives are inflected in masculine, feminine and neuter according to m. *-o* stem, f. *-ā* stem and nt. *-om* patterns, as in *newos, *newā, *newom 'new' (cf. Skt. *návas*, *návā*, *návam*, Gk. *né(w)os*, *né(w)ā*, *né(w)on*, Lat. *novus*, *nova*, *novum*). Other adjectival forms have identical masculine and feminine forms, but separate neuter (cf. Lat. *facilis, facile* 'easy'), and still others have all three identical in some cases (cf. Lat. *ferens* 'carrying' (< *ferentis)).

Adjectives were compared in three degrees, as in English *tall*, *taller*, *tallest*. Comparative forms are typically derived from positive forms through the suffixation of **-yes*, **-yos* (cf. Lat. *seniōr* 'older' (*senex*), Skt. *sánya* 'older' (*sána-*), and with **-tero-* (cf. Gk. *ponērós* 'wicked', comp. *ponēróteros*). Superlatives are often found with the suffixes *-isto-* and *-samo-*, though there are others. Some examples: Gk. *béltistos*, Go. *batista* 'best', Skt. *návistha-* 'newest' (*náva-*). For **-samo-*, cf. Lat. *proximus* 'nearest', *maximus* 'greatest', OIr. *nessam* 'next'. As with Gk. *béltistos*, Go. *batista*, adjectival comparison was occasionally carried out with suppletive forms, cf. Lat. *bonus, melior, optimus* 'good, better, best'.

Proto-Indo-European distinguished many different types of pronouns. A short sample of personal pronouns is given in table 1.2. Pronouns followed the same general inflectional patterns as nouns, though they have their own set of endings for many of the case forms, except personal pronouns, which are almost entirely different from nouns and did not mark gender. In addition to the personal pronouns 'I/we', 'you/you' (**eĝ(h)om*, *eĝō/*wei*, *ṇsmés; *tū, **tu/*yūs*, *usmés), Proto-Indo-European also had demonstrative pronouns with the form (m.) *so, (f.) *sā, (nt.) *tod and *is, *ī, *id. These also served the function of third person pronouns in many of the Indo-European languages. The first of these is represented in Skt. *sa, sā, tad*, Go. *sa, so, þata* and Gk. *ho, hē, tó*. The latter Proto-Indo-European demonstrative forms are represented in Lat. *is, ea, id* and in various forms in Sanskrit and Germanic such as Skt. nom. sg. nt. *id-ám*, acc. sg. m. *im-ám*, f. *im-ā́m*, and Go. acc. sg. *in-a*, nom. pl. m. *eis*, acc. pl. *ins*.

Interrogative and relative pronouns are also well represented, though it is not possible to reconstruct a single relative. From a PIE (anim.) *kʷis, (inanim.) *kʷid, which had either interrogative or indefinite meaning, we find Lat. *quis, quis, quid*, Gk. *tís, tís, tí*, Hitt. *kwis, kwit*, Skt. *kás, ká, kim*, and a number of variants of this stem with interrogative or indefinite meaning. In Italic, Tocharian, Hittite, Celtic and Germanic the root *$k^{w}is$, *$k^{w}id$ also functioned as a relative pronoun (as does Eng. *who*). In Indo-Iranian, Greek and Slavonic a different form *yos, *$yā$, *yod served the relative function (cf. Skt. *yás*, *yā́*, *yád*, Gk. *hós*, *hḗ*, *hó*). There is also a recoverable reflexive form *sew-, *sw (OCS *sę*, Lat. *se*, Go. *si-k*).

3.2.2 Verb Morphology

The Proto-Indo-European verb presents the analyst with many of the same problems as the noun. The various daughter languages show wide variation in formal categories and inflectional complexity; some of the ancient classical languages, especially Greek, Latin and Sanskrit, have highly diversified formal structure characterised by intricate relations of tense, mood, voice and aspect. Others, like Hittite and Germanic, have fairly simple morphological systems with few formal distinctions. We can contrast formal complexity by the following simple chart.

Verbal Categories

	Voices	Moods	Tenses
Greek	3	4	7
Sanskrit	3	4	7
Hittite	2	2	2
Gothic	2	3	2

As with the noun, we may take several paths to a reconstructed system. We can propose a full Proto-Indo-European system with losses and syncretisms in Hittite and Gothic, we may propose a simple Proto-Indo-European system with additive, accretionary developments in Greek and Sanskrit, or we may assume different periods of development and break-off from the parent language. Accepting this final alternative in effect prohibits us from reconstructing a single system which will underlie the others, but this is surely the most reasonable course. All we can do, then, is to present one version, surely quite late, of the Proto-Indo-European verbal system as traditionally reconstructed, recognising that many unanswered questions remain which are outside the scope of this chapter.

The classical reconstruction of the Proto-Indo-European verbal system posits two voices, four moods and from three to six tenses. In addition, there were person and number suffixes and a large number of derivational formatives by which additional categories were formed. The verb structure is as follows:

Voice refers to the relationship of the subject to the activity defined by the verb, i.e. whether the subject is agent, patient or both. In Proto-Indo-European there were two voices, active and medio-passive. An active verb is one in which the subject is typically the agent, but is not directly affected by the action (e.g. *John called Bill*). Medio-passive is a mixed category which includes the function of middle (= reflexive) and passive. When the subject of the verb is both the agent and the patient, the verb is in the middle voice (e.g. Gk. *ho païs loúetai* 'the boy washes himself', Skt *yájate* 'he makes a sacrifice for himself'). When the subject of the verb is the patient, but there is a different agent, the verb is in the passive voice (e.g. Gk. *ho païs loúetai hupò tễs mētrós* 'the boy is washed by his mother'). In general, the various Indo-European languages generalised either the middle or the passive function from the Proto-Indo-European medio-passive. For example, in Sanskrit the middle function dominates, the passive being late and secondary. In Greek the middle and passive are morphologically identical in all but the future and aorist tenses, with the middle dominating. Italic and Celtic have mostly passive use, though there are ample relics of the middle in deponent verbs like Lat. *loquitur* 'he speaks', OIr. *-labrathar* 'who speaks', as well as Lat. *armor* 'I arm myself', Lat. *congregor* 'I gather myself', and others. Germanic has no traces of the middle, and Hittite has a medio-passive with largely middle function.

Mood describes the manner in which a speaker makes the statement identified by the verb, i.e. whether he believes it is a fact, wishes it, doubts it or orders it. In Proto-Indo-European there were probably four moods: indicative, optative, conjunctive (known more commonly as subjunctive), and imperative. With the indicative mood the speaker expresses statements of fact. Indicative is sometimes marked by a vowel suffix (thematic class) and sometimes not (athematic class), e.g. Skt. *rud-á-ti*, Lat. *rud-e-t* 'he cries' (thematic); Skt. *ás-ti*, Lat. *es-t* 'he is' (athematic). The optative mood is used when the speaker expresses a wish or desire, and is also marked by a vowel which depends on the vowel in the indicative, e.g. OLat. *siet*, Gk. *eíē*, Skt. *syất* 'let him be'. The conjunctive is used when the speaker is expressing doubt, exhortation or futurity. Its theme vowel depends on the vowel of the verb in the indicative, though it is commonly with *e/o* ablaut. Some examples are Lat. *erō* 'I will be', *agam*, *agēs* 'I, you will/might drive', Gk. *íomen* 'let us go'. The final mood is the imperative, which is used when the speaker is issuing a command. The imperative was formed from the bare verbal stem, without a mood-marking vowel as with the other three. Imperatives are most common in the second person, though they are found in the first and third as well. Examples are (second person) Gk. *phére*, Skt. *bhára*, Lat. *fer* 'carry' (sg.) and *phérete*, *bhárata*, *ferte* (pl.). There were other imperative suffixes as well which need not concern us here.

Tense refers to the time of the action identified by the verb. The original Proto-Indo-European verb was probably based on aspectual rather than temporal relations (aspect refers to the type of activity, e.g. momentary, continuous, iterative, etc.), but traditionally these have been interpreted as tenses. We usually identify three tense stems, the present, the aorist and the perfect. The present identifies repeated and continuing actions or actions going on in the present (= imperfective aspect): Lat. *sum*, Gk. *eimí*, Skt. *ásmi* 'I am', or Lat. *fert*, Gk. *phérei*, Skt. *bhárati* 'he carries'. The aorist stem (= perfective aspect) marks actions that did or will take place only once, e.g. Gk. *égnōn* 'I recognised', Skt. *ádāt* 'he gave', Gk. *édeikse* 'he showed', Skt. *ánāiṣam* 'I led'. The final stem is the perfect stem (= stative aspect), which describes some state pertaining to the subject of the verb. Examples are Skt. *véda*, Gk. *oîda*, Go. *wáit* 'I know'.

The exact internal structure of the various tense systems is extremely complicated. A number of formal types exist, including stems characterised by ablaut, reduplication, prefixation (augment), infixation and a wide variety of derivational suffixes. An interesting fact is that though tense was not directly and explicitly marked in Proto-Indo-European, most of the daughter languages generalised tense as the defining characteristic of their respective verbal systems.

In addition to the tense, voice and mood categories, the Proto-Indo-European verb carried at the end of the verbal structure a set of endings which indexed first, second or third person and singular, plural or dual number. There were different sets of endings for different voices, tense stems and moods. Here we list only the principal 'primary' and 'secondary' endings; they are identical except for the final *-i*, an earlier particle which marks the primary endings. These endings were originally used with specific tenses and moods, but have been largely generalised in the daughter languages.

Verbal Endings

	Primary	*Secondary*
1st sg.	-mi (Skt. bhárāmi)	-m (Lat. sum)
2nd sg.	-si (Skt. bhárasi)	-s (OLat. ess)
3rd sg.	-ti (Skt. bhárati)	-t (Lat. est)
3rd pl.	-nti (Skt. bháranti)	-nt (Lat. sunt)

We can schematise the overall structure of the Proto-Indo-European verb as follows:

The Structure of the Indo-European Verb

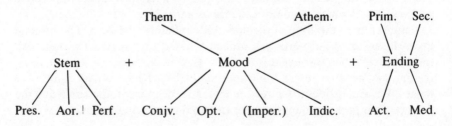

A few examples:

Lat.	am	ā	s	'you love'	(Pres. indic. 2nd pers. sg. act.)
	am	ē	s	'you might love'	(Pres. subj. 2nd pers. sg. act.)
	am	ā	ris	'you are loved'	(Pres. indic. 2nd pers. sg. pass.)
	am	ē	ris	'you might be loved'	(Pres. subj. 2nd pers. sg. pass.)
Gk.	paideú	ei	s	'you teach'	(Pres. indic. 2nd pers. sg. act.)
	paideú	ē	s	'you might teach'	(Pres. subj. 2nd pers. sg. act.)
	paideú	oi	s	'may you teach'	(Pres. opt. 2nd pers. sg. act.)
Skt.	bhár	a	ti	'he carries'	(Pres. indic. 3rd pers. sg. act.)
	á neṣ		vahi	'we two led ourselves'	(Aor. indic. 1st pers. du. mid.)
	sunu		yắma	'we might press'	(Pres. opt. 1st pers. pl. act.)

Besides the finite verb forms which we have been discussing, Proto-Indo-European also made use of a number of derivative forms which were non-finite, i.e. they did not stand as independent tensed predications. We include here a number of infinitive forms, which were originally noun forms in various oblique cases (mostly accusative and dative) and became reanalysed as part of the verbal system: cf. Skt. *dātum* (acc.), *dātavē* (dat.) 'to give'. There were also participial formations represented in most of the languages from Proto-Indo-European formations in *-nt-* (e.g. Go. *bairands*, Skt. *bháran-*, Lat. *ferens* 'carrying'), as well as others in *-wes-* (cf. Skt. *vidvás-* 'knowing'), *meno-* (cf. Gk. *hepómenos* 'following'), and *-to-* (cf. Lat. *amātus* 'loved'). These secondary formations, as well as a number of others such as gerunds, gerundives, supines and other verbal nouns, are widely represented and used throughout the Indo-European family.

3.3 Syntax

The reconstruction of syntax has lagged far behind the reconstruction of the phonological, morphological and lexical structures of Proto-Indo-European. This is initially surprising in light of the central role played by syntax and syntactic theory in modern linguistics. There are many reasons for this lag. Among them are the following:

(a) The lack of native speakers. Modern linguistics draws its data from the speech and intuitions of native speakers, but of course a reconstructed language has no such data source.

(b) The abstractness of syntax. Phonological, morphological and lexical units are far more concrete units than rules or patterns of syntax. Fewer theoretical notions are required in order to isolate concrete units, whereas in syntax, nothing exists pretheoretically. Syntax is an abstract set of principles, requiring abstract theories before even data organisation can begin.

(c) The structure of the descendant languages. The Indo-European daughter languages are of a highly inflecting type, and carry out a great deal of their 'syntax' in morphological expressions. Consider the difference between (1) and (2) in English:

(1) The boy sees the girl.
(2) The girl sees the boy.

The Latin equivalents to these sentences can have the words arranged in any order without affecting the agent/patient relations:

(1')	i	Puer	puellam	videt.
		Boy	girl	sees
	ii	Puellam	puer	videt.
		Girl	boy	sees
	iii	Videt	puer	puellam.
		Sees	boy	girl
			etc.	

(2')	i	Puella	puerum	videt.
		Girl	boy	sees
	ii	Puerum	puella	videt.
		Boy	girl	sees
	iii	Videt	puella	puerum.
		Sees	girl	boy
			etc.	

From these few examples we can readily see that the morphology/syntax division in inflected languages is quite a different matter from the same division in a language like English.

(d) The data. The Indo-European languages on which the reconstruction of Proto-Indo-European is based are simply not uniform enough to allow a straightforward account of syntactic patterns. The problem is no greater, and no less, than that found in phonology and morphology.

We will move now to a brief and highly selective review of some major features of Proto-Indo-European syntax. Because the citation of examples is extremely complicated, I will limit the data to the bare minimum.

3.3.1 Word Order

Late Proto-Indo-European was most likely a subject–object–verb (SOV) language with attendant adjective + noun (*good boy*), genitive + noun (*John's hat*), standard + marker + adjective (*John than bigger*) order, postpositions (*the world over*), and the preposing of relative clauses (*the who I saw man*). The reconstruction of these structural patterns is based on principles of typological inference developed largely by W. Lehmann (e.g. 1974), who extended the concepts of word order harmony formulated by J. Greenberg (1963) to historical syntax. According to these principles, there are major structural configurations in languages which are harmonious or compatible with each other. They take the form of statements like the following: if a language has some property P, then it will also have some property Q. For example, if a language is SOV in its basic sentence pattern, it will also have postpositions; if it is SVO, it will have prepositions.

Lehmann has put such 'implicational universals' to work in the reconstruction of Proto-Indo-European word order patterns. For example, Hittite, Vedic Sanskrit and Tocharian are SOV; Latin is predominantly SOV (Homeric Greek is apparently alternately SVO/SOV). Concentrating on Hittite, we find that it has postpositions and adjective + noun order, and dominant genitive + noun and relative clause + noun order. This seems to be ample evidence for an SOV Proto-Indo-European, a conclusion which is augmented by the existence of SOV-harmonic forms in otherwise SVO languages like relic postpositions in Slavonic and Baltic, as well as large numbers of formulaic postpositions in the Italic languages which, though they are mostly SOV, become SVO by the time of Vulgar Latin. The archaic-like nature of the frozen postpositions in Latin *mēcum* 'with me', *tēcum* 'with you' (not *cum mē, *cum tē, as expected; cf. *cum puellā* 'with the girl') or English expressions like *the world over* can be taken as evidence for early SOV structure, even in languages which show a move toward SVO structures. Discovering such patterns and drawing inferences for reconstruction depends crucially on the assumption that such marked structures as the Latin postpositions are indeed archaisms and not innovations.

There has been much criticism of the typological approach to syntax. For one thing, it has been noted that inflected languages have much freer word order possibilities than do languages like English, which rely on word order for marking grammatical function. According to this view, the word order issue is a false one, since word order serves mainly secondary functions like marking topic or focus relations

Another problem with the typological approach is the fact that the pure types are very rare (in the Indo-European family only Celtic is consistent, and it is VSO!). But the typological method has a built-in escape: languages which are internally inconsistent, like English with its SVO but adjective + noun structures, are said to be in transition from one type to another; the process is not yet complete. This begs the issue, because languages are always in such a transitional state. In other words, Greenberg's observations should be regarded as interesting tendencies and frequentalia, and should not be elevated to the status of explanatory devices. Furthermore, there is ample evidence that such implicational universals do not serve as reliable predictors of future syntactic change in a language.

Finally there is the matter of method. Typological inferences often are based on data being used in two directions, viz. if a language is SOV, one expects postpositions. And if a language is SVO but a stray postposition is found, one assumes that it must have been SOV at one time. There is also the issue of 'marked' vs. 'unmarked' structures. Determining that a language is SOV or SVO when both are present in the data requires a judgement that one of the structures is more natural, more basic, more regular than the other. The problem with ancient languages with no native speakers is that judgements about marked/unmarked structures often reduce to simple frequency counts, and this is not adequate.

3.3.2 Ergative–Nominative/Accusative Structure
It is clear from the daughter languages that late Proto-Indo-European was of the nominative/accusative type. That is, the agent of the verb was inflected in the nominative case, and the patient or goal was inflected in the accusative: cf. Lat. *Marc-us amat puell-am* 'Marcus loves the girl'. But as we saw in our discussion of early Proto-Indo-European noun morphology, there is significant evidence that Proto-Indo-European was at one time of the ergative type, i.e. a language in which the subject of a transitive verb is in a different case from the subject of an intransitive verb. There are many instances throughout the early Indo-European languages of agents in the genitive case: cf. OArm. *ēr nora* (gen.) *hraman aṙeal* 'he (of him) had received a promise', Lat. *attonitus serpentis* 'astonished by the serpent'. There are other cases where the real object of a verb of perception is in the accusative while the producer of the perceived act is in the genitive: cf. Skt. *vácam* (acc.) *śṛṇóti* 'he hears a voice' vs. *devásya* (gen.) *śṛṇóti* 'he hears a god'. These agentive genitives may at one time have been the subjects of intransitive verbs with genitive agents, as would be found with ergative languages. As Proto-Indo-European developed its complex nominal and verbal morphology, these genitives were reinterpreted as objects of transitive verbs and are now considered simply irregular formations. Schmalstieg (esp. 1980) has found traces of ergative syntax in a number of Indo-European dialects.

3.3.3 Some Syntactic Characteristics of Proto-Indo-European
Proto-Indo-European made use of a simple phrase structure principle by which the verb was the only obligatory constituent of a sentence. The subject of the verb was in the nominative, the object in the accusative and a number of other grammatical functions were served by the remaining cases. Verb structures could be expanded with case expressions of time, place-to, place-in, place-from, goal, possession and a number of other qualifiers. Conjunction of both noun phrases and other constituents was possible, including sentence conjunction. Simple sentences could be extended by the use of cases, adverbs and particles to indicate circumstance, purpose, result or manner. Particles were used to introduce different types of clauses (e.g. subordinate, interrogative, relative, co-ordinate). The modality of a sentence, as well as tense and aspect, were expressed inflectionally, though

they may have been originally marked only by particles. Finally, there is evidence for a well-developed noun-compounding system, represented chiefly by Sanskrit.

As a final note to the structure of Proto-Indo-European, it may be useful to take a brief look at a version of a reconstructed Proto-Indo-European sentence. This sentence is from Lehmann and Zgusta's (1979:462) reinterpretation of Schleicher's famous Indo-European fairy tale, which was written in 1868.

	Owis	ekʷōskʷe			
	Sheep	horses-and			
Gʷərēi	owis,	kʷesyo	wl̥hnā	ne	ēst
Hill-on	sheep,	of whom	wool	not	is
ekʷōns	espeket,	oinom	ghe	gʷr̥um	
horses	he-saw,	one	emph. prt.	heavy	
woĝhom	weĝhontm̥,	oinomkʷe	meĝam		
load	pulling,	one-and	great		
bhorom	oinomkʷe	ĝhm̥enm̥	ōku	bherontm̥	
burden	one-and	man	swiftly	carrying.	

'The sheep and the horses

On a hill, a sheep which had no wool saw horses, one pulling a heavy load, one carrying a great burden and one (carrying) quickly a man.'

4 Aspects of Proto-Indo-European Culture and Civilisation

When we reconstruct a proto-language, we are by implication also reconstructing a proto-culture and civilisation. But linguistic evidence alone is not sufficient to provide a complete picture of a proto-culture; it must be supplemented by information from archaeology, history, folklore, institutions and other sources. The question 'Who were the Proto-Indo-Europeans?' has been studied ever since the Indo-European family was established. Where was their homeland, when were they a unit, and what was the nature of their culture?

Many different areas of the world have been suggested for the Proto-Indo-European homeland. Central Asia was an early favourite because of the strong Biblical tradition that this was the home of mankind; the Baltic region, Scandinavia, the Finnic area, Western Europe, the Babylonian Empire, southern Russia, the Mediterranean region and a number of other places have been advanced as possibilities. The reason such a wide variety of views exists lies not only in the complexity and ambiguity of the issues, but also in the trends of the times and the prejudices of individual investigators, many of whom have been motivated by racial or ethnic considerations rather than scientific method. For example, many of the early researchers, lacking the insights of modern anthropology, believed that the obviously strong and warlike Indo-European people could only have been blond, blue-eyed Aryans who must have originated in Northern Europe, and not Asia or the Baltic region, for example. Such a confusion of the matters of race, culture and language, fuelled by religious prejudice and scientific immaturity, produced the many speculations on the homeland issue.

A famous argument about the homeland was made by Thieme (1953, summarised in 1958). Using the word for 'salmon' *$la\hat{k}s$ (Eng. *lox* < Yiddish *laks*), Thieme argued that these fish fed only in the streams of northern Europe in the Germano-Baltic region during Indo-European times. Since *$la\hat{k}s$ is recoverable with the meaning 'salmon' in Germanic and Baltic and 'fish' in Tocharian, this distribution suggests a northern homeland. In Indo-Iranian a form Skt. *lakṣá* 'one hundred thousand' is interpreted by Thieme as an extension of the uncountable nature of a school of salmon. Thieme concludes that the existence of this root in Indo-Iranian and Tocharian, where salmon are unknown, confirms the Germano-Baltic region as the original homeland.

Thieme uses similar argumentation with the reconstructed words for 'turtle' and 'beech tree'. There is a botanical beech line where the beech flourished about 5,000 years ago, as well as an area which defines the limits of the turtle at the time. Finding these roots in a number of Indo-European languages where the physical objects are unknown suggests the north European region again.

Of course the problem with such argumentation is that the botanical evidence for the beech line of 5,000 years ago is not conclusive. Also, it is well known that speakers frequently transfer old names to new objects in a new environment, as American speakers of English have done with the word *robin*. Thus the root *$bh\bar{a}go$- may have been used to designate trees other than the beech in some dialects.

This brief review provides us with some background to consider current thinking on the 'Indo-European Problem' (Mallory 1973). The most widely held view is that of M. Gimbutas, who has argued in a number of research articles (e.g. 1970) that the Proto-Indo-European people were the bearers of the so-called Kurgan or Barrow culture found in the Pontic and Volga steppes of southern Russia, east of the Dnieper River, north of the Caucasus, and west of the Ural mountains. The Kurgan culture (from Russian *kurgan* 'burial mound') is typified by the tumuli, round barrows or 'kurgans', which are raised grave structures from the Calcolithic and Early Bronze Age periods. Evidence from the Kurgan archaeological excavations gives clear evidence of animal breeding, and even the physical organisation of houses accords with the reconstructed Proto-Indo-European material. For example, Go. *waddjus* 'wall' is cognate with Skt. *vāya-* 'weaving', which reflects the wattled construction of walls excavated from the Kurgan sites.

Kurgan culture is divided into three periods, beginning in the fifth millennium BC. The Indo-Europeanisation of the Kurgan culture took place during the Kurgan II period, roughly 4000–3500 BC. Kurgan sites from this period have been found in the north Pontic region, west of the Black Sea in the Ukraine, Rumania, Yugoslavia and Eastern Hungary. During the Kurgan III period (c. 3500–3000 BC), Kurgan culture spread out across Central Europe, the entire Balkan area and into Transcaucasia, Anatolia and northern Iran. Eventually, it also spread into northern Europe and the upper Danube region. During the final period, Kurgan IV, waves of expansion carried the culture into Greece, West Anatolia and the eastern Mediterranean.

According to Gimbutas, the archaeological evidence attesting to the domesticated horse, the vehicle, habitation patterns, social structure and religion of the Kurgans is in accord with the reconstruction of Proto-Indo-European, which reflects a linguistic community from about 3000 BC.

In a recent work (Renfrew, 1987) it has been proposed that the older Indo-European languages were spoken as early as the seventh millenium BC in eastern Anatolia, and that they spread from there gradually throughout Europe through the introduction of farming. This view, which is based primarily on the archaeological record and a demographic model of processual spread, fits with the independently formulated linguistic speculations of Gamkrelidze and Ivanov (1984), who place the original Indo-Europeans in the same region, though a few millenia later.

Salient lexical items which give insight into Proto-Indo-European culture can be cited. In the remaining space we will note those items which are particularly useful in developing a view of Proto-Indo-European culture.
Physical Environment. Words for day, night, the seasons, dawn, stars, sun, moon, earth, sky, snow and rain are plainly recoverable. A number of arboreal units have been identified and successfully reconstructed. Words for horse, mouse, bear, wolf, eagle, owl, turtle, salmon, beaver, otter, dog, cattle, sheep, pig, goat, wasp, bee and louse can also be reliably postulated. It is interesting that no single word for river or ocean can be established.
Family Organisation and Social Structure. According to Friedrich (1966:29), Proto-Indo-European culture had patriarchal, patrilocal families that probably lived in small houses and adjacent huts. Villages were small, distant and presumably exogamous. There is excellent evidence for patriliny, and cross-cousin marriage was probably not permitted. Kinship terms are reconstructible for father, mother, brother, sister, son, daughter, husband's in-laws and probably grand-relatives. The word for husband means 'master' and the wife was probably 'a woman who learns through marriage'. Evidence for Proto-Indo-European patriarchal kinship comes not only from the lexicon, but also from epic songs, legal tracts and ethnological sources from the various ancient Indo-European languages.

There is widespread evidence of a word for tribal king, giving some indication that government was established.

Technology. The Indo-European languages confirm the technological advancements of the proto-culture. Evidence from farming and agricultural terms indicates small-scale farmers and husbandmen who raised pigs, knew barley, and had words for grain, sowing, ploughing, grinding, settlement and field or pasture. We can also safely reconstruct words for arrow, axe, ship, boat, gold, wagon, axle, hub and yoke, showing a rather advanced people with knowledge of worked metals and agriculture.

Religion and Law. From lexical, legal and other sources we find clear indications of a religious system among the Proto-Indo-European people. There is a word for god, and a designation for a priest; words for worship, prayer, praise, prophesy and holy give clear indications of organised religion. There is lexical evidence and evidence from ancient institutions for legal concepts such as religious law, pledge, justice and compensation.

Bibliography

General overviews of the Indo-European languages include Lockwood (1972) and Baldi (1983). Meillet (1937) is a lucid exposition of the principles of Indo-European linguistics, while Szemerényi (1980) is currently the most authoritative handbook.

For recent developments in the conception of Proto-Indo-European phonology, reference may be made to Lehmann (1952) and to the more recent suggestions by Gamkrelidze (1981) and Hopper (1981). Lehmann's often highly controversial statements on Proto-Indo-European syntax may be found in Lehmann (1974).

Pokorny (1951–9) sets the standard in Indo-European etymology and lexicography, while Buck (1951) is a resource of synonyms arranged by semantic class. For particular semantic areas in relation to Proto-Indo-European culture, see Friedrich (1966) and Thieme (1953; 1958). For the relation between the Proto-Indo-Europeans and the Kurgan culture, see Gimbutas (1970).

References

Baldi, P. 1983. *An Introduction to the Indo-European Languages* (Southern Illinois University Press, Carbondale)

Bomhard, A.R. 1984. *Toward Proto-Nostratic* (John Benjamins, Amsterdam)

Brugmann, K. 1903. *Kurze vergleichende Grammatik der indogermanischen Sprachen* (Trübner, Strassburg)

Buck, C.D. 1951. *A Dictionary of Selected Synonyms of the Principal Indo-European Languages* (University of Chicago Press, Chicago)

Friedrich, P. 1966. 'Proto-Indo-European Kinship', *Ethnology*, vol. 5, pp. 1–36

Gamkrelidze, T.V. 1981. 'Language Typology and Language Universals and Their Implications for the Reconstruction of the Indo-European Stop System', in Y.L. Arbeitman and A.R. Bomhard (eds.), *Bono Homini Donum: Essays in Historical Linguistics in Memory of J. Alexander Kerns* (John Benjamins, Amsterdam), pp. 571–609

—— and V.V. Ivanov. 1984. *Indoevropejskij jazyk i indoevropejcy* (Tbilisi State University, Tbilisi)

Gimbutas, M. 1970. 'Proto-Indo-European Culture: The Kurgan Culture During the

Fifth, Fourth, and Third Millennia B.C.', in G. Cardona, H.M. Hoenigswald and
A. Senn (eds.), *Indo-European and Indo-Europeans* (University of Pennsylvania
Press, Philadelphia), pp. 155–97
Greenberg, J.H. 1963. 'Some Universals of Grammar with Particular Reference to
the Order of Meaningful Elements', in J.H. Greenberg (ed.), *Universals of
Language* (MIT Press, Cambridge, Mass.), pp. 73–113
Hopper, P. 1981. ' "Decem" and "Taihun" Languages: An Indo-European Isogloss',
in Y.L. Arbeitman and A.R. Bomhard (eds.), *Bono Homini Donum: Essays in
Historical Linguistics in Memory of J. Alexander Kerns* (John Benjamins,
Amsterdam), pp. 133–42
Ivanov, V.V. 1965. *Obščeindoevropejskaja, praslavjanskaja i anatolijskaja jazykovye
sistemy* (Nauka, Moscow)
Kuryłowicz, J. 1927. 'ə indo-européen et ḫ hittite', in *Symbolae Grammaticae in
Honorem Ioannis Rozwadowski* (Drukarnia Uniwersytetu Jagiellońskiego,
Cracow), pp. 95–104.
Lehmann, W.P. 1952. *Proto-Indo-European Phonology* (University of Texas Press,
Austin)
—— 1974. *Proto-Indo-European Syntax* (University of Texas Press, Austin)
—— and L. Zgusta. 1979. 'Schleicher's Tale After a Century', in Bela Brogyanyi
(ed.), *Festschrift for Oswald Szemerényi on the Occasion of his 65th Birthday*
(John Benjamins, Amsterdam), pp 455–66.
Lockwood, W.B. 1972. *A Panorama of Indo-European Languages* (Hutchinson
University Library, London)
Mallory, J. 1973. 'A Short History of the Indo-European Problem', *Journal of Indo-
European Studies*, vol. 1, pp. 21–65.
Meillet, A. 1937. *Introduction à l'étude comparative des langues indo-européennes*,
8th ed. (reprinted by University of Alabama Press, University, Alabama, 1964)
Pokorny, J. 1951–9. *Indogermanisches etymologisches Wörterbuch* (Francke, Bern
and Munich)
Renfrew, C. 1987. *Archaeology and Language* (Jonathan Cape, London)
Schleicher, A. 1876. *Compendium der vergleichenden Grammatik der
indogermanischen Sprachen* (Böhlau, Weimar)
Schmalstieg, W.R. 1980. *Indo-European Linguistics: A New Synthesis*
(Pennsylvania State University Press, University Park)
Shields, K. 1981. *Indo-European Noun Inflection: A Developmental History*
(Pennsylvania State University Press, University Park)
Szemerényi, O. 1980. *Einführung in die vergleichende Sprachwissenschaft*, 2nd ed.
(Wissenschaftliche Buchgesellschaft, Darmstadt)
Thieme, P. 1953. 'Die Heimat der indogermanischen Gemeinsprache', in
Abhandlungen der geistes- und sozialwissenschaftlichen Klasse (Akademie der
Wissenschaften und Literatur, Wiesbaden), pp. 535–610
—— 1958. 'The Indo-European Language', *Scientific American*, vol. 199, no. 4,
pp. 63–74

2 Slavonic Languages

Bernard Comrie

The approximate present distribution of the Slavonic languages can be seen from the attached sketch-map. The languages currently spoken, according to their genetic relations within Slavonic (see below) are: South Slavonic: Bulgarian, Macedonian, Serbo-Croat, Slovene; West Slavonic: Czech, Slovak, Polish, Upper and Lower Sorbian (Lusatian); East Slavonic: Russian, Ukrainian, Belorussian (White Russian). In addition, two extinct Slavonic languages are known from texts: Polabian (a West Slavonic language spoken in northern Germany until around 1700) and Old Church Slavonic (Old Bulgarian) (a South Slavonic language attested by a huge volume of texts starting in the ninth century). In phonological and morphological structure the Slavonic languages are very close to one another, more so than the Romance languages. The same applies to their basic lexicon; for more abstract and technical vocabulary, however, there is considerable language diversity, reflecting different national policies towards loanwords and use of native word-forming techniques: thus Russian and Polish use the international word *teatr* 'theatre', while Czech uses *divadlo* (from a root meaning 'look') and Serbo-Croat has two words, the western variety preferring *kazalište* (from a root meaning 'show'), the eastern variety *pozorište* (from a root meaning 'see').

The earliest Slavonic texts are from the ninth century (though extant copies are later), in Old Church Slavonic. Since the final break-up of Common Slavonic unity is dated towards the beginning of our millennium, Old Church Slavonic is very close to Late Common Slavonic, although Old Church Slavonic does have distinctive South Slavonic (more specifically, Bulgarian-Macedonian) features. Two alphabets were in use in the early period, both providing a good fit to the phonemic system of Old Church Slavonic: Glagolitic and Cyrillic. Glagolitic is usually considered the older; the forms of its letters are quite distinctive, although similarities to the alphabets of other important Christian languages of the period are detectable. The Cyrillic alphabet is more closely modelled on Greek (see the chapters on Russian and Serbo-Croat for two modern Cyrillic alphabets). The Cyrillic alphabet continues in use among Slavonic peoples of traditional

Map 2.1: Approximate Distribution of Slavonic Languages in Europe

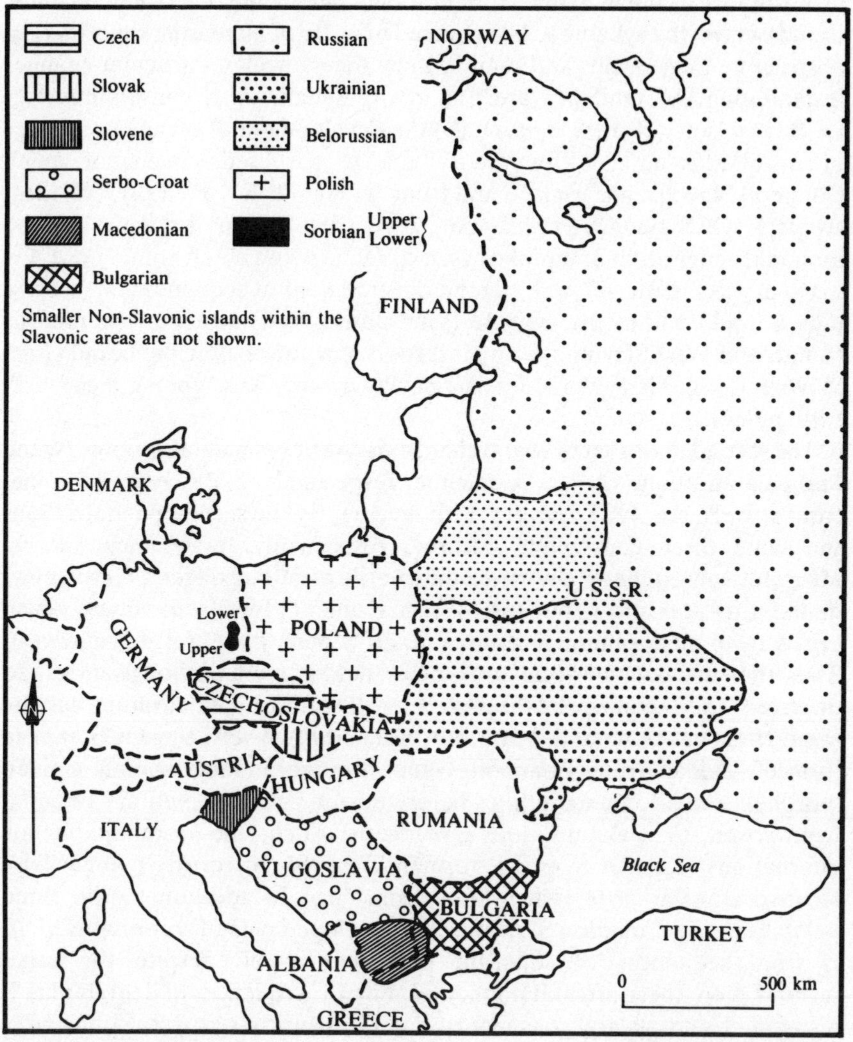

(adapted from Jakobson 1955)

Orthodox religion (i.e. for the East Slavonic languages, Bulgarian, Macedonian and the eastern variety of Serbo-Croat), while the others use the Roman alphabet.

Within the Indo-European family, the Slavonic languages are satem languages, with sibilant reflexes of PIE $\hat{k}$, e.g. PIE *$de\hat{k}m$ 'ten', OCS $des\c{e}t\tb$. An interesting development in the vowel system, of major importance for the later development of Slavonic, is the shift of PIE *i, *u to reduced vowels (jers), symbolised ь, ъ, e.g. OCS $m\tb gla$ 'mist' (cf. Lith. $migl\grave{a}$), OCS $sn\tb xa$

'daughter-in-law' (cf. Skt. *snuṣấ*). Two main sets of sound changes separate Proto-Indo-European from Common Slavonic. One is a tendency for sounds within the syllable to be arranged in order of increasing sonority (i.e. obstruents, then liquids and semi-vowels, then vowels). Particular changes instantiating this tendency are: (a) loss of syllable-final consonants, e.g. OCS *synъ* 'son' (cf. Lith. *sūnùs*); (b) the development of certain sequences of vowel plus nasal within the syllable to nasalised vowels, of which Common Slavonic has back **ǫ* and front **ę*, e.g. OCS *svętъ* 'holy' (cf. Lith. *šveñtas*), OCS *pǫtь* 'way' (cf. Lat. *pons*, gen. *pontis* 'bridge'); (c) the monophthongisation of diphthongs, e.g. OCS *iti* 'to go' (cf. Lith. *eīti*), OCS *suxъ* 'dry' (cf. Lith. *saūsas*); (d) the development of sequences of **o* or **e* plus a liquid within the syllable (symbolised **tort*) either by metathesis (South and West Slavonic) or by insertion of a vowel after the liquid (East Slavonic), e.g. OCS *glava*, Cz. *hláva,* Po. *głowa,* Rus. *golova* 'head' (cf. Lith. *galvà*).

The second major set of sound changes is a series of palatalisations. By the first palatalisation, **g*, **k*, **x* become, respectively, *ž*, *č*, *š* before original front vowels, e.g. OCS *živъ* (cf. Lith. *gývas*). By the second palatalisation, the same three consonants become, respectively, *ʒ* (a voiced dental affricate, subsequently de-affricated to *z* in most languages), *c* (voiceless dental affricate) and *s* (but *š* in West Slavonic) before front vowels newly arisen from monophthongisation, e.g. OCS *cěna* 'price' (cf. Lith. *káina*). Thus the first palatalisation took place before monophthongisation had occurred, the second palatalisation after. The third palatalisation has the same effect as the second, but occurs after front vowels, e.g. OCS *kъnęʒь* 'prince', a loan from Common Gmc. **kuningaz* 'king'. Since a given morpheme can occur sometimes before a back vowel, sometimes before a front vowel, the palatalisations give rise to synchronic morphophonemic alternations, e.g. OCS *mǫka* 'torment', *mǫčiti* 'to torture'; *noga* 'leg', locative singular *nozě* (where *ě* is from **āi*). In addition to the three palatalisations, Common Slavonic also developed palatal consonants *nj*, *lj*, *rj* from sequences of sonorant plus semi-vowel; despite the usual transcription, these are unit phonemes. Finally, sequences of dentals plus **j* also gave rise to palatal consonants, e.g. OCS *šyti* 'to sew' (cf. Lith. *siúti*).

In terms of nominal declension, the oldest Slavonic languages are conservative Indo-European languages. Three numbers are distinguished (singular, dual, plural), as are three genders (masculine, feminine, neuter) and seven cases (nominative, vocative, accusative, genitive, dative, instrumental, locative). The distinct declension classes and the distinction between substantival and pronominal declension are retained, though there are many analogies leading to the combination of similar declension classes (for instance, of masculine *o*-stems and *u*-stems, see below). An important innovation of the Common Slavonic period is the relevance of animacy to declension, whereby certain animate nouns (originally only some masculine singulars) replace the accusative by the genitive, e.g. OCS *bogъ* 'God', accusative *boga*, but *gradъ* 'city', accusative *gradъ*. An innovation within the morphology of adjectives is the development of pronominal adjectives, initially used only attributively and indicating a definite noun phrase, e.g. OCS *dobryjь člověkъ* 'the good man', cf. *dobrъ člověkъ* 'a good man'; Common Slavonic, like most of the modern languages (except Bulgarian and Macedonian), has no articles.

The verbal morphology of Common Slavonic represents a more radical departure from Proto-Indo-European. The morphological encoding of person and number in finite verbs is retained, as is the present/imperfect/aorist opposition. Morphologically expressed voice and mood distinctions are lost, except for that between indicative and imperative. There is no morphologically expressed future. The aspectual opposition between imperfective and perfective, so characteristic of the modern Slavonic languages (see further the chapter on Russian, pages 74–5), is already present, at least in embryonic form, from the earliest Slavonic texts. Various periphrastic verb constructions are found: the perfect, formed with the auxiliary 'be' and the past participle, occurs in all the languages, while the auxiliaries used for the future vary considerably from language to language.

Within the Indo-European family, the Slavonic languages are particularly close to the Baltic languages (Lithuanian, Latvian, Old Prussian), whence the frequent use of Lithuanian in this section for comparison with Slavonic. One particularly striking parallelism is the above-mentioned development of pronominal adjectives, cf. Lith. *geràsis žmogùs* 'the good man', *gēras žmogùs* 'a good man'. At one time these similarities were considered evidence for a single Balto-Slavonic branch of Indo-European, but now most scholars adhere rather to the view that such similarities, to the extent that they are not independent parallel developments, represent close contact between the two branches, rather than a period of common development.

As indicated above, the Slavonic languages subdivide into three groups, which can be identified on the basis of phonological criteria. The most salient characteristic of East Slavonic is the already cited insertion of an extra vowel in *tort* sequences (*polnoglasie*), as in Rus. *golova* 'head'. One salient characteristic of West Slavonic is the development of *tj* to c and of *dj* to ʒ (later de-affricated in most languages to z), e.g. PIE *medhjos*, Po. *miedza*, Cz. *meze*, cf. Rus. *meža*, OCS *mežda*, SCr. *mèđa*, Slovene *méja* 'boundary'; another is the development of *x* to š, rather than s, under the second and third palatalisations, e.g. Po. *szary*, Old Cz. *šěrý*, cf. Old Rus. *sěrъ*, Slovene *sęr* 'grey'. South Slavonic is a much less homogeneous grouping, and the only clear common phonological innovation is the development of Early Common Slavonic *jōns* (which occurs in a few morphological forms) to ę rather than to ě; indeed, the apparent unity of South Slavonic may well be in large measure an artefact of its physical separation from the other Slavonic languages, in particular Slovak, by the incursion of Hungarian and the expansion of Rumanian.

It is more difficult to say much that is interesting and reliable about Common Slavonic syntax. Most of the earliest texts are rather literal translations, especially from Greek, and it is therefore difficult to know to what extent word order, for instance, follows native Slavonic preferences or is calqued directly from the original. On the basis of the early textual evidence and comparison with later stages of the Slavonic languages, one can however state two generalisations that tie in intimately with the rich morphological system. Word order is grammatically free, i.e. there is no fixed order among subject, predicate, objects, adverbial modifiers etc.; the case inflections are usually sufficient to retrieve these grammatical relations, and variation in word order correlates primarily with pragmatic distinctions such as that between topic and comment (see further the chapter on Russian, pages 78–80). The rich morphological system also provides rich possibilities for agreement: thus, the verb agrees in person and number with its subject, and adjectives agree in gender, number and case with their head noun.

Later phonological, morphological and syntactic developments belong properly to the histories of the individual Slavonic languages, but the seeds of some of these later developments can already be seen in the Late Common Slavonic period, representing changes that had already begun in the Common Slavonic period but then took somewhat different paths in the different languages. Above, we have already discussed the different details of palatalisation and of *tort sequences in different branches of Slavonic. One major innovation of the early literary period that unites the Slavonic languages in type but divides them in detail is the subsequent development of the jers. In all Slavonic languages, a distinction is made between strong and weak jers, where in general a weak jer is one in word-final position or in a syllable preceding a full vowel, while a strong jer is one in a syllable preceding a weak jer. Weak jers are lost, while strong jers are strengthened to full vowels, but the precise full vowel to which each of the two jers is strengthened varies from language to language. In Common Slavonic *sъnъ 'sleep', the first jer is strong, the second weak. In Russian, strong ъ gives o, i.e. son; in Polish it gives e, i.e. sen. The loss of the jers has a major effect on the phonological structure of words in Slavonic languages, since it leads to consonant clusters that were previously impossible: thus Common Slavonic *gъdanьskъ is contracted from four syllables to one in Polish Gdańsk.

Another phonological development that characterises much of the Slavonic domain, especially East Slavonic and Polish, is the further development of a systematic opposition between plain and palatalised consonants. Weak ь, though lost as a segment, palatalises a preceding consonant, e.g. Rus. pjat´ 'five', cf. OCS pętь. In Common Slavonic, there is no possible palatalisation opposition before o, whereas language-particular developments in Russian and Polish give rise to just this contrast: from the Common Slavonic stem *nes- 'carry' Russian has /ńos/ '(he) carried' (cf. *nos* 'nose'), while Polish has *niosę* (phonemically /ńosē/) 'I carry'.

The rich nominal morphology of Common Slavonic is remarkably stable over most of the Slavonic territory. Only Bulgarian and Macedonian have completely lost morphological case. The dual has been lost in all Slavonic languages except Slovene and Sorbian. Most languages have undergone some simplification of the remaining distinctions, the main line of innovation being the loss of minor declension types in favour of the three main declension classes (*o*-stems, *a*-stems, *i*-stems), though in some instances the actual surviving inflection is taken from the minor class (e.g. the most common Polish suffixes for genitive and dative of masculine *o*-stems are *-u* and *-owi*, originally from the *u*-stems).

The morphology of the verb has undergone more radical shifts. Here, Bulgarian and Macedonian prove to be most conservative in retaining the rich Common Slavonic system, although both have also innovated in the development of special periphrastic verb constructions to indicate events not directly witnessed by the speaker (*preizkazvane*), e.g. Bulgarian *toj bil peel* 'he was (they say) singing', cf. *toj peeše* 'he was singing'. The aorist and imperfect have been ousted by the originally compound perfect in most Slavonic languages: apart from Bulgarian and Macedonian, these verb forms survive only in Sorbian and in literary Serbo-Croat. The aspectual opposition between imperfective and perfective has developed in all Slavonic languages (including Bulgarian and Macedonian) into a fully-fledged morphological opposition.

Bibliography

Jakobson (1955) is an introductory survey of the family and the individual languages, including comparative grammar. De Bray (1980) gives a concise grammar of each of the modern literary languages and Old Church Slavonic, with comparative and historical commentary and a good, up-to-date bibliography. Though rather dated, Entwistle and Morison (1964) is the only comprehensive comparative grammar available in English. Bräuer (1961–) is an excellent condensation of traditional Slavonic comparative grammar lore, but the morphology volumes to date unfortunately cover only noun declension. Vaillant (1950–77) is a solid comparative grammar. Schenker and Stankiewicz (1980) deals with each of the literary languages, including Old Church Slavonic and Cassubian, and is useful equally for the languages not given separate sections in this volume.

References

Bräuer, H. 1961–. *Slavische Sprachwissenschaft* (Walter de Gruyter, Berlin)
De Bray, R.G.A. 1980. *Guide to the South Slavonic Languages*; *Guide to the West Slavonic Languages*; *Guide to the East Slavonic Languages*, 3 vols. (Slavica, Columbus, Oh.) (= *Guide to the Slavonic Languages*, 3rd ed.)

Entwistle, W.J. and W.A. Morison. 1964. *Russian and the Slavonic Languages* (Faber and Faber, London)

Jakobson, R. 1955. *Slavic Languages: A Condensed Survey* (King's Crown Press, New York)

Schenker, A.M. and E. Stankiewicz (eds.) 1980. *The Slavic Literary Languages: Formation and Development* (Yale Concilium on International and Area Studies, New Haven, Conn.)

Vaillant, A. 1950–77. *Grammaire comparée des langues slaves*, 5 vols. (vols. 1–2, IAC, Paris; vols. 3–5, Klincksieck, Paris)

3 Russian

Bernard Comrie

1 Historical Background

Russian, together with Ukrainian and Belorussian, is a member of the East Slavonic group within the Slavonic branch of Indo-European. Although the three languages are now considered distinct literary languages, they are very close to one another, with a high degree of mutual intelligibility. At the time of the emergence of writing in East Slavonic, around the year 1000, there was just a single language, conventionally called Old Russian. In terms of the development of Russian as a modern literary language and of the separation of Ukrainian and Belorussian, there are two strands that must continually be borne in mind: the relation between native East Slavonic forms and forms borrowed from South Slavonic, and the relations among regional variations within East Slavonic.

Although there is some controversy concerning the possible independent, native development of writing in Russian, it is generally agreed that writing was introduced to Russia together with Christianity towards the end of the tenth century. The liturgical language that was introduced in this process was Old Church Slavonic, a South Slavonic language. At this period Old Church Slavonic and Old Russian were presumably easily mutually intelligible, yet still there were clear differences between them, namely the criterial differences between East and South Slavonic (see page 59). At this early period, much of the writing was of religious content (biblical and liturgical translations, saints' lives) or was written by monks (for instance, historical chronicles), and in such writing the attempt was made to write Church Slavonic, avoiding local East Slavonic dialect peculiarities. In practice, the Russian monks writing these manuscripts often erred by allowing East Slavonic forms to creep into their texts, but many of the religious texts of this time are very close to canonical Old Church Slavonic. Parallel to this writing in Church Slavonic, secular writing also developed, in particular for legal purposes (law codes, contracts, wills, treaties), later also personal messages. The language of these secular documents is much closer to the East Slavonic of the time, although inevitably, since any scribe was trained in Church Slavonic, numerous Church Slavonic forms crept into secular texts. Thus

Old Russian of this early period was characterised by diglossia between native East Slavonic (the low variety) and Church Slavonic (the high variety).

With the passage of time, the divergence between the two varieties became gradually less, in particular with many Church Slavonic forms gaining acceptance into even the lowest forms of language. A break in this process was marked by the second South Slavonic influence. A number of South Slavonic clerics were appointed to important ecclesiastical offices in Russia in the late fourteenth and early fifteenth centuries, and one effect of their influence was a return, in religious writing, to a more correct imitation of canonical Old Church Slavonic. While South Slavonic forms already accepted into lower styles remained, the higher styles now followed an archaic Church Slavonic language far removed from the spoken language of the period.

By the eighteenth century, in particular through the modernisation and secularisation efforts of Peter the Great, need was felt for a written language that would be closer to the educated spoken norm. The brilliant polymath M.V. Lomonosov, in his *Russian Grammar* (1755), set out a theory of three styles. According to this theory, there should be a high style, i.e. Church Slavonic, which would be used (in addition to religious purposes) for high poetic genres; a low style, almost purely East Slavonic (except for fully assimilated Church Slavonic features), to be used for personal correspondence and low comedy; and a middle style, to be used for lyric poetry, literary prose and scientific treatises. The modern standard language is closest to the middle style, though recent suggestions assign a much greater role to the spoken language of the aristocracy in its development. In any event, the modern standard language is already established by the time of A.S. Pushkin (1799–1837), the first of the great writers of Russia's nineteenth century. Although the language has continued to develop during the intervening two centuries, which have included the major social upheaval of the October Revolution (1917), the modern Russian literary language is still defined chronologically as the language from Pushkin to the present day.

The coexistence of East Slavonic and South Slavonic forms from the earliest Old Russian to the present day is one of the salient characteristics of the language. It may be compared with the coexistence of Anglo-Saxon and Norman French elements in English, with the exception that East and South Slavonic are much closer to one another genetically than are English and French. In modern Russian, it is common to find doublets, i.e. derivatives of the same Common Slavonic root in both East Slavonic and Church Slavonic forms, the Church Slavonic form usually having a more abstract or learned connotation. One of the main differences between East Slavonic and South Slavonic is the treatment of Common Slavonic sequences of *o/e* followed by a liquid between consonants, symbolised **tort*. In East Slavonic, this sequence yields *torot*, while in South Slavonic it yields *trat*. In modern

Russian, alongside East Slavonic *golová* 'head', there is also South Slavonic *glavá* 'chief; chapter'. (Note that in English *head* is of Anglo-Saxon origin, whereas *chief* and *chapter* are of Romance origin.) Another distinction between the two groups of Slavonic languages is the treatment of Common Slavonic **tj*, **dj*, which give East Slavonic *č*, *ž*, but South Slavonic *šč* (more accurately: *št*, but pronounced *šč* in Russian Church Slavonic), *žd*: contrast the East Slavonic form *gorjáčij* 'hot' with the present participle *gorjáščij* 'burning', which, like all modern Russian present participles, is of Church Slavonic origin. Since Common Slavonic had, within the paradigm of the same verb, some forms with just **t* and others with **t* followed by **j*, this gives rise to morphophonemic alternations in modern Russian, either between *t* and *č* (East Slavonic forms, e.g. *platít'* 'to pay', *plačú* 'I pay') or between *t* and *šč* (Church Slavonic forms, e.g. *sokratít'* 'to abbreviate', *sokraščú* 'I shall abbreviate'). In addition to East Slavonic and Church Slavonic doublets of the above kinds, there are also some instances where the Church Slavonic form has completely supplanted the native form, e.g. *sládkij* 'sweet', cf. Old Russian *solodъkъjь*.

At the time of the oldest Russian texts, the main dialect division was between Northern and Southern Russian, the dividing line running approximately along the latitude of present-day Moscow. The cultural centre of the south was Kiev; the north had several centres, the most important being Novgorod. In texts from the northern area, a number of regional features occur, one of the most salient being the neutralisation of *c* and *č* into a single affricate, usually *c*. It is probable that at this early period north and south were already divided by what is still one of the major dialect divisions in Russian, namely the pronunciation of Common Slavonic **g*, the north having a plosive [g], the south a fricative [ɣ]; the age of this feature is suggested, among other things, by the fact that modern Ukrainian and Belorussian share this feature with Southern Russian dialects. Unfortunately, the Cyrillic alphabet has no way of distinguishing between the plosive and fricative sounds, so textual evidence is inconclusive.

The linguistic separation of Ukrainian and Belorussian runs parallel to their political separation. In the mid-thirteenth century, Russia proper fell under Tatar domination, and subsequently what are now the Ukraine and Belorussia fell under Lithuanian, subsequently Polish hegemony. The distinctive features of Ukrainian are most marked, with Belorussian often occupying an intermediate position between the other East Slavonic languages. During the period of political separation, innovations that began in the Ukraine were in general unable to penetrate to Russian, and vice versa. One of the main characteristics of Ukrainian is the development of Common Slavonic **ě*, which in standard Russian ultimately merged with *e*, to *i*, e.g. Old Russian *lěto*, Russian *léto*, Ukrainian *líto* 'summer'. Another characteristic of Ukrainian is that consonants lose their palatalisation before reflexes of Old Russian *e* (Ukrainian *e*) and *i* (Ukrainian *y*). Belorussian has fewer unique characteristics, one being the affrication of palatalised *t*, *d* to *ć*, *ź*, just as in Polish.

Meanwhile, in Russian proper, another phonological development of major importance for the dialectal composition of the language was taking place, namely *ákan'e*. This refers to the pronunciation of Old Russian unstressed *o* as *a*, e.g. of *vodá* 'water' as [vadá]. This change probably started somewhere in the south of Russia, but spread rapidly to cover the whole of the south, some central areas, and also Belorussia (but not the Ukraine, further evidence of its greater separateness). Lack of *ákan'e* is referred to as *ókan'e*. This phonological development ties in with a crucial political development. In the struggle against the Tatars, a key role came to be played by Muscovy, the area around Moscow, leading to the independence and unification of Russia (minus the Ukraine and Belorussia) under Moscow by the late fifteenth century. Although Moscow seems originally to have been part of the *ókan'e* dialect area, the city and surrounding area succumbed to the spread of *ákan'e*. Moscow's central position, coupled with the fact that it combined features of Northern dialects (in particular, the plosive pronunciation of *g*) and of Southern dialects (in particular, *ákan'e*), led to the formation of a new intermediate dialect grouping, the Central dialects, which lie at the basis of the modern standard language. Although the orthography still fails to record *ákan'e* (thus the word for 'water' is spelled *voda*), *ákan'e* was admitted as the norm in the middle style by Lomonosov and has since then been required in the standard language. The main dialect areas in Russian are thus: Northern (*ókan'e*, plosive *g*), Central (*ákan'e*, plosive *g*) and Southern (*ákan'e*, fricative *g*), with the standard language following the compromise Central dialect distribution of these features. Despite the huge area over which Russian is spoken, dialect differences, whether regional or social, are remarkably small and are, as in many other countries, becoming ever smaller with the spread of education.

In addition to examining Russian relative to its own internal divisions, it is also important to recognise that it is the major language of a multi-national state, the USSR (until 1917: the Russian Empire), and that it therefore interacts with over a hundred other languages, many of them genetically totally unrelated to Russian. In the USSR, Russian serves as the effective official language for all purposes other than local affairs in non-Russian-speaking areas. According to the 1979 census, Russian is spoken natively by 153.5 million people in the USSR, or 58.6% of the total population. It is dominant in European Russia and also in large parts of Siberia and the Far East, where Russian immigration over the last few centuries has resulted in the original inhabitants becoming often a small minority in their homeland. Of those Soviet citizens who are not native speakers of Russian, 61.3 million claimed fluent command of Russian as a second language, giving a total of 214.8 million first- and second-language speakers. (The number of Russian speakers outside the USSR is minimal in comparison with this total.)

2 Phonology

The segmental phonemes of Russian (stressed vowels, consonants) are set out in table 3.1; certain minor phonemes, which occur only in the speech of some speakers of the standard language, have been omitted. One striking feature of this phoneme inventory is the richness of the consonant system, in large measure due to the almost completely systematic opposition of palatalised and non-palatalised consonants, as in *brat'* 'to take' [brat´] versus *brat* 'brother' [brat]. The only non-palatalised consonants to lack palatalised counterparts are [c], [š], [ž]. Conversely, a few consonants are always palatalised with no non-palatalised counterpart: [č], [š:], [j]. (The functional yield of palatalisation with the velars is, incidentally, minimal.)

Table 3.1: Segmental Phonemes of Russian

Vowels

i	ɨ	u
e		o
	a	

Consonants

	Plain stop		*Affricate*	*Fricative*		*Nasal*	*Lateral*	*Trill*	*Semi-vowel*
Bilabial	p	b				m			
	ṕ	b́				ḿ			
Labio-dental				f	v				
				f́	v́				
Dental	t	d	c			n	l		
	t́	d̦				ń	ĺ		
Alveolar				s	z			r	
				ś	ź			ŕ	
Palato-alveolar			č	š	ž				
				š:					j
Velar	k	g		x					
	ḱ	ǵ		x́					

The vowels represented in table 3.1 are those found in stressed syllables. In Russian, stress is free (can occur in principle on any syllable of a word) and mobile (different forms of the same word can have different stresses). Thus lexical items can be distinguished solely by stress, e.g. *muká* 'flour', *múka* 'torment', as can morphological forms of the same lexical item, e.g. genitive singular *rukí*, nominative plural *rúki*, from *ruká* 'hand'. Although there are some principles of accentuation (e.g. perfective verbs with the prefix *vy-* always stress this prefix), there is much that is purely conventional, and even within the standard language there are many instances of alternative stresses. Within the stressed vowel system, the phonemic status of the *i/ɨ* opposition is debatable: in general, *ɨ* occurs only after non-palatalised consonants, *i* only after palatalised consonants and word-initially. One of the main characteristics of Russian phonology is that the vowel system of unstressed syllables is radically different, because of a number of vowel neutralisations affecting, for many speakers, all vowels except *u*. By the phenomenon of *ákan'e*, the *o/a* opposition is neutralised in unstressed syllables (for the position after a palatalised consonant, see below): word-initially and in the immediately pretonic syllable, both vowels appear phonetically as [ʌ], elsewhere as [ə], e.g. *golová* 'head' [gəlʌvá], *magazín* 'shop' [məgʌzín]. After palatalised consonants, all of *a/e/o*, for some speakers also *i*, are neutralised to give [ɪ], e.g. *mestá* 'places' [mʲɪstá], *časý* 'clock' [čɪsí] (this phenomenon is referred to as *íkan'e*; the precise

Table 3.2: Russian Alphabet

Printed		Handwritten		Transliteration
А	a	$\mathcal{A}$	*a*	a
Б	б	$\mathcal{B}$	*б*	b
В	в	$\mathcal{B}$	*в*	v
Г	г	$\mathcal{T}$	*г*	g
Д	д	$\mathcal{D}$	*д*	d
Е	е	$\mathcal{E}$	*е*	e
Ё	ё	$\mathcal{E}$	*ё*	ë
Ж	ж	$\mathcal{M}$	*ж*	ž
З	з	$\mathcal{Z}$	*з*	z
И	и	$\mathcal{U}$	*и*	i
Й	й	$\mathcal{U}$	*й*	j
К	к	$\mathcal{K}$	*к*	k
Л	л	$\mathcal{L}$	*л*	l
М	м	$\mathcal{M}$	*м*	m
Н	н	$\mathcal{H}$	*н*	n
О	о	$\mathcal{O}$	*о*	o
П	п	$\mathcal{T}$	*п*	p
Р	р	$\mathcal{P}$	*р*	r
С	с	$\mathcal{C}$	*с*	s
Т	т	$\mathcal{T}$	*т*	t
У	у	$\mathcal{Y}$	*у*	u
Ф	ф	$\mathcal{P}$	*ф*	f
Х	х	$\mathcal{X}$	*х*	x
Ц	ц	$\mathcal{U}$	*ц*	c
Ч	ч	$\mathcal{C}$	*ч*	č
Ш	ш	$\mathcal{U}$	*ш*	š
Щ	щ	$\mathcal{U}$	*щ*	šč
	ъ		*ъ*	"
	ы		*ы*	y
	ь		*ь*	'
Э	э	$\mathcal{Э}$	*э*	e
Ю	ю	$\mathcal{HO}$	*ю*	ju
Я	я	$\mathcal{Я}$	*я*	ja

nature of *íkan'e* is subject to a number of more specific constraints and also to some variation, even within the standard language).

The Russian writing system uses the Cyrillic alphabet (table 3.1). The writing system is based, like the Greek and Roman alphabets, on the alphabetic system, with as a basic principle one letter per phoneme. To assist the reader in converting the transliterations used in this section to a reasonably accurate phonetic representation, some details of divergences between phoneme and letter sequences will be noted. Although stress is phonemic in Russian, it is not usual to mark stress in writing; in this chapter, however, stress is always marked by an acute accent. Likewise, the diacritic on *ë*, which is always stressed, is usually omitted in writing Russian, but is systematically included here. Otherwise, for vowels, it should be noted that Russian orthography does not represent the effects of *ákan'e* and similar phenomena: thus the unstressed vowels of голова (*golová*) 'head' and магазин (*magazín*) 'shop' are distinguished orthographically, but not phonetically.

In pronunciation, Russian word-final obstruents are always voiceless, but orthographically voiced and voiceless obstruents are distinguished: thus рот (*rot*) 'mouth' and род (*rod*) 'birth' are both pronounced [rot]. Similarly, in Russian, sequences of obstruents assimilate in voicing to the last obstruent, but this is not shown in the orthography, e.g. гибкий (*gíbkij*) 'flexible' [gípkij]. The main complication in relating spelling to pronunciation, however, is the representation of palatalisation. It will be seen from comparison of tables 3.1 and 3.2 that Russian has no special letters for palatalised consonants. Rather, palatalisation is indicated by modifying the non-palatalised consonant letter as follows. Word-finally or before a consonant, palatalisation is indicated by adding the letter ь after the non-palatalised consonant, as in брать (*brat'*) 'to take' [braţ], тьма (*t'ma*) 'mist' [ţma]. Before a vowel, different vowel symbols are used to distinguish palatalised and non-palatalised consonants. After a non-palatalised consonant, the vowel letters а, э, ы, о, у (*a, è, i, o, u*) are used; after a palatalised consonant я, е, и, ё, ю (*ja, e, i, ë, ju*) are used; e.g. мать (*mat'*) 'mother' [maţ], мять (*mjat'*) 'to crumple' [ṃaţ]. The unpaired consonants ц, ч, ш, щ, ж, (*c, č, š, šč, ž*) are treated differently: after them one always writes а, е, и, у (*a, e, i, u*), which thus have no effect on the palatalisation status of the preceding consonant (both *o* and *ë* are used; after *c*, *y* is written in native words). Thus: шить (*šit'*) 'to sew' [šiţ], час (*čas*) 'hour' [čas]. The representation of the phoneme /j/ is also complex and intertwined with the representation of palatalisation. In syllable-final position, the special letter й (*j*) is used, e.g. мой (*moj*) 'my' [moj], война (*vojná*) 'war' [vʌjná]. Word-initially and after a vowel, the special letters я, е, ё, ю (*ja, e, ë, ju*) represent the sequence of /j/ plus vowel, e.g. яма (*jáma*) 'pit' [jámə], союз (*sojúz*) 'union' [sʌjús]. After a consonant, /j/ is represented by using the letter ь (*'*) (across prefix-stem boundaries, ъ (*"*)) followed by я, е, и, ё, ю (*ja, e, i, ë, ju*), e.g. пьяный (*p'jányj*) 'drunk' [p̂jánɨj], муравьи (*murav'í*) 'ants' [murʌv́jí]. Although the representation of palatalisation in Russian may seem complex, it does, given the richness of the consonant system and the relative poverty of the vowel system, enable the full range of phonemic oppositions to be maintained orthographically with a restricted set of distinct letters.

It will now be useful to consider some of the main historical phonological processes that have affected Russian in its development from Common Slavonic, in particular in that these relate to the morphophonemic alternations to be discussed below. The Common Slavonic nasal vowels, as in most Slavonic languages except Polish, were lost in Russian (before the earliest written texts), *ǫ becoming *u* and *ę becoming *a* with palatalisation of the preceding consonant, e.g. Common Slavonic *pǫtь 'way', *pętь 'five', Russian *put'*, *pjat'*. The Common Slavonic (and Old Russian) reduced vowels (jers) are lost in Russian as in the other Slavonic languages. In Russian, strong ъ and ь give *o* and *e* respectively; the weak jers are lost, but ь causes palatalisation of the preceding consonant, e.g. Old Russian *sъnъ*, genitive *sъna* 'sleep', modern *son*, *sna*; Old Russian *dьnь* 'day', genitive *dьnja*, modern *den'*, genitive *dnja*.

Another innovation in Russian is the shift of Old Russian *e* to *o* before non-palatalised consonants, but with retention of palatalisation in the preceding consonant. Thus Old Russian *nesъ* 'carried' gives modern *nës*. The effect of this change, like some of those already discussed (loss of *ę, loss of ь) is to increase the domain of the palatalisation opposition, since *nës* contrasts with *nos* 'nose'. One of the latest changes in the vowel system, and one not shared by all dialects of Russian, is the merger of Old Russian *ě* and *e* (of which the former probably had a closer pronunciation in Old Russian, as still in those dialects that retain it) to *e*. (Distinct orthographic symbols were retained until 1918.) This shift of *ě* to *e* post-dates the shift of *e* to *o* noted above and is thus not subject to it, thus further reinforcing the phonemic distinctiveness of the palatalisation opposition: Modern Russian has the triple *voz* (Old Russian *vozъ*) 'cart', *vëz* (Old Russian *vezъ*) 'transported', *ves* (Old Russian *věsъ*) 'weight'.

Other changes in the vowel system already referred to are *ákan'e* and related phenomena (e.g. *íkan'e*), leading to neutralisation of unstressed vowels. In the obstruent system, the voice opposition was neutralised word-finally by the devoicing of voiced obstruents, leading to the merger of Old Russian *rъtъ* 'mouth' and *rodъ* 'birth' in modern pronunciation as [rot], and by assimilation of obstruents to the voice of a following obstruent, so that Old Russian *gibъkъjь* 'flexible' gives the modern pronunciation [ǵípḱij].

One of the main characteristics of modern Russian is the large number of morphophonemic alternations. Indeed, it is perhaps not accidental how much of modern morphophonemic theory has been developed by Russian phonologists and by phonologists working on Russian: Trubetskoy, Jakobson, Halle; since Polish shares this typological feature with Russian one can enlarge the list to include Baudouin de Courtenay. Some of the alternations are inherited from Indo-European, in particular ablaut (see pages 47–8), as in the alternation between the stem vowels of *tekú* 'I flow' and *tok* 'current' (Indo-European *e/o* ablaut). The more systematic alternations, however, are those that have arisen through innovatory sound changes in Common Slavonic or Russian. The main Common Slavonic innovations relevant here are the palatalisations and other processes leading to the development of palatal consonants. Thus the first palatalisation gives rise to the modern Russian *k/č* alternation in *pekú* 'I bake', *pečёš'* 'you bake': the original segment is **k*, retained before the back vowel (Common Slavonic **ǫ*) in the first member of the pair, but palatalised before the front vowel (Common Slavonic **e*) in the second item. The shift of **sj* to **š* in Common Slavonic turns up in modern Russian in the alternation found in *pisát'* 'to write', *pišú* 'I write', where the second item in early Common Slavonic was, with morpheme breaks, **pis-j-ǫ*.

Post-Common Slavonic innovations that have given rise to morphophonemic alternations include the loss of the jers. Since strong jers develop to full vowels while weak jers are lost, and since a given Old Russian jer might be strong in some morphological forms of a word but weak in others, the Old Russian predictable alternation of strong and weak jers gives rise in the modern language to alternation between a full vowel and zero, as in *son* 'sleep', genitive *sna*, *den'* 'day', genitive *dnja*.

Ákan'e and related phenomena give rise to vowel alternations, given the mobile stress. Thus we find nominative singular *golová* 'head' [gəlʌvá], nominative plural *gólovy* [góləvi], genitive plural *golóv* [gʌlóf], with alternation of the vowels in the first two syllables, and alternation of the first vowel in nominative singular *seló* 'hamlet' [śiló], nominative plural *sёla* [śólə]. In morphophonemic transcription, the stems of these two words would be {golov-} and {śol-}. Lastly, final devoicing and consonant voice assimilation give rise to morphophonemic alternations. Final devoicing gives rise to alternations because in different morphological forms of the same word a consonant can appear now word-finally, now followed by a vowel, as in *rod* 'birth' [rot], genitive *róda* [ródə]. Voicing assimilation gives rise to alternations because of the alternation between vowel and zero resulting from the loss of the jers, as in *pryžók* 'jump' [prižók], genitive *pryžká* [prišká].

3 Morphology

Russian nominal morphology is illustrated in the chart of declension types, with examples of the four major types of noun declension and of adjective declension. The nominal morphology turns out to be typologically very close to that of the oldest Indo-European languages. In particular, the morphology is fusional: thus, in the declension of nouns, it is not possible to

Russian Declension Types

Singular:	a-*stem*	Masculine o-*stem*	Neuter o-*stem*	i-*stem*
Nominative	straná	stol	mésto	brov'
Accusative	stranú	stol	mésto	brov'
Genitive	straný	stolá	mésta	bróvi
Dative	strané	stolú	méstu	bróvi
Instrumental	stranój	stolóm	méstom	bróv'ju
Locative	strané	stolé	méste	bróvi
Plural:				
Nominative	strány	stolý	mestá	bróvi
Accusative	strány	stolý	mestá	bróvi
Genitive	stran	stolóv	mest	brovéj
Dative	stránam	stolám	mestám	brovjám
Instrumental	stránami	stolámi	mestámi	brovjámi
Locative	stránax	stoláx	mestáx	brovjáx

Adjective Singular:	Masculine	Neuter	Feminine
Nominative	stáryj	stároe	stáraja
Accusative	stáryj	stároe	stáruju
Genitive		stárogo	stároj
Dative		stáromu	stároj
Instrumental		stárym	stároj
Locative		stárom	stároj
Plural:			
Nominative		stárye	
Accusative		stárye	
Genitive		stáryx	
Dative		stárym	
Instrumental		stárymi	
Locative		stáryx	

segment one inflection encoding number and another encoding case, rather these two categories are encoded by a single formative, so that the final -*u* of dative singular *stolú* represents 'dative singular', rather than part of it representing 'dative' and some other part 'singular'. In the adjective declension, the inflections are fusional for gender as well as for number and case, so that the inflection of *stár-uju* encodes the complex 'feminine singular accusative'. In fact, with nouns, there is fusion of yet another category, namely that of declension type: thus in the *a*-stems -*u* indicates 'accusative singular', whereas in the *o*-stems it indicates 'dative singular'. Although there is a high correlation between gender and declension type, it is not absolute: most *a*-stem nouns are feminine, but those with clear male reference are masculine; nearly all *i*-stem nouns are feminine, but *put'* 'way' is an isolated exception, being masculine; a masculine noun with male reference might be either an *o*-stem or an *a*-stem, while a feminine noun might be either an *a*-stem or an *i*-stem. In addition to the major declension types, there are also minor types represented by just a handful of nouns (e.g. ten neuter nouns follow the pattern of *ímja* 'name', genitive *ímeni*), in addition to idiosyncratic irregularities, including in particular the personal pronouns (e.g. *ja* 'I', genitive *menjá*).

One important parameter in Russian nominal declension not revealed by the table is animacy. In Russian, animate nouns (i.e. nouns referring to humans or other animals), and also their attributes, have the accusative case like the genitive rather than the form given in table 3.3 if they are either masculine *o*-stems or plural (of any gender or declension type). Thus *stáryj stol* 'old table' has accusative *stáryj stol*, but *stáryj slon* 'old elephant' has *stárogo sloná*; likewise nominative-accusative plural *stárye stolý*, but nominative plural *stárye sloný* and accusative-genitive *stáryx slonóv*. An animate noun not belonging to the *o*-stems, such as *žába* 'toad', has accusative singular *žábu*, nominative plural *žáby*, accusative plural *žab*.

Although Russian nominal morphology may look complex in comparison with, say, English, it reflects a number of significant simplifications relative to Old Russian or Common Slavonic. Few categories have been lost altogether, these being the dual number and the vocative case. However, several Common Slavonic declension types have been lost through merger with the more common types, such as *u*-stems with *o*-stems, most consonant stems with one of the other declension types. In addition, there has been some neutralisation (syncretism) leading to simplification, the most noticeable such effect being the loss of gender distinctions in the plural: thus the modern nominative plural *stárye* represents the merger of three distinct Old Russian forms: masculine *starii*, feminine *staryě*, neuter *staraja*. In addition to the overall pattern of simplification, there has also been some complication. For instance, some masculine *o*-stems have a partitive genitive in -*u* distinct from the regular genitive in -*a*; some masculine *o*-stems form the nominative (and inanimate accusative) plural in -*á* rather than -*y*, e.g. *gorodá*, plural of *górod* 'city'. In addition, some forms continuing Old Russian types have been retained as idiosyncratic irregularities (e.g. the endingless genitive plural of masculine *o*-stems in *glaz* 'eye', genitive plural also *glaz*).

In Common Slavonic, there were two declensions of adjectives, the so-called simple declension (identical to noun declension) and the pronominal declension. In attributive usage, they were distinguished in terms of definiteness, e.g. Old Russian *starъ gorodъ* 'an old town', *starъjь gorodъ* 'the old town'. In modern Russian, only the pronominal adjective survives in attributive usage, as in *stáryj górod* '(the/an) old town', and it is this form, conventionally termed the long form, that is given in the table of declensions. In predicative usage, either the long form or the so-called short form, continuing the Old Russian simple declension of adjectives, may be used, i.e. *górod stáryj/star* 'the town is old', *straná krasívaja/krasíva* 'the country is beautiful'. Since the short form is only used predicatively, it does not decline, but does distinguish gender and number (singular masculine *star*, feminine *stará*, neuter *stáro*, plural for all genders *stáry* or *starý*).

Russian verbal morphology is rather less like that of the older Indo-European languages. Inflectionally, only a small number of categories are distinguished, as represented in the chart of conjugation types. Among the finite forms, the only mood distinct from the indicative is the imperative. Within the indicative, there is a binary morphological opposition between non-past (i.e. present-future) and past. In the non-past, verbs agree with their subject in person and number; in the past, they agree in gender and number. Of the non-finite forms, the infinitive is in common use, in particular after certain finite verbs, e.g. *ja xoču čitát'* 'I want to read'. Modern Russian also has participles (verbal adjectives) and gerunds (verbal adverbs), but use of these is primarily restricted to literary and scientific writing.

Russian Conjugation Types

	I Conjugation	*II Conjugation*
Infinitive	čitát' 'to read'	govorít' 'to speak'
Non-past:		
Singular 1	čitáju	govorjú
2	čitáeš'	govoríš'
3	čitáet	govorít
Plural 1	čitáem	govorím
2	čitáete	govoríte
3	čitájut	govorját
Past:		
Singular masculine	čitál	govoríl
feminine	čitála	govoríla
neuter	čitálo	govorílo
Plural	čitáli	govoríli
Imperative:		
Singular 2	čitáj	govorí
Plural 2	čitájte	govoríte

In addition to the categories represented in the chart, Russian has a further category, that of aspect, with an opposition between imperfective and perfective. The general morphological principle is as follows. Simple verbs without a prefix are usually imperfective, e.g. *pisát'* 'to write'. Attachment of a prefix to such a verb makes it perfective, e.g. *na-pisát'* 'to write', *o-pisát'* 'to describe'. Usually, for a given simple verb there is one (unpredictable) prefix which adds no semantic component other than that of perfectivity, so that *pisát'–napisát'* (likewise *čitát'–pročitát'* 'to read') can be considered an imperfective-perfective pair. Other prefixes do make other semantic modifications, e.g. *opisát'* means 'to describe', not just 'to write', but such verbs can be given imperfective counterparts by suffixation, thus giving a pair *opísyvat'–opisát'*. In addition, there are less common ways of forming aspectual pairs, such as suffixation of non-prefixed verbs, e.g. perfective *rešít'*, imperfective *rešát'* 'to decide'. In general, then, Russian verbs come in imperfective-perfective pairs, but it is often impossible to predict what the perfective counterpart of a given imperfective verb will be or vice versa.

While the meaning of tense is to locate a situation (action, event, state) in a certain time (for instance, past tense in the time before the present moment), the meaning of aspect is concerned rather with the subjective way of viewing the internal temporal constituency of the situation. More particularly, the perfective views a situation as a single whole, effectively as a point, while the imperfective views a situation as having internal constituency. This distinction can be clarified by some actual examples. In a narrative, one normally presents a series of events each of which is viewed as complete in itself, and here the perfective is appropriate, as in *ja vošël v kómnatu, sel i vzjal knígu* 'I entered the room, sat down and took a book'. In background description, however, one presents situations that are on-going throughout the whole of a narrative sequence, and here the imperfective is appropriate, as in *pápa sidél v zelënom kreslé i spal* 'Father was sitting in the green arm-chair and was sleeping' (sc. when I entered the room etc.). The imperfective is thus also ideal for habitual situations, which serve as a potential background to individual events, as in *kogdá ja byl máľčikom, ja sobirál počtóvye márki* 'when I was a boy I used to collect postage stamps'. Although there are differences of detail, the distinction between imperfective and perfective in Russian can be compared to that between imperfect and preterit in Romance languages; in non-habitual, non-stative meaning, the opposition can be compared to that between progressive and non-progressive in English — all of these are aspectual oppositions.

In Russian, this aspectual opposition applies throughout the verb system, in particular in the infinitive (e.g. *čitáť–pročitáť*), in the non-past (e.g. *čitáju–pročitáju*; here the imperfective has present meaning, the perfective future meaning), in the past (*čitál–pročitál*) and in the imperative (*čitáj–pročitáj*).

In addition to morphological forms, Russian also has a small number of periphrastic verb forms. The conditional is formed by adding the invariable clitic *by* to the past tense, e.g. *ja čitál by* (perfective: *ja pročitál by*) 'I would read'. The imperfective future uses the auxiliary *búdu* 'I will be' in the appropriate person and number with the imperfective infinitive, e.g. *on búdet čitáť* 'he will read, be reading'. (Only the verb *byť* 'to be' has a morphological future, namely *búdu* itself.) There is thus a certain discrepancy between the tense-aspect correlation in form and in meaning in the non-past. In form, *čitáju* and *pročitáju* go together in contrast to the periphrastic *búdu čitáť*, which has no perfective counterpart; in meaning, however, *čitáju* is the isolated form — Russian has no perfective present — while *búdu čitáť* and *pročitáju* form an aspectual pair.

Historically, this represents a considerable simplification of the Old Russian verb system, virtually the only complication being the fully-fledged development of the aspectual opposition. Gone completely are, in addition to the dual number, the Old Russian simple past forms (imperfect and aorist) inherited from Common Slavonic. The modern Russian past tense derives from an Old Russian perfect, somewhat similar to English *I have read*, except that the auxiliary 'be' rather than 'have' is used with the past participle. Thus Old Russian has a present perfect *jazъ esmь čitalъ* 'I have read', and also equivalent forms in other tenses, e.g. pluperfect *jazъ běxъ čitalъ* 'I had read'. Of these, only the present perfect survives to modern Russian; as elsewhere in Russian, the copula is lost in the present tense, giving modern Russian *ja čitál*, which, with the loss of all the other past tenses, now survives as the basic and only past tense. The fact that the form *čitál* is etymologically a participle (i.e. a verbal adjective) accounts for why it agrees in gender and number rather than in person and number with its subject.

4   Syntax

In this brief discussion of Russian syntax, attention will be focused on two features: agreement and word order. In order to follow the example sentences, two particular features of Russian syntax should be noted in advance. Russian lacks equivalents to the English definite and indefinite articles, so that a noun phrase like *sobáka* will sometimes be glossed as 'a dog', sometimes as 'the dog'. In copular constructions in the present tense, there is usually a zero copula, so that corresponding to English 'Viktor is a student' we have *Víktor studént*. In other tenses, however, there is an overt copula, as in *Víktor byl studéntom* 'Viktor was a student'; this overt copula usually governs the instrumental case of a predicate noun, although the nominative is also possible.

In Russian, most predicates must agree, in some combination of person, gender and number, with their subject; the only exceptions are adverbial predicates and predicate nouns (or noun phrases) with the zero copula, as in *Víktor/Léna zdes'* 'Viktor/Lena is here'. Finite verbs in the non-past tense agree with their subject in person and number, e.g. *ja čitáju* 'I read', *on/oná čitáet* 'he/she reads', *oní čitájut* 'they read', *mál'čiki čitájut* 'the boys read'; despite the rich agreement morphology on the verb, it is not usual in Russian to omit unstressed subject pronouns (in this respect Russian differs from many other Slavonic languages, including Polish, Czech and Serbo-Croat). Finite verbs in the past tense agree with their subject in gender and number, e.g. *ja/on čitál* 'I (male referent)/he read', *ja/ona čitála* 'I (female referent)/ she read', *oní čitáli* 'they read'. Predicate adjectives agree in gender and number with their subject, whether there is an overt or a zero copula, e.g. *Víktor glup* 'Viktor is stupid', *Léna glupá* 'Lena is stupid', *Víktor i Léna glúpy* 'Viktor and Lena are stupid', *Víktor byl glúpym* 'Viktor was stupid', *Léna bylá glúpoj* 'Lena was stupid', *Víktor i Léna býli glúpymi* 'Viktor and Lena were stupid' (the adjectives in the past-tense sentences are in the instrumental case, although the nominative or the short form would also be possible).

Attributive adjectives (including possessive and demonstrative adjectives) agree in number, gender and case with their head noun. Thus from nominative singular *bédnyj mál'čik* 'poor boy' we can form genitive *bédnogo mál'čika*, nominative plural *bédnye mál'čiki*, dative plural *bédnym mál'čikam*; taking a feminine noun, we have nominative singular *bédnaja dévuška* 'poor girl', genitive *bédnoj dévuški*, nominative plural *bédnye dévuški*; taking a neuter noun, we have *bédnoe seló* 'poor hamlet', genitive *bédnogo selá*. Agreement of possessive and demonstrative adjectives can be illustrated by: *étot mál'čik* 'this boy', genitive *étogo mál'čika*; *éta dévuška* 'this girl', genitive *étoj dévuški*; *náše seló* 'our hamlet', genitive *nášego selá*.

One particularly complex area of Russian syntax, reflecting an unusual interplay of agreement and government, is the syntax of noun phrases involving numerals. In Russian, the numeral 'one' is an adjective, agreeing in case, gender and number with its head noun, e.g. *odín mál'čik* 'one boy', genitive *odnogó mál'čika*; *odná bédnaja dévuška* 'one poor girl'; the plural form is used with nouns that occur only in the plural but refer to a single object, e.g. *odní nóžnicy* 'one (pair of) scissors'. The numerals 'two', 'three', 'four' in the nominative-accusative govern a noun in the genitive singular, while an accompanying adjective may stand in either the nominative plural or the genitive plural (usually the latter), e.g. *dva mál'čika* 'two boys', *dve bédnye/bédnyx straný* 'two poor countries', *tri/četýre mál'čika/straný/selá* 'three/four boys/countries/hamlets'; note that of these numerals, 'two' distinguishes masculine-neuter *dva* from feminine *dve*. In the other cases, these numerals agree in case with their head noun (and show no gender distinction, as is usual in Russian in the plural), e.g. dative *dvum/ trëm/četyrëm bédnym mál'čikam/stránam/sëlam*. Numerals from 'five' up to 'nine hundred' in the nominative-accusative govern a following noun (with attributes) in the genitive plural, e.g. *pjat' bédnyx mál'čikov/dévušek/sël* 'five poor boys/girls/hamlets'; in other cases, they agree with the head noun, e.g. dative *pjatí bédnym mál'čikam/dévuškam/sëlam*. The numeral 'thousand' may either follow this pattern or govern the genitive plural in all cases: *týsjača bédnyx mál'čikov* 'a thousand poor boys', dative *týsjače bédnyx mál'cikov/bédnym mál'čikam*. The numeral 'million' and higher numerals take a following genitive plural irrespective of case, e.g. *millión bédnyx dévušek* 'a million poor girls', dative *milliónu bédnyx dévušek*.

Apart from the idiosyncrasy of the genitive singular after the numerals 'two' to 'four' (with nominative or genitive plural attributes), the other patterns can all be described in terms of the interaction of attributive adjective syntax (attributive adjectives agree with their head) and measure-noun syntax (nouns of measure govern a following count noun in the genitive plural, e.g. *vedró červéj* 'a bucket of worms'): thus, the numeral 'one' behaves consistently as an adjective, while the numerals from 'million' on behave consistently as measure nouns, the numerals from 'five' to 'thousand' combining aspects of adjective and measure-noun syntax. The synchronically unusual system can best be understood in terms of its historical origin. In Old Russian, 'one' is an adjective, while all numerals from 'five' on are measure nouns; diachronically, adjective properties have been creeping up the number scale. In Old Russian, the numeral 'two' is followed by the dual; although the dual as a separate category has been lost in modern Russian, the synchronic genitive singular found after 'two' derives etymologically from a nominative dual, i.e. originally this was an instance of agreement; for a few nouns, the genitive singular and the form used after 'two' still differ in stress, e.g. *čas* 'hour', genitive *čása*, but *dva časá* 'two hours'. The use of the erstwhile dual, now genitive singular, after 'three' and 'four' is a later analogical development.

Turning now to word order, we may distinguish between word order within the noun phrase and word order within the clause (i.e. the order of major constituents within each clause). Within the noun phrase, word order is fairly rigid in Russian, in particular in the written language, especially in scientific writing. Adjectives, including demonstrative and possessive adjectives, precede the head noun, as in *stáraja sobáka* 'old dog', *mojá sobáka* 'my dog', *éta sobáka* 'this dog'. Genitives, on the other hand, follow the head noun, as in *sobáka Víktora* 'Viktor's dog'. Relative clauses follow the head noun, e.g. *sobáka, kotóruju ja vídel, ukusíla tebjá* 'the dog that I saw has bitten you'; this reflects the general tendency in Russian for non-adverbial subordinate clauses to follow main clauses (i.e. Russian, like English, is a right-branching language). We may also note at this point that Russian has prepositions rather than postpositions, e.g. *v dóme* 'in the house', *péred dómom* 'in front of the house'; prepositions govern various cases, other than the nominative.

With respect to the order of major constituents within the clause, Russian is often referred to as a free word order language. This means that, in general, any permutation of the major constituents of the clause produces a grammatical sentence with essentially the same meaning as the original order (in particular, with the same truth conditions). Thus alongside *Víktor celúet Lénu* 'Viktor kisses Lena', one can also say: *Víktor Lénu celúet*; *Lénu Víktor celúet*; *Lénu celúet Víktor*; *celúet Víktor Lénu*; *celúet Lénu Víktor*. In Russian, the morphology is nearly always sufficient to provide unique recovery of the grammatical relations of the various major constituents: in these examples, the nominative *Víktor* is unambiguously subject, while the accusative *Lénu* is unequivocally direct object. To say 'Lena kissed Viktor', one would have to change the cases to give *Léna celúet Víktora* (or any permutation of these three words). In some instances, agreement may reveal the grammatical relations, as in *mat' zaščiščáet snarjády* 'the mother defends the missiles', where the singular verb *zaščiščáet* allows *mat'* 'mother', but disqualifies *snarjády* 'missiles' as subject. It is actually quite difficult to construct sensible sentences where the morphology is insufficient to disambiguate, e.g. *mat' celúet doč'*, literally 'mother kisses daughter', where both nouns happen to have the same form for nominative and accusative and are of the same person and number. In such sentences, the most salient interpretation is 'the mother kisses the daughter', one of the pieces of evidence suggesting that the basic word order in Russian, as in English, is subject–object–verb. But whereas in English departures from this order produce either nonsense or sentences with different meanings (*Viktor Lena kisses*; *Lena kisses Viktor*), in Russian the main clue to grammatical relations is the morphology, thus giving rise to the phenomenon of free word order.

This does not mean, however, that there are no principles of word order in Russian. Word order of major constituents within the clause is governed by two main principles. The first is that the topic of the sentence, i.e. what the sentence is about, comes initially. The second is that the focus of the sentence, i.e. the essential new information communicated by the sentence, comes last. Thus word order in Russian is largely pragmatically determined. (A further pragmatic principle, this time shared with English, is that interrogative pronouns and relative pronouns occur clause-initially, as in *kogó ty vídel?* 'whom did you see?'; *mál'čik, kotórogo ja vídel* 'the boy that I saw'.) One way of illustrating these principles is to produce miniature dialogues where the choice of topic and focus in the final sentence is forced by the context. Imagine that we have a discourse about kissing. If we ask *who kissed X?*, then in the answer *X kissed Y*, *Y* must be the focus, since it is the new information communicated. Conversely, given the question *what about Y?*, in the answer the topic must be *Y*, since any reasonable answer to a question about Y must have *Y* as its topic. The following miniature dialogues illustrate pragmatic word order in Russian, in each case the relevant sentence being the last one of the discourse:

(a) -Víktor poceloval Lénu.   -Viktor kissed Lena.
     -A Róbert, kogó on   -And what about Robert, whom did he
     poceloval?   kiss?
     -*Róbert* poceloval Mǎšu.   -*Robert* kissed Masha.
(b) -Víktor poceloval Lénu.   -Viktor kissed Lena.
     -A Mǎšu, kto poceloval eë?   -And as for Masha, who kissed her?
     -*Mǎšu* poceloval Rǒbert.   -Rǒbert kissed *Masha*.

In each example, the topic is italicised and the focus marked with the diacritic ". In English, the final turns in (a) and (b) are distinguished by sentence stress, this stress falling in each case on the focus. In Russian, too, the sentence stress falls on the focus, but there is the added differentiation brought about by the word order, which can thus be used to indicate topic and focus even in writing, where sentence stress is not indicated. (In the spoken language, for emotive effect, departures from the 'focus-last' principle are possible, but such deviations would be quite out of place in a scientific treatise.)

Freedom of word order in Russian applies primarily to major constituents of the clause. Under certain circumstances it is, however, possible to extract constituents of major constituents for purposes of topic or focus, as in *knígi u menjá xoróšie*, literally 'books at me good', i.e. 'I have good *books*'.

In English, the variation in word order that is possible directly in Russian can sometimes be achieved by less direct means. Thus one of the differences in English between the active voice, as in *Viktor kissed Lena*, and the passive voice, as in *Lena was kissed by Viktor*, is topicalisation of the patient in the passive. In English the order subject–verb–object is fairly rigid, but since the passive voice presents the direct object of the active sentence as subject of the passive sentence, this change in voice effectively allows one to prepose the patient to give a close equivalent to Russian *Lénu pocelovál Víktor*. Russian does have a passive similar in form to that of English, e.g. *Léna bylá pocelóvana Víktorom*, but this construction is much less frequently used in Russian than in English — it serves primarily as an indicator of literary style — and, moreover, given the free word order of Russian it is possible to invert the order of the noun phrases to have the agent, though not subject, as topic, i.e. *Víktorom bylá pocelóvana Léna*!

This infrequent use of the passive in Russian as compared to English is a particular case of a general phenomenon distinguishing the two languages. English has a wide range of possibilities for the link between the grammatical relations of a sentence and its semantic roles. Thus the subject is agent in *Viktor kissed Lena*, but patient in *Lena was kissed by Viktor*; in *lightning killed the soldier*, the subject is a natural force. In Russian, the fit between semantic roles and grammatical relations is much closer. As already indicated, avoidance of the passive is one instance of this. The most natural Russian translation of *lightning killed the soldier* (and equally of *the soldier was killed by lightning*) is impersonal (subjectless), with neither 'lightning' nor 'soldier' as subject: *soldáta* (accusative) *ubílo mólniej* (instrumental), literally (apart from word order) 'it killed the soldier by lightning'. In yet further instances where English allows a given predicate to take grammatical relations with different semantic roles, Russian allows this only if the predicate is marked overtly to indicate the difference in semantic roles. Thus, in English the verb *close* can take an agentive subject transitively in *Lena closed the door* and a patient subject intransitively as in *the door closed*; in Russian, the second usage must be overtly distinguished by the reflexive clitic *-sja/-s'*: *Léna zakrýla dver'*; *dver' zakrýlas'*. In English, the same verb can be used in *the collective farmer sowed maize in the field* and in *the collective farmer sowed the field with maize*, while Russian requires different prefixes on the verbs: *kolxóznik poséjal kukurúzu v póle*; *kolxóznik zaséjal póle kukurúzoj*. The interaction among morphology, word order, grammatical relations, semantic roles and pragmatic roles is one of the major typological differences between the grammars of Russian and English.

Bibliography

Ward (1955) is a useful introduction to the structure of Russian and its historical and social setting. The selection of reference grammars available in English is rather poor, one of the best being Pulkina (n.d.); for those who read German, Isačenko (1968) is an excellent descriptive morphology, including the meanings of the morphological categories. Švedova et al. (1980) is the latest Academy grammar, a major improvement over previous Academy grammars, in particular in syntax, semantics and pragmatics. For individual topics, Halle (1959) is a pioneering work on the synchronic analysis of Russian morphophonemics; Forsyth (1970) is an excellent account of aspect in Russian; Krylova and Khavronina (1976) is an account of Russian word order intended primarily for advanced students of Russian.

For the history of the language, Vinokur (1971) is a concise account of the historical and sociological development, while Comrie and Stone (1978) deals with post-Revolutionary developments in the language, including those subject to current variation, against a background of social factors. A standard handbook for the internal history is Borkovskij and Kuznecov (1965), as is Avanesov and Orlova (1965) for dialectology.

References

Avanesov, R.I. and V.G. Orlova (eds.) 1965. *Russkaja dialektologija*, 2nd ed. (Nauka, Moscow)
Borkovskij, V.I. and P.S. Kuznecov. 1965. *Istoričeskaja grammatika russkogo jazyka*, 2nd ed. (Nauka, Moscow)
Comrie, B. and G. Stone. 1978. *The Russian Language Since the Revolution* (Clarendon Press, Oxford)
Forsyth, J. 1970. *A Grammar of Aspect: Usage and Meaning in the Russian Verb* (Cambridge University Press, London)
Halle, M. 1959. *The Sound Pattern of Russian* (Mouton, The Hague)
Isačenko, A.V. 1968. *Die russische Sprache der Gegenwart, Teil 1: Formenlehre* (Max Niemeyer, Halle (Saale))
Krylova, A. and S. Khavronina. 1976. *Word Order in Russian Sentences* (Russian Language Publishers, Moscow; translated from the simultaneously published Russian edition)
Pulkina, I.M. n.d. *A Short Russian Reference Grammar* (Moscow)
Švedova, N.Ju. et al. (eds.) 1980. *Russkaja grammatika*, 2 vols. (Nauka, Moscow)
Vinokur, G.O. 1971. *The Russian Language: A Brief History* (Cambridge University Press, London; translated from the Russian edition of 1959)
Ward, D. 1955. *The Russian Language Today* (Hutchinson University Library, London)

4 Polish

Gerald Stone

1 Historical Background

The West Slavonic languages include a subgroup, known as 'Lechitic', comprising Polish (its easternmost variety) and the other Slavonic languages once spoken throughout what is now north Germany as far west as the Lüneburg Heath. Most of the dialects of Lechitic were extinct by the late Middle Ages and are attested only by fragmentary evidence, principally in the form of place names; but its westernmost variety, which has been given the name 'Polabian' by philologists, survived until the eighteenth century and is recorded in a number of substantial texts. Unless we bestow separate status on Cassubian, a variety of Lechitic still spoken by perhaps as many as 150,000 people near the Baltic coast to the west of the Bay of Gdańsk, Polish is the only Lechitic language which survives to the present day. Cassubian, despite features testifying to its former independence, is now generally regarded as a dialect of Polish. Within West Slavonic the Lechitic subgroup on the one hand and the Czecho-Slovak on the other constitute the two extremities. A link between them is provided by Sorbian.

Our earliest evidence of the Polish language comes in the form of place names, tribal names, and personal names recorded in medieval Latin documents going back to the ninth century AD. Among the most useful records of this kind are the Papal Bull of Gniezno (1136) which contains 410 names and the Bull of Wrocław (Breslau) (1155) containing about 50 more. The same kind of evidence becomes even more plentiful in the thirteenth century, by which time we also find isolated words other than proper nouns imbedded in Latin texts and accompanied by Latin explanations. In about 1270 the Cistercian monks of Henryków, near Wrocław, wrote a history of their monastery (in Latin) and included several Polish words. Their history also contains the first known Polish sentence: 'daj ać ja pobruczę a ty poczywaj' ('Let me grind and you rest'), which is quoted to explain the etymology of the place name Brukalice.

It is only in the fourteenth century that we find entire Polish texts consisting of many sentences. The earliest of these are the undated *Kazania Świętokrzyskie* ('Holy Cross Sermons'), which are attributed to the middle

82

of the century or a little later. A translation of the Book of Psalms into Polish, known as the *Psałterz Floriański* ('St. Florian Psalter'), is reckoned to date from the end of the century, as are the *Kazania Gnieźnieńskie* 'Gniezno Sermons'. There are also court records, dating from 1386 onwards, in which the main account is written in Latin, but the actual words of depositions sworn by witnesses and litigants are in the original Polish. The number of such depositions dating from before 1500 exceeds 8,000 and collectively they constitute one of our main sources for the state of medieval Polish. There are, however, many other sources, mostly of a devotional and literary kind, dating from this period. They include a manuscript of the greater part of the Old Testament, known as *Biblia królowej Zofii* ('Queen Sophia's Bible'), dating from around 1455.

The spelling in these early texts is far from systematic and it is consequently, in particular, almost impossible to distinguish between the three series of sibilants: /tɕ/, /ɕ/, /ʑ/ : /tʃ/, /ʃ/, /ʒ/ : /ts/, /s/, /z/, which in modern Polish are written respectively: *ć, ś, ź : cz, sz, ż : c, s, z* (see section 2). However, the local features in most of these texts are far less prominent than one might expect them to have been in the speech of the areas they came from. Clearly, certain standardising processes had been at work. Nevertheless, some local features may be detected in almost any medieval text of reasonable size. To a large extent the medieval dialectal features can be correlated with those observed in modern dialects. For example, the feature *chw → f* (e.g. *chwała* 'glory' pronounced as *fała*) is known to most modern dialects with the exception of that of Great Poland (Wielkopolska). Therefore, medieval spellings with *f* (such as *fała* 'glory') indicate that the text in question could not have originated in Great Poland. The reconstruction of medieval dialectal divisions is greatly helped by the forensic records owing to the fact that they almost always include the exact date and place of origin. Most of the devotional texts can be assigned either to Little Poland (Małopolska) (e.g. The St. Florian Psalter) or to Great Poland (e.g. The Gniezno Sermons). The centre of gravity of the Polish state is known to have been in Great Poland until the reign of Kazimierz the Restorer (reigned 1034–1058), but in 1037 the capital was moved to Cracow, and the position of importance consequently acquired by Little Poland was maintained until, and even after, the further transfer of the capital to Warsaw in 1596.

The modicum of standardisation exhibited by our fourteenth- and fifteenth-century manuscripts attracted a lot of interest among Polish scholars in the first half of the twentieth century. It was asserted by one faction that the standard must have been based on the dialect of Great Poland, which even after 1037 retained the seat of the archbishop (at Gniezno) and exerted great authority. Others claimed that the new capital Cracow must have provided the variety on which the standard was based. (No one doubted that Mazovia, which with its capital, Warsaw, was united to Poland only in the sixteenth century, could have had no influence in the

Map 4.1: Traditional Regions of Poland

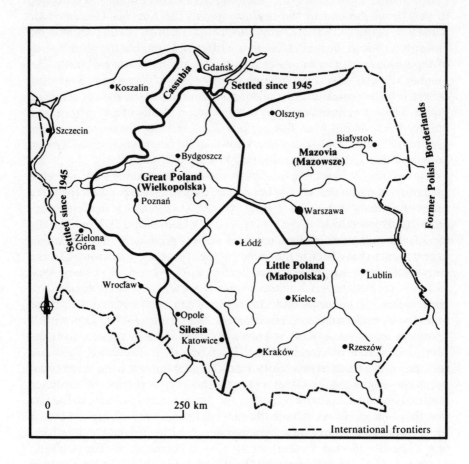

matter.) One of the crucial features in this argument was that known as *mazurzenie*, i.e. the neutralisation of the distinction between *c*, *s*, *z* and *cz*, *sz*, *ż* respectively. It was held that deliberate avoidance of this feature in the language of many scribes and later in printed books meant that the standard was based on a variety unaffected by *mazurzenie*. Dialectologists were able to show that Great Poland did not have *mazurzenie*, whereas (by the time dialectologists enquired, at least) Little Poland did. The question now turned on dating the arrival of *mazurzenie* in Little Poland. But the controversy was never settled.

The arrival of printing in Poland (the first book in Polish was printed in 1513) put an end to the untidy spelling system used by the scribes. The printers aimed for less ambiguity and more standardisation. The sixteenth century, known as the Golden Age of Polish literature, was also the age in which the first dictionaries and grammars appeared. The most important of these are Jan Mączyński's *Lexicon latinopolonicum* (Königsberg 1564), which contains 20,700 Polish words, and the *Polonicae grammatices institutio* (Cracow 1568) of Piotr Statorius (Stojeński). Also, at least five different treatises on spelling were published.

Towards the end of the fifteenth century the Polish vocalic system underwent a great change. It had hitherto involved the opposition of long and short vowels, but now vocalic quantity ceased to be a relevant phonemic distinction. The long vowels, in losing their length, acquired a new quality. At the beginning of the fifteenth century only the vowels /i/ and /u/ were unaffected by a quantitative distinction. Short /a/, /ɛ/, /ɔ/, and /ã/ were distinguished from long /aː/, /ɛː/, /ɔː/, and /ãː/. But by the sixteenth century there were ten qualitatively distinguished vowel phonemes: /a/, /ɑ/, /ɔ/, /o/, /u/, /i/, /e/, /ɛ/, /ɛ̃/, and /ɔ̃/. Books printed in the sixteenth century and later frequently made use of the acute accent to distinguish between /a/, and /ɑ/, /ɔ/ and /o/, /e/ and /ɛ/. In standard pronunciation, however, the ten-vowel system was eventually reduced to seven vowels, as the distinction between /a/ and /ɑ/, /o/ and /u/, and /e/ and /ɛ/ was neutralised. The last relic of the ten-vowel system is in the modern spelling system, which still uses *ó* for reasons of tradition (as in *wóz* 'cart, car', *gród* 'castle', etc.), though this letter now represents the same sound as the letter *u*.

With the First Partition of Poland in 1772 the Polish language entered a period of trial that was to last until the restoration of independence after the First World War. After 1795, when Poland disappeared from the map altogether, there were attempts by all the partitioning powers (Prussia, Austria and Russia) at one time or another to reduce the social functions of Polish and replace it with German or Russian. After 1848, however, language policy in the Austrian partition was modified to the advantage of the Poles and their language was henceforth able to thrive here. In the other two partitions users of Polish suffered numerous indignities. As a result of its prohibition from the schools a clandestine system of Polish instruction grew up to ensure the language's survival. Matters came to a head in May 1901 in a school in Września (Posnania), where the compulsory use of German during religious instruction led to a riot which attracted the attention of world public opinion.

By this time, owing to the practical advantages of knowing German or Russian and the influence of military service on the male population, a large proportion of educated Poles were bilingual. Bilingualism was most common in the Prussian partition, where educational standards were higher than in Russia or Austria. The existence of three separate administrations fostered the Polish language's existing tendency to regional variation. Some of the regional features first observed then have survived until recent times even in educated usage: e.g. *kurczak* 'chicken' (Warsaw) corresponding to *kurczę* elsewhere; *na polu* 'outside' (Cracow) corresponding to *na dworze* (Poznań) and *na dworze* or *na dworzu* (Warsaw); *listonosz* 'postman' (Cracow) corresponding to *listowy* (Poznań) and *listonosz* or *bryftrygier* (Warsaw).

After the First World War Polish was restored to its position as the language of the Polish state, but there were also many speakers of other languages living in Poland. At the 1931 census a population of 32,107,000 was recorded, of whom only 21,993,000 gave Polish as their native language. This situation was completely changed in the upheaval brought about by the Second World War. The population according to the first census held within the post-war frontiers (1946) was 23,930,000. Since then it has expanded to over 35 million, of whom almost all have Polish as their native language. The national minorities total about one per cent of the population. At the same time, there are millions of Polish speakers living outside Poland, including over 300,000 in the USSR and perhaps as many as six million in the USA.

2 Phonology

The segmental phonemes of Polish are set out in table 4.1.

Table 4.1: Segmental Phonemes of Polish

Vowels	Oral		Nasal	
	i	u		.
	ɛ	ɔ	ɛ̃	ɔ̃
	a			

Consonants	Plain stop	Affricate	Fricative	Nasal	Lateral	Trill	Semi-vowel
Bilabial	p b			m			w
	pʲ bʲ			mʲ			
Labio-dental			f v				
			fʲ ɣ				
Dental	t d	ts dz	s z	n	l		
Alveolar		tʃ dʒ	ʃ ʒ			r	
Pre-palatal		tɕ dʑ	ɕ ʑ	ɲ			
Post-palatal	kʲ gʲ						j
Velar	k g		x				

As in the case of Russian, the richness of the consonant system is striking. However, certain Russian oppositions between palatalised dentals (t:tʲ; d:dʲ; r:rʲ) have no counterpart in Polish. On the other hand, Polish has an additional type of opposition, viz. that between tʃ and tɕ, dʒ and dʑ, ʃ and ɕ, ʒ and ʑ. This distinction depends less on the precise portion of the roof of the mouth involved in the articulation than on the fact that tʃ, dʒ, ʃ and ʒ are articulated with the tip of the tongue, whereas tɕ, dʑ, ɕ and ʑ are produced with the middle of the tongue.

The functional load of dʒ is very light, since it is largely restricted to loanwords, but the rest of these oppositions have a substantial yield. Some have a role in the morphological system, e.g. *duży* /duʒi/ 'big' (masculine nominative singular) : *duzi* /duʑi/ 'big' (masculine personal nominative plural); *lepszy* /lɛpʃi/ 'better' (masculine nominative singular) : *lepsi* /lɛpɕi/ 'better' (masculine personal nominative plural).

Double consonants are not uncommon in Polish and their phonological function is well attested, e.g. *lekki* /lɛkki/ 'light' (masculine nominative singular) : *leki* /lɛki/ 'medicines'. Phonetically they may be double or long, but there are no cases of the opposition of morphologically indivisible long and short consonants. The example given breaks down into *lek-* (stem) and *-ki* (ending). Loss of this distinction (e.g. the pronunciation of *lekki* as /lɛki/) is a regional feature of Great Poland (Wielkopolska) and Silesia.

The distribution of the nasal vowels in restricted. They may only occur at the end of a word or before fricatives, e.g. *chodzę* /xɔdzɛ̃/ 'I walk', *gęś* /gɛ̃ɕ/ 'goose', *mąż* /mɔ̃ʃ/ 'husband'. (The nasal vowel *letters*, however, appear before consonants of all kinds and are therefore phonetically misleading.) In addition to /ɛ̃/ and /ɔ̃/ other nasal vowels may occur, but only before fricatives, e.g. *tramwaj* [trãvaj] 'tram', *inspektor* [ĩspɛktɔr] 'inspector', *triumf* [triũf] 'triumph'. Before fricatives the vowels /ɛ̃/ and /ɔ̃/ may be spelled *en*, *em*, *on* or *om*, e.g. *sens* /sɛ̃s/ 'sense', *konferencja* /kɔ̃fɛrɛntsja/ 'conference'. Before plosives and affricates, however, only the sequence oral vowel (abbreviated as V) plus nasal consonant (phonemes /n/, /ɲ/ and /m/) (abbreviated as N) may occur. Therefore, with the exception of /ɛ̃/ and /ɔ̃/ at the end of a word, nasal vowels are positional variants of VN. Clearly, [ĩ], [ã], [ũ] are not phonemes, and even the phonemic status of /ɛ̃/ and /ɔ̃/ depends solely on their occurrence at the end of a word before a pause, e.g. *tą* /tɔ̃/ 'that' (instrumental feminine singular) is distinct from *to* /tɔ/ 'that' (nominative neuter singular), *ton* /tɔn/ 'tone' and *tom* /tɔm/ 'volume'; *listę* /listɛ̃/ 'list' (accusative singular) is distinct from *listem* /listɛm/ 'letter' (instrumental singular); *piszę* /piʃɛ̃/ 'I write' is distinct from *pisze* /piʃɛ/ 'he writes'. However, no one, not even actors, consistently pronounces /ɛ̃/ at the end of words. *Piszę* 'I write', for example, may be realised as /piʃɛ/, in which case it becomes indistinguishable from *pisze* 'he writes'. On the other hand, no speaker of the standard language consistently denasalises final /ɛ̃/ and the possibility of making the distinction always exists. Therefore /ɛ̃/ is a phoneme. There is even less doubt in the case of /ɔ̃/, since denasalisation of final /ɔ̃/ is less common.

The distinction between voiced and voiceless paired consonants (i.e. between /b/ and /p/, /d/ and /t/, /v/ and /f/, /dz/ and /ts/, /z/ and /s/, /dʒ/ and /tʃ/, /ʒ/ and /ʃ/, /dʑ/ and /tɕ/, /ʑ/ and /ɕ/, /g/ and /k/) is neutralised at the end of a word. Thus, for example, *Bóg* /buk/ 'God' and *buk* /buk/ 'beech' are homophones. At the end of a word only the voiceless member of the pair can occur, but this feature is not reflected in the spelling, as we may see from such examples as *ząb* /zɔmp/ 'tooth', *nóg* /nuk/ 'feet' (genitive plural), *mosiądz* /mɔçɔnts/ 'brass', *mąż* /mɔ̃ʃ/ 'husband', *ród* /rut/ 'breed'.

With few exceptions, Polish words are stressed on the penultimate syllable. Thus, for example, *ziemia* 'earth' is pronounced as ['ʑɛm̩a], *sprawiedliwość* 'justice' as [spraɣɛ'dlivɔçtɕ] and *sprawiedliwośći* 'justice' (genitive, dative or locative singular) as [spraɣɛdli'vɔçtɕi]. The exceptions are mainly words of Greek origin, such as *muzyka* ['muzika] 'music', or of Latin origin, such as *uniwersytet* [uɳi'vɛrsitɛt] 'university', but even a few Slavonic words are irregular, such as *rzeczpospolita* [ʒɛtʃpɔ'spɔlita] 'commonwealth'. In addition, the first and second persons plural of the past tense of verbs have antepenultimate stress, e.g. *byliśmy* ['biliçmi] 'we were', *wiedzieliście* [ɣɛ'dʑɛliçtɕɛ] 'you knew' (masculine personal plural).

The Polish writing system uses an alphabet based on Latin, making liberal use of digraphs and diacritics. The Latin language and its alphabet were introduced to Poland simultaneously with Christianity in the tenth century AD. Gradually the alphabet was adapted to make it fit Polish.

Table 4.2: The Polish Alphabet

A	a	M	m
Ą	ą	N	n
B	b	Ń	ń
C	c	O	o
Ć	ć	Ó	ó
D	d	P	p
E	e	R	r
Ę	ę	S	s
F	f	Ś	ś
G	g	T	t
H	h	U	u
I	i	W	w
J	j	Y	y
K	k	Z	z
L	l	Ź	ź
Ł	ł	Ż	ż

Note: In addition to the 32 letters shown above, Q q, V v and X x may occasionally be found in foreign words, e.g. *Quebec*, *vademecum*, *Pax*. The digraphs *ch*, *cz*, *rz*, *sz*, *dz*, *dź*, *dż*, for the purpose of alphabetic order, are treated as sequences of separate letters.

The vowel letters *i* and *y* do not represent separate phonemes. They both stand for the phoneme /i/, but have separate functions in reflecting the quality of the consonant immediately preceding. Thus, for example, the

written sequences *ci, dzi, si, zi, pi, bi, mi, fi, wi, ni* correspond respectively to
/tɕi/, /dʑi/, /ɕi/, /ʑi/, /pi/, /bi/, /m̪i/, /f̪i/, /ɣi/, /n̪i/, whereas *cy, dzy, sy, zy, py, by, my, fy, wy, ny* represent /tsi/, /dzi/, /si/, /zi/, /pi/, /bi/, /mi/, /fi/, /vi/, /ni/.
Except in words of foreign origin or in onomatopoeic words, the letter *i* is
rarely or never written after the letters *d, t, cz, dz, sz, ż, ch, ł, r.* Subject to
exceptions of the same kind, the letter *y* does not occur after *k, g,* or *l.*

The phoneme /tɕ/ is represented by *ć* or *ci,* the phoneme /dʑ/ by *dź* or *dzi,*
the phoneme /ɕ/ by *ś* or *si,* the phoneme /ʑ/ by *ź* or *zi,* and the phoneme /n̪/
by *ń* or *ni.* There is an orthographical convention whereby *ć, dź, ś, ź* and *ń*
are written only at the end of a word (as in *być* /bitɕ/ 'to be') or immediately
before another consonant (as in *ćma* /tɕma/ 'moth'). Elsewhere (i.e. before a
vowel), *ci, dzi, si, zi* and *ni* are used (as in *ciemny* /tɕɛmni/ 'dark', *siano*
/ɕanɔ/ 'hay', and *ziarno* /ʑarnɔ/ 'grain'). If the vowel following is /i/, it is not
shown separately in the spelling. For example, *ci* /tɕi/ 'to you', *nikt* /n̪ikt/
'nobody', *musi* /muɕi/ 'he must', *zima* /ʑima/ 'winter'. In such cases the letter
i has a double function: it participates with the consonant letter in the
representation of the consonant and also stands for the vowel /i/. Any other
vowel, however, is shown separately in the spelling. In our examples
ciemny, siano and *ziarno* (see above) the letter *i* is relevant only to the
representation of the consonant.

The bilabial and labio-dental consonants /p̪/, /b̪/, /m̪/, /f̪/ and /ɣ/ can only
occur immediately before a vowel, e.g. *biały* /b̪awi/ 'white'. In the sixteenth
century they could occur at the end of a word and their palatalised quality
was then sometimes indicated by means of a diacritic. The gradual process
whereby they were replaced in this position by their non-palatalised
counterparts was complete by the nineteenth century. As a result, we
sometimes find palatalised and non-palatalised labials alternating in the
stems of certain nouns, e.g. *gołąb* (nom. sg.) 'dove': *gołębia* (gen. sg.);
Wrocław (nom. sg.): *Wrocławia* (gen. sg.). This tendency has gone even
further in the north-east, including Warsaw, where even before vowels the
palatalised labials are often replaced by the sequence non-palatalised labial
+ /j/, e.g. not /b̪awi/ but /bjawi/.

The following are some of the less obvious graphemic-phonemic
correspondences:

Grapheme	Phoneme
ą	finally and before fricatives: /ɔ̃/ e.g. *mąż* /mɔ̃ʃ/ 'husband', *idą* /idɔ̃/ 'they go'
	before dental plosives and affricates: /ɔn/ e.g. *kąt* /kɔnt/ 'angle', *zając* /zajɔnts/ 'hare'
	before /k/ and /g/: /ɔn/ (phonetically [ɔŋ]) e.g. *łąka* [wɔŋka] 'meadow'
	before /p/ and /b/: /ɔm/ e.g. *dąb* /dɔmp/ 'oak'
	before /w/: /ɔ/ e.g. *wziął* /ɣʐɔw/ 'took'
ę	(i) finally and before fricatives: /ɛ̃/ e.g. *chcę* /xtsɛ̃/ 'I want', *często* /tʃɛ̃stɔ/ 'often'
	(ii) finally (colloquially): /ɛ/ e.g. *chcę* /xtsɛ/ 'I want'

(iii)   before dental plosives and before dental and alveolar affricates: /ɛn/ e.g. *okręt* /ɔkrɛnt/ 'ship', *nędza* /nɛndza/ 'poverty', *tęcza* /tɛntʃa/ 'rainbow'

(iv)   before pre-palatal affricates: /ɛn̠/ e.g. *pięć* /pɛn̠tɕ/ 'five'

(v)   before /k/ and /g/: /ɛn/ (phonetically [ɛŋ]) e.g. *ręka* [rɛŋka] 'hand'

(vi)   before bilabial plosives: /ɛm/ e.g. *postęp* /pɔstɛmp/ 'progress'

(vii)   before /w/ and /l/: /ɛ/ e.g. *wzięli* /vʑɛli/ 'they took'

c	/ts/ e.g. *noc* /nɔts/ 'night'
ch h }	/x/ e.g. *suchy* /suxi/ 'dry', *błahy* /bwaxi/ 'trivial'
ć ci }	/tɕ/ e.g. *być* /bitɕ/ 'to be', *ciemny* /tɕɛmni/ 'dark'
cz	/tʃ/ e.g. *czas* /tʃas/ 'time'
ł	/w/ e.g. *łapać* /wapatɕ/ 'to catch'
rz ż }	/ʒ/ e.g. *rzeka* /ʒɛka/ 'river', *żagiel* /ʒagˌɛl/ 'sail'
ś si }	/ɕ/ e.g. *oś* /ɔɕ/ 'axis', *siano* /ɕanɔ/ 'hay'
sz	/ʃ/ e.g. *szok* /ʃɔk/ 'shock'
ó u }	/u/ e.g. *róg* /ruk/ 'corner', *mur* /mur/ 'wall'
w	/v/ or /ɣ/ e.g. *kawa* /kava/ 'coffee', *wiara* /ɣara/ 'faith'
ź zi }	/ʑ/ e.g. *luźny* /luʑni/ 'loose', *zima* /ʑima/ 'winter'

In the speech of a rapidly diminishing minority of Poles the archaic variant [ł] in place of normal [w] may be heard. The articulation of this dental lateral involves raising the back of the tongue. It is similar to the Russian non-palatalised /l/. Until recently Polish [ł] was obligatory in stage-pronunciation and it is still used by many actors. Regionally, it is mainly associated with the speech of Poles from the eastern areas now in the USSR, but it may also be encountered as a dialectal feature in the Tatra Mountains. The change [ł] > [w] began several centuries ago, but is still not complete.

Another feature characteristic of speakers from the eastern parts of the Polish speech area is the distinction of two separate phonemes /h/ and /x/, whereas most speakers have only one, viz. /x/. The phoneme /h/, which is a voiced laryngeal fricative, usually corresponds to the letter *h*. It is consequently possible in this type of pronunciation to make distinctions such as that between *hełm* [hɛłm] 'helmet' and *Chełm* [xɛłm] (a town in eastern Poland). For the vast majority of Poles these two words are homophones, both being pronounced [xɛwm].

The distinction between voiced and voiceless consonants is often neutralised as a result of assimilation, but the effects of assimilation are not always shown in the orthography. The orthography reveals that there was a time in the past when assimilation could operate progressively (i.e. towards the end of the word), e.g. *przy* /pʃi/ 'near'; but the active processes of assimilation are now only regressive (i.e. towards the beginning of the word), e.g. *prośba* /prɔʑba/ 'request'. Regressive assimilation may take place not only within the body of a word but also at the boundary between words. For example, *jak dobrze* 'how good' is pronounced /jag dɔbʒɛ/, *naród polski* 'the Polish nation' is pronounced /narut pɔlski/. This kind of assimilation is found on all social levels in all parts of Poland. However, if the second word begins with a vowel or a sonant (/m/, /n/, /r/, /l/, /w/), the presence or absence of assimilation by voicing is a regional feature distinguishing the north-east (including Warsaw) from the south and west (including Cracow and Poznań). In the north-east voicing is absent, e.g. *tak mało* 'so little' is pronounced /tak mawɔ/, *róg ulicy* 'the corner of the street' is pronounced /ruk ulitsi/. The corresponding variants in the south and west are /tag mawɔ/ and /rug ulitsi/. This variable is unaffected by social level. (Prepositions ending in a voiced consonant, however, are not affected by this type of variation. Their final consonants remain voiced before vowels and sonants in all parts of Poland.)

The results of the historical progressive assimilation of /v/ within the body of the word also varies regionally regardless of social factors. The pronunciation of such words as *twój* 'your', *kwiat* 'flower' with /f/ or /f̦/ (/tfuj/, /kf̦at/) is found in all parts of Poland except the eastern borderlands, Great Poland and Pomerania, where we hear /tvuj/, /kɣat/, etc.

We now come to consider some of the sound changes which have taken place in Polish and which distinguish it from the other Slavonic languages:

(i) The Common Slavonic nasal vowels were inherited by Polish and wherever the letters *ę* and *ą* are written today we may conclude that there was once a nasal vowel. However, as we have seen, these letters nowadays represent phonetically nasal vowels only in certain positions. The earliest records indicate that the Common Slavonic nasal vowels *ę* and *ǫ* were still distinguished in Polish until the beginning of the fourteenth century. During the course of this century, however, they appear to have coalesced as a single nasal vowel, written with the letter *ǿ*. Depending on prosodic factors, however, this single nasal underwent new changes, so that by the beginning of the sixteenth century (or perhaps even earlier) there were again two nasals (now written *ę* and *ą*). The present-day spelling system still reflects the state of the nasals in the sixteenth century. Of course, there is no correlation between the Polish letter *ę* and Common Slavonic *ę*, nor between Polish *ą* and Common Slavonic *ǫ*. For example, Polish *ręka* 'hand', *zięć* 'son-in-law', *rząd* 'row', *ząb* 'tooth' correspond to Common Slavonic **rǫka*, **zętь*, **rędъ*, **zǫbъ*, respectively.

(ii) The Common Slavonic reduced vowels or *jers* (*ъ* and *ь*) in strong positions give Polish *e*. In weak positions they are lost. The distinction between *ъ* and *ь*, whether strong or weak, survives in the quality of the preceding consonant. For example, **pьsъ* > *pies* 'dog', but **vьsь* > *wieś* 'village'; **sъnъ* > *sen* 'sleep', but **dьnь* > *dzień* 'day'.

(iii) In early Polish consonants located immediately before the front vowels (*e*, *i*, *ĕ*, *ь*, *ę*) were palatalised. In the case of the labials and labio-dentals this has resulted in the existence of pairs of consonants distinguished from each other solely by the feature 'palatalised' (i.e. the raising of the middle of the tongue to the hard palate). This is the only feature distinguishing /ḅ/ from /b/, /p̣/ from /p/, /v̦/ from /v/, /f̦/ from /f/ and /m̦/ from /m/. In the case of the dentals *s*, *z*, *t*, *d* and *n*, however, the change eventually involved more than the addition of the feature 'palatalised': /s/ > /ç/, /z/ > /ʑ/, /t/ > /tç/, /d/ > /dʑ/, /n/ > /ɲ/. For example, **osь > oś* 'axis', **zemja > ziemia* 'earth', **tęžьkъjь > ciężki* 'heavy', **kъdĕ > gdzie* 'where', **dьnь > dzień* 'day'. In each case the place of articulation of the resultant sound is entirely different from that of its origin (see table 16.1). Nevertheless, the native speaker, owing mainly to morphological alternations, feels that the relationship between the members of these pairs is the same as that between the non-palatalised and palatalised members of the labial and labio-dental pairs. The same is true of the pairs /w/ : /l/ and /r/ : /ʒ/, in each of which the phonological distinction also originally stems from the palatalisation of the second member before front vowels. Nowadays, however, neither member of either pair is palatalised.

(iv) Polish, in common with the other Lechitic languages, is affected by changes in certain Common Slavonic vowels if they were followed by the dental consonants *s*, *z*, *t*, *d*, *r* or *l*, and these consonants were themselves not followed by a front vowel. Thus, in this position, *e* > *'o* (i.e. *o* with palatalisation of the preceding consonant), e.g. **sestra > siostra* 'sister', **berǫ > biorę* 'I take'. In the same conditions, *ĕ* > *'a* (i.e. *a* with palatalisation of the preceding consonant), e.g. **lĕsъ > las* 'forest', **vĕtrъ > wiatr* 'wind'. In all other positions *e* and *ĕ* coalesced as *e*, e.g. **večerъ > wieczór* 'evening', **bĕgati > biegać* 'to run'. This is one of several sound changes that have led to morphophonemic vowel alternations.

3   Morphology

Polish nominal morphology is illustrated in the chart of declension types, with examples of the four main types of noun declension and of adjective declension. Although there is a high correlation between gender and declension type, it is not absolute: most *a*-stems are feminine, but those with clear male reference are masculine, e.g. *mężczyzna* 'man'. There are, in addition, subsidiary types such as that exemplified by *źrebię* 'foal', which has genitive singular *źrebięcia* and nominative plural *źrebięta*. The only noun belonging to this declension which is not neuter is *książę* 'prince'.

Two important interrelated distinctions in Polish nominal declension not revealed by the table are animate/non-animate and masculine personal/non-masculine personal. Masculine *o*-stem nouns and adjectives referring to human beings and other animals (and their attributes) in the singular have

Polish Declension Types

Singular:	a-*stem*	Masculine o-*stem*	Neuter o-*stem*	i-*stem*
Nominative	głowa	ptak	słowo	noc
Vocative	głowo	ptaku	słowo	nocy
Accusative	głowę	ptaka	słowo	noc
Genitive	głowy	ptaka	słowa	nocy
Dative	głowie	ptakowi	słowu	nocy
Instrumental	głową	ptakiem	słowem	nocą
Locative	głowie	ptaku	słowie	nocy

Plural:				
Nominative	głowy	ptaki	słowa	noce
Vocative	głowy	ptaki	słowa	noce
Accusative	głowy	ptaki	słowa	noce
Genitive	głów	ptaków	słów	nocy
Dative	głowom	ptakom	słowom	nocom
Instrumental	głowami	ptakami	słowami	nocami
Locative	głowach	ptakach	słowach	nocach

Adjective

Singular:	Masculine	Neuter	Feminine
Nominative	stary	stare	stara
Vocative	stary	stare	stara
Accusative	stary	stare	starą
Genitive	starego		starej
Dative	staremu		starej
Instrumental	starym		starą
Locative	starym		starej

Plural:	
Nominative	stare
Vocative	stare
Accusative	stare
Genitive	starych
Dative	starym
Instrumental	starymi
Locative	starych

an accusative case coinciding in form with the genitive singular. This is demonstrated by the example *ptak* 'bird' in the chart of declension types. In all other cases, the accusative singular of masculine *o*-stems coincides with the nominative singular. Thus, for example, *stary dom* 'an old house' has accusative singular *stary dom*, but *stary Polak* 'an old Pole' has *starego Polaka*. Masculine *a*-stems, such as *kolega* 'friend', like all other *a*-stems, have an accusative singular ending in -*ę*, e.g. *kolegę*. But adjectives agreeing with such nouns have an accusative singular coinciding with the genitive, e.g. *starego kolegę*. The masculine adjectival forms shown in the chart of declension types are those appropriate to a non-animate noun.

In the plural, however, the criterion is not whether the noun is animate, but whether it refers to a group embodying the two features 'masculine' and 'human'. If it does, the accusative plural has the same form as the genitive plural. If not, the accusative plural is the same as the nominative plural. Thus, for example, the accusative plural of *stary Polak* is *starych Polaków*, whereas the accusative plural of *stara Polka* 'an old Polish woman' is *stare Polki*, coinciding with the nominative plural. The masculine personal subgender is also manifested in the endings of the nominative plural. Some masculine personal nouns have the nominative plural ending *-owie*, e.g. *synowie* (nom. pl. of *syn* 'son'). Others have an ending which has evolved from the Common Slavonic nominative plural ending *-i*, but which in Polish is written *-i* or *-y*, depending on the nature of the preceding consonant, e.g. *chłopi* (nom. pl. of *chłop* 'peasant'), *Polacy* (nom. pl. of *Polak* 'Pole'). Masculine personal adjectives in the nominative plural can have only the *-i/-y* ending, e.g. *słabi* (from *słaby* 'weak'). This ending, whether used with nouns or adjectives, involves stem-consonant alternations, most of which result from the Common Slavonic second palatalisation of velars (see page 324) or from the Polish palatalisation of consonants before front vowels, but some of which are the result of analogy. Thus, for example, *k* alternates with *c* (e.g. *Polak:Polacy*), *g* with *dz* (e.g. *szpieg* 'spy' : *szpiedzy*), *s* with *ś* (e.g. *prezes* 'chairman' : *prezesi*), and (in adjectives only) *ż* with *ź* (e.g. *duży* 'big' : *duzi*), *sz* with *ś* (e.g. *lepszy* 'better' : *lepsi*).

Polish Conjugation Types

Infin.	Conjugation 1 pisać 'to write'	Conjugation 2 lubić 'to like'	Conjugation 3 padać 'to fall'	Conjugation 4 jeść 'to eat'
Non-past:				
Sg. 1	piszę	lubię	padam	jem
2	piszesz	lubisz	padasz	jesz
2 or 3	pisze	lubi	pada	je
Pl. 1	piszemy	lubimy	padamy	jemy
2	piszecie	lubicie	padacie	jecie
2 or 3	piszą	lubią	padają	jedzą
Imperative:				
Sg. 2	pisz	lub	padaj	jedz
Pl. 2	piszcie	lubcie	padajcie	jedzcie

Past:	Masculine	Neuter	Feminine	
Sg. 1	pisałem	–	pisałam	
2	pisałeś	pisałoś	pisałaś	
2 or 3	pisał	pisało	pisała	

	Masculine personal	Non-masculine personal
Pl. 1	pisaliśmy	pisałyśmy
2	pisaliście	pisałyście
2 or 3	pisali	pisały

However, the masculine personal/non-masculine personal distinction is not shown in the ending of most nouns whose stem ends in *c*, *ć*, *dź*, *j*, *ń*, *ś*, *ż*, *l*, *cz*, *dż*, *dz*, *rz*, *sz*, or *ż*. Thus, for example, the nominative plural *żołnierze* 'soldiers' is not morphologically distinct from *kołnierze* 'collars'. Masculine personal nouns ending in the nominative singular in *-ec* have nominative plural *-cy*, e.g. *chłopiec* 'boy' : *chłopcy*. They are thus morphologically distinguished from non-masculine personal nouns like *dworzec* 'station' : *dworce*. But other nouns ending in *-c* are not distinguished, e.g. *szlachcic* 'nobleman' : *szlachcice*, cf. *szkic* 'sketch' : *szkice*.

Polish verbal morphology is in many ways similar to that of Russian, but conventionally four conjugational types are distinguished (as opposed to two in Russian), principally on the basis of the vowel occurring in the endings of the middle four members of the paradigm (*-e-*, *-i-*, or *-a-*) of the present tense. Conjugation 4 scarcely deserves separate status, as it includes only four verbs (viz. *umieć* 'to be able', *śmieć* 'to dare', *wiedzieć* 'to know', and *jeść* 'to eat') and their derivatives. Even these four differ in the third person plural (*umieją*, *śmieją*, *wiedzą*, *jedzą*). The paradigm of *być* 'to be' in

The Verb 'to be' in Polish

Infinitive   być 'to be'

Present:

Sg.	1	jestem
	2	jesteś
	2 or 3	jest
Pl.	1	jesteśmy
	2	jesteście
	2 or 3	są

Imperative:

| Sg. | 2 | bądź |
| Pl. | 2 | bądźcie |

Past:

		Masculine	Neuter	Feminine
Sg.	1	byłem	–	byłam
	2	byłeś	byłoś	byłaś
	2 or 3	był	było	była

		Masculine personal	Non-masculine personal
Pl.	1	byliśmy	byłyśmy
	2	byliście	byłyście
	2 or 3	byli	były

Future:

Sg.	1	będę	Pl.	1	będziemy
	2	będziesz		2	będziecie
	2 or 3	będzie		2 or 3	będą

the present tense is unique.

Most finite verbal forms are unambiguously first, second or third person, singular or plural, and it is consequently not usual for them to be accompanied by personal pronouns, except for the purpose of emphasis. Exceptions to this rule, however, are the honorific second person pronouns *pan* (masculine singular), *pani* (feminine singular), *panowie* (masculine plural), *panie* (feminine plural), *państwo* (mixed gender plural). They are used with forms of the verb which are identical with those used in the third person. Therefore, unless the pronouns are expressed, the meaning is unambiguously third person. For example, *panowie piszą* 'you (m. pl.) are writing', but *piszą* 'they are writing'. These non-familiar address pronouns are all gender-specific and thus inevitably involve sexual discrimination.

The Polish personal pronouns (apart from the second person honorifics *pan* etc., already mentioned) are: *ja* 'I', *ty* 'you' (singular familiar), *on* 'he, it' (m.), *ona* 'she, it' (f.), *ono* 'it' (nt.), *my* 'we', *wy* 'you' (plural, familiar; or singular, honorific), *oni* 'they' (masculine personal), *one* 'they' (non-masculine personal). The most widespread type of non-familiar address is with one of the pronouns, *pan*, *pani* etc. (see above) in conjunction with a verb in the same form as for the third person, e.g. *pan pisze* 'you are writing', but *wy* with forms of the second person plural is used to address one person by peasants and members of the Polish United Workers' Party. Most Poles address older kin with *ty* and the corresponding verbal forms, but in the country *wy* often has this function, e.g. *coście powiedzieli, matko?* 'what did you say, mother?'. In this type of address masculine personal forms are used, even if the addressee is a female. In some families kinship terms are used as second person pronouns to address older kin in conjunction with verbs in the same form as the third person, e.g. *co mama powiedziała?* 'what did you say?' (lit. 'what did mummy say?').

The past tense (as may be seen from the chart of conjugation types) is derived from the same stem as the infinitive, e.g. *pisa-*, to which are added *-ł-* or *-l-* (denoting 'past'), a vowel (including zero) denoting gender and number and an ending (including a zero ending) denoting person. Historically, the form ending in *ł/l* is a participle; the ending is part of the present tense of the auxiliary *być* 'to be'. The erstwhile independence of the ending is demonstrated by the fact that it need not follow the *ł/l* participle, but may appear elsewhere in the sentence, e.g. *gdzieście byli?* or *gdzie byliście?* 'where have you been?'.

The aspectual system is similar to that of Russian (see page 74–5). Non-past imperfect verbs (e.g. those in the chart of conjugation types) have present meaning. Non-past perfective verbs have future meaning, e.g. *napiszę* 'I shall write'. The imperfective future is expressed periphrastically using the auxiliary *będę* 'I shall be' in the appropriate person and number with the imperfective infinitive, as in Russian, e.g. *będzie pisać* 'he will write, be writing', or with the *ł/l* participle, e.g. *będzie pisał*. The participle agrees in number and gender with the subject.

The conditional is formed by the addition of the invariable clitic *by* to the past tense. Most commonly it is inserted between the *ł/l* participle and the personal ending, e.g. *pisałbym* 'I should write', *panowie pisaliby* 'you would write' (m. plural). There is also a past conditional formed by the addition of the present conditional of the verb *być* 'to be' to the *ł/l* participle, e.g. *byłbym pisał* 'I should have written', *byłabyś pisała* 'you would have written' (familiar, feminine singular).

The pluperfect also exists, though it is extremely rare and is found only in a formal literary style. The *ł/l* participle of the auxiliary *być* is added to the past tense, e.g. *pisałem był* 'I had written, been writing'.

There are two declined participles (one active, one passive). The active declined participle is derived from the present stem of imperfective verbs by means of the morpheme *-ąc-* to which the adjectival endings are added, e.g. *piszący* 'writing' (masculine nominative singular). The passive declined participle, which may be formed from both imperfective and perfective verbs, is derived from the past (or infinitive) stem by means of the morpheme *-t-* or *-n-* followed by the adjectival endings, e.g. *kryty* 'hidden', *pisany* or *napisany* 'written'. The present undeclined (adverbial) participle is identical with the active declined participle minus the adjectival endings, e.g. *pisząc* 'writing'. There is also a past undeclined (adverbial) participle, which is derived from the past stem by the addition of *-wszy*, e.g. *napisawszy* 'having written'. It may be formed only from perfective verbs.

The passive need not involve the use of the passive participle. It may also be expressed by means of a finite form of the verb accompanied by the reflexive particle *się*, e.g. *książka się drukuje* 'the book is being printed' (lit. 'the book prints itself'). Such expressions may also be impersonal, e.g. *mówi się* 'it is said', *drukuje się książkę* (accusative). There are, in addition, impersonal constructions involving the use of special forms of the passive participle ending in *-no* or *-to*, e.g. *zaczęto taniec* 'the dance has been begun', *zamknięto okno* 'the window has been shut', *podano herbatę* 'tea is served'. As in the personal counterparts of these constructions (*podali herbatę* 'they served tea' etc.) the object is in the accusative.

The morphology of numerals in Polish is complicated by the fact that their gender system is different from that of nouns. In particular, the numeral 'two' manifests a fourfold distinction between *dwa* (masculine non-personal and neuter), *dwie* (feminine), *dwaj* (or *dwóch* or *dwu*) (group consisting exclusively of male persons), and *dwoje* (one man and one woman). (However, *dwoje* is also used with nouns which exist only in the plural or denote young creatures, including children.) Although this degree of subtlety is restricted to this numeral and words for 'both', the morphological specification of groups consisting exclusively of male persons is characteristic of numerals generally and in contradistinction to nominal gender, which only specifies groups containing at least one male person.

4 Syntax

Main verbs agree in number and person with their subjects. For example, *urzędnik pisze* 'the official is writing' (3 singular), *urzędnicy piszą* 'the officials are writing' (3 plural). Past tense verbs, in addition, agree in gender with their subject. For example, *urzędnicy pisali* 'the officials were writing' (3 plural, masculine personal), *nauczycielki pisały* 'the teachers (feminine) were writing' (3 plural, non-masculine personal), *koty siedziały* 'the cats were sitting' (3 plural, non-masculine personal). In the case of composite subjects the two features 'masculine' and 'personal' may be supplied separately by two nouns one of which is masculine (but not human) and the other of which is human (but not masculine). Thus: *nauczycielka i kot siedzieli* 'the teacher (feminine) and the cat (masculine) were sitting'.

Adjectives agree in number, case and gender with the nouns they modify, e.g. *Jadwiga jest chora* 'Jadwiga is ill' (feminine nominative singular), *mam młodą córkę* 'I have a young daughter' (feminine accusative singular). Nouns which refer to male human beings may, for expressive purposes (positive or negative), be used in the non-masculine personal form, e.g. *morowe chłopy* 'fine lads' (instead of masculine personal *morowi chłopi*). In such cases, both adjectives and past tense verbs may agree with the expressive form, e.g. *jakieś idioty to wymyśliły* 'some idiots have dreamed that up' (rather than *jacyś idioci to wymyślili*). Certain essentially expressive words hardly ever or never appear in the masculine personal form, e.g. *Szwab* 'German' (derogatory) always has plural *Szwaby*. (*Szwabi* or *Szwabowie* means 'Swabians' i.e. 'inhabitants of Swabia').

From some masculine nouns referring to professional posts and titles it is possible to derive feminine counterparts, e.g. from *nauczyciel* 'teacher' (masculine) we derive *nauczycielka* 'teacher' (feminine). Words like *nauczycielka* are straightforward feminine nouns and take normal feminine agreement. In some other cases, however, particularly those of professions which until recently were mainly the preserve of men, there is no feminine form. Therefore, the originally masculine noun is now usually of common gender, i.e. it is masculine when referring to a man and feminine when referring to a woman. This is so, for example, in the case of *doktor* 'doctor', *inżynier* 'engineer', *ambasador* 'ambassador', *architekt* 'architect'. It is possible, when referring to a woman, to retain masculine agreement, e.g. *nasz doktor wyjechał* 'our doctor has gone away' *may* refer to a woman. But in practice the predominant tendency is to avoid ambiguity by using feminine agreement, e.g. *nasza doktor wyjechała*. Similarly, when the syntax demands an oblique case, it is permissible to decline such nouns according to the masculine paradigm, but a sentence such as *oddałem książkę redaktorowi* 'I returned the book to the editor' will normally be taken to imply that the editor is a man. Therefore, the usual practice, if one of these nouns refers to a woman, is to leave it undeclined, e.g. *oddałem książkę redaktor*, thereby leaving no room for doubt as to the editor's sex.

Some collective nouns ending in *-stwo*, e.g. *państwo* 'ladies and gentlemen', *wujostwo* 'uncle and aunt', decline as singular nouns, but take plural, masculine personal agreement. For example, *Doktorostwo Kowalscy byli u nas wczoraj* 'Doctor and Mrs Kowalski were visiting us yesterday', *ci państwo przyszli* 'that lady and gentleman have arrived'. This syntactic property is one of the features distinguishing *państwo* 'ladies and gentlemen, Mr and Mrs etc.' from *państwo* 'state', which takes neuter singular agreement.

The numeral 'one' takes agreement in the singular, e.g. *jeden dzień* 'one day', *jedna kobieta* 'one woman', and itself agrees in gender and case with the noun it modifies. It also has a plural form *jedne/jedni* meaning 'some' or 'certain'. In compound numerals ending in 'one' *jeden* is invariable, e.g. *kupiliśmy dwadzieścia jeden książek* 'we bought twenty-one books'. The numerals 'two', 'three' and 'four' take the plural and agree in gender and case with the noun they modify, e.g. *dwa konie* 'two horses' (masculine non-personal nominative and accusative), *dwie książki* 'two books' (feminine nominative and accusative). The masculine personal category (i.e. *exclusively* masculine) is expressed by means of the forms *dwaj* 'two', *trzej* 'three', *czterej* 'four', e.g. *czterej urzędnicy pisali* 'four officials were writing', or by means of a genitive subject, e.g. *czterech urzędników pisało* 'four officials were writing'. The current tendency is for the latter type to become increasingly common at the expense of the former type. In the case of numerals from 'five' upwards, if the subject is masculine personal (exclusively) it *must* be in the genitive, e.g. *osiemdziesięciu czterech robotników pracowało* 'eighty-four workmen were working'. If the subject is not exclusively masculine personal, numerals from 'five' upwards are followed by the genitive plural e.g. *dwadzieścia ptaków odleciało* 'twenty birds flew away', unless they are composite and end in one of the numerals 'two' to 'four', in which case the form of the noun is determined by the last component, e.g. *dwadzieścia trzy ptaki odleciały* 'twenty-three birds flew away'.

The collective numerals *dwoje, troje, czworo, pięcioro* etc. have among their functions the possibility of referring to groups containing, but not consisting exclusively of, male persons. Thus, for example, the phrase *ich czworo* '(there are) four of them' (if it refers to adult human beings), reveals that there is at least one man and at least one woman in the group. When in the subject, the collective numerals are always followed by the genitive plural of the noun they modify.

One of the striking features of the Polish system of gender and agreement is the high degree of redundancy. The same information on gender and number may be repeated several times in the sentence. Even more striking, however, is the lack of non-specific forms. It is difficult to make any observation about any plural entity without sizing up its human or non-human and sexual properties. The word *osoba* 'person', which is always feminine, is a boon to those wishing to be non-specific about human groups. But from the problem of deciding whether one's interlocutor (even on the telephone) is male (requiring the address pronoun *pan* + masculine agreement) or female (requiring the address pronoun *pani* + feminine agreement) there is no escape.

Bibliography

Szober (1968) is a standard reference grammar in Polish, while Brooks (1975) is the best reference grammar available in English; Urbańczyk et al. (1978) is an encyclopedia covering all aspects of Polish. For pronunciation, Karaś and Madejowa is a dictionary of Polish pronunciation using the International Phonetic Alphabet, with an introduction in English; Puppel et al. (1977) is the only book of its kind presenting Polish pronunciation in English.

The standard history of the Polish language is Klemensiewicz (1974), while Klemensiewicz et al. (1965) is the standard historical grammar. For historical phonology, Stieber (1973) is a classic work, better than anything in Polish on this subject (including Stieber's own work). Westfal (1985) is a useful account of the language with historical explanations.

References

Brooks, M.Z. 1975. *Polish Reference Grammar* (Mouton, The Hague)

Karaś, M. and M. Madejowa. 1977. *Słownik wymowy polskiej PWN* (Państwowe Wydawnictwo Naukowe, Warsaw and Cracow)

Klemensiewicz, Z. 1974. *Historia języka polskiego* (Państwowe Wydawnictwo Naukowe, Warsaw)

——, T. Lehr-Spławiński and S. Urbańczyk. 1965. *Gramatyka historyczna języka polskiego*, 3rd ed. (Państwowe Wydawnictwo Naukowe, Warsaw)

Puppel, S., J. Nawrocka-Fisiak and H. Krassowska. 1977. *A Handbook of Polish Pronunciation for English Learners* (Państwowe Wydawnictwo Naukowe, Warsaw)

Stieber, Z. 1973. *A Historical Phonology of the Polish Language* (Carl Winter Universitätsverlag, Heidelberg)

Szober, S. 1968. *Gramatyka języka polskiego*, 10th ed. (Państwowe Wydawnictwo Naukowe, Warsaw)

Urbańczyk, S. et al. (eds.) 1978. *Encyklopedia wiedzy o języku polskim* (Ossolineum, Wrocław, Warsaw, Cracow and Gdańsk)

Westfal, S. 1985. *The Polish Language*, 2nd ed. (Veritas Foundation Publication Centre, London)

5 Czech and Slovak

David Short

1 Introduction

Czech and Slovak are by no means major languages on purely statistical grounds, with around 9.5 million and 4.5 million speakers respectively in Czechoslovakia itself, whereas Ukrainian, for example, has around 40 million speakers in the Soviet Union. Czechs and Slovaks are, however, to be found scattered worldwide, either diffused or in close-knit villages and some larger communities in Rumania, Yugoslavia, Hungary and Poland, due to local small-scale migrations or the vagaries of political frontiers, or Canada, the USA and South America, due to the modern tradition of economic or political emigration. These pockets add several hundred thousand to the total numbers of speakers; their languages, however, necessarily differ, through physical separation and the external influence of dominant languages in the alien environment, from the Czech and Slovak to be described in the following pages.

If not on statistical grounds, then historically Czech at least does have a claim as a major language: the Kingdom of Bohemia controlled, in the Middle Ages, a much vaster area than just the Lands of the Bohemian Crown (Bohemia and Moravia); Bohemian kings have been Holy Roman Emperors; and twice there have been Anglo-Bohemian dynastic links through marriage. More recently Czechoslovakia has been, between the wars, a major economic force in Europe. By contrast Slovakia has rarely enjoyed independence, coming closest to it briefly during the last war as a client state of Germany, and since 1968 when it became one of the two federated republics that now constitute Czechoslovakia.

The two languages are taken together in this volume because, despite the natural processes of divergence brought about by geography, geopolitical separation and exposure to different influences of neighbouring languages (Czech is heavily influenced by German, Slovak by Hungarian), the two languages share a great deal and are on average 90 per cent mutually intelligible. Now sharing a common state, Czechs and Slovaks are constantly exposed each to the other's language and mutual intelligibility is reinforced by, for example, labour mobility, military service and the media.

The similarities are highest, and increasing, at the lexical level (where there are also some of the most striking individual differences), while phonologically and morphologically the differences affect most words, though not enough to inhibit comprehension. The overall distinctiveness is, however, great enough for translations between the literatures to be a meaningful exercise.

2   The Historical Background

The written tradition in what is now Czechoslovakia goes back to the ninth century, with the Christian mission of Saints Cyril (Constantine) and Methodius to Great Moravia, where they prepared Slavonic translations of the central religious texts. At the time the Macedonian dialect of Slavonic which they used was readily comprehensible to all other Slavs. Although used for centuries afterwards in Eastern Orthodox Christianity, in the west it fell into disuse after the Slavonic monks were driven from the Sázava monastery in Bohemia in 1097. The existence of this early standardised literary language contributed to the general stability of the early literary tradition in Bohemia, but the Slavonic alphabets used in it, the Glagolitic created by St Cyril and the Cyrillic still used by Bulgarian, Macedonian and Serbian and the East Slavonic languages, were not widely employed. Czech and Slovak used a modified Latin alphabet, possibly because Cyril and Methodius were actually preceded by western missionaries from Italy, Bavaria and Ireland. The earliest texts show developing refinements of the Latin alphabet as it was adapted to express the non-Latin sounds of Czech, and the first attempt to systematise the orthography is generally attributed to the religious reformer Jan Hus (1373–1415). Amongst many other linguistic guidelines, Hus introduced systematically diacritics to replace the many cumbersome digraphs in use until then. His system was not adopted universally or immediately, but a version of it became generalised when adopted by the Czech Brethren, whose authority and literary output guaranteed its ultimate acceptance. This sixteenth-century 'Brethren' orthography differed from the modern in the use of g, $\check{g}$, j, w, v and au for j, g, $í$, v, u and ou respectively, and critically in the distribution of i and y. The modern values of the letters were established fairly painlessly in a sequence of nineteenth-century reforms, except in the case of i/y, which was a major controversy. The distinction between i and y as accepted in the modern orthographies is on etymological or morphological grounds and represents the victory of the 'iotist' camp in the nineteenth-century debate. The 'ypsilonists' gave precedence to phonetic considerations in certain critical environments. The iotist victory was assured once Josef Jungmann (1773–1847) and Josef Dobrovský (1753–1829) firmly adopted the new conventions, the matter being essentially settled about 1817–19. It was not laid to rest completely, however, until the death of the chief ypsilonist Jan

Nejedlý in 1834, though Jiří (Juraj) Palkovič (1769–1850) continued with the y-convention in Slovakia until his death.

Since the nineteenth century there have been further minor reforms, notably in the distribution of s and z medially and as prefixes, the two languages being not quite in step here. And recently the old i/y problem has resurfaced. Early in 1984 it seemed quite likely that y would be eliminated altogether in favour of i in Czech, except after d, t and n, which as hitherto would represent palatal stops before i and alveolar before y, and that ů would be replaced by ú. However, the public outcry over the consequences for language study and language learning, not to mention the continuing need to be able to read with ease texts in the prereform orthography which would be unlikely to be reprinted, has meant that the proposal has now been dropped.

The father of Slavonic studies, Josef Dobrovský, produced the first scientifically based modern grammar of Czech, at a time when the French Enlightenment and Austrian responses to it (the reforms of Josef II) had spurred on the National Revival and a new interest in the Czech nation and language. As his sources Dobrovský took both the best of the Humanist tradition, associated with the name of Jan Blahoslav (1523–71), the Kralice Bible (1579–93) and the printer Daniel Adam z Veleslavína (1546–99), and the living language of the rural Czech populace. The resultant grammar, still the basis of modern Czech, contained perforce many archaic features, and Dobrovský himself was not convinced that the language could be fully revived. It fell largely to Josef Jungmann to demonstrate, through translations of, amongst others, Milton's *Paradise Lost* and Goethe's *Herrmann und Dorothea*, that Czech was capable of high-style verse, and to provide Czech with a complete lexicon, his Czech-German dictionary of 1834–9. Czech was no longer a vehicle with limited capacity for expressing the full breadth of human communicational needs. Jungmann himself, and those who followed in the provision of technical terminologies, drew on some of the earlier vocabularies and on knowledge of other Slavonic languages as a source for rationally based loan-neologisms.

Meanwhile in Slovakia the language situation was also evolving. As part of Hungary, its official language had been Latin or Hungarian, while the Protestant liturgy continued to use Czech, the Czech of the Kralice Bible. The first attempted codification of Slovak was by Anton Bernolák (1762–1813), a Catholic priest, who produced a grammar based on a Western Slovak dialect, and a six-volume dictionary published posthumously in 1825–7. Bernolák's version of literary Slovak failed to gain wide approval, unlike the second attempt, by Ľudovít Štúr (1815–56), whose 1846 work, based on Central Slovak, found immediate favour. There have been changes since, in both the morphology and the lexicon of the standard, but the modern language still owes most to Štúr. Before Štúr and Bernolák there had been writing in 'Slovak' — various hybrids of Czech and local dialects written according to a variety of spelling conventions. It has recently become the practice to refer to these prestandardisation versions of the language as 'cultured (*kultúrna*) western/central/eastern Slovak'. Throughout the gestation and parturition of Slovak as an independent literary language there was also a continuous current which favoured the use of Czech, either as such, or in a mutation of a common Czechoslovak; the latter survived as a linguistic myth right through the First Republic.

In many ways Slovak is more modern than Czech, especially morphologically, for it has far fewer surviving redundant distinctions. Czech has more later phonological innovations, and even more still in its most progressive form, Common Czech, based on the Central Bohemian dialect. This has evolved into a remarkably distinct version of the national language.

Although there has been a strong tendency in the past to keep Slovak maximally distinct from Czech and free of Bohemicisms, there are some signs of a reverse tendency, due in part to the shift of the languages' centres of gravity away from the high literary towards the technical. Both languages resort to neologisms, and standardisation to international norms often means coincidence rather than further division. Added to that, Slovak, despite the opposition of purists, remains open to influences from Czech; Slovak influence on Czech is much slighter, though not yet fully appreciated.

3   The Alphabets, Orthography and Phonology of Czech and Slovak

Table 5.1: The Alphabets of Czech and Slovak

Czech	Slovak	Czech	Slovak
a, á	a, á	n, ň	n, ň
	ä	o, ó	o, ó
b	b		ô
c	c	p	p
č			
d, ď	d, ď	q	q
	dz	r	r, ŕ
		ř	
	dž	s	s
e, é, ě	e, é	š	š
f	f	t, ť	t, ť
g	g	u, ú, ů	u, ú
h	h	v	v
ch	ch	w	w
i, í	i, í	x	x
j	j	y, ý	y, ý
k	k	z	z
l	l, ľ, ĺ	ž	ž
m	m		

Typographically similar letters given on the same line, e.g. *a*, *á*, have no effect on ordering in the dictionary, those on separate lines, e.g. Slovak *a*, *ä*, are ordered separately. The three digraphs *ch*, *dz*, *dž* are treated in every respect as single letters. Although *d*/*d'*, *t*/*t'*, *n*/*ň* and *l*/*l'* are ordered indiscriminately in accordance with the following letter, i.e. *t'uhýk* will always precede *tuk*, the sounds represented by each member of the pairs are phonetically and phonologically distinct, as alveolar and palatal respectively. But because of certain spelling conventions a *d*, *t*, *n* or *l* may have the palatal values of *d'*, *t'*, *ň* and *l'*, notably before *ě* and *i* in Czech and (in most cases) *e* and *i* in Slovak. Note also the conventions whereby *d'* and *t'* use the hook ˇ instead of the apostrophe on capitals, in handwriting and on the Czech typewriter keyboard. Of the other consonants, *h* is a voiced glottal fricative, *c* and *dz* represent alveolar affricates, *č* and *dž* palato-alveolar affricates, *š* and *ž* palato-alveolar fricatives, and *ř* a rolled post-alveolar fricative (never the sequence of [r] + [ʒ] commonly attempted by non-Czechs in the name *Dvořák*). The letters *q*, *w* and *x* are confined to loanwords, though for perhaps obvious reasons only *x* is particularly common. In Slovak *g* is marginally more common than in Czech, thanks to a number of words containing /g/ that are not merely loans or onomatopoeic. By contrast *f* is more domesticated in Czech, having evolved as the voiceless counterpart of /v/, though it too is most frequent in loanwords. In circumstances parallel to the Czech devoicing of /v/ to /f/, Slovak has the bilabial /w/, not represented orthographically other than as *v* after any vowel or *u* after *o* in set morphological circumstances. The remaining consonant symbols have values similar to English, but the voiceless plosives represented by *p*, *t* and *k* are never aspirated.

Of the vowel symbols *ě* signals that a preceding *d*, *t* or *n* is to be pronounced as the appropriate palatal counterpart, or that a preceding *b*, *p*, *f*, *v* or *m* is to be pronounced [bj], [pj], [fj], [vj] or [mɲ]. Slovak *ä* represents a sound between /a/ and /e/, but is often indistinguishable from the latter, which the orthoepic norm allows. Slovak *ô* represents the diphthongal phoneme /uo/, and the circle on Czech *ů* is a historical convention appearing in circumstances where a long /u/ has evolved from a long /o/. Length in a vowel and Slovak syllabic /l/ and /r/ is otherwise marked by the 'acute accent'. Long *ó* occurs only in loanwords.

In addition to /uo/ (*ô*) Slovak has three other diphthongs represented by *ia*, *ie* and *iu*. Czech has one diphthong /ou/, spelled *ou* (contrast the Slovak *ou* sequence as [ow]).

Voice assimilation in clusters of consonants is important in Czech and Slovak, but is only sporadically reflected in the spelling. Voice assimilation in consonant clusters works right through both languages where paired consonants are involved, e.g. *bt* and *tb* will be pronounced /pt/ and /db/ respectively, and in Slovak also before *r*, *l*, *l'*, *m*, *n*, *ň* and *j* at word or morpheme boundaries. Czech and Slovak spelling is thus morphophonemic rather than phonetic.

One phonetic difference, not reflected in the orthography, is the presence and absence of the glottal stop in Czech and Slovak respectively; it appears in Czech between vowels and before words beginning with a vowel.

Both languages have fixed stress, on the first syllable, and this usually passes forward onto a preceding monosyllabic preposition.

4 The Evolution of Czech and Slovak

Among the early dialect divisions of Slavonic are the different resolutions of the *tort formula, as indicated on page 59. Importantly, Czech and Slovak here share the South Slavonic resolution, namely *trat, unlike Polish *trot; the only Czech/Slovak inconsistencies here are in variations of vowel length, brought about by different patterns of accent-shifting or the workings of analogy. Where they are distinct is in the related word-initial *ort formula: Central Slovak (the basis of the standard language) has fairly consistently *rat, while Czech has *rat or *rot according to whether the original tone had been rising or falling. Slovak is thus united to South Slavonic by an extra isogloss, cf. Cz. role 'field', rádlo 'plough', Slk. ral'a, radlo, Serbo-Croat ral, ralo.

The palatalisations (see page 58) produced two Czech/Slovak distinctions. Under the second palatalisation of velars ch yielded š in Czech as in West Slavonic generally, but s in Slovak (another feature shared with South Slavonic), hence Češi/Česi 'Czechs'. The affricate dz had two origins: from g by the second and third palatalisations, and from d + j. Whereas in Czech dz of either origin de-affricated to z (see page 324), suggesting near simultaneity of the two processes, in Slovak they must have been separated in time, since de-affrication only affected dz < g. The change of d + j to dz came about only after de-affrication was completed, leaving this second appearance of dz unchanged as the source of this Slovak-only phoneme.

To the Slavist knowing, say, Russian or Polish, a striking feature of Czech and Slovak is the absence of g from the native word stock and its replacement by h. This is a consequence of the realignment of consonantal parallelisms after the de-affrication of dž to ž. Prior to that there was symmetry between k:g (voiceless and voiced velar plosives) and č:dž (their post-palatalisation corresponding palatal affricates), with ch and its counterpart š standing to one side. Subsequently a voiced/voiceless relationship emerged between ž and š, not matched by g:ch. This led to the change g > h, leaving h:ch as a nearly matching pair of fricatives, differing slightly in the place of articulation (glottal and velar respectively). Before and after de-affrication the picture was thus:

Before: k:g   ch   After: k   h:ch
        č:dž   š   č   ž:š

The resolution of the jers (see page 60) is another area in which Czech and Slovak differ. Czech has all strong jers volcalised to *e*, while Slovak has essentially followed the Russian pattern, i.e. *e* for ь, *o* for ъ. Slovak also uses *a*, for which many conflicting theories have been advanced, as also for the explanation of the not infrequent cases of *o* for ь and *e* for ъ.

One of the more striking differences between Czech and Slovak (and also the easternmost dialects of Czech itself) is the outcome of the processes known in Czech as *přehláska* (approximately 'umlaut') whereby the back vowels *a/á*, *u/ú* and *o/ó* underwent a forward shift to *ě/ie*, *i/í* and *ě/ie*. The three sets of changes were not quite simultaneous, nor did they happen under exactly the same circumstances. The common factor was basically the influence of a preceding soft (palatalised) consonant, and although later developments, especially the effect of analogy, have 'undone' some of the effects, the consequences have been far-reaching phonologically (in the range of new syllable types), morphemically (in the increased incidence of root-vowel alternation, as in *pět/pátý* 'five/fifth' or *přítel/přátel* 'friend (nom. sg./gen. pl.)', cases where for $a > ě$, $á > ie > í$ the nature of a following consonant was also relevant) and morphologically. Here it led on the one hand to a proliferation of hard/soft oppositions in the declensional paradigms: *žena:duše* 'wife:soul', acc. sg., *ženu:duši*, *oknům:mořím* 'window:sea' dat. pl., ($\mathring{u} < ó$, $í < ie < ó$); and on the other hand it led, after the change of $ie > í$, to the obliteration of case-distinct forms in one particular large neuter paradigm (the contemporary *í*-declension, in which the only distinctively marked cases are those commonly associated with a consonant). Slovak was quite untouched by *přehláska*.

Czech and Slovak both possess syllabic liquids. The original **trt*, **tlt* have survived with fewer innovations in Slovak, while Czech has, in different circumstances, supporting vowels after *č* and *ž* with *r*, hence *čerpat* 'draw (water)', *žerd'* 'pole' to Slovak *črpat'*, *žrd'*, and after all consonants with *l*, except after labials where the *l* was of the soft variety, hence *žlutý* 'yellow', *dlouhý* 'long' to Slovak *žltý*, *dlhý*, but *vlk* 'wolf' and *plný* 'full' in both languages. As a consequence of the loss of the weak jers, many new consonantal clusters arose, often containing liquids. The picture is a complex one, with up to five different solutions to the problem, varying with position in the word and geographical distribution. Of most significance here are the initial and final positions, since this time it is Slovak which evolves supporting vowels, hence *luhat'* 'lie, fib', *l'ahostajný* 'indifferent', *ruvat'* 'tear', *ruman* 'camomile', *eržat'* 'neigh' correspond to the Czech *lhát*, *lhostejný*, *rvát*, *rmen*, *ržát* (where the initial liquids are only semi-syllabic, i.e. they do not attract the stress), and *niesol* 'he carried', *mysel'* 'mind', *vietor* 'wind' to the Czech *nesl*, *mysl*, *vítr* (where the liquids are syllabic and indistinguishable from original syllabic *l* and *r*). The failure of Slovak to evolve secondary final syllabic liquids underlies one of the contrasts in the absorption of loanwords in the two languages (there are of course others).

Where Czech spelling and pronunciation have here too a syllabic *l* or *r*, as in *menšestr* or *manšestr* 'corduroy', *metr* 'metre' or *triangl* 'triangle' — the instrument, Slovak has *menčester*, *meter* and *triangel*, and the orthoepic pronunciation of foreign toponyms etc. is analogously distinct (/menčestr/ vs./menčester/).

In the consonant systems mention must be made of the almost uniquely Czech phoneme represented by *ř*, a fully palatalised historically soft *r*.

This background account of the history of distinctive phonological features is by no means exhaustive, but there remains one more which cannot be overlooked, namely the so-called rhythmical law of Slovak. In essence this states that where two (historically) long syllables appear in succession, the second one shortens. This is most conspicuous in adjectival endings, which by the process of contraction were long. Contraction operated in most cases where there were two vowels in sequence separated by jot, hence in the adjectives **krásnъjь*, **krásnaja*, **krásnoje* 'beautiful (nom. sg. m., f., nt.)' gave *krásný, krásná, krásné*. By the rhythmical law the second long vowels shortened, hence modern Slovak *krásny, krásna, krásne*, which does not apply if the preceding syllable is short, as in *pekný* 'nice' (Cz. *pěkný*). Forms such as *krásne* are ambiguous in Slovak (on paper) as between some cases of the adjective (e.g. neuter singular nominative) and the adverb (equivalent to Czech *krásně*), but there is a pronunciation difference, the *n* of the adverb being palatal, that of the adjectival forms being alveolar. No Slovak *e* that has shortened in this manner causes prepalatalisation. The rhythmical law can be seen operating on various suffixes, such as *-ník*, as in *strážnik* 'policeman', cf. Czech *strážník*, as opposed to Slovak/Czech *hutník* 'smelter', or in diminutive formation, as in *národík, králiček*, from *národ* 'nation', *králik* 'rabbit' respectively, cf. Czech *nárůdek, králíček*. The Slovak rhythmical law is consistent throughout the word, i.e. it is not confined to shortening of final syllables, but there are some half-dozen morphologically governed circumstances when it is not observed. These include the third person plural of *i*-conjugation verbs, e.g. *chvália* 'praise' (*ia* is a diphthong and therefore long; diphthongs are generally covered by the rhythmical law otherwise), the genitive plural of some noun types, e.g. *piesní* 'songs', and adjectives formed from the names of animals, e.g. *vtáčí* 'birds'.

Both languages have evolved fixed stress, on the first syllable; this contrasts with Polish, where it is fixed on the penultimate, and Russian or Serbo-Croat, where it is mobile.

5 Morphology

Czech and Slovak have, like most of the Slavonic languages, been fairly conservative in their morphology, although they are by no means identical.

They both have three genders and a fully developed case system. There is one difference here, however, in that Slovak has lost the vocative (though remnants survive). The number system has become bipartite, singular and plural, with just a few remnants in Czech of the old dual declension surviving as anomalous plurals, chiefly associated with parts of the body. Standard literary Czech is the most conservative, Slovak and Common Colloquial Czech having proceeded further in the direction of eliminating redundant distinctions, notably in having a near-universal instrumental plural ending in *-mi* and *-ma* respectively (with an appropriate linking vowel where relevant). The latter *-ma* ending is a curiosity in that it comes from the instrumental dual, although the dual survives 'legitimately' only in the remnants mentioned.

The main distinctions between the two languages in noun morphology have come about because of the *přehláska* changes which affected Czech, while a not unimportant difference comes in the feminine hard *a*-declension where the more conservative Czech retains the products of palatalisation in the dative and locative singular, Slovak having evolved, like Russian, with forms which eliminate stem alternation; thus to the words *matka* 'mother', *kniha* 'book', *socha* 'statue' the dative/locative singular forms are *matce*, *knize*, *soše* and *matke*, *knihe* and *soche* in Czech and Slovak respectively.

Czech and Slovak Noun Declensions Compared

		Czech	Slovak
Masculine hard declension — animate			
Sg.	Nom.	chlap 'fellow'	chlap
	Voc.	chlape, synu 'son', bože 'god'[1]	
	Acc.	chlapa	chlapa
	Gen.	chlapa	chlapa
	Dat.	chlapovi, -u[2]	chlapovi
	Inst.	chlapem	chlapom
	Loc.	chlapovi	chlapovi
Pl.	Nom.	chlapi, sousedé 'neighbour', filologové 'philologist'	chlapi, občania 'citizen', filológovia
	Acc.	chlapy	chlapov
	Gen.	chlapů	chlapov
	Dat.	chlapům	chlapom
	Inst.	chlapy	chlapmi
	Loc.	chlapech, soudruzích 'comrade'	chlapoch

Masculine soft declension — animate			
Sg.	Nom.	muž 'man'	muž (declined as chlap)
	Voc.	muži, otče 'father'	
	Acc.	muže	muža
	Gen.	muže	muža
	Dat.	muži, mužovi	mužovi
	Inst.	mužem	mužom
	Loc.	muži, mužovi	mužovi

		Czech	*Slovak*
Pl.	Nom.	muži, otcové, učitelé 'teacher'	muži, otcovia, učitelia
	Acc.	muže	mužov
	Gen.	mužů	mužov
	Dat.	mužům	mužom
	Inst.	muži	mužmi
	Loc.	mužích	mužoch

Notes: [1] Subclasses of each paradigm may vary in one or more case. [2] Alternative forms exist, but may vary functionally.

Masculine hard declension — inanimate

Sg.	Nom.	hrad 'castle'	hrad
	Voc.	hrade	
	Acc.	hrad	hrad
	Gen.	hradu, lesa 'forest'	hradu, duba 'oak'
	Dat.	hradu	hradu
	Inst.	hradem	hradom
	Loc.	hradě, rohu 'horn, corner'	hrade, rohu, mieri 'peace'
Pl.	Nom.	hrady	hrady
	Voc.	hrady	
	Acc.	hrady	hrady
	Gen.	hradů	hradov
	Dat.	hradům	hradom
	Inst.	hrady	hradmi, listami 'leaf'
	Loc.	hradech	hradoch

Note: The ending -a in the gen. sing. is confined in Czech to a fairly small number of nouns; in Slovak it is the preferred ending for concreta.

Masculine soft declension — inanimate

Sg.	Nom.	stroj 'machine'	stroj
	Voc.	stroji	
	Acc.	stroj	stroj
	Gen.	stroje	stroja, čaju 'tea'
	Dat.	stroji	stroju
	Inst.	strojem	strojom
	Loc.	stroji	stroji
Pl.	Nom.	stroje	stroje
	Voc.	stroje	
	Acc.	stroje	stroje
	Gen.	strojů	strojov
	Dat.	strojům	strojom
	Inst.	stroji	strojmi
	Loc.	strojích	strojoch

Feminine hard declension

Sg.	Nom.	žena 'woman', hradba 'rampart'	žena, hradba
	Voc.	ženo	
	Acc.	ženu	ženu
	Gen.	ženy	ženy
	Dat.	ženě	žene
	Inst.	ženou	ženou
	Loc.	ženě	žene

		Czech	*Slovak*
Pl.	Nom.	ženy	ženy
	Voc.	ženy	
	Acc.	ženy	ženy
	Gen.	žen, hradeb	žien, budov 'building', záhrad 'garden', hradieb
	Dat.	ženám	ženám
	Inst.	ženami	ženami
	Loc.	ženách	ženách

Feminine soft declension — basic type

		Czech	*Slovak*
Sg.	Nom.	duše 'soul', ulice 'street', chvíle 'moment'	duša
	Voc.	duše	
	Acc.	duši	dušu
	Gen.	duše	duše
	Dat.	duši	duši
	Inst.	duší	dušou
	Loc.	duši	duši
Pl.	Nom.	duše	duše
	Voc.	duše	
	Acc.	duše	duše
	Gen.	duší, ulic, chvil	dúš, dielní 'workshop'
	Dat.	duším	dušiam
	Inst.	dušemi	dušami
	Loc.	duších	dušiach

Note: The fill vowel in the genitive plural is in Czech always -e-, whereas in Slovak there are several possibilities: *hradieb*, *vojen* 'war', kvapôk 'drop', *sestár* 'sister', *látok* 'material'.

Feminine soft declension — mixed type

		Czech	*Slovak*
Sg.	Nom.	dlaň 'palm (of hand)'	dlaň
	Voc.	dlani	
	Acc.	dlaň	dlaň
	Gen.	dlaně	dlane
	Dat.	dlani	dlani
	Inst.	dlaní	dlaňou
	Loc.	dlani	dlani
Pl.	Nom.	dlaně	dlane
	Voc.	dlaně	
	Acc.	dlaně	dlane
	Gen.	dlaní	dlaní
	Dat.	dlaním	dlaniam
	Inst.	dlaněmi	dlaňami
	Loc.	dlaních	dlaniach

Feminine i-declension

		Czech	*Slovak*
Sg.	Nom.	kost 'bone'	kosť
	Voc.	kosti	
	Acc.	kost	kosť
	Gen.	kosti	kosti
	Dat.	kosti	kosti
	Inst.	kostí	kosťou

		Czech	*Slovak*
	Loc.	kosti	kosti
Pl.	Nom.	kosti	kosti
	Voc.	kosti	
	Acc.	kosti	kosti
	Gen.	kostí	kostí
	Dat.	kostem	kostiam
	Inst.	kostmi	kosťami
	Loc.	kostech	kostiach

Neuter hard declension

Sg.	Nom./		
	Voc./		
	Acc.	město 'town'	mesto
	Gen.	města	mesta
	Dat.	městu	mestu
	Inst.	městem	mestom
	Loc.	městě, suchu 'drought', dobru 'good'	meste, suchu, dobre, vnutri 'interior', nebi 'sky'
Pl.	Nom./		
	Voc./		
	Acc.	města	mestá
	Gen.	měst	miest
	Dat.	městům	mestám
	Inst.	městy	mestami
	Loc.	městech, ložiskách 'deposit, bearing'	mestách

Neuter soft declension, equivalent to above

Sg.	Nom./		
	Voc./		
	Acc.	srdce 'heart'	srdce
	Gen.	srdce	srdca
	Dat.	srdci	srdcu
	Inst.	srdcem	srdcom
	Loc.	srdci	srdci
Pl.	Nom./		
	Voc./		
	Acc.	srdce	srdcia
	Gen.	srdcí, letišť 'airport'	sŕdc, polí 'field'
	Dat.	srdcím	srdciam
	Inst.	srdci	srdcami
	Loc.	srdcích	srdciach

Neuter 'long' soft declension

Sg.	Nom./		
	Voc./		
	Acc.	vysvědčení 'certificate'	vysvedčenie
	Gen.	vysvědčení	vysvedčenia
	Dat.	vysvědčení	vysvedčeniu
	Inst.	vysvědčením	vysvedčením
	Loc.	vysvědčení	vysvedčení
Pl.	Nom./		
	Voc./		
	Acc.	vysvědčení	vysvedčenia

	Czech	*Slovak*
Gen.	vysvědčení	vysvedčení
Dat.	vysvědčením	vysvedčeniam
Inst.	vysvědčeními	vysvedčeniami
Loc.	vysvědčeních	vysvedčeniach

Neuter '-nt-' declension

Sg. Nom./
Voc.   děvče 'girl', kníže (m.) 'prince'   dievča, holúbä 'young pigeon'
Acc.   děvče, knížete   dievča
Gen.   děvčete   dievčaťa
Dat.   děvčeti   dievčaťu
Inst. děvčetem   dievčaťom
Loc.   děvčeti   dievčati

Pl. Nom./
Voc./
Acc.   děvčata, knížata (nt.)   dievčatá   dievčence, holúbätá
Gen.   děvčat   dievčat   dievčeniec, holúbät
Dat.   děvčatům   dievčatám   dievčencom
Inst. děvčaty   dievčatami   dievčencami
Loc.   děvčatech   dievčatách   dievčencoch

alternative plurals

Animacy, as a subcategory of the masculine gender (only) in Czech and Slovak, shows some further important differences. The singular of the masculine nouns central to the inanimate-animate distinction is fairly similar, in having -a for the animate genitive singular and -ovi for the animate dative/locative singular, compare, e.g. *pána*, *pánovi*, *pánovi* 'mister' to *hradu* (gen.), *hradu (dat.)* and *hradě* (loc.) (In Czech alone the soft animate genitive, dative and locative forms coincide with those of the inanimate declension.) In common with general practice in the Slavonic languages, the animate genitive form is also used in the animate accusative. In the plural, however, the two languages differ in their expression of animacy: in Slovak it operates in a manner similar to the singular, i.e. the genitive form in the accusative, but in Czech it is expressed through the survival of the ancient nominative-accusative opposition, lost in the singular, cf. Czech *páni* (nom. pl.), *pány* (acc.), *pánů* (gen.) and Slovak *páni*, *pánov*, *pánov*. Another difference between Czech and Slovak is that while all nouns denoting living creatures that are grammatically masculine are 'animate' in both languages in the singular, the same applies in the plural only to Czech. In the Slovak plural it is confined to human males (cf. Polish). Another uniquely Slovak feature is the treatment of animacy in the peripheral masculine *a*-declension, which, other differences apart, has produced syncretism between the accusative and genitive singular, as one expects, but based on the accusative form. In Czech this declension retains most of the case distinctions of the central feminine *a*-declension.

	Masc. animate Czech/Slovak	Feminine a-decl. Czech/Slovak	Masculine a-decl. Czech	Slovak
Nom.	pán	žena	hrdina 'hero'	hrdina
Acc.	pána	ženu	hrdinu	hrdinu
Gen.	pána	ženy	hrdiny	hrdinu

This same distribution of endings in Slovak also applies to most native names ending in -o, e.g. *Botto, Bottu, Bottu*.

The basic neuter declensions in both languages are very conservative. On the Slovak side, however, there are three innovations worthy of mention: lengthening of the ending of the nominative/accusative plural, unless inhibited by the rhythmical law, e.g. *mesto* (nom./acc. sg.) but *mestá*, cf. Czech *město, města*; the extending of the feminine a-declension locative ending -*ách*/-*iach* to the neuters, e.g. *zenách/dušiach* (f.) and *mestách/poliach*, in contrast to Czech *městech/polích* which retain their affinity with the masculine (there is some penetration of a-declension endings into the neuter in Czech in the case of velar stems, e.g. *kolečkách* 'wheel' (diminutive), which avoids stem alternation of the type *kolečcích); and vowel lengthening before the zero ending of the genitive plural if not inhibited by the rhythmical law, e.g. *mesto* (nom. sg.), *miest*. This last is another feature shared with the a-declension, cf. *žena/žien*, and an interesting aspect of it is that it applies equally to a true stem vowel and any fill vowel which might appear, e.g. *okno/okien* 'window'. (Note that vowel lengthening often, as in these examples, means diphthongisation.)

Apart from the above, Czech noun morphology is generally more conservative than Slovak in the greater degree of preservation of the effects of the second palatalisation of velars, in the locative plural masculine (*jazycích* 'tongue', Slovak *jazykoch*) and the nominative plural animate, where it affects all three velar consonants: *žák/žáci* 'student', *Čech/Češi*, *vrah/vrazi* 'murderer'; in Slovak this only applies to the first two, hence: *žiak/žiaci, Čech/Česi*, but *vrah/vrahovia* (-*ovia*, Czech -*ové* is an alternative nominative plural masculine animate ending used with specific subclasses of nouns; a third is -*ia*, Czech -*é*).

Adjective declension is typified by the presence of long vowels in the ending (unless inhibited by the rhythmical law in Slovak as in the example following) as a result of contraction, cf. the disyllabic endings, in the nominative at least, in Russian, where contraction did not occur: Czech *krásný* 'beautiful' (m. sg.), *krásná* (f. sg.), *krásné* (n. sg.), *krásní* (m. anim. pl.), *krásné* (m. inanim. and f. pl.) and *krásná* (nt. pl.), Slovak *krásny* (m. sg.), *krásna* (f. sg.), *krasne* (nt. sg.), *krásni* (m. hum. pl.), *krásne* (all other plurals), Russian *krasnyj* (m. sg.), *krasnaja* (f. sg.), *krasnoje* (nt. sg.) and *krasnyje* (all plurals).

Apart from the operation of the rhythmical law in Slovak the other main differences between the Czech and Slovak adjectival declension can be

Adjective Declension

	Czech			Slovak		
Adjectival declension — hard						
Sg. Nom.	dobrý 'good'	-á	-é	dobrý	-á	-é
Voc.	dobrý	-á	-é			
Acc.	{ dobrý { dobrého	-ou	-é	{ dobrý { dobrého	-ú	-é
Gen.	dobrého	-é	-ého	dobrého	-ej	-ého
Dat.	dobrému	-é	-ému	dobrému	-ej	-ému
Inst.	dobrým	-ou	-ým	dobrým	-ou	-ým
Loc.	dobrém	-é	-ém	dobrom	-ej	-om
Pl. Nom.	{ dobré { dobří	-é	-á	{ dobré { dobrí	-é	-é
Voc.	{ dobré { dobří	-é	-á			
Acc.	dobré	-é	-á	{ dobré { dobrých	-é	-é
Gen.	dobrých			dobrých		
Dat.	dobrým			dobrým		
Ins.	dobrými			dobrými		
Loc.	dobrých			dobrých		
Adjectival declension — soft						
Sg. Nom.	cizí 'alien'	-í	-í	cudzí	-ia	-ie
Voc.	cizí	-í	-í			
Acc.	{ cizí { cizího	-í	-í	{ cudzí { cudzieho	-ej	-ie
Gen.	cizího	-í	-ího	cudzieho	-ej	-ieho
Dat.	cizímu	-í	-ímu	cudziemu	-ej	-iemu
Inst.	cizím	-í	-ím	cudzím	-ou	-ím
Loc.	cizím	-í	-ím	cudzom	-ej	om
Pl. Nom.	cizí			{ cudzie { cudzí	-ie	-ie
Voc.	cizí					
Acc.	cizí			{ cudzie { cudzích	-ie	-ie
Gen.	cizích			cudzích		
Dat.	cizím			cudzím		
Inst.	cizími			cudzími		
Loc.	cizích			cudzích		

Note: Pairs of forms joined by braces indicate variation by animacy, inanimate above, animate below. The masculine plural animate ending -í causes palatalisation of dental and velar stems in Czech, but not in Slovak.

explained by the relative conservatism of Slovak phonology, notably the absence of *přehláska* and the non-monophthongisation of *ie*, both affecting the soft adjectives and illustrated in, for example, the feminine and neuter singular forms *cudzia*, *cudzie*, Czech *cizí* 'alien, someone else's'.

It is worth noting that Czech retains a number of so-called short adjectives, e.g. *zdráv* 'healthy', *živ* 'alive', *jist* 'sure', *zvědav* 'curious', *vědom* 'aware', *bos* 'barefoot', which only occur in the predicate and in a narrow range of essentially idiomatic usages. Both Czech and Slovak have the short adjective *rád/-a/-o* which has no long counterpart and serves in conjunction with any verb to express the meaning 'like -ing'. Both languages show full adjective-noun agreement in case, number and gender including animacy. A curiosity on the Czech side is the special form of the instrumental plural in *-ýma*, used in agreement with the handful of nouns which retain *-ma* in that case — one of the dual remnants referred to earlier, occurring in *ruce–rukama* 'hands, arms', *nohy–nohama* 'feet, legs', *uši–ušima* 'ears', *oči–očima* 'eyes'.

An interesting morphological innovation is to be found in the declension of numerals in Slovak. The core system is as in Czech: *jeden* 'one' varies by gender and has case (and number) agreement (it actually declines in Czech like the demonstrative pronoun *ten*); *dva* 'two' has a special form *dve* (*dvě* in Czech) for feminine and neuter (contrast Russian, where *dve* is feminine only, with *dva* for masculine and neuter); *dva/dve*, *tri* 'three', *štyri* 'four' (*tři*, *čtyři* in Czech) 'three', 'four' all agree with their noun; *päť* (*pět*) 'five' and higher numerals take the genitive plural of the counted noun when the entire phrase is in any nominative or accusative slot in the sentence, otherwise there is case agreement (marked only rudimentarily in Czech) except after prepositions, when *päť* etc. do not decline. Slovak's innovation is in the possession of forms *dvaja*, *traja*, *štyria*, *piati* and onwards for use with animates; all such forms show agreement with the counted noun. The genderless *päť* and above may be used instead of *piati* etc., but the survival of the latter is ensured through the Slovak mutation of the expression of animacy, which has consistently distinctive forms in the nominative and the genitive-accusative. Hence not only *krásni muži–krásnych mužov*, but also *dvaja–dvoch*, *traja–troch*, *štyria–štyroch* and *piati–piatich*.

Verbal morphology in Czech and Slovak differs basically in consequence, again, of *přehláska* in Czech and the rhythmical law in Slovak. Slovak has, however, gone further than Czech in having consistent person markers, notably in having *-m* as the universal marker of first person singular. In both languages this has spread from a minor conjugation, the so-called athematic verbs (with the meanings 'be', 'have', 'know', 'eat' and 'give'), which formed a distinctive group in Proto-Slavonic and continue to exhibit various anomalous features, especially in Czech. Where Czech has not evolved the *-m* first person marker is in the conjugations here described as *e-*, *ne-*, *uje-* (the same endings also shared by the *je*-type): *e-*: *nést–nesu* 'carry', *brát–beru* 'take', *mazat–mažu/-i* 'smear', *péci–peču* 'bake', *umřít–umřu* 'die'; *ne-*: *tisknout–tisknu* 'print', *minout–minu* 'pass', *začít–začnu* 'begin'; *je-*: *krýt–kryji/-u* 'cover'; *uje-*: *kupovat–kupuji/-u* 'buy'. The original ending in these classes was *-u* (from the nasal *ǫ*), which has since given *-i* in cases where *přehláska* operated. The tolerance which the standard language has shown for a reversal of this *i*-ending to *-u*, by analogy with the majority, has varied from type to type, coming latest with those classes containing a final *-j-* in the present tense stem.

Slovak has long had *-t'* as the sole infinitive marker, whatever the shape of the remainder of the infinitive stem: *niest'*, *brat'*, but also *piect'*, while in the latter type Czech has had an anomaly in *-ci* (*péci*, *říci*, *moci* etc.), with forms in *-t* only in Common Czech. By a recent reform, however, the compelling force of analogy has led to a degree of upward mobility of the forms in *-t* (*péct*, *říct*, *moct*) towards their acceptance in the more colloquial version of the standard literary language.

Czech and Slovak, like Russian, but unlike Serbo-Croat, have moved right away from a complex tense system, still alive in Old Czech, to an aspect-based system, with pairs of verbs for all meanings that are acts, and single verbs for activities and states. The two members of the aspect category (perfective and imperfective) are much the same as for the other Slavonic languages: perfective for a single action seen as a whole, completed and potentially having consequences for subsequent actions, imperfective for an action in progress, repetition or the action *per se*, which may be completed but where consequence is immaterial. Differences of detail between Czech/Slovak and Russian relate in particular to the aspect form used in certain cases with explicitly expressed repetition; in Czech/Slovak the choice often hinges on the semantics of specific conjunctions and adverbs. The specific consequence for Czech/Slovak is the use of the perfective present (formally the same as the perfective future) in certain general or non-actual present time contexts, whereas it is normally the case that the only aspect in the present is the imperfective.

Having an aspect-based system, Czech and Slovak overcome the impoverishment of the tense system and the general Slavonic lack of sequence-of-tense rules by expressing anteriority, posteriority and simultaneity, in certain important subordinate clause types, e.g. after *verba dicendi*, by past, future and present tense forms, whatever the tense of the main clause: Czech *řekl/říká/řekne, že přijde* 'he said/is saying/ will say that he would/will come', *řekl/říká/řekne, že tam byl* 'he said/is saying/will say that he had/has been there', *řekl/říká/řekne, že nekouří* 'he said/is saying/ will say that he did/does not smoke'.

Both Czech and Slovak, unlike Russian, use auxiliary verbs in the past tense (omitted in the third persons), while in the conditional the auxiliary (evolved out of the aorist of *být* 'be') conjugates. A difference between Czech and Slovak is that the plural forms of the past *l*-participle do not mark gender in Slovak (cf. Russian), a simplification present only in colloquial Czech. Another difference of detail is in the greater refinement of the expression of the second person in the past tense in Czech, which can discriminate between not only the sex (gender) of the addressee, but also number and degree of familiarity, hence *byl jsi* 'you were' is singular familiar masculine, *byla jsi* singular familiar feminine, *byl jste* singular formal

Conjugation[1]

	Czech	Slovak
e-conjugation		
Infin.	nést 'carry'	niest'
Pres. sg.	nesu neseš nese	nesiem nesieš nesie
pl.	neseme nesete nesou	nesieme nesiete nesú
Imperative	nes nesme neste	nes nesme neste
Past	nesl	niesol
Transgressive	nesa nesouc nesouce[2]	nesúc
Past transg.	-nes -nesši -nesše[2]	
Pass. part.	nesen/-ý	nesený
ne-conjugation		
Infin.	vadnout 'fade'	vädnút'
Pres sg.	vadnu vadneš vadne	vädnem vädneš vädne
pl.	vadneme vadnete vadnou	vädneme vädnete vädnú
Imperative	vadni vadněme vadněte	vädni vädnime vädnite
Past	vadl	vädol
Transgressive	vadna vadnouc vadnouce	vädnúc
Past transg.	vadnuv vadnuvši vadnuvše	
Pass. part.	tištěn/tisknut/-ý[3]	-tisnutý
uje-conjugation		
Infin.	kupovat 'buy'	kupovat'
Pres. sg.	kupuji kupuješ kupuje	kupujem kupuješ kupuje
pl.	kupujeme kupujete kupují	kupujeme kupujete kupujú
Imper.	kupuj kupujme kupujte	kupuj kupujme kupujte
Past	kupoval	kupoval
Transg.	kupuje kupujíc kupujíce	kupujúc
Past transg.	na-kupovav -ši -še	
Pass. part.	kupován/-aný	kupovaný
i-conjugation		
Infin.	prosit 'ask for'	prosit'
Pres. sg.	prosím prosíš prosí	prosím prosíš prosí
pl.	prosíme prosíte prosí	prosíme prosíte prosia
Imper.	pros prosme proste	pros prosme proste
Past	prosil	prosil
Transg.	prose prosíc prosíce	prosiac
Past transg.	poprosiv -ivši -ivše	
Pass. part.	prošen/-ý	prosený
a-conjugation		
Infin.	volat 'call'	volat'
Pres. sg.	volám voláš volá	volám voláš volá
pl.	voláme voláte volají	voláme voláte volajú
Imper.	volej volejme volejte	volaj volajme volajte
Past	volal	volal
Transg.	volaje volajíc volajíce	volajúc
Past transg.	zavolav -avši -avše	
Pass. part.	volán/-aný	volaný

Notes: [1] This summary of the basic conjugational types cannot show the imbalance brought about by *přehláska*, particularly in the distribution of verbs among the *a*- and *i*-conjugations. Each class in both languages has various subtypes. [2] The present and past transgressives (the traditional term in Czech and Slovak grammars) are the gerunds of other Slavonic languages. The three forms in Czech are for masculine, feminine/neuter and plural, agreement being governed by the subject of the main clause. [3] Forms from the transitive verb *tisknout* 'print'; *vadnout* 'fade' is intransitive and therefore has no passive participle.

masculine, *byla jste* singular formal feminine, *byli jste* plural masculine or mixed, *byly jste* plural feminine (in speech the last distinction is not heard, thanks to the phonetic equivalence of *i* and *y*). Slovak distinguishes gender in the familiar singular: *bol/bola si*, but all other forms are *boli ste*.

6   Syntax

A complete description of Czech and Slovak syntax is beyond the scope of the present outline, but some features are worthy of special mention. These include the use and position of enclitics (mostly the auxiliary verbs and pronouns) and the expression of the passive. Both have a bearing on word order, on which more will be said in the concluding sentences.

Czech, and to a lesser degree Slovak, has quite strict rules on word order with enclitics. In a nutshell, these say that any enclitic will appear in the second grammatical slot (not merely second word) in the sentence, i.e. there must be at least one stressed word at the beginning of a sentence on which the stressless enclitics can lean. The critical first slot may be occupied by the subject, object, an adverb or conjunction (but not the weak coordinating conjunctions *a* 'and', *i* 'and even', *ale* 'but', *nebo* 'or'; this last constraint applies much less in Slovak). It may also be occupied by a subject pronoun, which will be there for emphasis, since subject pronouns are not normally required, person being adequately expressed in the verb, even in the past tense, thanks to the use of auxiliaries (unlike in Russian). Within the second, enclitic slot the ordering is also fixed: an auxiliary verb in the past tense or conditional (but not the imperfective future auxiliary) will always take precedence, followed by dative, then accusative (occasionally genitive) object pronouns, and finally certain enclitic adverbs or particles. Hence, in Czech, for example:

Včera	jste	mi	ji	však	nedal.
Yesterday	2nd pers. aux.	me (dat.)	it (f.)	though	not gave

'But yesterday you did not give it to me.'

The only refinements to this rule in Czech relate to the use of the reflexive pronouns *se/si* (accusative and dative respectively) either of which takes precedence over all other pronoun objects, and to the referentially vague *to* which, whether subject or object, i.e. nominative or accusative, stands in the accusative/genitive enclitic slot: *včera jste mi to neřekl* 'you did not tell me (it) yesterday', *Petrovi by se to* (subject) *nelíbilo* 'Peter would not like it/ that' (*líbit se* 'be pleasing'). The situation as described is beginning to break down, the enclitics, especially *se*, showing a tendency to be more closely associated with the verb phrase wherever it may stand. In Slovak the process has gone slightly further.

The passive in Czech and Slovak is only rarely expressed by the periphrastic form analogous to the English passive, although it is quite common in technical and some journalistic texts. Instead the shift of emphasis, or perspective, from 'Peter killed Paul' to 'Paul was killed by Peter' is carried by simple inversion of subject and object: *Petr zabil Pavla*, *Pavla zabil Petr*, an obvious possibility in a language where syntactic relations are explicit in the morphology and where there are relatively few constraints on word order. Very widespread in both languages are passive, quasi-passive and impersonal constructions, comparable to many passive-like constructions in English, based on verb phrases with *se*, here best interpreted as a passivising or intransitivising particle. They are used typically where no agent is (or can be) named (*talíř se rozbil* 'the plate broke/ got broken'), in the language of instructions (*cibule se tam dá nejdřív* 'the onion is put in first', *tato samohláska se vyslovuje dlouze* 'this vowel is pronounced long'), and in depersonalised accounts of events (*pivo se pilo, písničky se zpívaly a okna se rozbíjela* 'beer was drunk, songs were sung and windows were broken'); in this last type the same construction is available with intransitive verbs, always in the third person singular neuter (*nepracovalo se a šlo se domů brzy* 'no work was done and people went home early' lit. 'it was not being worked and it was gone home early')

Word order in Czech and Slovak, as was hinted above, is governed primarily by functional sentence perspective. That element which carries most emphasis, or most new information, is reserved to the end of the sentence. In general terms, the 'communicative dynamism' of an utterance builds up from low to high as the sentence unfolds. This allows maximum exploitation of 'free word order', which of course does not mean random word order. A great deal of work has been done on the subtleties of word order, ever since Vilém Mathesius and the Prague Linguistic Circle, and new theories and descriptions continue to appear. It has also been an area of study in contrastive, comparative and confrontational linguistics. It is perhaps worth noting that a major impulse here has undoubtedly been the very strong tradition of translating into Czech and Slovak: Czechoslovakia translates an average of 650 non-dramatic works of literature, 150 plays and 200 films (dubbed or subtitled) annually, and about 28 per cent of television time is spent on translated material. These are figures which can be matched by few other countries.

7 The Contemporary Language Situation

As with any modern language, Czech and Slovak show much variation in regional and social dialects. Czech divides into four main regional dialect groupings, Slovak into three.

The Czech macrodialects are: Bohemian, Central Moravian (Haná), Eastern Moravian or Moravian Slovak, and Silesian (Lach). The dialect differences have evolved in fairly recent times, mostly since the twelfth century, but particularly during the fourteenth to sixteenth centuries. Some prehistoric differences are also present, in the distribution of some lexical items, suffixes and vowel quantity in certain prosodically distinct word types: long in Bohemian *práh* 'threshold', *bláto* 'mud', *žába* 'frog', *bříza* 'birch', *moucha* 'fly', *vítr* 'wind', short in Central Moravian *prah*, *blato*, *žaba*, *březa*, *mucha*, *vjetr*.

One of the most important sound changes in the history of Czech was, as mentioned earlier, *přehláska*. That of *a* to *ě* was carried through in a decreasing number of environments the further east one goes through Moravia, while *u* > *i* is practically unknown anywhere in Moravia. One consequence of this is the much greater degree of similarity between 'soft' and 'hard' declensional paradigms than in standard Czech and a measure of interchange between them, words in *-sa*, *-za* and *-la* with originally hard *s*, *z*, and *l* tending to shift to the equivalent soft paradigm.

The Lach dialects separated from the rest of Czech by the retention of softness in the syllables *ďe*, *ťe*, *ňe*, the loss of distinctions of vowel quantity, and the development, as in Polish, of fixed stress on the penultimate.

Typical of the Bohemian dialects are the changes of *ý* into *ej* and *ú* into *ou*, which took over two centuries to complete, peaking in the sixteenth century. Eastern Moravian and the Lach dialects show no sign of this shift, cf. for *strýc* 'uncle' Cent. Boh. *strejc*, E. Mor. *strýc*, Lach *stryc*, and for *múka* 'fly' Cent. Boh. *mouka*, E. Mor. *múka*, Lach *muka*. (Note that the forms used in standard Czech are *strýc* and *mouka* respectively, though *strejc* is colloquial; few words with *ej* < *ý* have passed into the standard language whereas *ou* < *ú* is the norm except initially.) The same dialects were also unaffected by the Central Bohemian change of *aj* to *ej* in closed syllables and *é* to *í*, hence *daj* 'give (sg. imper.)' for Central Bohemian and standard Czech *dej* and *dobré mléko* 'good milk' for Central Bohemian *dobrí mlíko*. (Here standard Czech has *dobré mléko*, one of the reasons why Moravians are often heard to assert that they speak a 'better' Czech than the Bohemians.)

Eastern Bohemian was once distinguished by the loss of softness from labials before *e*, giving rise to syllables *pe*, *be*, *me*, *ve* where elsewhere Czech has /pje/, /bje/, /mňe/ and /vje/, though this feature has largely yielded to the more universal version of these syllables. By contrast, one of the features marking out the south-west group of Bohemian dialects is the survival of softness, again expanded to a *j*, even before *i*, as in *pjivo* 'beer'.

These days the most typical features of north-east Bohemian are the bilabial pronunciation of *v* in closed syllables, much as in Slovak, and, in morphology, the spread of the ending *-ej* in the instrumental singular of soft feminine nouns. The Giant Mountains area is renowned for the appearance of *e* before syllabic *r*: *perší* '(it) rains', *perkno* 'board' for standard *prší*, *prkno*.

The last major contributor to the distinctness of the Moravian centre, the Haná and related dialects, is a change of *ej* to *é* and *ou* to *ó*. The former is very widespread, since it affects *ej* from *ý*, *ej* from *aj* and cases where the *e* and the *j* straddle a morpheme boundary, hence Central Bohemian *dobrej strejc* 'good uncle' (from *dobrý strýc*), *dej* (from *daj*) and *nejsem* '(I) am not' (from *ne + jsem*) correspond to Haná *dobré stréc*, *dé* and *nésem*. Related changes in the short vowels produce so many local variants that the Moravian dialect area is fragmented on this basis alone into dialects with five-, six- or seven-member vowel systems in various combinations.

From all the foregoing it follows that the Eastern Moravian dialects have been the most conservative, untouched by many of the sound changes mentioned. In this, and in certain other respects, they represent a transition to Slovak.

The dialect situation in Slovakia is even more complex than in the Czech-speaking areas. Three macrodialects are usually pinpointed, but each has numerous subdivisions, partly understandable from a glance at the country's physical geography.

Since Central Slovak became the basis for the Slovak literary language, it is usually taken as the reference point against which to describe the other main dialect groupings. Not all of the features typical of the central dialects have been adopted by the standard language. Some of the distinctive Central Slovak features are as follows:

The reflexes of the jers and the so-called fill vowels vary more than in any other Slavonic language or dialect, with *e*, *o* or *a* in short syllables and *ie*, *uo* (orthographically *ô*) or *á* in long syllables; in Western Slovak, as in Czech, it is always *e*, and in Eastern Slovak predominantly so, with sporadic instances of *o*. The *ä* of the standard language (where /e/ is a tolerated alternative pronunciation) is replaced after labials by *e*, alternating with *ia* in cognate long syllables; in Western Slovak the alternation is between *a* and *á*, and in Eastern between *e* and *ia*. There are the four diphthongs of the standard language, with none in Western Slovak, and local survivals of *ie* and *uo* in Eastern dialects. The syllabic liquids occur in long and short syllables, but in Western Slovak they are only short as in Czech. In Eastern Slovak they have not even survived as syllabic and are always accompanied by a vowel, with considerable local variation. The standard language owes its rhythmical law to Central Slovak, since Western Slovak reveals no such vowel shortening, and phonological quantity has totally disappeared from Eastern Slovak. Central Slovak morphological features include the long *á* or *ia* ending in the neuter plural of nouns, the *e*-ending of soft neuter nouns in the nominative singular (*o* in Western and Eastern Slovak, hence *vreco* 'sack', *ojo* 'shaft' to Central and standard Slovak *vrece*, *oje*), the instrumental singular feminine ending *-ou* (*-ú* in the west, *-u* in the east), and two very distinctive adjectival endings: nominative neuter singular in *-uo*, contrasting with *-é* in the west and *-e* in the east, and the locative singular masculine and neuter ending *-om* as against *-ém* in most of the west and *-im* in the east. The third person plural of the verb 'to be' is generally *sa*, which also occurs in parts of the west, but the standard form has adopted *sú*, the Western Slovak form, comparable also with *su* in the east.

Two important Western Slovak features not mentioned (and there are others of course) are the absence of the soft /l'/ phoneme, and the curious extension of the third person singular of the verb *byt'* 'to be' in the negative (*neni*) into the function of simple negator, hence *neni som* 'am not', originally 'isn't am'.

Additional distinctive Eastern Slovak features include: stress on the penultimate, as in Polish, complete absence of phonological quantity, a change of *ch* [x] into *h*, and the adoption of a universal genitive and locative plural ending for all genders, usually *-och* (*bratoch* 'brother', *ženoch* 'woman', *mestoch* 'town' etc.) and locally *-of*.

The foregoing are only a sample of the most striking features and those which cover most of the respective macrodialect areas. What they do not reveal immediately is something which has provided material for numerous books and papers, namely that there are a number of similarities between Western and Eastern Slovak which make them jointly distinct from the Central macrodialect. It is now generally accepted that this is a consequence of the different route and chronology in the arrival of the Slavonic-speaking population of the area. A number of features which Central Slovak shares with South Slavonic suggests a period of contiguity with the South Slavs and that colonisation of Central Slovakia proceeded from the south. The full details of this prehistory are still the subject of debate.

In addition to the horizontal (geographical) division of Czech and Slovak into dialects, there is a vertical division into the more or less conventional range of styles, registers, social dialects, slangs and so forth. On the whole it is probably safe to say that Slovak is the less interesting of the two, though not for any lack of richness or variety. There is indeed a full range of linguistic variation, much of it still being described for the first time. The slightly greater interest of Czech stems from the fact, already mentioned, of a literary standard language rich in essentially archaic features, some of which are jettisoned in the colloquial (*hovorový*) versions of it, and the parallel existence of Common Czech, or Common Colloquial Czech (*obecná čeština*). This is phonologically and morphologically closely related to the Central Bohemian dialect, syntactically to the less strict versions of Colloquial Czech, with some other features often ascribed to the influence of

German, and lexically often quite distinct, i.e. there are many lexical items peculiar to Common Czech which have to be 'translated' into standard Czech, e.g. *táta* = *otec* 'father'. Although rooted in Central Bohemia, Common Czech has spread well beyond the frontiers of that dialect area, especially to the major urban centres and then outward from them. However, with this spread it is also ceasing to be a universal koine and other versions are being observed to arise, especially in Moravia. Here the influence of the distinctive local dialects proper has given rise to the fairly recent conception of a Common Moravian Czech. A great deal of work has been conducted in recent decades on analyses of urban speech (*městská mluva*) in a number of large towns, and this has shown how Common Czech is contributing to the disappearance of local dialects while taking on specific local variations of detail from them.

Czech and Slovak are also both very rich in slangs, and although there are large areas of difference, it is interesting to note that here, as with the standard languages, there is a degree of convergence. This is understandable when one appreciates the cross-mobility, within a unitary state, of such groups as students, members of the armed forces or those involved in the pop-music and other subcultures. This is not to suggest that here, or at any other level, the process of convergence will ever be more than partial.

Bibliography

The standard reference grammar of Czech is Havránek and Jedlička (1981), although this is soon to be superseded by an entirely new work from the Academy of Sciences. Mazon (1952) is a classic but dated reference work. Kučera (1961) is a structuralist phonology of literary and colloquial Czech.

For Slovak, there is a new descriptive grammar by Pauliny (1981), in addition to the classical reference grammar by Bartoš and Gagnaire (1972); Mistrík (1983) is a descriptive reference grammar, marred by quirky English.

Millet (1983) is an excellent external history of Czech since the National Revival, including a section on the emergence of Slovak.

References

Bartoš, J. and J. Gagnaire. 1972. *Grammaire de la langue slovaque* (Institut d'Études Slaves, Paris and Matica Slovenská, Bratislava)

Havránek, B. and A. Jedlička. 1981. *Česká mluvnice*, 4th ed. (Státní Pedagogické Nakladatelství, Prague)

Kučera, H. 1961. *The Phonology of Czech* (Mouton, The Hague)

Mazon, A. 1952. *Grammaire de la langue tchèque*, 3rd ed. (Institut d'Études Slaves, Paris)

Millet, Y. 1983. 'Continuité et discontinuité: cas du tchèque', in I. Fodor and C. Hagège (eds.), *Language Reform: History and Future*, vol. 2 (Helmut Buske, Hamburg), pp. 479–504.

Mistrík, J. 1983. *A Grammar of Contemporary Slovak* (SPN, Bratislava)

Pauliny, E. 1981. *Slovenská gramatika* (Slovenské Pedagogické Nakladatel'stvo, Bratislava)

6 Serbo-Croat

Greville Corbett

1 Historical Background

The line which divided Europe into east and west, Orthodox and Catholic, runs right through the part of the Balkans where Serbo-Croat (or Serbo-Croatian) is spoken. Various states have prospered at different times in this region, such as the Serbian medieval kingdom under rulers like Stefan Nemanja and Stefan Dušan and the unique city state of Dubrovnik (Ragusa). Parts of the territory have been under Venice, Austro-Hungary and the Turks. We can only hope to hint at the complex and turbulent history of the area.

The ancestors of the South Slavs arrived in the Balkans during the sixth and seventh centuries and within the next two centuries the first Slav states of the area sprang up. By this time too the main linguistic divisions were evident. There were two main sets of dialects: East South Slavonic would later develop into Bulgarian and the closely related Macedonian, while West South Slavonic was the basis for Slovene and Serbo-Croat. From the ninth century the Slovenes in the north-west were ruled by Bavarian and Austrian princes and so were separated from their Slavonic neighbours. In the remaining area, roughly equivalent to modern Yugoslavia excepting Slovenia and Macedonia, a range of dialects was spoken, which would give rise to modern Serbo-Croat.

Christianity was accepted in the ninth century, with certain political repercussions. The tenth-century Croatian kingdom looked to Rome in matters of religion. Serbia's adoption of Orthodoxy meant that it looked first to Constantinople and later, after the fall of Constantinople, to Moscow for support. Montenegro was also Orthodox. The picture was complicated by the invasion of the Turks, who defeated the Serbs at Kosovo in 1389, and by the resulting migrations of population. In the next century the Turks occupied Bosnia and Hercegovina, where a large proportion of the population adopted Islam, and Montenegro. By the time the Turks were finally removed (1878), Croatia was part of the Austro-Hungarian Empire, which took over Bosnia and Hercegovina. It was not until 1918 that the different groups were united into one state.

Three main dialect groups had emerged, which take their names from the interrogative pronoun 'what?': Čakavian (*ča?* 'what?'), Kajkavian (*kaj?*) and Štokavian (*što?*). Kajkavian was spoken in the north, Čakavian in the west and Štokavian in the east, centre and south-west. However, the dialectal, political and religious boundaries did not match in a straightforward way. Despite this troubled history there have been some remarkable flowerings of literature. When the Serbian Kingdom was at its height during the twelfth to fourteenth centuries, literature flourished, written not in the vernacular but in the Serbian version of Church Slavonic. In the west too, Church Slavonic was used at first, but by the sixteenth century major writers like Marulić, Hektorović, Zoranić and Lucić were using Čakavian. The rise of Dubrovnik brought Štokavian to the fore also in the sixteenth century. And in the eighteenth century, Kajkavian was widely used in Croatia around Zagreb.

This diversity of literary tradition, mirroring the dialectal fragmentation of the area, naturally impeded the development of a common literary language in the west. In the east, Turkish domination had severely hampered the development of the Serbian Church Slavonic tradition. Russian Church Slavonic was adopted in the eighteenth century and a hybrid language (Slavenoserbian) evolved, with elements of Russian Church Slavonic and vernacular Serbian. Its artificiality, contrary both to the aspirations of intellectuals influenced by the Enlightenment and to the needs of modern society, led to a movement towards a more popular language, which was brought to fruition by Vuk Karadžić (1787–1864). Karadžić rejected Slavenoserbian, insisting that the new literary language must be based on the vernacular and on a single dialect, the Štokavian dialect of East Hercegovina. He made his revolutionary proposals in his dictionary (1818), which also contained a grammar of the language. There had already been some movement in the west towards basing the literary language on Štokavian. The Zagreb editor Ljudevit Gaj (1809–72) and other intellectuals helped accelerate this trend. In 1850 the Literary Accord between Croats and Serbs was signed in Vienna. It justified the use of Štokavian (Hercegovinian dialect) as the literary language and gave rules for writing it. Reactions to the Accord varied; not surprisingly it aroused a great deal of hostility, but gradually it gained support. Yet the centuries of division between different dialects, religions, cultures and political groups could not be removed by such an agreement. In any case, the major task of adapting the chosen variant to all the functions of a modern literary language had still to be faced. Nevertheless the Accord crystallised a unifying trend. A major success associated with this trend was the reform of the writing system.

2   Writing System

The original alphabet was Glagolitic. In the eastern, Orthodox area this was replaced from the twelfth century on by Cyrillic. In the west, the Latin alphabet was introduced in the fourteenth century, under Catholic influence. However, Glagolitic remained in use in the west, particularly among priests on the Dalmatian coast and islands, even into this century. From the sixteenth century until the Second World War, some Moslem writers in Bosnia used the Arabic script.

Neither in the east nor in the west was the writing system satisfactory. The version of the Cyrillic alphabet employed was appropriate for Church Slavonic but not for the contemporary language, while the use of the Latin alphabet in the west was influenced by Italian or Hungarian practice (depending on the area), neither of which was a suitable model for a Slavonic language. In his dictionary of 1818, Vuk Karadžić justified and used a new version of Cyrillic. This was a major reform involving simplifying the alphabet, using a single letter per sound and adopting a phonemically based orthography. He eliminated several unnecessary letters and introduced six new ones. Despite initial angry opposition, his alphabet was adopted and, with one minor modification, is in use today.

The equivalent reform for the Latin alphabet was carried out a little later by Ljudevit Gaj, using diacritic symbols on the Czech model. With minor modifications, Gaj's alphabet is the present one. Unlike the Cyrillic alphabet it includes digraphs: *lj*, *nj* and *dž* (also *dj* though this latter is usually written *đ*). Single symbols exist for these but their use is restricted to certain academic publications. The digraphs cause little problem; the combination *l* + *j* does not occur, while *n* + *j* and *d* + *ž* are rare; an example is *nadživeti* 'to outlive', where *d* + *ž* represent separate sounds. The two modern alphabets are given in table 6.1.

Table 6.1: The Alphabets of Serbo-Croat

Latin		Cyrillic		Latin		Cyrillic	
A	a	А	а	L	l	Л	л
B	b	Б	б	Lj	lj	Љ	љ
C	c	Ц	ц	M	m	М	м
Č	č	Ч	ч	N	n	Н	н
Ć	ć	Ћ	ћ	Nj	nj	Њ	њ
D	d	Д	д	O	o	О	о
Dž	dž	Џ	џ	P	p	П	п
Đ	đ	Ђ	ђ	R	r	Р	р
E	e	Е	е	S	s	С	с
F	f	Ф	ф	Š	š	Ш	ш
G	g	Г	г	T	t	Т	т
H	h	Х	х	U	u	У	у
I	i	И	и	V	v	В	в
J	j	J	j	Z	z	З	з
K	k	К	к	Ž	ž	Ж	ж

The characters are arranged in the Latin order; the Cyrillic order is: А, Б, В, Г, Д, Ђ, Е, Ж, З, И, Ј, К, Л, Љ, М, Н, Њ, О, П, Р, С, Т, Ћ, У, Ф, Х, Ц, Ч, Џ, Ш. This Cyrillic list includes six characters not found in Russian Cyrillic; conversely, Russian has nine characters not used in Serbo-Croat. Note from the table that there is an exact correspondence, letter for letter, between the two alphabets of Serbo-Croat. The digraphs in the Latin version function as autonomous letters. This means that in a dictionary, all words beginning with *lj* are grouped together after all those with initial *l* (unlike English, where *thin* comes before *tin*); in a crossword, *lj* occupies a single square. The exact correspondence between the two alphabets means that transliteration is automatic; a typescript may be submitted in the Latin alphabet though it is to be printed in Cyrillic. This parallel use of the alphabets is found in the east, while in the west the Latin alphabet is found almost exclusively. There appears to be a trend in the east towards greater use of the Latin alphabet. In present-day Belgrade the two coexist with no apparent confusion: one sees shop windows with notices in both alphabets side by side, or a lecturer may begin labelling a diagram in one alphabet and then continue in the other.

The orthography of Serbo-Croat is based on the phonemic principle. Assimilations are indicated in spelling, for example, *redak* (masculine singular) 'rare' but *retka* (feminine singular); *top* 'gun' but *tobdžija* 'gunner'. If a consonant is dropped it is omitted in spelling, for example, *radostan* (masculine singular) 'joyful' but *radosna* (feminine singular). Though there are rare exceptions, this phonemic principle is applied (at the expense of the morphological principle) with unusual consistency.

3 The Contemporary Situation: Dialects and Varieties

Serbo-Croat is the major language of Yugoslavia; it is spoken in the Yugoslav republics of Bosnia and Hercegovina, Croatia, Montenegro and Serbia, by a total of over 17 million according to the 1981 census. Slovenia and Macedonia have their own languages but many Slovenes and Macedonians know Serbo-Croat (as do large numbers of the sizable populations of Albanians and Hungarians living in Yugoslavia and of the smaller groups of Bulgarians and Rumanians). Many hundreds of thousands of Serbo-Croat speakers now live abroad, notably in the United States and Australasia, and in West Germany and Sweden.

As stated earlier, there are three main dialects: Čakavian, Kajkavian and Štokavian. Each of these is in fact a set of related dialects. In contrast to their earlier importance, Čakavian and Kajkavian are spoken in relatively small areas, so we shall discuss them briefly. Čakavian survives along the Dalmatian coastal fringe, on the Adriatic islands, in Istria and in a small part of northern Croatia. As we shall see in the next section, it preserves an interesting accentual system; in morphology too it is more conservative than

Štokavian. Kajkavian is spoken around Zagreb in the north of Croatia, bordering on Slovenia. It shares several features with Slovene. Like Čakavian, it retains distinct dative, instrumental and locative plural endings, which are merged in Štokavian; another interesting archaic feature is the preservation of the supine to express purpose.

The main dialect, Štokavian, is spoken over the remainder of the Serbo-Croat area. It is divided first into New Štokavian (the innovating dialects, typically those which underwent the stress shift described in the next section) and Old Štokavian (those which did not). The most important of the Old Štokavian dialects are the Prizren-Timok dialects, which are spoken in the south-east of Serbia, bordering on Bulgaria and Macedonia. They have lost the infinitive and reduced the case system to three cases only and are therefore clearly transitional to Bulgarian and Macedonian. The Kosovo-Resava dialects run in a band from south-west to north-east, between the Prizren-Timok dialects and the rest of the Štokavian dialects, and share features with both.

Within New Štokavian, the traditional feature for distinguishing between dialects is the reflex of Common Slavonic *ě* (*jat´*), which may be *i*, *e* or *ije/je*. This gives three dialect groups: Ikavian, Ekavian and Ijekavian, in which the word, say, for 'child' is *dite*, *dete* and *dijete* respectively. The Ikavian dialect is found in Dalmatia, the west of Bosnia and Hercegovina and parts of Lika and Slavonia. It is no longer used as a literary language (though certain Ikavian features are established in the literary language). This leaves the two major dialects of New Štokavian: Ekavian is spoken in most of Serbia; Ijekavian is found in the western part of Serbia, Montenegro, the east of Bosnia and Hercegovina and in those parts of Croatia not previously mentioned. Ekavian is the basis of the eastern variety of the literary language, which has Belgrade as its centre; Ijekavian is the foundation of the western variety, whose focal point is Zagreb, even though Zagreb is in a traditionally Kajkavian area. The Ijekavian of Bosnia and Hercegovina, the starting point of the new literary language, is transitional between the two varieties. Montenegro is particularly interesting in that it is Ijekavian, but in terms of lexis belongs to the eastern variety of the literary language.

It is worth looking in a little more detail at the differences between the two main varieties of Serbo-Croat. As previously mentioned, the western variety is predominantly Ijekavian. This means that Common Slavonic *ě* is represented as *ije*, in long syllables, e.g. *snijeg* 'snow', and as *je* in short syllables: *snjegovit* 'snowy'. In Ekavian, *e* is found in both cases: *sneg*, *snegovit*. The western variety is written in the Latin alphabet, the eastern traditionally in Cyrillic, but now also in the Latin alphabet. The other most obvious area of difference is in lexis. Several very common objects are referred to by different words in the two varieties: 'bread' is *kruh* in the west, but *hleb* in the east; a 'train' is *vlak* in the west, but *voz* in the east. There are fewer borrowings in the west and correspondingly more calques and neologisms; we find, for example, *sveučilište* 'university' (based on *sve* 'all' and the root *uč-* 'teach, learn') whereas the east has *univerzitet*. Those words which have been borrowed into the western variety come predominantly from German, Latin and also Czech, while borrowings from Turkish, Greek and Russian are more common in the east. Words borrowed into both varieties may show differences in derivational morphology. Thus *student* 'male student' is found in both; 'female student' is *studentica* in the west, *studentkinja* in the east. Salient differences in inflectional morphology and in syntax will be pointed out in the appropriate sections.

While considerable differences exist, most of them are not absolute but are a matter of frequency of usage. Many features often quoted as characteristic of one variety actually occur in the other, though they are less common there. The whole question of the status of the two varieties is very sensitive, because of the cultural and political implications. To the outside linguist, the numerous shared features between the varieties added to the ease of mutual comprehension suggest one language with two varieties, and many Yugoslavs concur. But we must accept that some Yugoslavs feel it important, often for non-linguistic reasons, to recognise Croatian and Serbian as distinct languages. In what follows we will use Ekavian forms, but in the Latin alphabet.

4 Phonology

Serbo-Croat's inventory of segmental phonemes is one of the smallest in the Slavonic family, since it does not have the range of palatalised consonants found, say, in Russian. Generally 25 consonants are recognised. Of these *r*,

Table 6.2: Segmental Phonemes of Serbo-Croat

Vowels

	i	r	u
	e		o
		a	

Consonants

	Plain stop	Affricate	Fricative	Nasal	Lateral	Trill	Semi-vowel
Bilabial	p b			m			
Labio-dental			f v				
Dental	t d	c		n	l		
Alveolar			s z			r	
Palato-alveolar		č dž	š ž				
Palatal		ć đ		nj	lj		j
Velar	k g		h				

which is trilled, can be syllabic, as in *trg* 'square'. In addition there is a straightforward five-vowel system. The phonemes are presented in table 6.2, using the normal orthography, which does not distinguish syllabic *r* and which includes digraphs for single sounds.

The vowel system provides the most interesting feature of Serbo-Croat phonology, namely accentuation. The classical account goes back to Karadžić and his follower Daničić and is that found still in most modern descriptions. In this analysis, vowels (including syllabic *r*) vary according to length and pitch. Vowels may be long or short, both in stressed position and in positions after the stress. Pitch is differentiated only in initial stressed position, where there is an opposition between rising and falling tone. These possibilities are indicated using the symbols given in table 6.3. The top four

Table 6.3: Serbo-Croat Accentuation

		long	short
stressed syllables	falling tone	ˆ	˝
	rising tone	´	`
unstressed syllables		-	

symbols indicate the position of the stress, tone and length. Thus *govòriti* 'to talk' is stressed on the second syllable, where there is a short vowel with rising tone. On unstressed syllables length is indicated; the absence of a marker, as on the other three vowels of this example, indicates an unstressed short vowel. Long vowels are indicated as follows: *glèdalācā* (genitive plural) 'of the spectators'. The first vowel is stressed and has falling tone and is short; the second is unstressed and short; the other two are unstressed and long.

These symbols are used in dictionaries and grammars but are not printed in ordinary texts. We shall include them when discussing phonology and morphology but not in the syntax section. An indication is given in texts to avoid confusion, notably for the genitive plural, which in many nouns is identical to the singular, apart from vowel length. For example, *rȉbāra* (genitive singular) 'fisherman', *rȉbārā* (genitive plural). The first would be printed without accent, the second as *ribarâ*, using the circumflex. (This actually retains Karadžić's usage; the macron ⁻, given in our table, is a twentieth-century innovation in linguistic usage.) While the opposition of genitive singular to genitive plural is the most crucial distinction which depends on the accentual system, other morphological distinctions rest on it in some words. Furthermore, there is a small number of frequently quoted minimal pairs: *grâd* 'city', *grȁd* 'hail'; *pâs* 'belt', *pȁs* 'dog'; *kúpiti* 'to buy', *kȕpiti* 'to collect'; *pàra* 'para' (unit of currency), *pȁra* 'steam'.

There are severe restrictions on the distribution of tone and length, which are best understood in terms of historical development. Falling tone is found only on initial syllables and monosyllables always have falling tone. Apart from monosyllables, and a few recent borrowings, stress is never on the final syllable of a word. Long vowels occur in stressed position or after the stress. When we compare the position of the stress in Serbo-Croat with that of the other Slavonic languages which have free stress and which, in the main, preserve the Common Slavonic stress position (the East Slavonic languages and Bulgarian) then we find that normally the Serbo-Croat stress is one syllable nearer the beginning of the word, for example *sèstra* 'sister', as compared to the Russian *sestrá*.

Serbo-Croat had inherited quantitative opposition in vowels; of the other Slavonic languages only Slovene, Czech and Slovak preserve this opposition. There was also an opposition, for long vowels, between acute (´) and circumflex (ˆ) intonations; the origin of this opposition is open to debate, many claiming it is of Indo-European origin, others believing it dates only from Common Slavonic times. In very broad outline the development was as follows. The acute was replaced by a short vowel with falling pitch. A special rising tone, however, had arisen when the ultra-short vowels (jers) could no longer carry stress: *krāljь̀* > *krāljь* 'king'. This long rising accent, denoted ˜, and called the 'neo-acute', is preserved in Čakavian and Kajkavian dialects. In Štokavian, with the exception of some dialects in Slavonia, the neo-acute became identical with the long falling accent. At this stage, then, vowels were opposed in length (long or short only, after the loss of the jers). As a result of various changes, this opposition occurred in stressed position, immediately before the stress and in all post-tonic positions.

The crucial development took place around the fourteenth century in the central Štokavian dialects. The stress moved one syllable towards the beginning of the word, creating new rising tones. If the stress moved onto a long vowel, long rising tone resulted (´), and short rising (`) if the vowel was short. The modern restrictions on tone and length are explicable in terms of this change. Falling tone is found only on initial syllables since stress moved from all other syllables to produce rising tone. Monosyllables have falling tone because they were not involved in stress shifts. Stress is not found on final syllables because, of course, it has moved forward. Finally, length is found in stressed and post-tonic positions only, because the earlier additional position (immediate pretonic) was covered by the accentual shift.

This, then, is the classical account of Serbo-Croat accentuation and its development. However, an extensive survey by Magner and Matejka revealed that the Karadžić-Daničić system is not so well preserved in towns as in rural areas. The influx of population to urban centres with the resultant mixing of dialects has led to a less clear situation. In particular, many speakers do not distinguish length on unstressed (post-tonic) vowels.

5 Morphology

Serbo-Croat has been generally conservative, maintaining most of the categories of Common Slavonic and changing some of the actual forms remarkably little. However, there have also been some surprising innovations. Seven cases have been preserved, together with three genders, which are distinguished in the plural as well as the singular (unlike Russian). The dual number has been lost, but it has left its mark on the plural oblique case forms (a Serbo-Croat innovation). The chart given here shows the main types of noun declension, corresponding to those given for Russian.

Serbo-Croat Nominal Declension

	a-*stem*	Masculine o-*stem*	Neuter o-*stem*	i-*stem*
Singular:				
Nom.	žèna 'woman'	zákon 'law'	sèlo 'village'	stvâr 'thing'
Voc.	žèno	zákone	sèlo	stvâri
Acc.	žènu	zákon	sèlo	stvâr
Gen.	žènē	zákona	sèla	stvâri
Dat.	žèni	zákonu	sèlu	stvâri
Inst.	žènōm	zákonom	sèlom	stvârju/stvâri
Loc.	žèni	zákonu	sèlu	stvâri
Plural:				
Nom.	žène	zákoni	sèla	stvâri
Voc.	žène	zákoni	sèla	stvâri
Acc.	žène	zákone	sèla	stvâri
Gen.	žénā	zákōnā	sêlā	stvárī
Dat.	žènama	zákonima	sèlima	stvárima
Inst.	žènama	zákonima	sèlima	stvárima
Loc.	žènama	zákonima	sèlima	stvárima

In broad typological terms, the picture is similar to that of Russian: the morphology is fusional, and there is a high, but not absolute, correlation of gender with declensional class. When we look in more detail, however, we find interesting differences as compared to Russian. The vocative case is preserved, requiring a mutation of consonants for many masculine nouns. Thus *drûg* 'comrade', vocative singular *drûže*, *prèdsednīk* 'chairman', vocative singular *prèdsednīče*. These mutations go back to the first palatalisation (see page 58). The second palatalisation is well preserved too. It is found in the singular of feminine *a*-stems: *knjîga* 'book', dative and locative singular *knjîzi*; *réka* 'river', dative and locative singular *réci*. In addition, it occurs in the plural of masculine nouns: *ìzlog* 'shop window', nominative plural *ìzlozi*, dative, instrumental and locative plural *ìzlozima*; *tèpih* 'carpet', nominative plural *tèpisi*, dative, instrumental and locative plural *tèpisima*. The innovatory mutation *l/o* also affects nominal paradigms: *pèpeo* 'ash', genitive singular *pèpela*. When combined with a fleeting *a*, the reflex of both jers in 'strong' position, it can make forms from a single paradigm sound very different: *čìtalac* 'reader', vocative singular *čìtaoče*, accusative singular *čìtaoca*, genitive singular *čìtaoca*. These last examples illustrate the genitive-accusative syncretism found with animate nouns. In Serbo-Croat this is much more restricted than in Russian, being limited to masculine singular nouns. Note, however, that masculine plurals have an accusative form distinct from both and nominative and genitive. While Serbo-Croat preserves the vocative, it has all but lost the distinction between dative and locative. Probably the major innovation in the nominal paradigms is the genitive plural *-ā*, for most nouns except *i*-stems. The origin of this form is still subject to debate. An *ā* may also be inserted to avoid consonant clusters before this ending, for example, *stùdent* 'student', genitive plural *stùdenātā*.

There are various smaller declensional classes which complicate the picture: some consonant stems are preserved, though with regularised endings, and certain suffixes may be added or lost in the declension of masculine nouns. And as the first noun in our chart shows, the length and tone of the stressed syllable may change within a paradigm; furthermore, as in Russian, the position of the stress may move as well. Before leaving the declension of nouns, it is interesting to note that, with a very few exceptions, all Serbo-Croat nouns are declinable. Even borrowings ending in a vowel decline: *bìrō* 'office', genitive singular *biròa*, unless they are feminine. This contrasts with Russian, where nouns whose stem ends in a vowel (a considerable number) are normally indeclinable. On the other hand, most of the numerals in Serbo-Croat no longer decline, while in Russian they decline fully.

Many of the adjectival endings (as shown in the chart of adjectival declension) are similar to those of Russian, though contraction has applied to a greater extent. The accusative singular masculine form depends on the animacy of the noun. The forms given in brackets are optional additions; thus the genitive singular masculine and neuter is *mlâdōg* or, less usually, *mlâdōga*. Note that the three genders are distinguished in the direct cases of the plural. The forms given in the chart are the definite (pronominal, long) forms. Serbo-Croat retains indefinite forms, though these are distinguished by inflection in the masculine singular only; elsewhere the difference is normally one of length, the definite endings including a long vowel and the indefinite endings typically a short one. The distinction is best preserved in the nominative singular masculine: *dòbrī čòvek* 'the good man' contrasts with *dòbar čòvek* 'a good man'. Thus noun phrases are clearly marked for definiteness providing they include an attributive adjective and a masculine singular noun in the nominative case (or accusative-nominative). As in other Slavonic languages, though later than in most, the indefinite forms are being lost. The main reason why they are best preserved in the nominative, is that when the adjective is used predicatively it stands in the nominative and the

Serbo-Croat Adjectival Declension (Definite)

	Masculine	*Neuter*	*Feminine*
Singular:			
Nom.-Voc.	mlâdī 'young'	mlâdō	mlâdā
Acc.	as nom. or gen.	mlâdō	mlâdū
Gen.	mlâdōg(a)		mlâdē
Dat.	mlâdōm(e)		mlâdōj
Inst.	mlâdīm		mlâdōm
Loc.	mlâdōm(e)		mlâdōj
Plural:			
Nom.-Voc.	mlâdī	mlâdā	mlâdē
Acc.	mlâdē	mlâdā	mlâdē
Gen.		mlâdīh	
Dat.		mlâdīm(a)	
Inst.		mlâdīm(a)	
Loc.		mlâdīm(a)	

indefinite form is used. Definite forms are therefore attributive, indefinites could be attributive or predicative and are increasingly a sign of predicative usage. A secondary reason for the retention of the opposition in the masculine concerns case marking. Subjects and direct objects are clearly distinguished for animate nouns since, as mentioned earlier, animates have accusative forms identical to the genitive. For inanimates, however, nominative and accusative are identical. In actual text, a high proportion of subjects is definite, while most direct objects are indefinite. Therefore, for inanimate masculine nouns, the opposition of definite and indefinite forms helps to mark case.

When we move to verbal morphology, we find a plethora of forms. Serbo-Croat is moving from a system based on tense to one in which aspect has a

Serbo-Croat Conjugation Types

	I Conjugation	*II Conjugation*	*III Conjugation*
Infinitive	pèvati 'to sing'	nòsiti 'to carry'	trésti 'to shake'
Present:			
Singular 1	pèvām	nòsīm	trésēm
2	pèvāš	nòsīš	trésēš
3	pèvā	nòsī	trésē
Plural 1	pèvāmo	nòsīmo	trésēmo
2	pèvāte	nòsīte	trésēte
3	pèvajū	nòsē	trésū
Imperative:			
Singular 2	pèvāj	nòsi	trési
Plural 1	pèvājmo	nòsimo	trésimo
Plural 2	pèvājte	nòsite	trésite

central role, but it has not lost the redundant tense forms as most other Slavonic languages have. A concomitant change involves greater use of compound tenses. We start, however, with simple forms. The main conjugations are given in the chart of conjugation types (there are several variations on these forms which will be omitted).

Similarities with the present tense forms in the other Slavonic languages already given are evident. The main innovation is in the first person singular. The -*m* has spread from the very small group of athematic verbs to all the verbs in the language (with two exceptions: *mòći* 'to be able', first person singular *mògu*, and *htèti* 'to want', first person singular *hòću* or *ću*). As stated earlier, long vowels after the stress, which occur in all persons in the present tense, are shortened by many speakers. Serbo-Croat preserves two more simple tenses, the imperfect and the aorist, illustrated in the charts displaying these forms. Note that in the imperfect the stem may show a

The Imperfect Tense in Serbo-Croat

	I Conjugation	*II Conjugation*	*III Conjugation*
Infinitive	pèvati 'to sing'	nòsiti 'to carry'	trésti 'to shake'
Imperfect			
Singular 1	pèvāh	nòšāh	trésijāh/trésāh
2	pèvāše	nòšāše	trésijāše/trésāše
3	pèvāše	nòšāše	trésijāše/trésāše
Plural 1	pèvāsmo	nòšāsmo	trésijāsmo/trésāsmo
2	pèvāste	nòsāste	trésijāste/trésāste
3	pèvāhu	nòšāhu	trésujāhu/trésāhu

consonant mutation, as in the case of *nòšāh* from *nòsiti*; several verbs have two possible forms, while *imati* 'to have' has three: *imāh*, *imàdijāh* and *imađāh*. The imperfect indicates action in process in the past. It contrasts with the aorist, which is normally used for a completed single action in the past. Both tenses are particularly used for events witnessed by the speaker.

The Aorist Tense in Serbo-Croat

	I Conjugation	*II Conjugation*	*III Conjugation*
Infinitive	sàznati 'to find out'	kúpiti 'to buy'	istrésti 'to shake out'
Aorist			
Singular 1	sàznah	kúpih	istrésoh
2	sàzna	kûpī	ìstrēse
3	sàzna	kûpī	ìstrēse
Plural 1	sàznasmo	kúpismo	istrésosmo
2	sàznaste	kúpiste	istrésoste
3	sàznaše	kúpiše	istrésoše

In the aorist of third conjugation verbs, a mutation of velar consonants may occur in the second and third persons singular (first palatalisation), for example, *rèći* 'to say', first singular aorist *rèkoh*, second and third singular aorist *rèče*. In the first conjugation, some forms coincide with the imperfect — apart from post-accentual length. There is, however, little possibility of confusion, since the imperfect is formed only from imperfective verbs and the aorist usually, but not exclusively, from perfectives (hence the different illustrative verbs given in the chart of aorist tense forms). The notion of aspect is discussed in the chapter on Russian (pages 74–5). In broad outline, the aspectual system is similar in Serbo-Croat both in morphology (perfectives are typically derived from imperfectives by prefixation, and imperfectives from perfectives by suffixation) and semantics (the perfective views a situation as a single whole, the imperfective views a situation as having internal constituency). Given the basic aspectual meanings, it is not surprising that the imperfect is found with imperfective verbs and the aorist typically with perfectives. However, the increasing importance of the aspectual opposition imperfective-perfective, which duplicates the imperfect-aorist opposition, is leading to the supplanting of both tenses by a compound past tense, which can be formed from verbs of either aspect. We shall refer to it simply as the 'past tense'; it is sometimes referred to as the 'perfect'. For some speakers, particularly in Croatia, the past tense is replacing both the imperfect and aorist, the aorist being the better preserved.

Before going on to the past and other compound tenses, we should return for a moment to the present tense. Whereas in Russian, only imperfectives have a present tense (forms with the morphological appearance of the present formed from perfective verbs are future perfective), in Serbo-Croat there is a present perfective, distinct from the future. It is formed identically to the examples given in the chart of conjugation types, but from perfective verbs. Thus *istrésti* 'to shake out', first person singular present *istrésēm*. The perfective present has a range of uses, but is not used for events occurring at the moment of speech. In the example: *stȍ ne sȅdnēš?* (perfective present) 'why don't you sit down?', the addressee is evidently not actually doing so. This tense is frequently used in subordinate clauses; examples will be given in the syntax section.

Of the compound tenses, the past is easily the most important. It is formed using the past participle of the verb. This participle agrees in gender and number, as is illustrated using the verb *znȁti* 'to know'.

Forms of the Past Participle

	Masculine	Feminine	Neuter
Singular	znȁo (<znal)	znȁla	znȁlo
Plural	znȁli	znȁle	znȁla

The other component of the past tense consists of the present tense forms of the auxiliary verb bìti 'to be'. These agree in person and number, and they are enclitic (see section 6), though there are also long forms used for emphasis and in questions. Subject personal pronouns are normally omitted in Serbo-Croat unless they are under contrastive or emphatic stress. If there is no nominal subject or other preceding word in the sentence, the participle precedes the enclitic, which cannot of course stand in first position. The past tense paradigm is therefore as that given for znàti 'to know'. The past tense

The Past Tense in Serbo-Croat

Infinitive	znàti 'to know'

Past Tense

Singular 1	znào/znàla sam
2	znào/znàla si
3	znào/znàla/znàlo je
Plural 1	znàli/znàle smo
2	znàli/znàle ste
3	znàli/znàle/znàla su

can be formed from imperfective verbs, like znàti, and such forms have largely supplanted the imperfective tense. The past tense can also be formed from perfectives in just the same way: sàznati 'to find out', sàznao sam 'I found out', (such forms replace the aorist). Compare písala je písmo (imperfective) 'she was writing a letter', napísala je písmo 'she wrote a letter'.

While the past is easily the most common tense for reference to past events, there is in addition a pluperfect tense. This can be formed from the imperfect of bìti plus the past participle, for example bèjāh pèvao 'I had been singing'. As elsewhere, the past can replace the imperfect, so an alternative formation with the past tense of bìti is bìo sam pèvao. The pluperfect occurs infrequently. If the aorist of bìti is combined with the past participle, then the conditional results: pèvao bih 'I would sing'. These auxiliary forms are again enclitics. The inflections of the aorist are being lost in this usage and the uninflected form bi is taking over (as has happened in Russian, see page 341). There is also a past conditional: bìo bi rèkao 'he would have said'. This tense is found in the western variety but has practically died out in the east.

All the compound tenses discussed so far use the auxiliary bìti. In contrast, the future tense is formed with the verb htèti 'to want' together with the infinitive. Normally the short forms of htèti are used (singular cú, ćeš, će, plural ćemo, ćete, ćē), for example, žèna će znàti 'the woman will know'. These short forms are enclitic, so that if no subject is expressed the infinitive is likely to precede: dóći ću 'I will come'. If an infinitive in -ti precedes the auxiliary, the -ti is not pronounced. This is reflected in the spelling in the east: *znàću* 'I will know'; the pronunciation is the same in the west, but only the *i* is dropped in the spelling: *znȁt ću*. The long forms of *htȅti* can be used for emphasis: *hòću dóći* 'I **will** come', and in questions: *hòću li dóći?* 'shall I come?'. As our examples show, the future is formed with verbs of both aspects: *znȁti* is imperfective and *dóći* is perfective. Particularly in the east, the infinitive is frequently replaced by *da* plus verb in the present tense; we return to this topic in the next section.

There are two other future tenses. The first, sometimes called the 'future exact', is formed from a second set of present tense forms of *bȉti* 'to be' (singular: *bȕdēm, bȕdēš, bȕdē*; plural: *bȕdēmo, bȕdēte, bȕdū*) plus the past participle. It is used only in subordinate clauses, especially those introduced by *ȁko* 'if' and temporal conjunctions such as *kȁd* 'when': *ȁko bȕdeš dòšao* 'if you come'. In the case of perfective verbs, the present perfective can be used instead; this normally happens in the western variety. The future exact is much more common in the east. The other future tense, which is very rare, is formed from the future of *bȉti* 'to be' and the past participle. It indicates supposition: *bȉćete čȕli* 'you will have heard' ('I suppose you have heard').

Of all the tenses described, the ones which form the backbone of the system in the modern language are the present, the past (*znȁo sam* 'I knew') and the future (*znàću* 'I will know'). Each of these can be formed from perfective and imperfective verbs, giving six possibilities, which cover most situations. As aspect has gained in significance, tenses other than the main ones have been reduced to marginal status. It will be interesting to observe how many of them survive and for how long.

In contrast to the wealth of tense forms, the inventory of non-finite verbal forms is limited. There are two indeclinable adverbs, termed 'gerunds'. The present gerund is formed from imperfective verbs (*pȅvati* 'to sing' gives *pȅvajūći* 'singing') and denotes action contemporaneous with that of the main verb. The past gerund, normally formed from perfective verbs (*sàznati* 'to find out': *sàznāvši* 'having found out'), is for an action prior to that of the main verb. There is also the past passive participle, formed more frequently from perfective verbs than imperfectives, for example, *kúpiti* 'to buy', *kûpljen* 'bought'. The past passive participle takes adjectival endings and, with *bȉti* 'to be' as auxiliary, forms the passive voice.

6   Syntax

Two particularly interesting aspects of Serbo-Croat syntax (enclitics and the replacement of the infinitive by a subordinate clause) have already been mentioned and will be described in more detail. In addition, we shall give brief consideration to agreement.

Serbo-Croat enclitics are already familiar to many non-Slavists through the work of Wayles Browne, who showed the problems they posed for transformational theory. Enclitics must come in second position in a clause.

There are six 'slots', each of which may be filled by one enclitic, in the strict order given in table 6.4. As examples, consider the following: *gde ste me videli?* (enclitics II, V) 'where did you see me?'; *želim mu ih dati* (III, V) 'I wish to give them to him'; *našao ga je* (V, VI) 'he found it'; *sećate li me se?* (I, IV, V) (*sećati se* is a reflexive verb which governs the genitive) 'do you remember me?'

Table 6.4: Serbo-Croat Enclitics

I	Interrogative particle: li
II	Verbal auxiliaries: sam, si, smo, ste, su (not *je*)
	ću, ćeš, cé, ćemo, ćete, će
	bih, bi, bi, bismo, biste, bi
III	Dative pronouns: singular: mi, ti, mu, joj (reflexive *si* in west only)
	plural: nam, vam, im
IV	Genitive pronouns: singular: me, te, ga, je
	plural: nas, vas, ih
V	Accusative pronouns: identical to the genitive pronouns with the addition of the reflexive *se*
VI	Third singular form of *biti*: je

There are two special rules concerning *je*, the third person singular of *biti*. If the combination *se je* is expected, then *je* is dropped. *Vratiti se* 'to return' is a reflexive verb; the expected third singular masculine of the past tense would be *vratio se je*, but we find *vratio se* 'he returned'. This is now an absolute rule in the east but occasional forms with *se je* still occur in the west. The other special rule prohibits the combination **je je*, where the first is the accusative case of the personal pronoun (third singular feminine) and the second is the third singular of *biti*. Instead, the first is replaced by the form *ju*, for example, *video ju je* 'he saw her'.

Earlier it was stated that enclitics stand in 'second' position. The expected interpretation of this statement might be after the first accented constituent. This interpretation would fit the examples given so far, as well as sentences like: *taj pesnik mi je napisao pesmu* 'that poet wrote me a poem'. If an initial constituent is separated by a pause, enclitics will then occur in second position counting from the pause: *ove godine, taj pesnik mi je napisao pesmu* 'this year, that poet wrote me a poem'. In some cases an initial long constituent is disregarded though there is no pause. More surprisingly, the enclitics may stand after the first accented word, even though by doing so they split a constituent: *taj mi je pesnik napisao pesmu* (lit. 'that to me is poet written poem') 'that poet wrote me a poem'; similarly: *jedan je hodža imao kuću...* ('one is priest had house') 'one (Muslim) priest had a house...'.

Enclitics are found in the other Slavonic languages, though Serbo-Croat has preserved them particularly well and has created new ones, such as the clitic forms of *hteti*. Our next point of interest, however, is unusual in Slavonic (being found only in Bulgarian and Macedonian in addition to Serbo-Croat) but shared with other language of the Balkans (e.g. Rumanian and Greek — see pages 167–8). Mainly in the eastern variety, Serbo-Croat tends to replace the infinitive by a construction consisting of the conjunction *da* plus a verb in the present tense. The infinitive with purposive meaning is most likely to be replaced, so that examples like: *Jovan je došao da kupi knjigu* (lit. 'Jovan came that he buys a book') 'Jovan came to buy a book', occur freely in the western variety as well as in the east. With verbs like *želeti* 'to wish', both constructions occur: *Jovan želi da kupi knjigu/ Jovan želi kupiti knjigu* 'Jovan wishes to buy a book', but the first is more likely in the east and the second in the west. The construction with *da* has spread into the ordinary future: *Jovan će da kupi knjigu* 'Jovan will buy a book'. This is common in the east, much less so in the west, where one would expect the infinitive: *Jovan će kupiti knjigu*. Broadly speaking, as one moves eastwards, so the infinitive becomes rarer, though there is considerable variation even among individuals. In eastern dialects transitional to Bulgarian and Macedonian the infinitive is effectively excluded.

The last area to consider is agreement. Like the other Slavonic languages described, Serbo-Croat shows agreement of attributive modifiers with their head nouns in gender, number, case and, to a limited extent, in animacy. Main verbs agree in person and number with their subjects, participles in gender and number. There are various complications. For example, a few nouns are of different gender in the singular and the plural: *to* (nt. sg.) *oko* 'that eye'; *te* (f. pl.) *oči* 'those eyes'. Then there is a class of nouns ending in *-a*, which have the appearance of feminines but refer to males. In the singular, these are masculine: *naš gazda* 'our master'. In the plural, both masculine and feminine agreements are found: *naši/naše gazde* 'our masters'. Furthermore, a small group of nouns, instead of having a normal plural paradigm, takes another singular. Thus *dete* (nt. sg.) 'child' has the form *deca* 'children', which declines like the feminine singular noun *žena* in the chart of nominal declension. Agreement with *deca* is singular or plural, depending on the construction: *majka ove* (gen. sg. f.) *dece* 'the mother of these children'; *deca spavaju* (pl.) 'the children are sleeping'.

Since Serbo-Croat retains the original gender distinctions in the plural, there are rules for agreement with conjoined noun phrases, which may be of different genders. If all conjuncts are feminine, then feminine agreements are found (all these examples are from works by the Nobel prize-winning novelist, Ivo Andrić): *nad njim su stajale* (f. pl.) *Jelenka* (f.) *i Saveta* (f.) 'over him were standing Jelenka and Saveta'. In all other cases, the masculine plural is used even if no masculine is present: *znanje* (nt. sg.) *i intuicija* (f. sg.) *su kod njega sarađivali* (m. pl.)... 'knowledge and intuition worked together in him...'. Conjoined neuter singulars similarly require a masculine plural predicate. Similar rules are found in Slovene.

However, Serbo-Croat has made an interesting innovation. If the conjuncts are all of feminine gender, but at least one is of the -*i* declension (like *stvar* in the chart of nominal declension), then masculine agreements may be found: *službena revnost* (f. sg., -*i* declension) *i lična sujeta* (f. sg.) *zanosili* (m. pl.) *su ih...* 'professional zeal and personal vanity carried them away...'. The *i*-stem declension includes a large proportion of abstract nouns and few animates. It appears, therefore, that Serbo-Croat is moving towards a position in which the feminine plural will be required for agreement with conjoined nouns referring to females, the feminine will be optional for other feminine nouns and the masculine will be used under all other circumstances.

This last construction typifies the particular interest of Serbo-Croat for the linguist. The preservation of the original gender distinctions in the plural is an example of its conservatism; there are, as we have seen, various forms still found in Serbo-Croat which have been lost in most of the other Slavonic languages. On the other hand, the innovation permitting masculine agreement with feminine nouns (depending on their type) is, like other innovations we have noted, a surprise and a challenge for the linguist.

Bibliography

Partridge (1972) is a solid grammar in textbook form, with brief but helpful background notes. Descriptive grammars include Meillet and Vaillant (1969), with thorough coverage of morphology but somewhat dated, and Leskien (1914), a landmark in its time. The following deal with accent: Lehiste and Ivić (1963), an extensive acoustical study; Magner and Matejka (1971), a challenge to traditional accounts, perhaps overstated, though a good entry point to the extensive literature on the subject; Gvozdanović (1980), an acoustical study, with a useful introduction to the phonology of Serbo-Croat. The *Publications of the Yugoslav Serbo-Croatian-English Contrastive Project* (1968–) contain papers covering a range of topics, especially in syntax and lexicon; for instance, *Contrastive Analysis of English and Serbo-Croatian*, vol. 1 (1975) includes a paper by W. Browne giving a detailed account of clitics.

For the history of the language, Naylor (1980) provides a clear account of the external history of Serbo-Croat; Popović (1960) lays particular emphasis on the early period and on contacts with other languages; while Vaillant (1928–79) is a historical grammar of wider scope than its title suggests. Ivić (1958) provides a survey of Serbo-Croatian dialects by one of Yugoslavia's foremost linguists.

Acknowledgement

I am very grateful to all of the following for helpful comments on an earlier draft of this chapter: W. Browne, P.V. Cubberley, P. Herrity, Milka and Pavle Ivić, D.J.L. Johnson, Lj. Popović and R.D. Sussex.

References

Gvozdanović, J. 1980. *Tone and Accent in Standard Serbo-Croatian (With a Synopsis of Serbo-Croatian Phonology)* (Österreichische Akademie der Wissenschaften, Vienna)

Ivić, P. 1958. *Die serbokroatischen Dialekte: ihre Struktur und Entwicklung, I: Allgemeines und die štokavische Dialektgruppe* (Mouton, The Hague)

—— 1986. *Word and Sentence Prosody in Serbocroatian* (MIT Press, Cambridge, Mass.)

Lehiste, I. and P. Ivić. 1963. *Accent in Serbocroatian: An Experimental Study* (University of Michigan, Ann Arbor)

Leskien, A. 1914. *Grammatik der serbokroatischen Sprache, I: Lautlehre, Stammbildung, Formenlehre* (Carl Winter, Heidelberg)

Magner, T.F. and L. Matejka. 1971. *Word Accent in Modern Serbo-Croatian* (Pennsylvania State University Press, University Park and London)

Meillet, A. and A. Vaillant. 1969. *Grammaire de la langue serbo-croate*, 2nd ed. (Champion, Paris)

Naylor, K.E. 1980. 'Serbo-Croatian', in A.M. Schenker and E. Stankiewicz (eds.), *The Slavic Literary Languages: Formation and Development* (Yale Concilium on International and Area Studies, New Haven, Conn.), pp. 65–83

Partridge, M. 1972. *Serbo-Croat: Practical Grammar and Reader*, 2nd ed. (Izdavački zavod Jugoslavia, Belgrade)

Popović, I. 1960. *Geschichte der serbokroatischen Sprache* (Otto Harrassowitz, Wiesbaden)

Publications of the Yugoslav Serbo-Croatian-English Contrastive Project (1968–) (Institute of Linguistics, University of Zagreb, Zagreb)

Vaillant, A. (1928–79), *La Langue de Dominko Zlatarić, poète ragusain de la fin du XVIe siècle*, 3 vols. (Institut d'Études Slaves, Paris and Serbian Academy of Sciences, Belgrade)

7 Greek

Brian D. Joseph

1 Historical Background

The Greek language forms, by itself, a separate branch of the Indo-European family. It is one of the oldest attested Indo-European languages, being attested from c. 1400 BC in the Mycenaean Greek documents found on Crete (and from somewhat later, on the Greek mainland) written in the Linear B syllabary. Except for a break in attestation between the end of the Mycenaean empire (c. 1150 BC) and roughly 800 BC, a period sometimes referred to as the 'Dark Ages' of Greek culture, Greek presents a continuous record of attestation for the linguist, right up to the present day.

Commonly called *Greek* in English, based on the term *Graeci* used by the Romans to label all the Greeks (though originally the name may have properly applied only to a tribe in the north-west of Greece), the language is also referred to as *Hellenic*, from the Greek stem Ἑλλην-*, used in the *Iliad* to refer to a Thessalian tribe but in Herodotus (and elsewhere) to designate the Greeks as a whole as opposed to barbarians; indeed, the Greeks themselves have generally referred to their language as ἑλληνική, though contemporary Greeks also use the designation ρωμαίικα, an outgrowth of their connection historically with the Eastern Roman Empire based in Constantinople.

Within Indo-European, Greek can be classified as a 'centum' language, for it shows a distinct set of reflexes for the Indo-European labio-velars, opposed to a single set of reflexes for the Indo-European palatals and velars combined; thus, Greek shows a root πρια- 'buy' (cf. also Mycenaean *qi-ri-ja-to* 'bought' showing the labio-velar preserved as ⟨q⟩) from Proto-Indo-European *$k^w riH_2$- (cf. Sanskrit root *krī*- 'buy'), a noun κρέας 'meat' from Proto-Indo-European *$krewH_2s$ (cf. Sanskrit *kravis*- 'raw flesh'), and a root κει- 'lie (down)' from Proto-Indo-European *$\hat{k}ei$- (cf. Sanskrit root *śī:*- 'lie'), in which the plain *k of the proto-language and the palatal *$\hat{k}$ show a merger while the labio-velar *k^w is kept distinct. Greek also shows some particular

*Greek forms are cited throughout in the Greek alphabet. See table 7.1 for the pronunciation of the letters.

144

affinities with Armenian and Indo-Iranian, sharing with these branches, for example, the past-tense morpheme *e- (the 'augment'), and the use of the negator *$m\bar{e}$: (Greek μή), and with Armenian alone the vocalisation of the Indo-European 'laryngeal' consonants in initial position, and some notable parallels in vocabulary (e.g. ἀλώπηξ 'fox' = Arm. *aluēs*, where no other Indo-European language has precisely this form, or πρωκτός 'anus' = *erastank'* 'buttocks'). Moreover, Greek preserves the Indo-European vowel system (with long and short *a *e *i *o *u) more faithfully than any other language in the family.

Differentiating Greek from the other members of the Indo-European family, though, are several particular features. In morphology, Greek innovated a (past and future) passive marker -θη- and elaborated the infinitival system. With regard to phonology, Greek alone in Indo-European shows voiceless aspirates (in the ancient language) as the continuation of the Indo-European voiced aspirate consonants (e.g. φερ- 'carry' from *$bher$-, cf. Sanskrit *bhar*-); in addition, Greek lenited Indo-European *s to h in many environments, ultimately losing it intervocalically (e.g. ἑπτά 'seven' from *$sept\underset{.}{m}$, cf. Latin *septem*, or γένε-ι 'in, at, to a race, kind (dat. sg.)' from *$genes$-i, cf. Sanskrit *janas-i* 'in the people (loc. sg.)'). Also, Greek deleted original word-final stops (e.g. μέλι 'honey' from *$melit$, cf. Hittite *milit* 'honey').

Moreover, although Common Greek preserved the Indo-European labio-velars as such, to judge in part from their preservation in Mycenaean (cf. *qi-ri-ja-to* above), the ancient language is characterised by a number of complex dialectal developments with *k^w, *g^w and *g^wh. Labial reflexes occur in some environments and in some dialects (e.g. pan-Greek interrogative stem πο- from *k^wo-, Aeolic (Boeotian) πέτταρες 'four' from *$k^wetw\underset{.}{r}$-), dental reflexes in other environments, also dialectally conditioned (e.g. τίς 'who' from *k^wis, and non-Aeolic (Attic) τέτταρες 'four'), and even velar reflexes in some dialects when adjacent to *u or *w (e.g. εὐχ- 'wish' from *ewg^wh-). Further Greek-particular developments setting the language off from other Indo-European languages include a number of complex treatments of clusters of obstruent + *y and of clusters of resonant (*r *l *m *n *y *w) + *s (examples below in section 4.1). A final diagnostic feature for Greek within Indo-European is a three-way distinction in reflexes of the laryngeal consonants, represented by ε, α, and ο in Greek; this feature is likely to represent the continuation of a three-way Proto-Indo-European contrast in the laryngeals, but by some accounts, it is a significant Greek innovation (perhaps morphologically induced).

The early attestation of Greek and the archaic nature of the Homeric epic corpus together serve to make Greek extremely important for the understanding and reconstruction of all aspects of Proto-Indo-European language and culture. In addition, the literary output of writers of Greek has throughout the ages been of utmost importance to Western culture so that

Greek has a special place in a variety of humanistic pursuits, including the history of linguistics because of the native Greek grammatical tradition developed by the Alexandrians in the Hellenistic era. Finally, the long and relatively continuous attestation of the Greek language gives it a significance for general historical linguistics, as it offers a 'window' on the nature of language change which few other languages can provide.

With such a long historical record for the language, it is convenient, as well as conventional, to break the span up into several major periods of development. These periods are defined in part by external, especially political and historical, factors, but also reflect real linguistic developments. These periods are:

(a) Mycenaean Greek (c. 1500–1150 BC)
(b) Classical Greek, including Homeric Greek (c. 800–300 BC)
(c) Hellenistic Greek, including New Testament Greek (c. 300 BC–AD 300)
(d) Middle Greek, comprising Byzantine Greek (c. AD 300–1100) and Medieval Greek (c. AD 1100–1600)
(e) Modern Greek (c. AD 1600 to the present).

With such a long period of attestation for Greek, it is of course natural to find that there are some significant differences between Greek of the fourteenth century BC and Greek of the twentieth century AD, and these differences are chronicled in the sections to follow. At the same time, though, there are some aspects of the language, occasionally isolated ones though some fit into a system, which show remarkable continuity and stability over some 3,500 years. Among these are the past tense augment ε-, still found in stressed positions in the modern language, the personal endings in the present active and medio-passive present and past (excepting the third person plural), the general structure of the nominal and verbal systems and numerous lexical items, including some which have changed neither phonetic form (excepting the realisation of accent) nor meaning, e.g. ἄνεμος 'wind'.

2 Greek in its Geographic and Social Context

Greek has been spoken in the southern Balkans since early in the second millennium BC, according to conventional accounts of the coming of the Greeks to the area. Arriving most likely in waves of different tribes over a period of several centuries, the Greeks absorbed some autochthonous groups, traces of whose language(s) can probably be seen in numerous place names and terms for native flora and fauna containing the sequences -νθ- and -σσ-, among others (e.g. Κόρινθος, μίνθη 'mint', Παρνασσός etc.), and possibly also in Indo-European-like words with a somewhat aberrant phonology for Greek (e.g. ἀλείφ-ω 'I anoint' with a prefixed ἀ- and a voiceless aspirate consonant, both unexpected if the word were inherited directly from Proto-Indo-European into Greek, versus inherited Greek λίπος 'fat', from an Indo-European root *leip-). Greek has remained in the Balkans since that early period, although it has spread to other areas as well.

In ancient times, Greek colonies were established in Cyprus (perhaps as early as the twelfth century BC) and southern Italy (c. eighth century BC), and there have been Greek speakers continuously in these places up to the present day. Similarly, colonies established in western Asia Minor were continuously peopled by Greek speakers up to the beginning of the twentieth century, when population exchanges in the 1920s between Greece and Turkey led to the relocation of most of the Greeks back to Greece. All of these settlements were renewed with further Greek speakers throughout the Hellenistic period, when Greek spread as the lingua franca for all of the eastern Mediterranean, the Middle East and into Central Asia as far east as Persia and India. Some of the pockets of Greek speakers established in that period remain to this day, for example in Alexandria (Egypt).

In the Middle Greek period, the geographic domain of Greek became somewhat more restricted, with important centres still in Constantinople, Asia Minor in general, Alexandria, Cyprus, and elsewhere in the general eastern Mediterranean area, including the Ukraine. The modern era has seen the reduction in the number of Greek speakers in all these areas except Cyprus, but also the expansion of Greek into the 'New World'. There are now significant Greek-speaking communities in America (especially the urban centres of the East), in Canada, in Britain and in Australia. The speakers in Greece, Cyprus and elsewhere in the Mediterranean together with those in the 'Hellenic diaspora' number some 12 million today (c. nine million in Greece).

Despite the rather widespread geographic distribution of Greek throughout its history, it is Balkan Greek, i.e. Greek of the southern Balkans including the Greek islands and Crete, that is of primary importance here. The dialect diversity in ancient times, with four main dialect groups (Attic-Ionic, Aeolic, Arcado-Cyprian, and West Greek (comprising Northwest Greek and Doric)) as well as the earlier Mycenaean Greek (problematic in terms of its connections with these dialect groups), centred more on matters of detail in phonological and morphological development rather than on broad structural aspects. Thus, Attic, the dialect of Athens and the preeminent dialect from a cultural and political standpoint, and more generally the Attic-Ionic branch of Greek, constitute the primary representative of Ancient Greek. Moreover, Attic-Ionic provided the basis for the Hellenistic koine (ἡ κοινὴ διάλεκτος 'the common dialect'), which showed considerable uniformity across the whole area of its use. This koine, in turn, provided the basis for the Middle and Modern Greek dialects, with the exception of Tsakonian, spoken in the eastern part of the Peloponnesus, which derives from the ancient Doric dialect. Finally, the language of the modern Hellenic diaspora, while incorporating features, mainly lexical items, from the local dominant languages, has nonetheless remained true to its Attic-Ionic origin in terms of general structural characteristics.

Focusing on Balkan Greek is important for another reason. This particular geographic setting is crucial for understanding the development of the language in the late Middle Greek and early Modern Greek periods, and especially for understanding many of the differences, to be discussed in more detail below, between these later stages of the language and its earlier stages. Greek in these later stages shows numerous linguistic features that are found as well in other languages of the Balkans, such as Albanian, Rumanian, Macedonian, Bulgarian and to a somewhat lesser extent, Serbo-Croat. These features include various mergers of nominal case functions, especially possessive and indirect object functions in a single form, the formation of a future tense with a form of the verb 'want' (e.g. Modern Greek θά from earlier impersonal θέλει 'wants' + verbal particle νά), the widespread use of finite complement clauses where many other languages (and indeed, earlier stages of the languages in question, for the most part) would use non-finite forms and others of a more particular nature.

The exact nature of the relation between developments of this sort in Greek and parallel developments in the other Balkan languages is not clear; some scholars argue that Greek underwent the changes as part of its natural development and that (many of) these changes spread to the other languages from Greek, while others argue that their appearance in Greek is the result of the importation of foreign features into the language through contact with the other Balkan languages. It is more likely, though, that no single explanation can be found to be valid for all of these common features, and that some may have begun in Greek and spread from there, others may have made their way into Greek from elsewhere, and others may even be the result of a combination of Greek-internal developments enhanced or guided along a particular path through language contact.

One final aspect of the social setting of Greek that is vital to an understanding of the language concerns the extent to which a high- versus low-style distinction, inherent, probably, in all languages, has come to pervade Greek language use. In Ancient Greek, there is evidence for a distinction at least between the literary language in which most of the classical works (drama, poetry, philosophy etc.) were written and the colloquial language as evidenced in numerous inscriptions; recent investigations into the inscriptions of the Athenian ἀγορά ('marketplace') have indicated that colloquial usage was marked by pronunciations which came to be more current in later stages of the language, e.g. [i:] for [e:] and a spirantal pronunciation of the voiced stops, and observations contained in Plato's dialogue *Cratylus* provide confirmation of this point. Similarly, the

Greek of the non-literary papyri of Hellenistic Egypt gives a good indication of what must have been true colloquial usage through numerous hypercorrections and mistakes in approximating 'correct', i.e. high-style, Attic Greek.

In later stages of Greek, though, a consciously archaising tendency on the part of many Middle Greek writers to 'Atticise', i.e. emulate Classical Attic Greek spelling, morphology, syntax and usage, served to create a large stylistic rift in the language. Consequently, there were writers in the Middle Greek era who wrote in a language not unlike Classical Attic Greek (though it must be noted that mistakes abound!), while others wrote in a form more in line with colloquial usage of the day, the result of several centuries of natural linguistic development from the Hellenistic koine. Even in such a speech form, though, numerous learned borrowings occur, owing to the prestige enjoyed by the archaising style. Accordingly, even 'pure' colloquial Greek, what has come to be called Demotic (Greek: δημοτική), at all times in the post-classical period has incorporated many historically anomalous and anachronistic elements; this is, of course, an expected development in a language with a long literary history available to speakers and writers at all times (compare the situation in India with regard to Sanskrit and the modern Indic languages, the Romance languages and Latin, and the Slavonic languages and Old Church Slavonic).

In the case of Greek, though, with the founding of the Greek national state in the 1820s and the desire at the time for a unified form of a national language, this stylistic rift has become institutionalised and politicised. The debate over which form of Greek to use in this context, the consciously archaising so-called 'puristic' Greek (Greek: καθαρεύουσα 'purifying') or the form more based in the colloquial developments from the koine, the Demotic Greek, has occupied much of the linguistic and political energy of the Greeks since the 1820s; the current official position on the 'language question' (Greek: τὸ γλωσσικὸ ζήτημα) is in favour of the Demotic, with the now-standard language being based generally on the southern (i.e. Peloponnesian) dialect.

3   Writing Systems for Greek

Greek has been written in a variety of writing systems throughout its history. The earliest written Greek is found in the syllabic system known as Linear B, in which Mycenaean Greek documents were written, generally on clay tablets. A syllabic system, related in some way to that of Linear B (though the exact details of the relationship are controversial) was also used in Cyprus in ancient times to write many of the ancient Cyprian dialect inscriptions. In addition, Greeks in Asia Minor in medieval times occasionally used the Arabic alphabet and even the Hebrew alphabet to write Greek.

The most enduring writing system for Greek, though, is the Greek alphabet. Adapted from the old North Semitic alphabet (traditionally, according to the Greeks themselves, transmitted through the Phoenicians) and embellished with separate signs for vowel sounds, the Greek alphabet has served the Greek language well for some 2,800 years since its introduction into Greece in the tenth or ninth century BC.

The system is basically a one-letter-to-one-phoneme system, though there are some 'double letters' representing clusters and at all stages some distinctive oppositions are either not represented at all (e.g. [a] versus [aː] in Ancient Greek) or represented only secondarily via clusters of letters (as with [d] versus [ð], spelled ⟨ντ⟩ and ⟨δ⟩, respectively, in Modern Greek). Also, diacritics to represent pitch accent in Ancient Greek were not introduced until Hellenistic times (c. 200 BC) by the Alexandrian grammarians, and changes in the accentual system, from a pitch accent to a stress accent, left the writing system with more diacritics than needed for Middle and Modern Greek (though a recent official orthography has been adopted with but a single accentual diacritic). Moreover, the phonetic values of the letters have changed over time, so the current orthography is not as well matched with the phonological system as in earlier stages. Table 7.1 gives the information about the former and current phonetic values and transcriptions of the letters of the Greek alphabet.

Table 7.1: The Greek Alphabet, with Transliteration and Pronunciation for Ancient (Attic) Greek and (Standard) Modern Greek, plus Diphthongs and Clusters

Capital letter	Small Letter	Ancient phonetics	Usual transliteration	Modern pronunciation	Usual transliteration
A	α	[a]	a	[a]	a
B	β	[b]	b	[v]	v
Γ	γ	[g]	g	[j] (/— i, e) [γ] (elsewhere)	y g(h)
Δ	δ	[d]	d	[ð]	d(h)
E	ε	[ɛ]	e	[ɛ]	e
Z	ζ	[zd]	z	[z]	z
H	η	[ɛː]	eː, ē	[i]	i
Θ	θ	[tʰ]	th	[θ]	th
I	ι	[i]	i	[i]	i
K	κ	[k]	k	[k]	k
Λ	λ	[l]	l	[l]	l
M	μ	[m]	m	[m]	m
N	ν	[n]	n	[n]	n
Ξ	ξ	[ks]	x	[ks]	ks, x (as in box)
O	o	[o]	o	[o]	o
Π	π	[p]	p	[p]	p

Capital letter	Small Letter	Ancient phonetics	Usual transliteration	Modern pronunciation	Usual transliteration
Ρ	ϱ	[r]	r	[r]	r
Σ	σ (ς ##)	[s]	s	[s]	s
Τ	τ	[t]	t	[t]	t
Υ	υ	[y]	y, u	[i]	i
Φ	φ	[pʰ]	ph	[f]	f
Χ	χ	[kʰ]	ch, kh	[χ]	h, x (IPA value)
Ψ	ψ	[ps]	ps	[ps]	ps
Ω	ω	[ɔ:]	o:, ō	[o]	o
	αι	[ai̯]	ai	[ɛ]	e
	αυ	[au̯]	au	$\begin{cases} [av] \\ (/\_\_ +voice) \\ [af] \\ (/\_\_ -voice) \end{cases}$	av af
	ει	[e:]	ei	[i]	i
	ευ	[ɛu̯]	eu	$\begin{cases} [ev] \\ (/\_\_ +voice] \\ [ef] \\ (/\_\_ -voice) \end{cases}$	ev ef
	οι	[oi̯]	oi	[i]	i
	ου	[o:]	ou	[u]	u
	υι	[yi̯]	yi, ui	[i]	i
	γ before γ χ ξ	[ŋ]	n(g, kh, ks)	[ŋ]	n(g, h, ks)
	γκ	[ŋk]	nk	$\begin{cases} [(ŋ)g] \\ (medially) \\ [g] (initially) \end{cases}$	(n)g g
	μπ/μβ	[mp/mb]	mp/mb	$\begin{cases} [(m)b] \\ (medially) \\ [b] (initially) \end{cases}$	(m)b b
	ντ/νδ	[nt/nd]	nt/nd	$\begin{cases} [(n)d] \\ (medially) \\ [d] (initially) \end{cases}$	(n)d d
	τζ	------	------	[dz]	dz
	(##)ʿ	[h]	h	Ø	Ø
	(##)ʼ	Ø (absence of #h)		Ø	Ø

4 Structural Features of Greek

Although five different periods were distinguished for the purposes of outlining the internal and external history of the Greek language over the approximately 3,500 years of its attestation, for the purpose of giving the major structural features of the language, it is more useful to examine the ancient language in contrast with the modern language. In general, then, the relevant distinction is between Classical Greek and Post-Classical Greek, for most of the changes which characterise the difference between these two stages of the language are already under way and evident in the koine of the

Hellenistic period. Similarly, the differences between Middle Greek and Modern Greek are not great, and some scholars even date the beginning of the modern era to around the tenth or eleventh centuries AD. Accordingly, the whole post-classical period can be treated in a unified fashion, with the understanding that what is described in the modern language is the end-point of a long period of development from the classical language, and the stages of Hellenistic and Middle Greek defined earlier represent way stations on the road to Modern Greek; references to individual stages in particular developments, though, are made whenever necessary or appropriate.

4.1 Phonology

The consonant inventory of Ancient Greek included three distinctive points of articulation — labial, dental and velar — and three distinctive manners of articulation among the stops — voiced, voiceless unaspirated and voiceless aspirated. As noted above, in Common Greek (c. 1800 BC) and in Mycenaean Greek, there were also labio-velar consonants, which later merged with the labial, dental and velar stops under the conditions alluded to earlier. In addition, Greek had a single sibilant [s] (with [z] as an allophone before voiced consonants), the resonants [r] (with a voiceless allophone [r̥] in initial position) and [l], the nasals [m] and [n] (with [ŋ] as an allophone before velar consonants) and the glottal fricative [h]. There may have been an affricate [dᶻ], though most of the evidence concerning the pronunciation of the letter ⟨ζ⟩ suggests it represented a true cluster of [z + d] not a unitary affricated segment (cf. spellings such as Διόζοτος for *Διὸς δοτός, literally 'given by Zeus'). The Common Greek [j] and [w] had been eliminated in many positions by Classical Greek, though they did remain as the second element of several diphthongs in the classical language; moreover, [j] is found in Mycenaean in several positions (e.g. *jo-i-je-si* 'so they send', interpretable 'alphabetically' as ὡς ἱενσι), and [w] occurs in many of the dialects (e.g. Mycenaean *wo-i-ko*, Doric, Thessalian and Arcadian ϝοικος, where the letter ⟨ϝ⟩ ('digamma') represents [w], to be compared with Attic οἶκος 'the house').

By contrast to this relatively straightforward and simple consonant inventory, the vowel system of Ancient Greek was most complex. Length was distinctive and several degrees of height were distinguished as well; moreover, there were numerous diphthongs. The system of monophthongs is summarised in table 7.2 and the diphthongal system is given in table 7.3. It should be noted that the front rounded vowels ([y] and [yː] of table 7.2) are characteristic of the Attic-Ionic dialect only; the other dialects had back [u] and [uː] corresponding to these Attic-Ionic vowels. Furthermore, the gaps in the short diphthongs (absence of [ei̯] and [ou̯]) are the result of early sound changes by which *ei̯ became [eː] and *ou̯ became [oː]. Finally, the long diphthongs were somewhat rare and had a very low functional load; in

Table 7.2: Ancient (Attic) Greek Monophthongs (IPA Symbols)

i iː y yː			
e eː		o oː	
ɛː		ɔː	
	a aː		

Table 7.3: Ancient (Attic) Greek Diphthongs (IPA Symbols)

	eu̯	yi̯	eːi̯	eːu̯
ai̯	au̯		aːi̯	aːu̯
oi̯			oːi̯	

fact, early on in the classical period, [eːi̯], [aːi̯], and [oːi̯] lost their off-glide and merged with the corresponding long pure vowels.

Although there are dialectal differences in the consonants, these tend not to be in the consonantal inventory but rather have to do more with the outcome of the Common Greek labio-velars (e.g. labials generally in Aeolic versus conditioned (before front vowels) dental reflexes or (elsewhere) labial reflexes in other dialects, as in πέτταρες/τέτταρες 'four' cited above), and the outcome of complex cluster developments involving obstruent plus glide combinations and resonant or nasal plus *s*. For example, generally speaking — there are several exceptional cases — *t* + *y* yielded a geminate *-ss-* (graphic ⟨σσ⟩) in Ionic, Doric in general, Arcadian and part of Aeolic, a geminate *-tt-* (graphic ⟨ττ⟩) in Attic and part of Aeolic (Boeotian), and various spellings (⟨ζ⟩, ⟨ττ⟩, ⟨θθ⟩, which may represent developments of something like [ts]) in Central Cretan (Doric), as in the feminine adjectival ending (from *-e(n)t-ya*) (χαρί-)εσσα (Ionic), (Παδο-)εσσα (Arcadian), (οἰνοῦ-)ττα (Attic), (χαριϝ-)ετταν (Boeotian), (ἑα-)σσα (Doric), (ια-)τταν (Central Cretan). Similarly, for certain classes of words and with some obscuring of dialect distribution due to analogies and some borrowings, there is a major split in the Greek dialects concerning the outcome of *t* before the vowel *i*, with West Greek and part of Aeolic (Thessalian and Boeotian) preserving *t* in this context and the other dialects assibilating it to *s*, as in Doric εἶτι '(s)he goes' versus Attic-Ionic εἶσι.

The vowel systems of the ancient dialects, however, show considerable variation, with alternations of length and quality and in the outcome of contractions serving to distinguish the dialects from one another. Particularly notable is the raising and fronting of Common Greek *aː* to [æː] and ultimately [ɛː] in the Attic-Ionic dialect; thus one finds Attic-Ionic μήτηρ 'mother' versus Doric (for example) μάτηρ from Common Greek *maːteːr*. The fronting of [u] to [y] in Attic-Ionic has already been noted. Lengthening (often due to the loss of *s or *y in a cluster with a resonant) and contraction (of combinations of e and o) gave rise in Attic-Ionic to the long closed ([eː] and [oː]) vowels and likewise in parts of Doric (e.g. Corinthian and Delphian) and Thessalian and Boeotian (both Aeolic), while in Lesbian (Aeolic) and Arcadian and the rest of Doric (e.g. Cretan, Laconian) long open vowels ([ɛː] and [ɔː]) are found as the corresponding elements. For example, Attic-Ionic has εἰμί [eːmi] 'I am' from Common Greek *esmi, while Doric has ἠμί [ɛːmi]; similarly, Attic-Ionic has τρεῖς [treːs] 'three' from Common Greek *treyes, while Doric has τρης.

Among the peculiarities of Ancient Greek phonotactics, the following are to be noted: [r] could not occur in initial position; one finds instead the unvoiced allophone [r̥] (which has sometimes been described as an aspirated r). In final position, only [r], [s], [n] and vowels were permitted. Geminate consonants were permitted, though geminate labial and velar stops occur most often in onomatopoeic, nursery and expressive words. Lastly, Ancient Greek tolerated numerous consonant clusters, including a variety of initial clusters: any stop plus r or l is permitted (including #τλ-); all but *βν-, *βμ-, *γμ-, *θμ-, *πμ-, *τν-, *φμ- and *χμ- are found for stop plus nasal clusters, though φν- occurs only in a single onomatopoeic form, and τμ-, δν- and κμ- are quite rare; two stops are permitted initially if they differ in point of articulation but agree in manner and the second stop is a dental, though the voiced such clusters (βδ- and γδ-) were found in only a small number of words; and clusters of s plus as many as two consonants occur (e.g. σχίζω 'cut', σπλάγχνα 'innards', σκνίπτω 'pinch, nip', etc.).

The Ancient Greek accentual system was based on a pitch accent. There were a high pitch (the acute, Greek ὀξύς, marked with the diacritic ⟨ˊ⟩), a low pitch (the grave, Greek βαρύς, marked with the diacritic ⟨ˋ⟩), and a contour pitch (the circumflex, Greek περισπομένος, marked with the diacritic ⟨ˆ⟩) which consisted of an acute plus a grave on the same syllable and occurred only on long vowels or diphthongs. At most, one high pitch, either an acute or circumflex, occurred per word (except for some special developments with enclitics), and all non-high syllables were considered grave.

Accent placement was predictable (for the most part — some exceptions exist) only in finite verb forms and in declined forms of certain nouns, e.g. those with antepenultimate accent in their lexical form; for such forms, the accent is said to be 'recessive', i.e. as far from the end of the word as permitted. Also, the placement of accent was predictable in certain morphologically definable formations, e.g. compounds with εὐ- 'well, easy' had recessive accent, verbal adjectives in -τος were accented on the final syllable, etc. In other contexts, accent placement was unpredictable and was therefore an element of the underlying (lexical) form of the word in question, though there were some regularities in the realisation of the accent (e.g. circumflex if the accent fell on a long penultimate syllable when the ultima was short). Thus, accent was distinctive in the Ancient Greek phonological system, for some words were distinguished only by the type of accent on a given syllable (e.g. locative adverbial οἴκοι 'at home' versus nominative plural οἶκοι 'houses') and others only by the placement of the accent (e.g. τιμά 'two honours' versus τίμα '(you) honour!').

An overriding principle in the placement of the pitch accent in Ancient Greek is the so-called 'Dreimorengesetz' (Law of Three Morae), by which the accent could only occur on the antepenultimate, penultimate or ultima syllable and never earlier in the word than that. With a few exceptions, this restriction can be stated in terms of morae (hence the name 'Dreimorengesetz'), so that Ancient Greek was probably a mora-timed language (note also that syllable quantity mattered for purposes of the ancient poetic metres). This restriction gave rise to certain of the predictable aspects of the placement of accent, especially in those forms which had recessive accent. For example, a noun such as θάλαττα 'sea' was lexically accented on the antepenultimate syllable, as indicated by the citation form (nominative singular); in the genitive singular, though, the final syllable is long (θαλάττης) and as a result, the accent cannot stand on the antepenultimate syllable. Instead, it predictably is pulled forward to the penultimate, so that it does not stand more than three morae from the end. Similarly, a finite verb form such as κελεύω 'I order' was predictably accented on the penultimate syllable because the ultima is long and finite forms have recessive accent; the first person plural present form κελεύομεν and the first person singular past form ἐκέλευσα, however, are both accented on the antepenultimate syllable because the ultima is short. By contrast, the perfect middle participle of this verb, a non-finite form, had penultimate accent (e.g. in the nominative singular masculine form) even though the ultima was short, i.e. κεκελευμένος. In this way, therefore, accent placement in the verb serves also as a correlate of the morphosyntactic category of finiteness; recessive accent correlates with the presence of person and number markings on the verb, but not with the absence of such markings, in general.

With regard to the morphophonemics of Ancient Greek, three types of alternations must be distinguished: vowel alternations that represent a remnant — by then fully morphologically conditioned — of the Indo-European ablaut patterns (see pages 47–8), alternations caused by the sound changes that separate Greek from Proto-Indo-European and that distinguish the individual dialects of Greek itself, and alternations due to natural processes such as assimilation.

Within paradigms, except for a few irregular verbs (e.g. εἶ-μι 'I go' versus ἴ-μεν 'we go') with alternations between e-grade and zero-grade retained from the proto-language, the vowel alternations one finds in Greek are those of length. This situation occurs in a few verbs (e.g. δί-δω-μι 'I give' versus δί-δο-μεν 'we give', actually a remnant of Proto-Indo-European full-grade/zero-grade ablaut transformed in Greek into simply a length distinction) and in a large number of nominal forms of the consonant stem declension (e.g. nominative singular τέκτων 'carpenter' versus genitive singular τέκτον-ος, nominative singular ποιμήν 'shepherd' versus genitive singular ποιμέν-ος, masculine adjective ἀληθής 'true' versus neuter ἀληθές, etc.).

Across paradigms, between derivationally related forms of the same root, one finds alternations in vowel quality as well as quantity. For example, the inherited e/o-ablaut is found in numerous Greek pairs of related forms, such as λέγ-ω 'I say' versus λόγ-ος 'word', φέρ-ω 'I bear' versus φόρ-ος 'tribute, (tax) burden' (and compare also the related form φώρ 'thief (i.e. one who bears off something)' for a length alternation); moreover, it has a grammatical function still in forms such as present tense λείπ-ω 'I leave' versus perfect λέ-λοιπ-α 'I have left' (and note the zero-grade reflex in past ἔ-λιπ-ον 'I did leave'). This e/o-ablaut interacts with the development of the labio-velars to give etymologically related (but probably synchronically unrelated) pairs such as θείνω 'I strike' from *gʷhen-yo: versus φόνος 'murder' from *gʷhon-os. Transformations of the Indo-European ablaut due to sound changes are also to be found, such as in the masculine stem τέκτον- 'carpenter' versus the feminine τέκταινα 'carpentress', where the -o-/-αι- alternation results from an alternation which in pre-Greek terms would have been *-on-Ø versus *-n̥-ya (with -αιν- from *-n̥y-).

Among the sound changes that left traces in morphophonemic alternations, one noteworthy one that operates in noun paradigms is the loss of final stops. Thus one finds such alternations as γάλα 'milk' (nominative singular) versus γάλακτ-ος (genitive singular), or λέων 'lion' (nominative singular) versus λέοντ-ος (genitive). Similarly, the loss of medial *s created paradigmatic alternations such as γένος-Ø 'race, kind' (nominative singular) versus γένε-α (nominative plural), from *genes-a. Across paradigms, the developments of clusters with *y gave rise to derivational alternations, since *-ye/o- was an especially common present tense formative — compare ταραχ-ή 'trouble, disorder' with the related verb ταράττ-ω (Ionic ταράσσ-ω) 'disturb, trouble' from *tarakʰ-yo:, for example — and since *-y- figured in other derivational processes, as with the formation of certain comparative adjectives (e.g. μέγ-ας 'big' versus μείζων 'bigger' from *meg-yo:n). Furthermore, in dialects with the assibilation of t to s before i, one finds such alternations as πλοῦτ-ος 'wealth' versus πλούσ-ιος 'wealthy'. In addition, the *-s- formative, which appeared in some past tense forms, created alternations in vowel quality with the dialectal resolution of resonant plus s clusters, e.g. νέμ-ω 'I distribute' versis ἔ-νειμ-α 'I distributed' (Doric ἔ-νημ-α, both from *e-nem-s-a).

Finally, many morphophonemic alternations are the result of more or less natural processes that take effect when certain segments come together as the result of word formation processes. For example, assimilation in voicing is common, as seen in the pair ἄγ-ω 'I lead' versus ἄξ-ω (i.e. ak-s-o:) 'I will lead' where -s- is the marker for future tense, or in the pair κρύπ-τω 'I hide' versus κρύβ-δην 'secretly'. Similarly, deaspiration before -s- occurs, as in γράφ-ω 'I write' versus γράψ-ω (i.e. *grap-s-o:*) 'I will write', and assimilation in aspiration to a following aspirate is found as in τρίβ-ω 'I rub' versus ἐ-τρίφ-θην 'I was rubbed' (cf. also τρίψ-ω 'I will rub').

The phonology of Ancient Greek has been described in such detail here because it provides the appropriate starting point for a discussion of Post-Classical Greek phonology. The relation is not merely chronological here, for in Post-Classical Greek and on into Modern Greek, one finds that many of the same general phonological characteristics occur in the language, but with different realisations. For example, by the Hellenistic period, systematic shifts in the consonant inventory were under way — to be completed later in Post-Classical Greek — which nonetheless preserved the earlier three-way contrast but with new distinctive oppositions established. The voiced stops became voiced spirants and the voiceless aspirates became voiceless spirants, while the voiceless plain stops remained the same (in general). Thus one finds in Post-Classical Greek the system:

v p f
δ t θ
γ k χ

replacing the earlier *b p pʰ/d t tʰ/g k kʰ* system. In addition, *z* became a distinctive sound (with phonemic status) and *h* was lost.

A [j] reentered the language, originally as an allophone of [γ] before front vowels and of unstressed [i] before vowels, but now it (probably) has phonemic status in the modern language. Similarly, throughout the post-classical period, new voiced stops (*b, d, g*) arose, first as allophones of voiceless (and original voiced) stops after homorganic nasals, and later as distinctive segments (although their synchronic status is still somewhat controversial) through further sound changes that obscured the original conditioning factors. Thus the verb ἐντρέπομαι 'I feel misgivings about' has yielded Modern Greek ντρέπομαι [drεpomε] 'I feel ashamed' through the stages *endrep- > edrep-* (with reduction of nasal plus stop clusters, a process still present but now sociolinguistically and stylistically conditioned, and still found in many of the regional dialects) > *drep-* (with loss of unstressed initial vowels, a sound change of Middle Greek). In addition, borrowings have provided new instances of voiced stops in the language (e.g. more recently μπάρ 'bar', ντάμα 'queen (in cards)', γκαράζ 'garage' etc., but some even as early as Hellenistic times).

Finally, in Middle Greek a *ts* and a *dz* were added to the language, partly through dialectal affrications and borrowings from other languages. These sounds probably represent unitary sounds (affricates) in the modern language, but a cluster analysis cannot be ruled out entirely for them.

The major changes in the vowel system were also beginning in the Hellenistic period, though, as noted above, some of the innovative pronunciations may have been associated with an originally non-standard sociolect of Attic Greek in the late classical period. The principal changes are as follows: length became non-distinctive; the diphthongs monophthongised, with [ai̯] becoming [ɛ], [yi̯] and [oi̯] becoming [i] (presumably through a stage of [y], still present probably as late as the tenth century AD), and the off-glide in [e(ː)u̯] and [au̯] becoming fully consonantal, realised as [f] before voiceless sounds and as [v] before voiced ones, and several of the height distinctions were neutralised with a tendency for vowels to move to [i]. The result is that the Modern Greek vowel system (and that of late Middle Greek as well) consists of five short 'pure' vowels: *i e a o u*. Sequences which are diphthong-like, though perhaps still to be analysed as true sequences of vowels, have arisen through the loss of intervening consonants, as with λέει ([leï]) '(s)he says' from Ancient Greek λέγει through the Middle (and careful Modern) Greek pronunciation [léyi], and through borrowings (e.g. τσάϊ 'tea', λαοῦτο 'lute', etc.). Nonetheless, there are some words that are probably best analysed as having underlying diphthongs, e.g. γάϊδαρος 'donkey', which would violate the modern equivalent of the 'Dreimorengesetz' if it were /γáiðaros/.

Since the vowel length came to be non-distinctive in the later stages of Greek, it is not surprising that the principles upon which accent placement was based would change, inasmuch as vowel quantity mattered for Ancient Greek accent placement. Modern Greek generally has accent placed in the same positions in words as Ancient Greek, and the 'Dreimorengesetz' still holds now though as a 'three syllable rule'. The realisation of accent has changed, though, and Modern Greek now has a stress accent, not a pitch accent, with prominent stress corresponding to the earlier high (acute or circumflex) pitch (and note that by Middle Greek, the basis for poetic metre was syllable counting, with a 15-syllable line being the preferred metrical unit). Modern Greek thus has some of the same accent shifts as Ancient Greek, as for example in ἄνθρωπος 'man' (nominative singular) versus ἀνθρώπου (genitive), but because of the absence of a phonological motivation for them, numerous levellings have occurred, resulting in stable stress throughout a paradigm (as in πράσινος 'green' (nominative singular masculine) versus πράσινου (genitive) from Ancient Greek πράσινος/πρασίνου, and in dialectal forms such as ἄνθρωπου for standard ἀνθρώπου). The recessive accent rule for finite verb forms no longer holds in general, but is valid for the simple past and imperfect tenses of verbs which are stem-stressed (as opposed to end-stressed) in the present (e.g. νομίζω 'I think' versus νόμιζα 'I was thinking', νομίζαμε 'we were thinking', νόμισα 'I thought', νομίσαμε 'we thought'). Stress placement, though, is distinctive, as shown by pairs such as κοπή 'cutting' – κόποι 'troubles, reward', κύριος 'master' – κυρίως 'above all, chiefly', among others.

The major change in phonotactics concerns new final sequences which have entered the language through borrowings (e.g. final [l] in γκόλ 'goal' from English, final [z] in γκαράζ 'garage' from French, final [p] in the current slang expression εἶμαι ἄπ 'I am up (in spirits)' from English, etc.). One noteworthy change in allowable clusters, though, affected combinations of voiceless stops and combinations of Ancient Greek voiceless aspirated stops. Both types of clusters, e.g. πτ- and φθ-, have converged, through what has been described as a manner dissimilation, on the combination of voiceless fricative plus voiceless (unaspirated) stop. Thus earlier πτ has yielded φτ [ft], as in πτέρον 'feather' > φτέρο (with regular loss of final *n* as well), and earlier φθ has also yielded φτ, through a stage of [fθ], as in φθάνω > φτάνω 'I arrive'. The effects of the diglossia alluded to earlier can be seen especially clearly in this aspect of the phonology, for in many words of learned origin, the non-dissimilated clusters remain and both cluster types occur as stylistic variants within one and the same speaker's idiolect even, because of the stylistic mixing induced by the diglossic situation.

For the most part, the later stages of Greek preserved the same types of morphophonemic alternations as Ancient Greek, though again with different phonetic realisations. Thus one now finds alternations such as γράφ-ομε 'we write' versus γράψ-αμε 'we wrote' with an *f/p* alternation (Ancient Greek *pʰ/p* alternation), ἀνοίγ-ω 'I open' versus ἄνοιξ-α 'I opened' with a *γ/k* alternation (Ancient Greek *g/k* alternation), where the structure of the alternations is the same but the segments involved have changed in part. Various morphological changes in the noun in particular have undone many of the Ancient Greek nominal alternations, as with Ancient Greek φλέψ (i.e. [pʰlep-s]) 'vein' (nominative singular) versus φλέβ-α (accusative) being remade to a paradigm with φλέβα [fleva], the continuation of the old accusative form, serving as the nominative and accusative form. One can still find the Ancient Greek alternations preserved relatively intact, though, in the archaising linguistic forms of early Post-Classical Greek on through Middle Greek and into Modern Greek; such forms are not — and probably never were — in current colloquial usage, however.

A final point about Post-Classical Greek phonology concerns some of the major differences that characterise the Modern, and to a large extent the Middle, Greek dialects. Characteristic of the northern dialect zone (north of Attica on the mainland, though excluding the urban Thessaloniki dialect, and the islands of the northern Aegean including Thasos, Samothraki, Lemnos and Lesbos, and also the more southerly Samos) is the raising of unstressed mid vowels and the deletion of unstressed high vowels. Thus one finds paradigms such as present [pirmén] '(s)he waits' (cf. standard περιμένει), imperfect [pirímini] '(s)he was waiting' (cf. standard περίμενε). This syncope has also given rise in these dialects to consonant clusters not found in the standard language and the more southerly and eastern dialects (e.g. [éstla] 'I sent' for standard ἔστειλα). Another isogloss distinguishing the regional dialects is the presence of palatalisations (especially [č] for [k] before front vowels) in the southeastern dialects (of Chios, the Dodekanese islands including Rhodes, and Cyprus), in Cretan and in Old Athenian (the dialect of Attica before the establishment of the standard language in the 1820s, which still survives in a few isolated pockets), but not in the northern dialects (in general, though [š] for [s] before front vowels is common) nor in the standard language, based as it is on the Peloponnesian-Ionian (Island) dialect.

4.2 Morphology

It is safe to say that the general character of Greek morphological structure has remained fairly stable over the 3,500 years of our knowledge of the language, though, of course, there have been numerous significant changes as well. Greek has been a fusional language throughout all stages in its development; in Middle and Modern Greek, though, there is a distinct tendency in the direction of analytic expressions, examples of which are given below *passim*. To illustrate the fusional character of the language, one need only consider the nominal ending -ους (Ancient Greek [-oːs], Modern Greek [-us]), for it marks accusative case, plural number and masculine gender, all in a single unanalysable unit, for the so-called *o*-stem nouns. Moreover, even though there is a nominal ending -ου and another nominal ending -*s*, so that one might attempt to analyse -ους as -ου plus -*s*, such an analysis cannot work: -ου marks genitive singular for masculine *o*-stem nouns and -*s* marks nominative singular for certain masculine and feminine consonant stem nouns in Ancient Greek and for masculine nouns in general in Modern Greek.

The relevant morphological categories for the Greek nominal system, comprising nouns, adjectives and pronouns, are as follows. In Ancient Greek, there were five cases (nominative, accusative, genitive, dative and vocative), three numbers (singular, dual and plural), and three genders (masculine, feminine and neuter). In Modern Greek, by contrast, there are four cases (nominative, accusative, genitive and vocative), two numbers (singular and plural), and the same three genders. The loss of the dative is under way as early as Hellenistic Greek, though this change was not completed until well into the Middle Greek era (in part because of the pressure from the learned language in which the dative was retained). In Modern Greek, the genitive case has assumed some of the typical functions of the earlier dative case, e.g. the expression of indirect objects, but one also finds, in keeping with the analytic tendency noted above, indirect objects expressed in a prepositional phrase (σ(έ) 'in, at, to', from Ancient Greek είς 'in, into', plus accusative). It is worth noting as well that the genitive plural is obsolescent in Modern Greek for many nouns and for many speakers, with periphrases of the preposition άπό 'from' plus accusative being used instead.

In both Ancient and Modern Greek, these nominal morphological categories were realised in different ways depending on the class of noun involved. In Ancient Greek, the assignment to inflectional class was based on phonological characteristics of the nominal stem, so that one finds o-stem nouns, a:-stem nouns and consonant stem nouns (including i- and u-stems as consonantal); within these stem classes, all three genders were represented, though feminine o-stems were rare as were masculine a:-stems (neuter a:-stems being non-existent). In Modern Greek, the assignment to inflectional class is by and large based on gender, not phonological stem shape, so that in general, the masculine nouns are inflected alike, especially in the singular, with -s in the nominative singular versus -Ø in the accusative singular and -Ø

Nominal Inflection in Ancient and Modern Greek

	Feminine a:-stem γνώμα:- 'opinion'	Masculine o-stem λόγο- 'word'	Neuter o-stem δῶρο- 'gift'	Feminine Consonant stem φλέβ- 'vein'	Masculine φύλακ- 'watchman'	Neuter σῶματ- 'body'
Ancient Greek						
Nom. sg.	γνώμη	λόγος	δῶρον	φλέψ	φύλαξ	σῶμα
Acc. sg.	γνώμην	λόγον	δῶρον	φλέβα	φύλακα	σῶμα
Gen. sg.	γνώμης	λόγου	δώρου	φλεβός	φύλακος	σώματος
Dat. sg.	γνώμηι	λόγωι	δώρωι	φλεβί	φύλακι	σώματι
Voc. sg.	γνώμη	λόγε	δῶρον	φλέψ	φύλαξ	σῶμα
Nom. du.	γνώμα:	λόγω	δώρω	φλέβε	φύλακε	σώματε
Acc. du.	γνώμα:	λόγω	δώρω	φλέβε	φύλακε	σώματε
Gen. du.	γνώμαιν	λόγοιν	δώροιν	φλεβοῖν	φυλάκοιν	σωμάτοιν
Dat. du.	γνώμαιν	λόγοιν	δώροιν	φλεβοῖν	φυλάκοιν	σωμάτοιν
Voc. du.	γνώμα:	λόγω	δώρω	φλέβε	φύλακε	σώματε
Nom. pl.	γνῶμαι	λόγοι	δῶρα	φλέβες	φύλακες	σώματα
Acc. pl.	γνώμα:ς	λόγους	δῶρα	φλέβας	φύλακας	σώματα
Gen. pl.	γνωμῶν	λόγων	δώρων	φλεβῶν	φυλάκων	σωμάτων
Dat. pl.	γνώμαις	λόγοις	δώροις	φλεψί	φύλαξι	σώμασι
Voc. pl.	γνῶμαι	λόγοι	δῶρα	φλέβες	φύλακες	σώματα
Modern Greek						
Nom. sg.	γνώμη	λόγος	δώρο	φλέβα	φύλακας	σώμα
Acc. sg.	γνώμη	λόγο	δώρο	φλέβα	φύλακα	σώμα
Gen. sg.	γνώμης	λόγου	δώρου	φλέβας	φύλακα	σώματος
Voc. sg.	γνώμη	λόγε	δώρο	φλέβα	φύλακα	σώμα
Nom. pl.	γνώμες	λόγοι	δώρα	φλέβες	φύλακες	σώματα
Acc. pl.	γνώμες	λόγους	δώρα	φλέβες	φύλακες	σώματα
Gen. pl.	γνωμών	λόγων	δώρων	φλεβών	φυλάκων	σωμάτων
Voc. pl.	γνώμες	λόγοι	δώρα	φλέβες	φύλακες	σώματα

Note: Accentuation in Modern Greek forms follows current official monotonic orthography, with a single accentual diacritic. The colon (:) for length in the Ancient Greek forms is given here only to indicate pronunciation; it was not a part of the Ancient Greek orthography.

in the genitive singular, and the feminines are inflected alike, again especially in the singular, with a -∅ ending in the nominative and accusative singular versus -s in the genitive singular. As with most changes between Ancient and Modern Greek, the beginnings of this shift in inflectional class assignment can be seen early in the post-classical period. In the chart given here the inflection of six nouns is given for Ancient and Modern Greek by way of illustrating the basic patterns for these stages and of highlighting the differences between the two. Although the nominal system of Greek, especially the ancient language, shows a goodly number of inflectional categories and markers, it is the verbal system that presents the greatest morphological complexity in the language. Moreover, despite a number of reductions in this complexity between Ancient and Modern Greek, especially in the realm of non-finite verbal forms, Modern Greek still has a verbal system that is, in basic character, very like its ancient source.

Ancient Greek, for instance, distinguished three persons in verbal inflection, and three numbers (singular, dual and plural), although the combination of first person with dual number was not realised inflectionally in the language at all. A significant distinction was made in the verbal system between finite and non-finite forms, with the relevant morphological distinction for finiteness being the presence of person and number markings; as noted above in the section on accentuation, though, recessive accent placement also served to distinguish finite from non-finite forms. Among the non-finite forms were several different infinitives and several different participles, as enumerated below, differing in voice, aspect and tense, and two verbal adjectives (denoting capability and obligation, respectively).

As indicated, there were inflectional categories for voice, with active, passive and middle voice being distinguished. The middle voice indicated reflexive action (though there were also available in the language overt reflexive pronominal forms), or more generally, action one undertook on one's own behalf or to one's own benefit. For example, the active βουλεύω means 'to take counsel' while the middle βουλεύομαι means 'to take counsel with oneself, to deliberate', and the active λούω means 'to wash' while the middle λούομαι means 'to wash oneself, to bathe'. The passive was formally distinct from the middle only for future tense and simple past (aorist) forms. In addition, there were four moods, an indicative, a subjunctive, an optative (used in the expression of potentiality and for past time in indirect discourse, for example) and an imperative, all fully inflected for all the voice, number and person categories, as well as most of the temporal/aspectual categories described below.

Finally, Ancient Greek is usually described as having seven 'tenses', a present, a future, a (present) perfect, a pluperfect, a future perfect (which is usually passive), an imperfect past and a simple past (known as the aorist). In actuality, these 'tense' forms encoded two different types of distinctions — a purely temporal one of present time versus future time versus past time, and an aspectual one of action that is continuous (imperfective) versus action that is completed (perfective) versus action that is simply taking place (aoristic). The three-way distinction is realised fully in past time forms only, incompletely in the present, and via a formal merger of two categories in the future. These relations are summarised in table 7.4 below (adapted from Goodwin and Gulick 1958):

Table 7.4: Ancient Greek Tense-Aspect Relations

Tense Aspect	*Present*	*Past*	*Future*
Continuous	present	imperfect	future
Simple			
occurrence	(no realisation)	aorist	future
Completed	perfect	pluperfect	future perfect

Illustrative examples are: present γράφω 'I am writing', perfect γέγραφα 'I have written', imperfect ἔγραφον 'I was writing', aorist ἔγραψα 'I did write, I wrote', pluperfect ἐγεγράφη 'I had written', future γράψω 'I will be writing (continuous aspect), I will write (simple occurrence)', and future perfect γεγράψεται 'it will have been written'.

The non-finite forms show the aspectual nature of the category oppositions especially clearly, for one finds a present infinitive and participle, an aorist infinitive and participle, and a perfect infinitive and participle, corresponding to the continuous, simple and completed aspectual distinctions in the finite verbal system. In addition, though, there is a future infinitive and participle, so that the non-finite system too shows some purely temporal as well as aspectual distinctions. As with the different moods, the non-finite forms occur in all voices, so that there are 11 different infinitival types and a like number of participles.

Many of the complexities of this system are retained in Post-Classical Greek and on into Modern Greek, though in some instances, there is only apparent, and not actual, continuity. Some of the differences are the result of responses to system-internal pressures, as for example, with the changes in the voice and aspect categories, while others may have been, at least in part, induced by external factors, as with the changes in the non-finite system and the future tense. Many, however, are in keeping with a tendency toward analytic expressions where Ancient Greek had synthetic ones.

The only difference in person and number categories is that, as in nominal inflection, the dual number category has been eliminated, its demise evident as early as Hellenistic Greek. The moods too have been altered. The optative began to fall into disuse in the Koine period, partly as a result, no doubt, of sound changes leading to partial homophony (in four of eight forms) with the subjunctive and (less so) with the indicative. Similarly, it is a matter of some debate even today as to whether Greek now has a distinct subjunctive mood, for there is no formal difference between the continuation of the old present indicative and present subjunctive due to various sound changes, and virtually all 'subjunctive' uses are marked with a verbal particle νά, giving an analytic counterpart to the Ancient Greek synthetic subjunctive (e.g. νὰ γράψεις versus ancient γράψῃς 'that you (might) write'). Finally, where Ancient Greek had synthetic forms for non-second person imperatives, Modern Greek has, again, analytic forms, marked by the particle ἄς, though distinct (synthetic) second person imperative forms remain.

Greek maintains an opposition among active, middle and passive voices, though from a formal standpoint, the middle voice and passive voice are never distinct; the cover term medio-passive is thus perhaps more appropriate. This development seems to be a natural outgrowth of the Ancient Greek system in which the distinction was realised formally only in the aorist and future tenses but in no others. Thus in Modern Greek, and earlier stages of Post-Classical Greek as well, a form such as πλύθηκα, a medio-passive aorist of the verb πλύνω 'wash', can mean 'I was washed (by someone)' or 'I washed myself', with the context of the utterance generally being the only determinant of which of these interpretations is preferred.

The Ancient Greek tenses all remain in Modern Greek, but here the continuity is apparent only. In the Koine period, the perfect tense system was eliminated, with the simple past (aorist) taking over some of the old perfect functions and various periphrastic (i.e. analytic) constructions (e.g. εἰμί 'be' plus the perfect participle) taking over other of its functions. Thus there was a period in the post-classical language in which there was no formal perfect tense system. By the middle of the Middle Greek period, approximately the tenth century, though, a pluperfect arose, formed with the aorist of 'have' plus one continuation of the Ancient Greek infinitive (e.g. εἶχα γράψαι 'I had written', later εἶχα γράψει); this construction was originally used, in late Hellenistic and early Middle Greek, as a conditional but later passed over into a true pluperfect meaning. The relation between it and the *habeō* + infinitive/participle formations found in Vulgar Latin and Romance is uncertain, but some influence through Balkan Roman cannot be discounted. From that pluperfect, a new perfect system, with the full range of inflectional categories, was spawned; a present perfect was created consisting of the present of 'have' plus this continuation of the old infinitive, and later a future perfect was formed with the Middle and Modern Greek future formants, an imperative perfect arose, etc. The Modern Greek perfect system, therefore, represents a considerable elaboration within the Post-Classical Greek verbal system, and though only indirectly connected with them, parallels the Ancient Greek perfect system forms.

Similarly, Modern Greek has a future tense, just as Ancient Greek had, but again one finds an analytic expression in place of the earlier synthetic one, with only an indirect connection between the two forms. In the case of the future, though, as opposed to the perfect, there seems never to have been a period in which the future tense failed to exist as a formal category in the language. Within the Hellenistic period, the use of the older synthetic future, e.g. γράψω 'I will write', became obsolescent, with various periphrases arising to compete with it, including the present of 'have' plus a continuation of the infinitive and other quasi-modal constructions (e.g. μέλλω 'be about to' plus infinitive). With the passage of the 'have' forms into the incipient perfect system, as just described, a new future periphrasis arose, by the tenth century, completely ousting the earlier synthetic form. This was a future based on the verb 'want' (θέλω); as with the perfect, the relation between this form and similar ones found in virtually all the Balkan languages is controversial. In the medieval period, an unusual variety of future formations with this verb can be found, consisting of combinations of inflected forms of θέλω plus uninflected (infinitival) main verbs, uninflected (i.e. invariant third person singular) forms of θέλω plus inflected forms of main verbs, inflected forms of θέλω plus inflected forms of a main verb, the optional use of the verbal particle νά and so forth; representative examples of these patterns would be θέλω γράψει(ν) (infinitive), θέλει (invariant) (νά) γράψω, θέλω (νά) γράψω, all meaning 'I will write'. Ultimately, the formation of the type θέλει νά γράψω won out, and through various reductions, the modern standard and widespread dialectal future particle θά (e.g. θά γράψω 'I will write') was created.

Going along with these future formations were parallel conditional formations consisting of a past tense of the auxiliary-like verb plus a form of the main verb (compare the ἔχω 'have' plus infinitive future and εἶχα plus infinitive conditional of early Post-Classical Greek). These conditional formations have no formal category correspondent in Ancient Greek (the modal particle ἄν with the optative mood is the Ancient Greek potential/conditional expression), so that here too one finds an elaboration within the earlier tense/mood system.

The aspectual system too has undergone various rearrangements from the Ancient Greek system. In this case, the internal pressures within the system, partly as a result of the incomplete realisation of the aspect system within the tense system (see table 7.4) were a major factor in the developments. The basic opposition of continuous versus punctual aspect has been maintained throughout the development of Post-Classical Greek and, with the new periphrastic formations, has been extended to the future tense as well (e.g. θά γράφω 'I will be writing' versus θά γράψω 'I will write', in Modern Greek, or θέλω γράφει(ν) versus θέλω γράψει(ν) in Middle Greek). The completed aspect category now finds expression in the new perfect system, though one can still find uses of the simple past (aorist) which signal completed action as opposed to simply past action, as with the 'pro futuro' use of the aorist (e.g. ἔφυγα 'I'm about to leave' lit. 'I (have) left; my leaving is over and done with').

Finally, Modern Greek, as well as Post-Classical Greek in general, maintains the Ancient Greek distinction of finite versus non-finite forms, though this opposition has undergone perhaps the greatest series of restructurings of any part of the verbal system. In particular, the realisation of the opposition has changed considerably. In Ancient Greek the imperative patterned with the finite forms in terms of accent placement and person/number markings, while in Modern Greek it patterns instead with the non-finite forms; like the participles (and unlike, for example, the indicative), the imperative allows only enclitic pronoun objects and not proclitic ones, and like the participles (and again unlike the indicative), it is arguably marked only for number and not for person (cf. singular δές '(you) see!' versus plural δέσ-τε '(you) see!' where the only formal difference is -∅ versus -τε and the only semantic difference singular versus plural) — recall that non-second person imperative forms of Ancient Greek gave way to analytic expressions with the particle ἄς in later Greek. Moreover, the number of participles has been reduced, so that Modern Greek has only a present (continuous aspect) medio-passive participle (e.g γραφόμενος 'being written') and a present (continuous aspect) active participle, also called a gerundive, which generally serves only as an adverbial adjunct modifying the surface subject of a sentence (e.g. γράφοντας '(while) writing').

Similarly, the category of *infinitive* has been eliminated entirely from the language, although the indications are that it was maintained until approximately the sixteenth century as at least a marginal category. The details of this development are discussed more in the following section on syntax. The only remnant of the earlier infinitive is in the new perfect system, for the second part of the perfect periphrasis (γράψει in ἔχω γράψει 'I have written') continues a Middle Greek analogical replacement for the Ancient Greek aorist infinitive (so also in the medio-passive, e.g. ἔχει γραφθεῖ 'it has been written' from Middle Greek ἔχει γραφθῆν(αι)). There is no synchronic justification, though, for treating these remnants as categorically distinct within the morphology, and they perhaps are to be considered now as the punctual aspect counterparts to the continuous aspect participles (thus γράψει versus γραφθεῖ as γράφοντας versus γραφόμενος). In both the case of the reduction of the participle and the case of the demise of the infinitive, the Modern Greek situation represents the end-point of a long and gradual process whose roots are to be found in Hellenistic Greek usage of the non-finite forms.

4.3 Syntax

A considerable amount of space has been spent on the phonology and morphology of Greek, both from a synchronic standpoint for relevant periods and from a diachronic standpoint, in part because it is possible to give a fairly complete picture of these components of a language in a relatively short space. With regard to the syntax, it is of course impossible to do justice to any stage of the language in anything less than a full-sized monograph (and it is worth noting that there are numerous lengthy works dealing with individual constructions in single periods of the language). Nonetheless, a few of the especially noteworthy aspects of the syntactic combinations of the language can be mentioned, along with a sketch of their development over the centuries.

Perhaps one of the most elaborate parts of the Ancient Greek syntactic system was the system of verbal complementation. Not only were there so many non-finite forms — infinitives and participles — available which were utilised in forming complements to main verbs, but there were also a good number of finite forms, differing, as has been described, in aspect and mood, which could combine with a variety of subordinating conjunctions to form verbal complements. Thus a major part of the description of Ancient Greek syntax must deal with the question of how the moods, aspects and non-finite forms were actually used. Not surprisingly, there is a fairly complex set of sequence of tense conditions governing allowable combinations of main verb and dependent verb, especially in indirect discourse and in conditional sentences.

One significant development in the verbal complementation system in later stages of Greek is the demise of the infinitive, mentioned above in its purely morphological context. From as early as Hellenistic Greek, finite clause complements are found in places in which Classical Greek had used an infinitive (or even participle). For example, in the New Testament, a finite clause complement is found in competition with an infinitive with the adjective ἄξιος 'worthy, deserving', a context in which only an infinitival complement could appear in Classical Greek:

(a) οὗ   οὐκ εἰμὶ   ἄξιος   τὸ ὑπόδημα τῶν ποδῶν   λῦσαι
                                                                    (Acts 13.25)
     whose not am/1 sg. worthy the-sandal   the-feet/gen. loosen/infin.
     '(One) of whom I am not worthy to loosen the sandal from his feet.'

(b) οὗ οὐκ εἰμὶ ἐγὼ ἄξιος ἵνα λύσω   αὐτοῦ τὸν ἱμάντα τοῦ
                                                           ὑποδήματος   (Jo. 1.27)
                  I/nom.   that loosen/1 sg. subj. his   the-thong/acc.
                                                           of-the-sandal

The spread of finite complementation, most usually introduced by the particle ἵνα (later Greek νά through an irregular stress shift and regular sound changes) but also with the true complementisers such as the neutral ὅτι (comparable to English *that*), at the expense of infinitival complements continued throughout the post-classical era, working its way through syntactically defined classes of construction type (e.g. like-subject complements versus unlike-subject complements) and within each such class diffusing across the range of governing lexical items. By Middle Greek, the only productive uses of the infinitive were with the verbs ἔχω and θέλω in the perfect and future periphrases, respectively, though a few sporadic uses of the infinitive with other verbs (e.g. (ἠ)μποϱῶ 'can') and as an adverbial adjunct are to be found as well.

The spread of finite complementation is complete, though, in Modern Greek, and there are no instances of non-finite complementation remaining. Thus from the standpoint of typology, Modern Greek, unlike its predecessors, is a language in which all complement verbs are fully finite, marked for person, number and tense/aspect. Greek thus now diverges considerably from the Indo-European 'norm', but interestingly, as noted earlier, converges on this point with the other languages of the Balkans; in fact, Greek, along with Macedonian, shows the greatest degree of infinitive loss among all the Balkan languages. As with the other Balkan areal features, the extent to which the developments with the infinitive represent an internal development in Greek (and the other languages) or a contact-induced one is debated; in this case, a combination of internal and external factors seems to provide the best account for this phenomenon within each language, Greek included, and within the Balkans as a whole.

It is to be noted, moreover, that the replacement of the infinitive by finite expressions with a verbal particle ties in with the general trend towards analytic constructions seen in the morphology. Other syntactic reflexes of this move towards analysis include comparison productively via the particle πιό with an adjective in Modern Greek versus a bound suffix -τεϱος in Ancient Greek (e.g. ἀξιώτεϱος 'more worthy' > πιό ἄξιος), and the expression of indirect objects with a prepositional phrase (σ(έ) plus accusative) versus the Ancient Greek dative case alone.

The developments with the moods and the tenses and the infinitive between Ancient and Modern Greek show also a trend towards the development of a system of preverbal particles, for example the future particle θά, the subjunctive and infinitival replacement particle νά, the non-second person imperatival ἄς (from earlier ἄφησε 'let', itself an imperative). A further reflection of this development is to be seen in the pronominal system of Modern Greek as compared with that of Ancient Greek. While Ancient Greek had both strong forms of the personal pronouns and weak (clitic) forms, the weak forms were restricted to the oblique (non-nominative) cases only, and use of the clitic genitive forms in the expression of possession was somewhat limited; true possessive adjectives were substitutable for the clitic forms in all persons and numbers and were the preferred variant in the first and second person plural. In Modern Greek, by contrast, there is now a set of nominative clitic pronominal forms (though they are restricted to use just with the deictic particle νά 'here (is)!' and the interrogative particle ποῦ(ν) 'where (is)?') and the primary means of expressing possession is with clitic genitive forms of the personal pronouns for all persons and numbers. Thus in Ancient Greek one finds both ὁ σὸς ἀδελφός (lit. 'the your brother') and ὁ ἀδελφός σου (lit. 'the brother of you') for 'your brother', while Modern Greek has only the latter type.

Similarly, the clitic object pronouns (both accusative and genitive) of Ancient Greek have been expanded in use in Modern Greek. In particular, they are now quite commonly used to cross-index definite and specific objects, as in:

(a) τόν   εἶδα   τόν Γιάννη
    him/acc. clit.   saw/1 sg.   the-John/acc.
    'I see John.'

(b) τοῦ   (τό)   ἔδωσα   τοῦ Γιάννη   τό βιβλίο
    him/gen. clit.   it/acc. clit.   gave/1 sg.   the-John/gen.   the-book/acc.
    'I gave the book to John.'

This feature represents another way in which Modern Greek diverges from Ancient Greek in the direction of the other Balkan languages (though again the causes for the divergence and convergence are subject to debate). For some speakers of Greek, this clitic doubling is obligatory at least for indirect objects, while for others it is an optional process with an emphatic function.

Two relatively stable elements of the syntax of Greek over the centuries are to be found in the syntax of the nominal system — the use of the definite article and adjectival position. The development of a definite article took place within the history of Greek, for in Homeric Greek, the form which became the Classical definite article is generally used as a demonstrative pronoun, and a few traces of this usage survive in the classical language. The definite article in classical times came to be used also as a means of substantivising virtually any part of speech or phrasal category, including adverbs (e.g. τοῖς τότε 'to the (men) of that time' (lit. 'the (dat. pl. masc.) then')), infinitives, whether alone or in a verb phrase (e.g. τὸ δρᾶν 'the acting, action', τὸ βίαι πολίτων δρᾶν 'acting in defiance of citizens'), and so on. Moreover, virtually any type of modifier, whether adverb, prepositional phrase, noun phrase or adjective, could be placed between the article and a modified noun. This construction with the definite article and modified nominals is to be found throughout the history of Greek, so that in Modern Greek in place of the 'articular infinitive' one finds nominalised finite clauses (e.g. τό νά εἶναι ῞Ελληνας 'the (fact of) being a Greek'), extended prenominal modifiers (though these can have a bookish feel, e.g. ὁ μορφομένος στό Παρίσι γειτονάς μου 'my educated-in-Paris neighbour'), etc.

As just noted, adjectives could in Ancient Greek, and still can in Modern Greek, appear prenominally. Throughout the history of Greek, there has been an important contrast in the position of an adjective based on its function. An adjective standing outside the article had, and still has, a predicative function, defining a clause without the necessity for an overt copular verb, e.g.:

(a) καλὸς   ὁ ἀδελφός   (b) ὁ ἀδελφὸς καλός
    good (nom. sg. m.)   the-brother (nom. sg.)
    'The brother is good.'

When the adjective occurs between the article and the noun or if no article is present, then the adjective has attributive function, and a noun phrase is defined:

(a) ὁ καλὸς ἀδελφός   (b) καλὸς ἀδελφός
    'the good brother'   'a good brother'

Other aspects of Greek word order have remained more or less stable throughout its development. In particular Greek has always enjoyed a relatively free ordering of the major constituents of a sentence, with grammatical relations and relations among constituents being encoded in the inflectional morphology, although certain patterns seem to be preferred in particular contexts (e.g. verb–subject–object order in the modern language in sentences presenting wholly new information).

4.4 Lexicon

At all points in its history, the Greek lexicon has incorporated a large number of native (inherited) lexical roots and stems. As noted earlier, some of these have remained more or less intact over the years, e.g. ἄνεμος 'wind', ἄλλος 'other'; more usually, though, words in Modern Greek show the effects of regular sound changes, e.g. γράφω 'I write' (with [γ] and [f] for earlier [g] and [pʰ]), μέρα 'day' (Ancient Greek ἡμέρα), changes in form and meaning, e.g. χῶμα 'bank, mound (Ancient Greek); soil (Modern)' and morphological reshapings (e.g. φύλακας versus φύλαξ — see the chart of nominal inflection). Finally, many words in the later language are built up out of native elements but with no direct ancestor in the ancient language, e.g. πιστοποίηση 'guarantee', and the many modern scientific terms built out of Greek morphemes by non-Greek speakers and reborrowed back into Greek, e.g. ἀτμοσφαῖρα 'atmosphere'.

At the same time, though, there has always been also in Greek a significant number of foreign elements. Ancient loans from Semitic (e.g. χιτών 'tunic', σαγήνη 'large drag-net'), Anatolian (e.g. κύανος 'dark blue enamel', κύμβαχος 'crown of a helmet'), and other languages of the ancient Near East can be identified, and as noted in section 2 above, there may be numerous words in Ancient Greek taken over from the languages indigenous to Greece before the arrival of the Greeks proper. During the

Hellenistic period, a major source of loanwords into Greek was Latin. During the later periods, one finds first an influx of Venetian (Italian) words and somewhat later an admixture of some Slavonic and Albanian words but mainly Turkish lexical items and phrases. More recently, loans from French and especially English have entered the language in great numbers. One final important source of borrowings in Greek has always been Greek itself; due to the long literary record of the language and the importance placed from a sociolinguistic standpoint on the literary language (recall the discussion of Greek diglossia in section 2), there has always been pressure to borrow from the literary language into the colloquial language, so that Modern Greek now has an internal lexical stratification parallel to what is found in Slavonic or Romance.

Bibliography

With the possible exception of English, there has probably been more written on the Greek language than on any other language. Consequently, giving references for information on Greek in its various aspects is difficult. None the less, it is possible to identify a number of basic and representative works on the language.

Grammars of the Ancient language abound, and the most detailed available, though a bit difficult to use because of a somewhat odd arrangement of facts, is Schwyzer (1939) and Schwyzer and Debrunner (1950). This work, moreover, contains much information on the historical development of the language and on the ancient dialects. For practical purposes, the more pedagogically oriented grammars of Smyth (1920) or Goodwin and Gulick (1958) contain sufficient information for the understanding of the structure of the language. Vilborg (1960) offers a grammatical sketch of Mycenaean Greek, as does Ventris and Chadwick (1973). More specialised works include Lejeune (1972) (on the historical phonology in general, including Mycenaean), Sommerstein (1973) (a generative treatment of Attic phonology), Teodorsson (1974) (also on Attic phonology) and Chantraine (1973) (on the morphology, especially diachronically). The basic treatment in English of the dialects is Buck (1955).

For the Hellenistic period, the best grammars available are Moulton (1908) and Blass and Debrunner (1961), both of which deal primarily with New Testament Greek.

For Greek of the Byzantine and Medieval periods, unfortunately no standard grammar is available. Perhaps the best general statement on Greek of that period is the (relatively brief) description found in Browning (1982). More is available on the modern language, and many of the historically oriented works fill in some of the gaps in the literature on Middle Greek, Mirambel (1939; 1959) are standard structuralist treatments of Modern Greek, and Householder et al. (1964) provides a useful account in English. Though now a bit outdated, however, Thumb (1964) is the best general work available in English, providing much on the dialects and general historical development of Modern Greek as well as numerous sample texts. Newton (1972) is a study within the generative framework of Greek dialect phonology, including, to a certain extent, the dialect bases of the standard language. Warburton (1970) and Sotiropoulos (1972) provide a modern treatment of the verb and noun respectively. As yet there is no full-length generative study of Greek syntax, though there is a growing body of such literature (see Kalmoukos and Phillipaki-Warburton (1982) for some references, many in English).

Finally, there are several general surveys of the Greek language, covering all or most of the stages in its development. Meillet (1920) and Palmer (1980) focus more on the earlier stages, though both treat Middle and Modern Greek as well. Browning (1982) focuses primarily on the later stages, but gives the necessary background on the early stages too. Mention can also be made of Costas (1936), Atkinson (1933), Thomson (1966), and Householder and Nagy (1972).

References

Atkinson, B.F.C. 1933. *The Greek Language* (Faber and Faber, London)

Blass, F. and A. Debrunner. 1961. *A Greek Grammar of the New Testament and Other Early Christian Literature* (Cambridge University Press, Cambridge; translated and revised by R. Funk from the 9th-10th ed. of *Grammatik des neutestamentlichen Griechisch*, Vandenhoeck and Ruprecht, Göttingen)

Browning, R. 1982 *Medieval and Modern Greek* (Cambridge University Press, Cambridge)

Buck, C.D. 1955. *The Greek Dialects*, revised ed. (University of Chicago Press, Chicago, reprinted 1973)

Chantraine, P. 1973. *Morphologie historique du grec*, 2nd ed. (Klincksieck, Paris)

Costas, P. 1936. *An Outline of the History of the Greek Language with Particular Emphasis on the Koine and the Subsequent Periods* (reprinted by Ares Publishers, Chicago, 1979)

Goodwin, W. and C. Gulick. 1958. *Greek Grammar* (Blaisdell, Waltham, Mass.)

Householder, F., K. Kazazis and A. Koutsoudas. 1964. *Reference Grammar of Literary Dhimotiki* (Mouton, The Hague)

Householder, F. and G. Nagy. 1972. *Greek. A Survey of Recent Work* (Mouton, The Hague)

Kalmoukos, X. and I. Philippaki-Warburton. 1982. 'Βιβλιογραφικό σημείωμα των εργασιών σχετικά με την σύνταξη και την μορφολογία της Νέας Ελληνικής που έχουν εκπονηθεί κατά το πρότυπο της γενετικής μετασχηματιστικής γραμματικής' ('Bibliographic Notice of Works Concerning the Syntax and Morphology of Modern Greek which have been Produced According to the Model of Generative-Transformational Grammar'), *Mantatoforos*, vol. 20, pp. 8–17

Lejeune, M. 1972. *Phonétique historique du mycénien et du grec ancien* (Klincksieck, Paris)

Meillet, A. 1920. *Aperçu d'une histoire de la langue grecque*, 2nd ed. (Hachette, Paris)

Mirambel, A. 1939. *Précis de grammaire élémentaire du grec moderne* (Société d'Édition 'Les Belles Lettres', Paris)

―――― 1959. *La langue grecque moderne: description et analyse* (Paris)

Moulton, J. 1908. *A Grammar of N.T. Greek* (T. and T. Clark, Edinburgh)

Newton, B. 1972. *(The Generative Interpretation of Dialect: A Study of Modern Greek Phonology* (Cambridge University Press, Cambridge)

Palmer, L. 1980. *The Greek Language* (Humanities Press, Atlantic Heights, NJ)

Schwyzer, E. 1939. *Griechische Grammatik, I: Lautlehre, Wortbildung, Flexion* (C.H. Beck, Munich)

―――― and A. Debrunner, 1950. *Griechische Grammatik, 2: Syntax und syntaktische Stilistik* (C.H. Beck, Munich)

Smyth, H. 1920. *A Greek Grammar for Colleges* (American Book Co., New York)

Sommerstein, A. 1973. *The Sound Pattern of Ancient Greek* (Basil Blackwell, Oxford)

Sotiropoulos, D. 1972. *Noun Morphology of Modern Demotic Greek* (Mouton, The Hague)

Teodorsson, S.-T. 1974. *The Phonemic System of the Attic Dialect, 400–340* BC (= Studia Graeca et Latina Gothoburgensia XXXVI, Göteborg)

Thomson, G. 1966. *The Greek Language,* 2nd ed. (Heffer, Cambridge)

Thumb, A. 1964. *A Handbook of the Modern Greek Language: Grammar, Texts, Glossary* (Argonaut Inc., Chicago; translated from the 2nd ed. of *Handbuch der neugriechischen Volkssprache. Grammatik. Texte. Glossar*, Karl I. Trübner, Strassburg)

Ventris, M. and J. Chadwick. 1973. *Documents in Mycenaean Greek*, 2nd ed. (Cambridge University Press, Cambridge)

Vilborg, E. 1960. *A Tentative Grammar of Mycenaean Greek* (= Studia Graeca et Latina Gothoburgensia IX, Göteborg)

Warburton, I. 1970. *On the Verb in Modern Greek* (Mouton, The Hague)

8 URALIC LANGUAGES

Robert Austerlitz

The term 'Uralic' refers to a language family with one large branch, Finno-Ugric, and one smaller one, Samoyedic. Each branch is further subdivided into sub-branches and these into individual languages. *Finno-Ugric* is often used in its wider meaning of Uralic. Though this is sanctioned by usage, it will be avoided here. Equally inaccurate is a vague association of Uralic with Turkic languages. (See page 228.) Ural-Altaic is a superstructure, a unit larger than a family (also called stock or phylum).

The best known Uralic languages are Hungarian, with some fourteen million speakers, Finnish with some five million, and Estonian with about one and a half million. These are also the populations which are most thoroughly integrated into the European cultural and economic community.

Hungarian and Finnish are related only remotely, while Finnish and Estonian are related much more intimately. The network which unites the entire family genetically can be seen in figure 8.1.

In terms of numbers of speakers of the remaining Uralic languages, Mordva is the largest, followed by Mari and Udmurt.

In terms of positions on today's political map, only Finnish and Hungarian are spoken completely outside the confines of the USSR. The bulk of the speakers of Lapp live in Norway and Sweden; about 1,500 live in Finland and another 1,500 in the Soviet Union. All of the other Uralic languages are spoken in the Soviet Union. For general geographical locations, see the accompanying map.

In terms of very broad cultural features, the Hungarians are Central Europeans, the Finns, and to some extent, the Lapps are Fenno-Scandians, the Estonians and the other Baltic-Finnic speakers are Balts. The Mari, Mordva and Udmurt are agrarian populations. Komi culture occupies an intermediate position between that of the central-Russian agrarians and a sub-Arctic form of living. The Ob-Ugrians and the Samoyeds were, until this century, sub-Arctic peoples, as were the northernmost Lapp.

The family tree of the Uralic languages (figure 8.1) shows that this is a closely-knit family in the accepted sense. Only two questions are still awaiting resolution: (1) The precise position of Lapp within the family. This

Figure 8.1: The Uralic Language Family

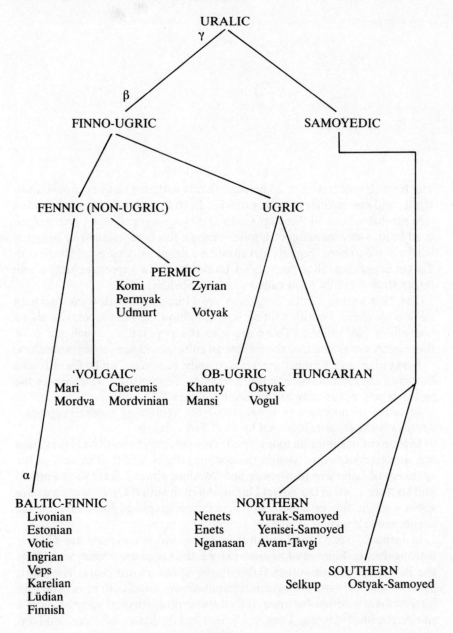

Map 8.1: Location of Uralic Languages

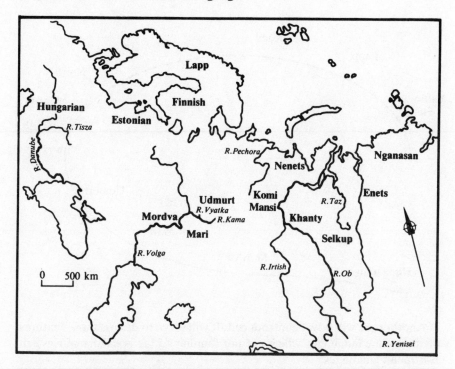

group of languages has been considered Baltic-Finnic (node α), Finno-Ugric (node β), a separate branch of Uralic (node γ) and a 'mixed language', a vague term which generates further questions. (2) The precise relationship between Mordva and Mari.

The Uralic languages can also be plotted along an ear-shaped geographical arc extending from Fenno-Scandia and the Baltic in the West, extending eastward over the Kola peninsula into the basins of the Pechora, Ob and Yenisey rivers. At that point the arc is broken. It begins again in the Volga-Kama basin and ends, after another break, into the Carpathian basin (see figure 8.2). The model of this arc can also serve as a device for visualising the order in which the forebears of the speakers of today's Uralic languages separated out of early family groupings and ultimately out of the original proto-language. The generally accepted order is: Samoyed (estimates of the date of separation range from the fourth to the second millennium BC); Ugric, which split into an early form of Hungarian on the one hand and the language which later developed into Khanty and Mansi on the other. The last group to split up was Permic, around the seventh or eighth century AD. Hypothetical dates for the formation of the individual Baltic-Finnic languages as well as the proto-history of the Mari and the Mordva remain in dispute.

Figure 8.2: Schematic Location of Uralic Languages

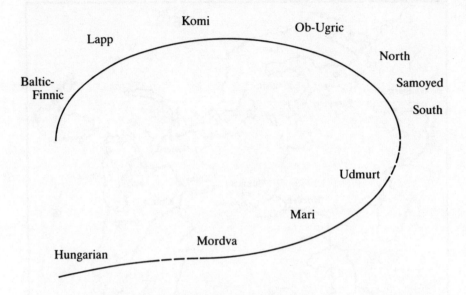

Another arc will now be introduced. It will serve to discuss those features of the Uralic languages which are not familiar to the speakers of western European languages.

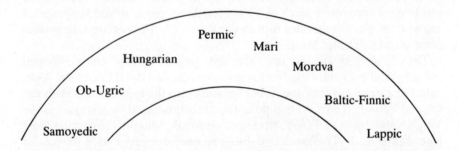

Consonant gradation is a prominent phenomenon in Baltic-Finnic and Lapp. Thus, -*nt*- (strong grade) in Finnish *anta-vat* 'they give' alternates with -*nn*- (weak grade) in *anna-n* 'I give'. Originally, the strong-weak opposition correlated with open versus closed syllable, as in this Finnish example. Traces of this phenomenon can be found in Mordva and Mari. It is absent from the other languages.

The only typically Uralic grammatical feature found in the Permic languages is the so-called negative conjugation: Komi *o-g mun* 'I do not go', *o-z mun* 'you (sg.) do not go', *e-g mun* 'I did not go'. In this construction it is not the main verb (*mun* 'to go'), but the auxiliary negative verb (present *o-*, past *e-*) which is conjugated (*-g* 'I', *-z* 'you (sg.)'). Mari, Mordva, some of the Baltic-Finnic languages, and the Samoyedic languages (except Selkup) also have such a device for negating the verb.

Vowel harmony occurs in Hungarian, in some of the Baltic-Finnic languages and in various degrees of development elsewhere (Mordva, Mari, Khanty, Samoyedic). It is absent from Permic and Lapp. The rules of vowel-harmony require that only specific subclasses of vowels coexist in a non-compounded word. Thus, in Finnish, the sign of the third person plural is *-vat* and *-vät* as in *anta-vat* 'they give' and *kyntä-vät* 'they plough' (read *y* as *ü*); cf. Hungarian *lop-nak* 'they steal' vs. *tör-nek* 'they break'. The vowel of the suffix adjusts to the vowels contained in the stem. The specific subclasses of vowels are determined by physiological factors, basically the position of the tongue (front/back) and of the lips (rounded/unrounded).

The grammatical category of the dual ('two of a kind') plays an important role in Ob-Ugric, in Samoyedic and in Lapp. The following Mansi example will also illustrate the possessive suffix of the third person singular, *-et-* 'his/her', and the instrumental case, *-l* 'with': *aamp-ay-et-l* 'with his two dogs' (*-ay-* is the dual, 'two'). In Lappic, the dual occurs only in pronouns and in the verb. The dual, then, is found only in the languages at the two extremes of the arc and can be thought of as closing the circle.

Another typological feature, reference to a specific object within the verbal complex (also called the objective conjugation), is more difficult to place on the arc: it predominates on the left (Ugric, Samoyedic) but is also found in Mordva. The details of this feature differ strongly from one subgroup to another. Essentially, it signals the presence of a specific object, e.g. Hungarian *lop-j-uk* 'we steal it' as against *lop-unk* 'we steal' (without reference to a specific third-person object in the latter).

Mordva and Hungarian also have a definite article. In Hungarian *a ház* 'the house' the article *a* precedes the noun and is separable from it (*a kék ház* 'the blue house'), as in English. In Mordva *kudo-ś* 'house-the' the article is suffixed, as in the Scandinavian languages and some Balkan languages.

The basic and still prevalent rule of word order in the Uralic languages is subject–object–verb (SOV). However, this rule is rigid only in Ob-Ugric and in Samoyedic — on the left side of the arc — while Baltic-Finnic languages are basically SVO. The other languages have so-called free word order. Thus, in Hungarian, all permutations are possible: *A fiúk krumplit lopnak* 'the boys are stealing potatoes' (lit. 'the boys potato[-object] steal'), *krumplit lopnak a fiúk, lopnak a fiúk krumplit, lopnak krumplit a fiúk, a fiúk lopnak krumplit* and *krumplit a fiúk lopnak* can all occur under specific circumstances. The nuances of meaning expressed are in the areas of emphasis and focus. Those languages which lack this sort of syntactic elasticity have other ways of expressing emphasis and focus, generally particles which attach to specific parts of the sentence.

All of the Uralic languages have a set of spatial cases which convey such meanings as 'in', 'from', 'to' etc. The languages richest in this respect are Hungarian and Permic. In Baltic-Finnic and Lapp one such local case, the partitive, which originally meant 'from' has acquired the additional function of partitive object, as in French, e.g. Finnish *juo-n maito-a* 'I am drinking milk' (lit. in French, *bois-je lait-du)*' as against *juo-n maido-n* 'I am drinking (the) (entire quantity of) milk (which has already been specified in the discourse)'. The *-n* in *maido-n* is the accusative case marker. The more archaic function of the partitive (*-a*) can be seen in *taka-a* '(movement) from behind (something)'; contrast *taka-na* '(which is) behind'. Also in Finnish, all negative objects must be in the partitive, e.g. *e-n juo maito-a* 'I do not drink milk'; a sentence such as **e-n juo maido-n* (with the object in the accusative) is impossible.

Some of the salient features of the sound systems of the Uralic languages are: (1) word stress on the first vowel of the word, with the notable exception of Udmurt, where it falls on the last (and less striking exceptions in Mordva, Mari, Komi and Permyak); (2) vowel systems with reduced vowels: Mari, Ob-Ugric, Northern Samoyedic; (3) vowel systems with front rounded vowels (*ü, ö*): Baltic-Finnic, Mari, Hungarian (and, in a less developed form, in Khanty). Vowel systems with back unrounded vowels: Estonian (and some other Baltic-Finnic languages), Permic. A vowel system with both front rounded and back unrounded vowels is found in Selkup. (4) A correlation of palatalisation: Mordva, Permic, Samoyedic. (5) Rich systems of affricates: Hungarian, Permic, Selkup. (6) A correlation of voice in the obstruents: Hungarian, Permic, Lapp (rudimentary in Mordva).

Each Uralic language has a constellation of typological features of the kind discussed above which is unique unto itself and which lends it its own particular profile. The features themselves evolved and crystallised during the historical development of each individual language for a variety of reasons — the economy of the phonology and grammar of each language, stimuli from other, related or unrelated, languages or combinations of the two. One task of the specialist is to peel off the layers of each Uralic language and to find correspondences among subsets of related languages. Such correspondences eventually permit the reconstruction of a parent language. By the same token, it is the task of the specialist to identify innovations in each language.

One tractable approach to the history of each of the Uralic languages is the study of loanwords — vocabulary items which entered each individual language in the course of its history as a result of contact with other languages and cultures. All of the Uralic languages have loanwords from Slavonic, acquired relatively recently. All of the Finno-Ugric languages have loans from Iranian or perhaps even Indo-Iranian, acquired so long ago that it is thought that they entered the proto-language and were passed on to its descendants along with the native vocabulary. One such item is Finnish *sata*, Hungarian *száz* 'hundred', an item which has implications for early commercial contacts between the two parties.

Table 8.1 gives a synoptic view of the lending and the borrowing parties.

Table 8.1: Loanwords in Uralic Languages

	Later Iranian	East Turkic	West Turkic	Baltic	Germanic Older	1200–	Slavonic
Samoyedic	+	+					+
Ob-Ugric	+	+					+
Hungarian	+	+	+			+	+
Permic	+	+	+				+
Mari	+	+	+				+
Mordva	+	+	+	+			+
Baltic-Finnic				+	+	+	+
Lapp				+	+	+	+

The systematic comparison of the Finno-Ugric languages amongst themselves has provided a glimpse into both the structure of an earlier, hypothetical Proto-Finno-Ugric language and, through it, of some aspects of the culture of the population which spoke this language. Analogously, the same has been done for the Samoyedic languages. The comparison of Proto-Finno-Ugric with Proto-Samoyedic, then, affords an insight into the still earlier Proto-Uralic hypothetical language. Table 8.2 displays the data on

Table 8.2: A Proto-Uralic Reconstruction

URALIC							
	SAMOYEDIC		South	Kamassian Selkup	t'en čɔt, tən	Proto-Samoyedic: *cən	Proto-Uralic: *sənе
			North	Nganasan Enets Nenets	taŋ ti/tino- teʔ/ten-		
	FINNO-UGRIC	UGRIC	Ob-Ugric	Khanty Mansi Hungarian	ton, lan, jan taan, tən ín/ina-	Proto-Finno-Ugric: *sone, *soone, *səne	
		FENNIC	Permic	Udmurt Komi	sən sən		
			(Volgaic)	Mari Mordva	šün, śün san		
			Balto-Finnic	Livonian Estonian Finnish	suón/suonə- soon/soone- suoni/suone-		
	LAPP			Lapp	suodnâ/suonâ-		

which such a step-by-step comparison is carried out. The word in question is thought to have meant 'vein' but may also have meant something like 'sinew' and thus carries suggestions about the use of the objects denoted — archery, fishing equipment and the like. What can be reconstructed in the area of vocabulary has analogues in grammar. Proto-Uralic probably had a nominative (or absolute case, with no overt marker), an accusative, a genitive, at least three local cases (locative, allative, ablative), adverbial cases (with such meanings as 'with'), aspect (or tense) in the verb, an imperative and possibly an impersonal form of the verb.

Bibliography

Harms (1974) is a careful, comprehensive survey of the family. Among more extensive surveys, Hajdú (1975) provides a historically orientated introduction; Comrie (1981) discusses the phonology, grammar, typology and sociolinguistics of the Uralic languages of the USSR; Collinder et al. (1957) provides descriptive sketches and texts from thirteen languages — to be used with caution. Décsy (1965) is the basic text, on historical and comparative principles and rich in detail; the comparative grammar by Collinder (1960) is idiosyncratic but comprehensive.

References

Collinder, B. 1960, *Comparative Grammar of the Uralic Languages* (Almqvist & Wiksell, Stockholm)
—— et al. 1957. *Survey of the Uralic Languages* (Almqvist and Wiksell, Stockholm)
Comrie, B. 1981. 'Uralic Languages', in B. Comrie, *Languages of the Soviet Union* (Cambridge University Press, Cambridge, pp. 92–141
Décsy, Gy. 1965. *Einführung in die finnisch-ugrische Sprachwissenschaft* (Otto Harrassowitz, Wiesbaden)
Hajdú, P. 1975. *Finno-Ugrian Languages and Peoples*, translated and adapted by G.F. Cushing (André Deutsch, London)
Harms, R.T. 1974. 'Uralic Languages', in *The New Encyclopaedia Britannica: Macropaedia*, vol. 18 (Encyclopaedia Britannica, Chicago), pp. 1022–32

9 Hungarian

Daniel Abondolo

1 Introduction

Hungarian (native name *magyar*) is the only Uralic language spoken in central Europe. In terms of number of speakers, Hungarian ranks twelfth among the languages of Europe: c. 10 million in Hungary and c. three million elsewhere in Europe, mostly in Rumania, Czechoslovakia and Yugoslavia. There are also about one million Hungarian speakers elsewhere, mostly in the United States and Canada.

Because it is a Uralic language, Hungarian is typologically unlike the majority of European languages. But paradoxically, Hungarian is also atypical among the Uralic family. It is by far the largest, disproportionately so, in the sense that more than half of all speakers of Uralic languages speak Hungarian. It has both a rich vocalism (14–15 vowels) and a rich inventory of voiced/voiceless oppositions in its consonantism (which includes four affricates). Most of its inflectional morphemes are innovations. Its syntax boasts an impressive set of coordinating conjunctions. The array of foreign elements in its lexicon rivals that of Gypsy (Romany). Unlike Finnish, Hungarian has no close relatives; the Ob-Ugric languages, traditionally bundled together with Hungarian into the Ugric subgroup of the Uralic family, are radically different from Hungarian in their phonology, syntax and vocabulary.

This singular character is due to one decisive difference: migration by the Proto-Hungarians, first southward from the Uralic Urheimat into the maelstrom of cultures in the South Russian steppe, then westward into the heart of Roman Christian Europe.

This rudimentary sketch outlines only a few of the more salient features of Hungarian grammar and lexicon. In order to compress the presentation without sacrificing accuracy of detail, the following typographic conventions have been observed: suffixes are written to the right of a hyphen (-) if inflectional, of an equals sign (=) if derivational. A double equals sign (==) marks a coverb to its left.

2 Sounds and Orthography

2.1 Vowels

The short vowels are *i*, *e*, *a*, *o*, *u* and the front rounded *ü*, *ö*, marked with umlaut as in German. These seven vowels are sounded much as in German, with two important exceptions: *e*, which is an open vowel resembling the *a* of English *mat*; and *a*, which is pronounced with a slight rounding of the lips, as in English *chalk*.

Nearly one half of Hungarian speakers distinguish an eighth, short *e*-type vowel like that of English *met*; this sound is written throughout this chapter (and in Hungarian dialectology) as *ë*, for example: *szëg* 'carpenter's nail' (rhymes with English *beg*). For speakers who distinguish this sound, this word differs in pronunciation from the verb *szeg-* 'break' somewhat as English *set* differs from *sat* (in the Hungarian words, however, both vowels are equally short).

The long vowels are indicated in the orthography with an acute accent (*í*, *é*, *á*, *ó*, *ú*) or, if marked with umlaut when short, with a double acute accent, a diacritic unique to Hungarian (*ű*, *ő*). Phonetically, these seven long vowels are simply longer versions of their short counterparts, again with two important exceptions: (1) *é* is *not* a long version of *e* (which would be the *ä* of literary German *gäbe*), but rather a long high *e*-sound similar to the first *e* of German *gebe*; and (2) *á* is not a long version of *a*, which would have lip-rounding as in English *caught*, but rather is a long open unrounded *a*-sound as in German *Gabe*. The vowel system of Hungarian is set out in table 9.1.

Table 9.1: Hungarian Vowel Phonemes

i	ü	u		í	ű	ú
(ë)	ö	o		é	ő	ó
e	.	a				á

The salient assimilatory phenomenon associated with the Hungarian vowels is called vowel harmony. This is a mechanism which, at one time, regulated the quality (front vs. back) of vowels within the word, but which today affects only suffixal vowels. Over-simplifying, we may state that stems containing only front vowels select front-vowel variants of suffixes (e.g. *szűr-tök* 'you (pl.) strain'), while other stems select back vowel variants (e.g. *szúr-tok* 'you (pl.) pierce'). An important exception is the class of verb roots whose sole vowel is *i* or *í*, most of which take back vowel suffix forms (e.g. *ír-tok* 'you (pl.) write'). Note also that oblique stem vowels of nouns (see section 3.2) play a decisive role in suffix vowel selection, e.g. *híd-ról* 'off (the) bridge' (and not *híd-ről: this noun has an oblique stem *hida-* with back vowel *a*).

Vowel harmony also affects the roundedness of vowels in certain suffixes. For example, the second person plural suffix (*-tök/-tok* above) is *-tëk* after unrounded front vowels: *ér-tëk* 'you (pl.) arrive'.

Another prevalent vowel alternation is that of the short mid vowels (*o*, *ö*, *ë*) with zero. This alternation is evident in allomorphy such as that of the accusative suffix, which is *-ot/-öt/-ët* (according to vowel harmony, cf. above) after labials, velars, apical stops and affricates and consonant-final oblique stems, but *-t* after vowels and apical continuants (*r, l, ly/j, n, ny, sz, s, z, zs*). Sample accusative forms:

ostrom-ot	'siege'
hercëg-ët	'duke'
ökr-öt	'ox' (citation form *ökör*)
korbács-ot	'scourge'
lakat-ot	'(pad)lock'
ládá-t	'crate'
hajó-t	'ship'
jege-t	'ice' (citation form *jég*)
mája-t	'liver' (citation form *máj*)
lakáj-t	'lackey'
gúny-t	'mockery'

2.2 Consonants

The consonant system and its regular orthographic representations are given in table 9.2.

Table 9.2: Hungarian Consonantism

phonemes					*orthography*			
		r					r	
	l	j				l	j,ly	
m	n	ń			m	n	ny	
p	t	t́	k		p	t	ty	k
b	d	d́	g		b	d	gy	g
f	s	š	h		f	sz	s	h
v	z	ž			v	z	zs	
	c	č				c	cs	
	ʒ	ǯ				dz	dzs	

In modern Hungarian, *j* and *ly* (originally a palatal lateral) are pronounced alike. Noteworthy are the oppositions palatal vs. non-palatal among the oral and nasal stops (t vs. t́, d vs. d́, n vs. ń) and sibilant vs. shibilant among the apical fricatives and affricates (s vs. š, z vs. ž, c vs. č, ʒ vs. ǯ). From the historical point of view, the development of the opposition of voice (p vs. b, f vs. v etc.) is particularly striking (within Uralic, it is developed fully only in the rather distantly related Permic languages — see the chapter on Uralic languages).

The most conspicuous assimilatory phenomena affecting the consonants centre on the above outlined three oppositions. Thus: (1) unpalatalised /t/ followed by palatal /ń/ yields the palatal sequence /t́ń/, e.g. *cipő-t nyer* /cipőt́ńer/ 'wins (a pair of) shoes'; (2) sibilant /z/ followed by shibilant /ž/ yields the shibilant sequence /žž/, e.g. *tíz zsaru* /tīžžaru/ 'ten cops'; (3) distinctively voiced /z/ followed by distinctively voiceless /s/ yields the voiceless sequence /ss/, e.g. *tíz szarka* /tīssarka/ 'ten magpies'.

Other assimilatory phenomena include (a) combinations of the above three types; thus (1+3) /t/ + /d/ yields /d́d́/, e.g. *cipő-t gyárt* /cipőd́d́ārt/ 'manufactures shoes', (2+3) /z/ + /š/ yields /šš/, e.g. *tíz saru* /tīššaru/ 'ten (pairs of) sandals'; and (b) adaffrication, e.g. /t/ + /š/ yields /čč/, e.g. *rét=ség* /rēččēg/ 'meadow +(collective/abstract suffix)' = 'meadowlands'.

3 Inflection

3.1 Conjugation

Every Hungarian conjugated verb form may be analysed as consisting of three parts: (1) a stem, followed by (2) a tense/mood suffix, followed by (3) a person-and-number suffix. The four forms of the verb *mën-* 'go' listed below, all with second person plural subject, illustrate the four tenses/moods occurring in the present-day language:

present	mën-Ø-tëk	'you (pl.) go'
past	mën-te-tëk	'you (pl.) went'
conditional	mën-né-tëk	'you (pl.) would go'
subjunctive	mën-je-tëk	'you (pl.) should go; go!'

The suffix of the present tense is zero (-Ø-). The suffixes of the past, conditional and subjunctive are subject to considerable formal variation, conditioned by the phonological and grammatical make-up of the morphemes which flank them. Compare the various shapes of the subjunctive suffix (-ja-, -je-, -já-, -j-, -zé-, -s-, -Ø-) in the following forms (the list is not exhaustive):

vár-ja-tok	'you (pl.) should wait'
mér-je-tëk	'you (pl.) should measure'
vár-já-l	'you (sg.) should wait'
vár-j-on	'(s)he/it should wait'
néz-zé-l	'you (sg.) should watch'
mos-s-on	'(s)he/it should wash'
mos-Ø-d	'you (sg.) should wash it'

The person suffixes present a complex and intriguing picture. Each person suffix refers not only to the person and number of the subject (as, for example, in Latin, Russian or Finnish), but also to the person — but not the number — of the object. Certain suffixes are explicit and unambiguous with regard to the person of the object; for example, the first person singular suffix -$l_a^e k$ refers explicitly, and exclusively, to a second person object: *lát-lak* 'I see you' (more precisely, *lát-Ø-lak* 'see-present-I/you'). On the other hand, certain other suffixes are ambiguous with regard to object person and indeed need not refer to any object whatsoever. For example, the form *lát-Ø-nak*, built with the third person plural suffix -$n_a^e k$, may be translated as 'they see me', 'they see you', 'they see us', or simply 'they (can) see (i.e. are not blind)'. The form *lát-Ø-nak* is explicit with regard to object person only in a negative sense: the object cannot be a specific third person object known from the context, that is, this form cannot mean 'they see him/her/it/them'.

One way to think about object-person marking in Hungarian is to arrange the persons (first, second, and third) on a concentric model with first person (the speaker) at the centre (figure 9.1). A form such as *lát-Ø-lak* 'I see you'

Figure 9.1

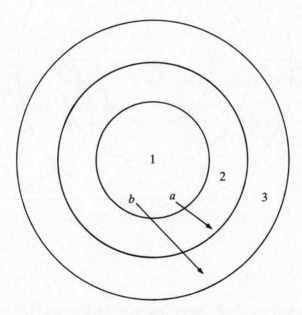

may then be plotted on the model as an arrow which starts at the centre (subject = first person) and points outward (object = second person); see arrow *a* in figure 9.1. All forms having such centrifugal orientation on the model are unambiguous with regard to object person. It follows, therefore, that there is a separate form meaning 'I see him/her/it/them', namely *lát-Ø-om*, symbolised by arrow *b* in figure 9.1.

Similarly, the form *lát-Ø-ja* '(s)he/it sees him/her/it/them' is also unambiguous with regard to object person, since the object is invariably third person. Such a form is also centrifugal in orientation, since there is an unlimited supply of potential third person subjects. The arrow representing this form points outward into the realm of other third person objects, schematically 3*a* in figure 9.2:

Figure 9.2

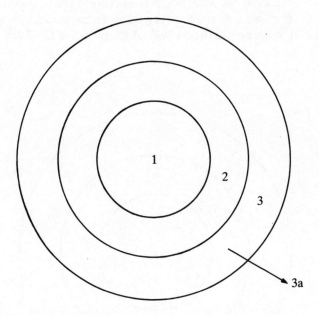

Conversely, suffixes which are ambiguous with regard to object person show only inward-pointing arrows on the concentric model and may therefore be termed centripetal. For example, the form *lát-Ø-nak* cited above may refer to a first or a second person object (arrows *a* and *b* in figure 9.3) or to no object at all (point *c* in figure 9.3).

Figure 9.3

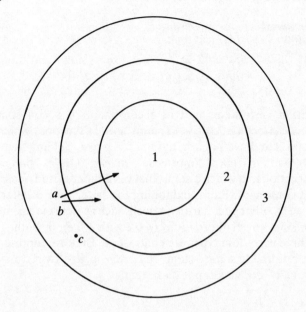

The seven singular forms of the present tense of the verb *lát-* 'see' may therefore be presented synoptically as in figure 9.4.

Figure 9.4

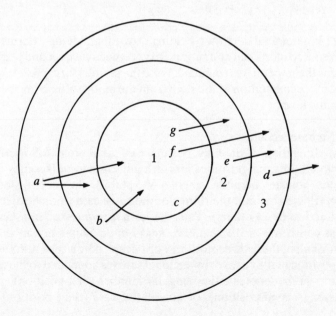

These forms (*a* to *g* in figure 9.4) are:

	Centripetal		Centrifugal
(a)	lát-Ø-Ø	(d)	lát-Ø-ja
(b)	lát-Ø-sz	(e)	lát-Ø-od
(c)	lát-Ø-ok	(f)	lát-Ø-om
		(g)	lát-Ø-lak

All Hungarian verb stems end in a consonant or a consonant cluster. Alternations characteristic of verb stems are (1) syncope, which deletes a short mid vowel to the left of a stem-final *z*, *l*, *g* or *r*, yielding stem alternates such as *rögtönöz-/rögtönz-* 'improvise', *hízelëg-/hízelg-* 'flatter'; and (2) *v*-stem alternations, in which a stem-final *v* is either deleted or assimilates to a following consonant. Stems exhibiting the latter type of alternation are characterised by other peculiarities as well, such as stem extension (with =*sz* or =V*d*) or stem vowel alternations (*o ö ë* with *ó ő é*), or both.

Below, three verb stem types are contrasted. They are represented by (a) *ver-* 'beat', a non-alternating stem, (b) *pëdër-/pëdr-* 'twirl', a syncopating stem and (c) *tëv-* 'do, make, put', a *v*-stem.

	a	*b*	*c*
1	ver=és	pëdr=és	tëv=és
2	ver-Ø-tëk	{ pëdr-Ø-ëtëk / pëdër-Ø-tëk }	të=sz-Ø-tëk
3	ver-né-tëk	{ pëdr-ené-tëk / pëdër-né-tëk }	tën-né-tëk
4	ver-je-tëk	pëdër-je-tëk	tëgye-tëk
5	ver-j-Ø	pëdër-j-Ø	tégy-Ø

Form 1 is a nominal derivate: 'beating', 'twirling', 'doing'. Forms 2, 3 and 4 are present, conditional and subjunctive, respectively, second person plural; form 5 is the imperative (singular). Note the parallel forms (b2, b3). In forms c4 and c5, segmentation of the stem from the mood suffix is impossible at the phonemic level.

3.2 Noun inflection

Every Hungarian noun may be analysed as a stem followed by three inflectional slots, i.e. positions in which inflectional suffixes may occur. The first slot indicates number (singular vs. plural), the second slot indicates person (possessor) and the third slot indicates case (direct object, indirect object and some 14 others). Thus the form *hajóimon* 'on my ships' may be seen as consisting of the sequence *hajó-i-m-on* 'ship-s-my-on'.

Any or all of these three slots may be occupied by a zero suffix. According to its position in the chain of inflectional suffixes appended to the noun stem, this zero suffix denotes either singular number (first position), absence of possessor (second position), or nominative case (third position). Thus we have: *hajó-Ø-m-on* 'ship-Ø-my-on' = 'on my ship', *hajó-k-Ø-on* 'ship-s-Ø-on' = 'on ships', *hajó-i-m-Ø* 'ship-s-my-Ø' = 'my ships'. Notice that the plural suffix is *-i-* when second position is occupied by a person/possessive suffix but *-k-* when second position is occupied by zero (i.e. no possessor).

The case suffixes may be classified into two basic groups, local and non-local. The local cases form a neat system defined by concrete spatial and kinetic oppositions such as interior vs. exterior, stationary vs. moving etc., shown schematically in table 9.3.

Table 9.3: Locative Cases

		Stationary		Moving Approach		Depart
Interior		1 $-b_a^e n$	2	$-b_a^e$	3	$-b\acute{o}l$
	Surface	4 $-n$	5	$-r_a^e$	6	$-r\acute{o}l$
Exterior	Proximity	7 $-n_a^\acute{e} l$	8	$-h_{\ddot{o}}^{\ddot{e}} z$	9	$-t\acute{o}l$
	Terminus		10	$-ig$		

A few concrete examples will illustrate the meanings of these cases. Within the category 'moving/approaching' (the middle column in table 9.3) four degrees of intimacy are distinguished: suffix 2 (illative) indicates movement into an interior, e.g. *fal-ba* 'into (the) wall'; suffix 5 (sublative) indicates movement onto a surface, e.g. *fal-ra* 'onto (the) wall'; suffix 8 (allative) indicates movement into an immediate proximity, e.g. *fal-hoz* '(moving) over to the space immediately next to (the) wall'; and suffix 10 (terminative) indicates movement as far as, but no farther than, a point in space, e.g. *fal-ig* 'as far as (the) wall but no farther'.

The non-local cases normally express primary syntactic or adverbial functions, e.g. subject, direct and indirect object, possessor or instrument. The traditional names of these cases can be quite misleading; the so-called dative ($-n_a^e k$), for example, may mark not only the indirect object, but also the possessor or a predicate construed with an infinitive. Note the dative form of the noun *katona* 'soldier' in the sentences:

(1) Odaadta a katonának. 'He gave it *to the soldier*.'
(2) A katonának nehéz az élete. '*A soldier's* life is difficult.'
(3) Katonának lenni nehéz. 'To be *a soldier* is difficult.'

The other non-local cases are: nominative ($-\emptyset$); accusative ($-t$); essive ($-_u^{\ddot{u}} l$, e.g. *cél-ul* '(considered) as a goal'); causal/final (*-ért*, indicating the efficient or final cause, e.g. *hazá-ért* '(sacrificed his life) for (the) fatherland'); instrumental ($-v_a^\acute{e} l$, e.g. *olló-val* 'with (a pair of) scissors'); and translative

(-vá, indicating transformation into another state, e.g. *só-vá* '(turned) into salt'). The *v* initial in the last two suffixes assimilates to a preceding consonant, e.g. *olló-m-mal* '(pair of) scissor(s)-my-with' = 'with my scissors', *kenyér-ré* '(turned) into bread'.

In contrast to verb stems, noun stems may end in either a consonant or a vowel. The vowel may be any save *o*, *ö*, *ë* or *á*; the consonant may be any save *dz*, but *dzs*, *zs*, *ty*, *f* and *h* are rare.

All stems with final *a* or *e* exhibit lengthening of this vowel before most suffixes, whether declensional or derivational. Examples: *alma/körte* 'apple'/'pear', *almá-m/körté-m* 'my apple'/ 'my pear', *almá=s/körté=s* 'containing apples'/'containing pears'. This is by far the largest class of vowel-final noun stems. It contains more than 1,200 underived stems (like *alma* and *körte* above) and thousands of derivates such as *jár=da* 'sidewalk' (from the verb *jár-* 'be in motion, walk'), *cukor=ka* 'bonbon' (from *cukor* 'sugar'), *pëng=e* 'blade' (from the verb *pëng-* 'ring, clang').

There is also a closed set of nearly 500 stems which exhibit a special stem form only when followed by certain suffixes. This special stem form, termed here for convenience the 'oblique stem', differs from the nominative singular (citation form) by the presence of a stem-final *a* or *e*, the absence of a stem-penultimate *o*, *ö* or *ë* or both. For example: from their nominative singular forms, it would appear that the nouns *dal* 'song' and *fal* 'wall' are parallel in shape and, presumably, inflectional pattern. This is not so, however, because *fal*, unlike *dal*, has an oblique stem with final *a*, namely *fala-*; compare the accusative forms *dal-t*, *fala-t*. Similarly, *nyomor* 'misery' and *gyomor* 'stomach' display different inflectional patterns because the latter noun has an oblique stem which lacks the penultimate *o*, namely *gyomr-*; compare the accusative forms *nyomor-t*, *gyomr-ot*. Finally, some noun stems (about 115) exhibit both types of alternation simultaneously, e.g. *sátor* 'tent', in the oblique stem of which we find at once the absence of the penultimate *o* and the presence of final *a*; contrast *sátra-m* 'my tent' with *mámor-om* 'my rapture'.

Nouns whose oblique stems have final *a* or *e* may be subclassified according to additional alternations. For example, it was noted above that the oblique stem of the noun *fal* 'wall' differs from its nominative singular only by virtue of a stem-final *a*; this is not the case with the noun *falu* 'village', whose oblique stem has not only a final *a* but also *v* instead of *u*, namely *falva-*, as in the form *falva-k* 'villages'. Contrast a stem such as *kapu* 'gate', which has no oblique stem and therefore forms its plural simply as *kapu-k* 'gates'. Another characteristic subtype of oblique-stem alternation involves the long vowels *á* and *é*, which when penultimate in the oblique stem occur as short *a* and *e*, e.g. *madár* 'bird', oblique stem *madara-*, thus: *madara-k* 'birds'.

Broadly speaking, the oblique stem of a noun occurs only to the left of derivational suffixes and older declensional suffixes. This distribution in the present-day language reflects the historical fact that most nouns which now exhibit oblique stems date from at least Ugric and often Finno-Ugric or even Uralic times. An important exception to this distribution is the derivational suffix =*i*, which normally requires the nominative singular form of the stem, e.g. *madár=i* 'avian', *fal=i* 'wall-' as in *fal=i óra* 'wall-clock'.

4   Derivation

Both the verb and the nominal are capable of extensive derivation. Examples of nominal derivation: *ház* (oblique stem *háza-*) 'house'; *ház=i* 'domestic'; *háza=s* 'married'; *ház=i=as* 'homely'; *háza=tlan* 'houseless', especially in the construction *háza=tlan csiga* 'houseless snail' = 'slug'; *háza=cska* 'cottage'; *ház=beli* 'tenant'. Examples of verbal derivation: *fog-* 'seize, grasp'; *fog=ad-* 'accept'; *fog=an-* 'become pregnant, conceive'; *fog=dos-* 'handle, paw at'; *fog=lal-* 'occupy'; *fog=lal=koz-* 'occupy oneself'.

Combined verbal and nominal derivatives are extremely common, e.g. *öle=l=és* 'embrace (noun)', cf. *öle=l-* 'embrace (verb)' and *öl/öle-* 'lap, space between shoulders and knees'; *ad=ag=ol-* 'measure out', cf. *ad=ag* 'portion' and *ad-* 'give'.

Verbal derivation is especially enriched by the coverbs, which are a special class of adverb-like forms. Like preverbs in Slavonic languages, Hungarian coverbs are connected with aspect; like verbal prefixes in German, they are not always to be found in preverbal position (see section 6). The change in meaning effected by the addition of a coverb may be obvious (e.g. *jön* 'comes': *vissza==jön* 'comes back') or less than obvious (e.g. *meg==jön* 'comes (back) to one's proper place (as was hoped/expected)'). Often, the role played by a coverb (or by its absence) is entirely outside the limits of the sentence in which it occurs/is lacking; for example, in the sentence pair

(1) Mikor vetted meg azt a cipőt?
(2) Mikor vetted Ø   azt a cipőt?

both translatable as 'when did you buy those shoes?', sentence (1) is a sincere request for information, while sentence (2) may veil criticism of the shoes' appearance.

5   Lexicon, History

The existence of Hungarian independent of its closest congeners Mansi and Khanty is reckoned to be some 2,500 to 3,000 years old. Evidence of early forms of Hungarian may be found in documents only for the last millennium of this period. The earliest such documents are Arab, Persian and Byzantine political and geographical tracts in which Hungarian personal and tribal names are cited in isolation. While extremely useful as historic and linguistic sources, such documents contain no connected passages of Hungarian. The oldest source to contain a running text in Hungarian is the *Halotti Beszéd* (Funeral Oration), c. 1200, a free — and elegant — translation of a Latin text contained in the same codex.

The first 1,500 to 2,000 years of the Hungarian language can be studied only indirectly, through the historiography of neighbouring peoples and with the aid of the tools of archaeology, philology, and linguistics. For example, the frequent denomination of the Hungarians as 'Turks' in various early sources (e.g. *toúrkoi* in the mid-tenth century *De Administrando Imperio* of Constantinos Porphyrogennetos) suggests that from the seventh to the ninth centuries at least a part of the Hungarians were under Turkic dominance.

It is the evidence of loanwords, however, which paints the most vivid picture of this long period in Hungarian chronology and culture. The trajectory of migration, first southward, then westward, from the Urals to the Carpathian basin, can be traced in reverse by unpeeling, one by one, the layers of foreign elements in the Hungarian lexicon.

Immediately beneath the rich top layer of pan-Europeanisms such as *atléta* 'athlete', *pësszimista* 'pessimist' are hundreds of loans originating in or mediated through German. Thus, from the eighteenth and nineteenth centuries: *copf* 'braid; pigtail', *púdër* '(cosmetic) powder', *fasírt* 'ground meat' (*falschiert(es) Fleisch*)), *vigéc* 'commercial traveller (slang)' (*wie geht's*), *priccs* 'cot'; from the sixteenth and seventeenth centuries: *lakáj* 'lackey', *prés* 'wine-press', *tucat* 'dozen', *pisztoly* 'pistol'. Older still (twelfth to fifteenth centuries) are such loans as *hercëg* 'duke', *kastély* 'castle', *tánc* 'dance', *céh* 'guild', *polgár* 'Bürger', *ostrom* 'siege, attack' (*Sturm*).

Of loanwords from the Romance languages, the most recent (and thinnest) layer is borrowed from Rumanian. Although the oldest known Rumanian loanword in Hungarian, *ficsúr* 'dandy, fop', dates from the fourteenth century, most are from the sixteenth to the eighteenth centuries: *cimbora* 'pal, crony', *poronty* 'brat', *málé* 'polenta, corn-cake', *tokány* 'a kind of ragoût', *cujka* 'a kind of fruit brandy'.

The richest stock of Romance vocabulary is from Italian. Hungarian-Italian contacts grew in breadth and intensity from military, then trade contacts with Venice in thirteenth-century Dalmatia through the Angevin dynasty (1308–86), culminating in the decidedly Tuscan-oriented rule of Mathias I, 'Corvinus' (ruled 1458–90). Examples: *dús* 'luxurious' (from Venetian *dóse* 'doge', probably by way of Croatian), *paszomány* 'braiding, piping', *piac* 'market-place', *lándzsa* 'lance', *pálya* 'course, track'.

There is also a small set of loanwords from Old French and Provençal dating from the twelfth and thirteenth centuries (later French influence, in the eighteenth and nineteenth centuries, was filtered through Vienna and therefore through German; cf. *púdër* above). Although the earliest French contacts were monastic (Benedictines, Cistercians, Premonstratensians), the earliest Old French loanwords are secular in meaning, e.g. *lakat* '(pad)lock' (*loquet*), *mécs* 'wick' (*mèche*), *kilincs* 'latch' (*clinche*).

Religious vocabulary, not surprisingly, is overwhelmingly Latin in origin, e.g. *templom* 'house of worship', *mise* 'mass', *ostya* 'Host', *angyal* 'angel'. The list extends even to terms exclusively Protestant in implementation, e.g. *ëklézsia* 'congregation', *kollégium* 'dormitory' (originally 'seminary'). Although Latin loanwords belong primarily to the area of Christian terminology, numerous other semantic areas may also be cited, e.g. schooling (*tinta* 'ink', *tábla* 'blackboard', *lénia* 'ruler'), medicine and horticulture (*kúra* 'course of treatment', *petrezselyëm* 'parsley') or jurisprudence (*juss* 'patrimony' from Latin *ius*). Even a few Latin adverbs survive in present-day colloquial Hungarian: *persze* 'of course' (*per sē*), *plánë* 'especially' (*plānē* 'smoothly; really'); note also *ipse* 'fellow, chap' (*ipse* 'he himself'). The time-frame for Latin influence on the Hungarian lexicon is extremely broad: Latin was (at least nominally) the official language of the Kingdom of Hungary from its inception (1001) until the mid-nineteenth century. On the other hand, direct ties to the Christian East were tenuous and short-lived, a fact reflected in the very small number of words borrowed directly from the Byzantine Greek: *paplan* 'quilt', *iszák* 'knapsack', *katona* 'soldier' and perhaps a few others.

The two largest and most important sets of loanwords are those from Slavonic and Turkic languages. It is not surprising, given the geographical location of Hungary, that loans from the Slavonic languages are both numerous (c. 500) and central to basic vocabulary. Examples drawn only from the Hungarian word stock beginning with *p-* are *pad* 'bench', *palack* 'bottle', *pálinka* 'distilled spirits', *pap* 'clergyman', *pëcsënye* 'roast', *patak* 'brook', *pëlënka* 'diaper', *poloska* 'bedbug', *pók* 'spider', *puszta* 'bare, deserted'. Slavonic languages served as mediators for terminology of both Byzantine(-Christian) and Roman Christian culture. Examples of the former: *terëm* '(large public) room', *pitvar* 'porch', *palota* 'palace', *kërëszt* 'cross'; of the latter: *malaszt* 'grace', *apáca* 'nun'. The intensity and variety of contact with different forms of Slavonic may be inferred from doublets internal to Hungarian such as *vacsora* 'evening meal', *vëcsërnye* 'Vespers'; *rozsda* 'rust', *ragya* 'mildew; rust (on plant)'; *mëgye* 'county', *mezsgye* 'boundary-mark between ploughed fields'; *család* 'family', *cseléd* 'servant'.

The Turkic component of the Hungarian lexicon is a unique amalgam of elements borrowed from several different Turkic peoples over a span of some 1,500 years. The most recent layer dates from the Ottoman (Osmanli) occupation (sixteenth and seventeenth centuries); this layer is quite thin (about 30 words), e.g. *zseb* 'pocket', *findzsa* 'demi-tasse', *korbács* 'scourge', *kávé* 'coffee'. An earlier layer, also quite thin, of Turkic loanwords dates from the two or three centuries following the arrival of the Hungarians in Europe (tenth to thirteenth centuries). The words of this layer are borrowed from the languages of the Pechenegs and the Cumans, e.g. *csősz* 'field-guard', *koboz* 'a type of lute', *orosz* 'Russian'.

By far the most numerous and culturally significant, however, are the loanwords taken from Turkic languages during the Hungarian migration westward across southern Russia. Some 300 such loanwords entered during this period (roughly fifth to ninth centuries). A small sampling reveals the cultural breadth and depth of this Old Turkic component of the Hungarian lexicon: *dél/dele-* 'south, noon', *idő* 'time', *szél/szele-* 'wind', *szám* 'number', *ok* 'cause', *tanú* 'witness', *ír-* 'write', *bocsát-* 'forgive', *sátor/sátra-* 'tent', *sëprő* 'broom', *szék* 'chair', *gyümölcs* 'fruit', *szőlő* 'grape', *bor* 'wine', *bika* 'bull', *ökör/ökr-* 'ox', *borjú/borja-* 'calf', *ünő* 'heifer', *disznó* 'pig', *gödény* 'pelican', *kar* 'arm', *boka* 'ankle', *gyomor/gyomr-* 'stomach', *köldök* 'navel', *szakáll/szakálla-* 'beard', *szeplő* 'freckle'.

Older still are three thin layers of Iranian loanwords acquired at the earliest stages of the Hungarian migration. To the most recent of these three layers belong *vám* 'tithe, toll, customs-station' and *vásár* 'bazaar' from Persian; older are *híd/hida-* 'bridge' and *asszony* 'woman (as opposed to girl)', from Alanic (= Old Ossete); and oldest are *tehén/tehene-* 'cow', *tej/teje-* 'milk', *nemez* 'felt', and perhaps *vászon/vászna-* 'linen', from an Iranian language which cannot be precisely identified.

But the oldest layers of the Hungarian vocabulary are of course not borrowed at all; rather, they are descended from the common Ugric, Finno-Ugric or Uralic lexical stock. To these layers belong hundreds of basic vocabulary items from such semantic domains as kinship (*fiú/fia-* 'son', *mëny/mënye-* 'daughter-in-law', *vő/veje-* 'son-in-law', *öcs/öccs(é)-* 'younger brother'); parts of the body (*fej/feje-* 'head', *szëm* 'eye', *nyelv/nyelve-* 'tongue', *ín/ina-* 'tendon', *epe* 'gall', *máj/mája-* 'liver'); natural phenomena (*ég/ege-* 'sky', *hajnal* 'dawn', *tél/tele-* 'winter', *jég/jege-* 'ice', *tó/tava-* 'lake'); animals, hunting and fishing (*fogoly/fogly-* 'partridge', *fajd* 'grouse', *íj/íja-* 'bow', *nyíl/nyila-* 'arrow', *hal/hala-* 'fish', *háló* 'net'); and primary functions and activities expressed by monomorphemic verbs (*lësz/lëv-* 'become', *él-* 'live', *hal-* 'die', *öl-* 'kill', *mëgy/mën-* 'go', *jön/jöv-* 'come', *ëszik/ëv-* 'eat', *iszik/iv-* 'drink').

The statistically preponderant component of the Hungarian lexicon is neither borrowed nor inherited. These words are constructions built from mostly native elements during the independent existence of Hungarian; they range in age and type from unconscious and doubtless quite old onomatopoeic and affective vocabulary (e.g. *rëcs=ëg* 'creak, squeak', *krák=og* 'caw', *mëk=ëg* 'bleat', *hömpöly=ög* 'billow, surge') to conscious creations which often can be attributed to a particular language reformer who either sired or fostered them, for example *vissz+hang* 'back+sound' = 'echo' (Dávid Baróti Szabó, 1739–1819), *könny+elmű* 'light+minded' = 'heedless' (Ferenc Kazinczy, 1759–1831). Thousands of such new terms survived but briefly, e.g. *ibl=any* 'violet+(suffix)' = 'iodine' (Pál Bugát, 1793–1845); in this and countless similar instances, the Hungarian term which prevailed is the Europeanism (*jód* 'iodine').

The creation of new vocabulary of this sort, termed language renewal (*nyelvújítás*), was practised even by its harshest critics, e.g. Ferenc Verseghy (1757–1822) who, on the analogy of verb/noun pairs such as *tag=ol-/tag* 'dismember/member', introduced such new coinages as *gúny* 'mockery', *pazar* 'spendthrift', by subtracting the final *ol*-sequence from the verbs *gúnyol* 'mock' and *pazarol* 'squander'.

6 Syntax

In the noun phrase, demonstratives alone agree in number and case with their head, e.g. *ez-ëk-ben a nagy görög ládá-k-ban* 'in these large Greek crates', where *nagy* 'large' and *görög* 'Greek' lack the plural and inessive suffixes *-(ë)k* and *-bán*. Cumulative plural subjects are usually construed with a singular predicate, especially if they are members of a coherent semantic set, e.g. *a só mëg a bors itt van a ládá-ban* 'the salt and pepper are (lit: is) here in the crate'.

The elements of a Hungarian sentence are ordered according to the textually and contextually determined factors of topic (what is assumed) and focus (the central component of the comment about the topic). Focus position is immediately to the left of the finite verb; topic position is normally sentence-initial. Thus in the sentence *a pék elfutott* 'the baker ran away', the baker (*a pék*) is the topic and 'away' (*el*) is the focus of the comment about him. By relocating the coverb *el*, the baker can be made into the focus: *a pék futott el* 'it is the baker who ran away'. The coverb can also be placed in sentence-initial position and thus be topicalised: *el a pék futott* 'as for (running) away, it is the baker (who did that)'.

The situation is much more complex, however, since certain grammatical and semantic categories are inherently associated with focus, for example negation in the examples *a pék nem futott el* 'the baker did not run away', *nem a pék futott el* 'it is not the baker who ran away', *el nem a pék futott* 'as for (running) away, it is not the baker (who did that)'. Different stress patterns produce different types of contrastive focus, e.g. *a pék nem 'elfutott, hanem 'befutott* 'the baker didn't run *away*, he ran *in*', or *a pék nem el'futott, hanem el'sétált* 'the baker didn't *run* away, he *sauntered* away'. For many speakers, stress also plays a role in the rendering of aspect. Thus if both verb and coverb receive stress in the sequence *a pék futott el* cited above, the meaning is something like 'the baker was (in the act of) running away'.

Bibliography

Three general works on Hungarian can be recommended: Simonyi (1907) is still the best introduction, encyclopaedic and circumstantial; Sauvageot (1971) is an insightful overview, primarily historical; Benkő and Imre (1972) is a general work, whose best chapters are those by Hajdú and Imre. Lotz (1939) is an unsurpassed reference grammar. Given the importance of derivation in Hungarian, the reverse-alphabetised dictionary by Papp (1969) is indispensable.

References

Benkő, L. and S. Imre (eds.) 1972. *The Hungarian Language* (Mouton, The Hague and Paris)
Lotz, J. 1939. *Das ungarische Sprachsystem* (Ungarisches Institut, Stockholm)
Papp, F. 1969. *A magyar nyelv szóvégmutató szótára/Reverse-Alphabetized Dictionary of the Hungarian Language* (Akadémiai Kiadó, Budapest)
Sauvageot, A. 1971. *L'Édification de la langue hongroise* (Klincksieck, Paris)
Simonyi, S. 1907. *Die ungarische Sprache* (Karl J. Trübner, Strassburg)

10 Finnish

Michael Branch

1 Introduction

Finnish (native name *suomi*) is one of a group of closely related and to some extent mutually intelligible languages, known collectively as Baltic-Finnic. They are spoken mainly in the Republic of Finland, the Karelian ASSR (USSR), the Estonian Soviet Socialist Republic, and adjacent areas of the Russian and Latvian Soviet Socialist Republics. The other languages in the group and the numbers of peoples speaking them (according to the 1979 Soviet census figures) are: Karelian, 138,400; Vepsian, 8,100; Ingrian, 700; Estonian, 1,019,900. Of historical interest, but almost extinct are Votic (c. 30) and Livonian (c. 500). Finnish and Estonian are also spoken by migrants and descendants of migrants in Sweden and North America. Of the present-day population of Finland, c. 4,900,000, the vast majority, speak Finnish as their first language. Of the total population of Finland approximately 300,000 Finnish citizens speak Finland-Swedish as their first language and, depending on the statistical source, between 1,500 and 5,000 speak Lapp (*sami*); most speakers of Finland-Swedish and the Lapp dialects of Finland are also competent in Finnish.

The relationship of Finnish to the other major Finno-Ugric language, Hungarian, is described elsewhere in this book (see pages 177–8). Attempts to reconstruct anything more than a relative chronology of the two languages' separate development from ancient Finno-Ugric origins are inevitably speculative, and indeed there remain many uncertainties even about the historical development of the Baltic-Finnic languages. Until recently, scholars had assumed that speakers of a language of Finno-Ugric origin, 'Pre-Finnic', had migrated from regions to the east and southeast, reaching the area of present-day Estonia about 500 BC. There they were thought to have lived for several centuries in close contact first with Ancient Balts and then with groups of East Germanic peoples. According to this theory, about two thousand years ago a group of people speaking 'Proto-Finnic' — a development of 'Pre-Finnic' — was thought to have divided into smaller units which slowly migrated in various directions: south and south-east, north across the Gulf of Finland into Finland proper, and north-east around the Gulf into Ladoga Karelia and thence into eastern Finland or further north and north-east into Olonets and Archangel Karelia. It was further thought that the northern lands into which these groups had migrated were largely empty of population apart from groups of Lapps, who had moved north ahead of the Baltic-Finnic newcomers and who spoke a language that derived, probably through borrowing, from 'Pre-Finnic'.

In recent years, comparative multidisciplinary research has led to substantial revision of this theory. Archaeologists have shown that Finland has been continuously inhabited for at least 8,000 years; comparative linguists and ethnographers now believe that speakers of Germanic and Baltic languages have inhabited various parts of the lands now occupied by speakers of the Baltic-Finnic languages for at least the last 3,500 years. Thus the early theory of a clearly stratified hierarchy of language contact and development has given way to one of a mosaic of sporadic contacts over a far longer time and probably of greater influence in shaping the grammar, syntax and lexicon of the Baltic-Finnic languages than had earlier been thought possible.

A number of dialects, from which present-day Finnish took shape, were probably being spoken in southern and western Finland in the early centuries AD. The available evidence indicates an area of small, isolated settlements, inhabited by hunters and fishermen; wandering northwards they began to combine pastoralism with food gathering and then slowly adapted to a primitive agricultural way of life, largely dependent on burn-beat cultivation. In the southern coastal regions contacts were formed with traders coming from the east and Vikings from the west. Although fragments of Christianity began to penetrate from the east during the late dark ages, the inhabitants' religious world-view appears to have been shamanistic, and it was not until the twelfth century, with the Swedish Crusades, that efforts were made to replace this ancient world-view with that of Roman Catholic Christianity. At the same time a centrally based system of government was instituted which demanded faith in the Christian deity, loyalty to a ruler, service to those in authority and the payment of taxes. The confluence in Finland of influences from various directions and their impact on Arctic and sub-Arctic cultures account for the present-day east-west distribution of linguistic, anthropological and ethnographical distinctive features along an axis running north-west from the region of Viipuri in the south to Oulu in the north; historically and politically this division was fixed by the Treaty of Schlüsselburg signed between Sweden and Novgorod in 1323. Although there have been various changes in the frontier since then (notably in 1595, 1617, 1721, 1743, 1809 and 1944), none of these has altered in any significant way the east-west linguistic, anthropological and ethnographical division.

Since the late middle ages the dominant political and cultural influences that have shaped — and preserved — Finnish were religion and nationalism.

The earliest written record known to survive in a Baltic-Finnic language is a spell written in a Karelian dialect, and dated to the thirteenth century. Although there is sufficient evidence from secular and non-secular sources to show that Finnish was in use as a written language during the late middle ages, when the Church of Rome was still dominant, the earliest surviving specimens of continuous passages in Finnish date from the 1540s with the publication in 1542 of Bishop Mikael Agricola's *Abckiria* ('ABC book'), the first known printed book to appear after the declaration of the Reformation in Finland in 1527. This was followed by various liturgical and biblical works written or translated in a 'literary' language which was codified from dialects spoken in south-west Finland and which was to remain the canonical form of Finnish until the early nineteenth century.

The growth of a national consciousness that began at the end of the eighteenth century awoke among a small but influential number of intellectuals a desire to cultivate a distinctive Finnish national identity rooted in the Finnish language. This ideal gained powerful momentum early in the nineteenth century when Finland became a Grand Duchy in the Russian Empire, and the following generation of nationalists took as their aim the elevation of Finnish to equal standing with Swedish as a language of government, trade, commerce, education and culture. This aim was achieved in 1863 with the issue of the Language Edict. A literary language, codified in the course of the nineteenth century, retained much of the old canon, although its structure and lexicon were revised and standardised to take account of the dialects of Eastern Finland that had acquired prominence through the publication in 1835 and 1849 of Elias Lönnrot's compilation of oral epic poems, *Kalevala*.

Finnish shares with Hungarian a rich vocalism, but unlike Hungarian it has relatively few consonant phonemes. It is an agglutinative language with a complex but consistent regularity in its morphophonology; inflectional suffixes, of which a large number have cognates in most other Finnic-Ugric languages, account for a wide range of grammatical functions, while a large stock of derivational suffixes provides a productive source of word creation. Of particular interest in the structure of Finnish is the case system and the variety of finite and non-finite verbal categories. (In the present description of the characteristic features of Finnish, the typographic conventions used in the chapter on Hungarian have been observed (i.e. suffixes are written to the right of a hyphen (-) if they are inflectional, or to the right of an equals sign (=) if they are derivational.))

2 Phonology and Orthography

The orthography of standard Finnish is for the most part phonetic. With three exceptions each letter represents a single phoneme; with two exceptions all sounds are marked orthographically. If a letter is written twice, it indicates that quantity is double the length of a single sound.

2.1 Vowels

Finnish has eight monophthong phonemes and sixteen diphthong phonemes. The short front vowels are *ü* (*y* in orthography), *ö* and *ä*; *i* and *e* are regarded as 'neutral' vowels in respect of vowel harmony; the back vowels are *u*, *o* and *a*. The front vowel *ä* is pronounced as in English *bad*; the other two front vowels are pronounced as in German. The back vowels are pronounced as in English *pull*, *hot* and *father*. The neutral vowels *i* and *e* are as in English *hit* and *pet*. Each of these sounds can be pronounced long, doubling the quantity but not changing the quality.

Table 10.1: Finnish Vowel Phonemes

Monophthongs	i		y	u		ii		yy	uu
	e		ö	o		ee		öö	oo
		ä		a			ää		aa
Diphthongs	ei		äy	eu					
	äi								
	ui								
	ai			au					
	oi			ou					
	öi		öy						
	yi								
	ie								
			yö	uo					
				iu					

With the exception of certain recent loanwords, the vowels in a Finnish word are subject to partial assimilation. This phenomenon, known as *vowel harmony*, requires that all the vowels of a word are front or back depending on the category of the vowel in the first syllable of the word. In compound words vowel harmony affects each lexical component separately, e.g. *työaika*: *työ* 'work' + *aika* 'time'. This assimilatory phenomenon determines suffix-vowel selection in those inflectional and derivational suffixes which allow front/back vowel opposition: e.g. *pöydä-llä* 'on the table' but *tuoli-lla* 'on the chair'. In compound words vowel harmony in suffixes is determined by the vowel category of the final lexical component. Each neutral vowel word has a fixed requirement for front or back suffixal forms determined on historical grounds: e.g. *silmä-llä* 'with an eye' but *silla-lla* 'on the bridge'; *elä-mä-llä-än* 'by his/her life' but *ehdo-i-lla-an* 'on his/her conditions'. On the basis of such oppositions some scholars classify the neutral vowels as each having front and back allophones: the /e/ opposition has a cognate in

Estonian front *-e* and back *-õ-*, while the /i/ variation can be compared with a similar phenomenon in Hungarian (see pages 186–7).

2.2 Consonants

The consonant system has 15 phonemes and 13 letters. Letters preceded by an asterisk (*) occur only in foreign toponyms and commercial brand names or in very recent loans; for many speakers the pronunciation of these sounds will vary between the non-Finnish sound and an assumed Finnish correspondent. A hyphen to the right of a consonant (e.g. h-) indicates that it occurs only in syllable-initial position, to the left (-h) only in syllabic-final positions; hyphens on either side (-d-) indicate that the sound can occur only in a word-medial position. Underlining indicates that the item also occurs as a long sound and in orthography is written twice.

Table 10.2: Finnish Consonant Phonemes

Phonemes					Orthography				Recent loans		
	r					r					
	l	j				l	j				
m	n	-ŋ-/-ŋŋ-			m	n	nk/ng				
p	t		k	-ʔ	p	t	k	∅	*b	*d- *g-	
	-d-					d					
	s		h- -h			s	h	h	*f	*š	
v					v(w)						*z
									*ts/*c *tš		

The pronunciation of the consonant phonemes is close to that of English. The lack of voiced/unvoiced opposition among the stops, of an apical sibilant *s* (Finnish *s* is more palatalised than general European *s*) and of an unvoiced labio-dental *f*, however, results in less marked opposition between the distinctive categories. Thus Finnish *v* is more labialised than in English. The final-position glottal stop /ʔ/ represents a former /k/ that occurred word-finally after /e/ and as a component of suffixes marking the final sound of the short infinitive (e.g. *haluta* 'to want') and certain negative and imperative forms. In spoken Finnish the glottal can be heard if followed by a vowel sound; otherwise it assimilates with a following consonant to form a long sound: e.g. *perhe saapuu* pronounced /perhessaapuu/ 'the family arrives'; *en käytä maitoa* /enkäytämmaitoa/ 'I don't take milk'. Partial assimilation occurs at word juncture where a final dental nasal is followed by a bilabial stop, e.g. *talonpoika* /talompoika/ 'farmer'.

2.3 Quantity and Syllable Structure

Opposition between a long and short sound is an important distinctive feature (e.g. *tapan* 'I kill', but *tapaan* 'I meet'; *tuli palaa* 'the fire burns' but *tuuli palaa* 'the wind returns'). A syllable may have only one vowel sound. The minimum component of a syllable is a vowel (i.e. a short or long monophthong or a diphthong). A syllable ending in a vowel is classified as 'open': e.g. *vai/ke/a* 'difficult', *sa/no/a* 'to say', both of which have three syllables. The second syllable type, classified 'closed', comprises [vowel +consonant] or [consonant+vowel+consonant]: e.g. *Hel/sin/ki/in* 'to Helsinki', which has four syllables. Variation in the 'open' or 'closed' status of a syllable is determined by the addition of inflectional and derivational suffixes and frequently causes a phonological change at the word stem (see sections 3.1.1 and 3.1.2).

2.4 Stress
The main stress falls on the first syllable of a word, with decreasing secondary stress on the third and fifth syllables; similarly sentence intonation is generally falling, although there may be a small rise at the beginning of the final word or constituent.

3 Inflection

3.1 The Word Stem
Morphophonemic alternation at the juncture of the word stem is a characteristic feature of Finnish. It is determined by the phonology and environment of derivational and inflectional suffixes and accounts for the 85 declension classes and 45 conjugation classes identified in the definitive dictionary of Finnish, *Nykysuomen sanakirja*. In respect of morphophonemic alternation this classification into nominal and verbal categories is functional, serving the purpose of convenient grammatical description. In effect, the 130 classes listed in the *Nykysuomen sanakirja* represent the narrow realisation of regular phonemic change conditioned by specific morphological and phonemic environments.

The phonemic features underlying this complex set of realisations at the end of the word stem are consonant gradation, total or partial consonant assimilation, vowel mutation, and vowel loss (Holman's terminology). They can operate either singly or in various combinations. The environment in which they operate is determined by stress, which varies according to the syllable in which the stem juncture is located (see section 2.4), and by the phonology of the set of suffixes added to the word. In distinguishing between various forms of the narrow realisation account must also be taken of the historical development of Finnish and in certain cases of the irregular selection of alternative forms to avoid ambiguity. An example of this is the change, or lack of change, in situations where the sounds /t/+/i/ combine, yielding either *-si-* at a very early period (e.g. *ves-i-llä* 'on the waters', *halus-i* 'wanted') but *-ti-* at a later period (e.g. *tina* 'tin', *vuot-i* 'leaked'). The difference between the noun forms is explained by historical period (i.e. the change *ti* > *si* had ceased to be effective by the time the Germanic **tina-* had entered Finnish), but it is the need to avoid homonymic clash that accounts for the variation in the verbal forms (**vuosi* would conflict with the noun *vuosi* 'year').

Suffixes are added to an oblique stem. Every Finnish word has an oblique stem ending in a vowel. In many words this is the only stem and for nominals it is often identical with the nominative case which is also the dictionary referent (e.g. *yö* 'night', *talo* 'house', *asema* 'station', *ruskea* 'brown'). For those verbs which have only one oblique stem the stem is identified by removing the infinitive marker from the dictionary referent, i.e. the short 1st infinitive (e.g. *syödä* → *syö-* 'eat', *sanoa* → *sano-* 'say', *lähteä* → *lähte-* 'depart'). In certain nominals, however, the vowel of the oblique stem differs from that of the nominative: e.g. *järve-* 'lake' but nominative *järvi*, *suure-* 'large' but nominative *suuri*. In such cases the stem vowel should be considered primary and the vowel of the nominative stem as the result of sound change in final, unmarked positions. As with the /t/+/i/ feature discussed above, such change is historically determined, as can be seen from comparison of *risti* 'cross', which has the oblique stem *risti-* (a Slavonic loan adapted to the prevailing phonological system of early Finnish by simplification of the initial consonant cluster through consonant loss and of the final cluster through the addition of *-i*). Since *risti* entered Finnish at a time when the *-e* > *-i* change in final unmarked position was no longer operative on new items, the nominative form also functions as the oblique stem.

Several classes of Finnish nominals have, in addition to an oblique stem ending in a vowel, a second oblique stem that ends in a consonant; the stem to which suffixes are added is determined by the morphophonemic environment. Nominals of this type fall into two main categories: those in which the nominative ends in a vowel and those in which it ends in a consonant; in each sub-category the stem to be used is environmentally determined. Examples of the first category are: *tuli* 'fire', vowel stem *tule-* (e.g. genitive *tule-n*), consonant stem *tul-* (e.g. partitive *tul-ta*); *pieni* 'small', (*piene-*, gen. *piene-n*, partitive *pien-tä*); *lumi* 'snow', vowel stem *lume-* (e.g. gen. *lume-n*), consonant stem *lun-* (e.g. partitive *lun-ta*). Examples of consonant-ending nominatives are *sydän* 'heart', vowel stem *sydäme-* (e.g. gen. *sydäme-n*), consonant-stem *sydän-* (partitive *sydän-tä*); *punainen* 'red', vowel stem *punaise-*, consonant stem *punais-* (e.g. *punaise-n*, *punais-ta*).

Reference has already been made to verbs that have only one oblique stem. Similarly, however, there are categories of verbs which also have vowel and consonant stems, whose selection is determined by comparable morphophonemic environmental features. An example of the verb type with a single oblique stem is *puhua* 'to speak' (e.g. *puhu-n* 'I speak', *puhu-kaamme!* 'let us speak'). Sub-categories of the two-stem type are illustrated by *ansaita* 'to earn' and *levätä* 'to rest': vowel stems *ansaitse-* (e.g. *ansaitse-n* 'I earn'), *lepää-* (e.g. *lepää-t* 'you. (sg.) rest'); consonant stems *ansait-* (e.g. *ansait-kaa!* '(you pl.) earn!'), *levät-* (e.g. *levät-kööt!* 'let them rest').

3.1.1 Consonant Gradation

Alternation caused by consonant gradation affects the stops /k/, /p/ and /t/. The type of alternation depends on the length of the stop and on whether it occurs alone and intervocalically or as the first or second component of an intervocalic cluster of which the other consonant is /m/, /n/, /ŋ/, /l/, /r/, or /h/. Alternation is classed as qualitative or quantitative; a qualitative alternation changes the sound, whereas in a quantitative alternation it is the length of the stop that changes. The operation of alternation is dependent on the status of the stem syllable as determined by the morphophonemic environment: an open syllable requires the strong grade of the alternation, a closed syllable the weak grade, though subsequent changes have sometimes obscured the original environment. Thus there is in Finnish a strong/weak gradation correlation with open/closed syllable form (see page 206). The most common examples of gradation are illustrated in table 10.3.

Table 10.3: Finnish Consonant Gradation

		Strong		Weak	
Quantitative					
kk	~ k	akka-	~	akassa	(inessive 'old woman')
pp	~ p	piippu-	~	piipusta	(elative 'pipe')
tt	~ t	matto-	~	maton	(genitive 'mat')
Qualitative					
t	~ d	vete-	~	vedestä	(elative 'water')
k	~ Ø	ruoka-	~	ruoan	(genitive 'food')
k	~ v	suku-	~	suvulla	(adessive 'family')
p	~ v	lupa-	~	luvatta	(abessive 'promise')
mp	~ mm	kampa-	~	kamman	(genitive 'comb')
nt	~ nn	tunte-	~	tunnen	('I feel')
nk	~ nŋ	hanke-	~	hangella	(adessive 'snow crust')
lt	~ ll	multa-	~	mullassa	(inessive 'soil')
rt	~ rr	saarta-	~	saarramme	('we surround')

Less frequent forms of gradation in standard Finnish are *ht ~ hd, lke ~ lje, rke ~ rje, hke ~ hje*; further variations occur in dialects.

3.1.2 Other Changes at the Stem

Partial consonant assimilation affects intervocalic *-t-* and causes the change *-t-* → *-s-* in an environment in which it is followed by *-i-* (allowing for the variation described in section 3.1). In nominals this environment arises most commonly from the change of final *-e* → *-i* and from the suffixing of the oblique plural marker, e.g. stem *käte-* 'hand', nominative singular *käsi*, adessive plural *käs-i-llä* 'with the hands'. In verbal forms the environment usually arises from the suffixing of the imperfect *-i-* marker to those categories of verbs that have a consonant stem (see section 3.1), e.g. consonant stem *levät-* 'rest', imperfect *lepäs-i* 'rested'.

Total consonant assimilation at the stem occurs only in verbal morphology and affects the consonant stems ending in *-t-*, *-n-*, *-l-* and *-r-* when suffixes are added to mark the active indicative past participle (*-nut/-nyt*), the active potential mood suffix (*-ne-*), the 1st short infinitive *-ta/-tä* suffix type, and the passive-impersonal present voice of verbs of the same category. In the case of past participles and the potential, total assimilation also occurs in *-s-* consonant stems. The influence of total assimilation in these occurrences is either regressive or progressive. In the case of *-t-* stems, assimilation is regressive after suffixing of the past participle and potential markers (e.g. *levät-* → *levän-nyt, levän-ne-*) but is progressive in its influence on the infinitive and passive-impersonal forms (e.g. *levät-ä, levät-ään*). Total assimilation is progressive in all four verbal forms where the stem consonant is *-n-*, *-r-* or *-l-* (e.g. *pan-* 'put, place' → *pan-nut, pan-ne-, pan-na, pan-naan*; *kuul-* 'hear' → *kuul-lut, kuul-le-, kuul-la, kuul-laan*; *sur-* 'grieve' → *sur-rut, sur-re-, sur-ra, sur-raan*) and in the two forms affecting consonant stems in *-s-* (e.g. *pes-* 'wash' → *pes-syt, pes-se-*).

Vowel mutation or vowel loss at the word stem is caused by the suffixing of *-i-*; in nominals this arises most commonly from the oblique plural suffix, in verbs the *-i-* sound functions as the imperfect tense suffix and as a component of the conditional mood suffix (*-isi-*). In most instances the result of this suffixing is phonemically determined irrespective of nominal or verbal categories. The short stem vowels subject to loss or mutation are *-a-*, *-ä-*, *-e-* and *-i-*. In two-syllable words stem *-a-* labialises if the vowel of the first syllable is *-a-*, *-e-* or *-i-* (e.g. *kirja-* 'book', inessive plural *kirjo-i-ssa; maksa-* 'pay', 3rd person singular imperfect *makso-i*); if the vowel of the first syllable is labial (*-o-* or *-u-*), the stem vowel is lost (e.g. *kunta-* 'group(ing), region', inessive plural *kunn-i-ssa; osta-* 'buy', imperfect *ost-i*). Where the stem vowel of a two-syllable word is *-e-* or *-ä-*, the vowel is always lost (e.g. *isä-* 'father', adessive plural *is-i-llä; kiittä-* 'thank, praise', imperfect *kiitt-i, saare-* 'island', adessive plural *saar-i-lla; näke-* 'see', imperfect *näk-i*).

In nominals only a stem *-i-* mutates to *-e-* (e.g. *viini-* 'wine', inessive plural *viine-i-ssä*). In verb forms only, stem vowels *-a-* and *-ä-* mutate to *-e-* in the formation of the stem form of the passive-impersonal voice (e.g. *hoita-* 'care for', passive-impersonal present *hoide-taan; estä-* 'prevent', passive-impersonal *este-tään*). Both these features also occur in all other syllables of nominals and verbs respectively in the specific categories described. Apart from these specific categories, the short stem vowels discussed above are normally lost in words of more than two syllables when an *-i-* is added; the only exception is *-a-* which in certain vowel and consonant environments may labialise (e.g. *asia-* 'thing', adessive plural *asio-i-lla*).

The result of suffixing *-i-* markers to a long monophthong or diphthong is shortening of the monophthong or mutation of the diphthong. In the case of all long monophthongs, irrespective of the syllable in which the stem is located, the *-i-* sound becomes the second component of the resulting diphthong (e.g. *maa-* 'land', inessive plural *ma-i-ssa*; *saa-* 'obtain', imperfect 3rd person singular *sa-i*; *saappaa-* 'boot', inessive plural *saappa-i-ssa*; *pelkää-* 'fear', conditional present 3rd person singular *pelkä-isi*; *venee-* 'boat', inessive plural *vene-i-ssä*; *kaunii-* 'beautiful', adessive plural *kauni-i-lla*; *talkoo-* 'group work', adessive plural *talko-i-lla*). A diphthong can occur as a stem vowel in monosyllabic words only. From a synchronic point of view the effect of an *-i-* marker on such stems (unless the second component of the diphthong is also *-i-*) appears to work differently, causing loss of the first component of the diphthong (e.g. *yö-* 'night', inessive plural *ö-i-ssä*; *luo-* 'create', imperfect 3rd person singular *lo-i*; *tie-* 'road, way', adessive plural *te-i-llä*). As each of these diphthongs has evolved from a long monophthong, however (i.e. **öö*, **oo*, **ee* respectively, cf. Estonian cognates *öö*, *loo-*, *tee*), the effect of suffixing the *-i-* sound is historically consistent with the long-monophthong examples. Where diphthong stems end in *-i-*, the stem *-i* can be assumed to have been lost (e.g. *voi-* 'be able', imperfect 3rd person singular *vo-i*). In dialects, alternative realisations of these sound changes are common. A rare example of an alternative realisation becoming established as the canonical form is the imperfect and conditional present of *käy-* 'go, visit' (e.g. 3rd person singular *kävi*, *kävisi*). More common is the destabilising influence of alternative realisations on the standard language, illustrated by the variants *myi-* and *möi-* as acceptable forms for many speakers of the imperfect of *myy-* 'sell'.

3.2 Verbal Morphology and Usage

The finite forms of the Finnish verb comprise two voices, active and passive-impersonal. Each voice has four moods: indicative, potential, conditional and imperative. The indicative mood has four tenses, two primary and two secondary. The primary tenses are the present-future (non-preterite in Holman's classification) and the imperfect; the secondary tenses, formed with the auxiliary *olla* 'to be' and a past participle, are the perfect and pluperfect. The potential, which conveys the possibility of something happening, and the conditional each have one secondary form based on the auxiliary *olla* and a past participle. Apart from certain fixed forms of expression, the potential mood has fallen out of common use in the modern spoken language and occurs with decreasing frequency in modern written usage. Various secondary forms of the imperative can also be construed but their realisation in normal usage is very rare; the use of the imperative in certain specific situations is also decreasing (see section 3.2.2).

3.2.1   Active Voice

In the active voice an inflected verb form can comprise up to four components in fixed sequence. Slot 1: *stem* (including any embedded derivational suffix). Slot 2: *tense/mood suffix*. Slot 3: *number-and-person suffix* (historically both items are present but have undergone partial fusion in the 1st and 2nd persons). Slot 4: *enclitic suffixes*. Back/front variation occurs in vowel components as a result of vowel harmony. Depending on the particular emphasis of a statement and the syntactic environment, the 1st or 2nd personal pronoun can also be used as a separate item in other parts of the sentence either before or after the verb, depending on the nature of the emphasis required. When the subject of the 3rd person is the personal pronoun *hän* 'he, she' or *he* 'they (animate)', the pronoun must be used (except in the imperative mood). The variation in the use of the personal pronouns is probably explained by the fact that the suffixes of the 1st and 2nd persons evolved from suffixing pronominal items to the verb, whereas 3rd-person forms of the active voice appear to derive from an active present participle suffix. Some scholars argue that the [verb + personal suffix] structure of the 1st and 2nd person markers has its realisation in the 3rd person in the passive-impersonal voice, and would prefer to classify the latter as the 4th person of the active voice (see section 3.2.2).

The basic verbal morphological structure, excluding Slot 4, is illustrated in the chart given here, in which the present-future tense of the verb *puhua* 'to speak' is conjugated.

The Present-future Tense of *puhua*

Personal pronoun	Slot 1 Stem	Slot 2 Tense/mood suffix	Slot 3 Number/person suffix	Example
[minä]	puhu-	-Ø-	-n	puhun
[sinä]			-t	puhut
hän			stem vowel lengthens	puhuu
[me]			-mme	puhumme
[te]			-tte	puhutte
he			-vat/-vät	puhuvat

This paradigm structure applies to all verb types in the present-future tense with variation only in the formation of the 3rd person singular. Instead of lengthening the stem vowel, verbs with long-vowel or diphthong stems mark the 3rd person singular by -Ø (e.g. stems *jää-* 'remain', *syö-* 'eat', *luetteloi-* 'classify' → 3 sg. *jää*, *syö*, *luetteloi*).

In the imperfect, the tense suffix (Slot 2) is -*i*-, in the potential present the mood suffix (Slot 2) is -*ne*-, and in the present conditional it is -*isi*-, e.g.

imperfect: *puhu-i-n*, *puhu-i-t*, *hän puhu-i* etc. ('I spoke' etc.). In all forms of the imperfect the 3rd p. singular marker is -Ø- (see section 3.1.2).

potential: *puhu-ne-n*, *puhu-ne-t*, *hän puhu-ne-e*, etc. ('I might speak' etc.). As discussed above (see section 3.1.2), a morphophonemic feature of the potential in certain verb types is the use of a consonant stem with regressive or progressive assimilation at the stem juncture (e.g. *tule-* 'come' → potential *tullen*; *nouse-* 'rise' → *nousset*).

conditional: *puhu-isi-n*, *puhu-isi-t*, *hän puhu-isi*, etc. ('I should speak' etc.).

The secondary forms of the active indicative, potential and conditional are formed with the appropriate tenses or moods of the auxiliary *olla* and an active past participle formed from [verb stem + suffix *-nut/-nyt*, plural *-neet*]. Where the participle is formed from a consonant stem, regressive or progressive assimilation at the stem juncture occurs in specific morphophonemic environments (e.g. *ole-* 'be' → *ollut*, plural *olleet* 'been', see section 3.1.2). The conjugation of the auxiliary *olla* follows the above pattern but with two differences: the 3rd person forms of the present-future tense are *on* and *ovat* respectively, and in the potential mood the auxiliary is the cognate *liene-* 'might be', e.g.

perfect: *olen*, *olet*, *hän on puhu-nut*, *olemme*, *olette*, *he ovat puhu-neet*;
pluperfect: *olin puhunut*, etc.; potential perfect: *lienen puhunut*, etc.;
conditional perfect: *olisin puhunut*, etc.

Negation in all the above forms is based on a negative auxiliary: [*e-* + person marker] (i.e. *en*, *et*, *hän ei*, *emme*, *ette*, *he eivät*). Tense or mood is indicated by the form of the principal verb. In the present tense this is [verb stem + orthographically unmarked glottal] (e.g. *en puhu*). The imperfect negative is indicated by [negative verb + past participle of the principal verb] (e.g. *en puhunut*, *emme puhuneet*). In the potential and the conditional it is the mood stem that follows the negative auxiliary verb (e.g. potential *hän ei puhune*, *he eivät puhune*; conditional *en puhuisi*, *emme puhuisi*, *he eivät puhuisi*).

Structurally the fourth mood, the imperative, comprises similar components although they have a different morphophonemic realisation. Thus *sano-* 'say' has the forms: 2nd person singular [*sano-* + orthographically unmarked glottal]; 3rd person singular *sano-koon*; plural *sano-kaamme*, *sano-kaa*, *sano-koot* (front vowel variants: *-köön*, *-käämme*, *-kää*, *-kööt*). Similarly, the negative employs an auxiliary *äl-* (thus *äl-ä*, *äl-köön*, etc.) followed by a form of the principal verb, e.g. [*sano-* + orthographically unmarked glottal], in the 2nd person singular, and by the form [principal verb + *-ko/-kö*] (e.g. *sanoko*) in all other forms, e.g. *älä sano* but *älkäämme sanoko*). The function of the imperative tends to be instructional in the 1st person plural and in the second persons, but exhortative in the third persons. In normal modern speech the use of the passive-impersonal voice is more common for the persuasive or exhortative imperative in the 1st person plural. Thus the grammatical imperative *menkäämme!* 'let's go!' is likely to be used in situations where orders are expected to be given and obeyed, whereas in ordinary social situations the passive-impersonal *mennään!* is preferred.

3.2.2 Passive-impersonal

The morphological structure of the passive-impersonal voice has the same pattern as the active voice forms; morphological differences concern the stem (Slot 1) and the number-person suffix (Slot 3). Historically the stem appears to have embedded in it a derivational suffix which once generated a reflexive or medio-passive function. The mood and tense markers are identical with those of the active voice. According to some scholars the person component of the number-person suffix consists of items cognate with the historical form of the 3rd person singular pronoun *hän*. The passive-impersonal verb paradigm is illustrated by *sanoa* 'to say' and *lähteä* 'to depart'.

The Passive-impersonal Voice of *sanoa* and *lähteä*

Present/future	sano-taan	lähde-tään
Imperfect	sano-ttiin	lähde-ttiin
Potential	sano-tta-neen	lähde-ttä-neen
Conditional	sano-tta-isiin	lähde-ttä-isiin
Past participle	sano-tt-u	lähde-tt-y

The negative auxiliary is the 3rd person singular *ei*, while the mood and tense are marked by the appropriate passive-impersonal stem (e.g. present-future *ei sanota*, conditional *ei lähdettäisi*). Regular variation in stem forms and in the length and form of vowels and consonants is explained by the working of consonant gradation, various forms of assimilation, mutation and loss of vowels and consonants (see sections 3.1.1, 3.1.2).

All verbs can occur in the passive-impersonal voice irrespective of their transitivity or intransitivity. In modern literary Finnish a very common function of this voice is to express impersonal general statements of the kind introduced in German by *man* or in French by *on* (e.g. *täällä puhutaan suomea* 'Finnish spoken here'). In modern colloquial language, the use of the passive-impersonal in sentence-initial position is the usual way of expressing the 1st person plural imperative (e.g. *syödään!* 'let's eat!'). When preceded by the personal pronoun *me* 'we', a passive-impersonal form commonly — and in some social groups, always — replaces the active first person plural forms (e.g. *me lähdetään kotiin junalla* 'we shall go home by train', *me oltiin siellä kaksi viikkoa* 'we were there for two weeks'). In active functions of this kind the object of a transitive verb is also marked (e.g. *me nähtiin sinut koulussa* 'we saw you in school', *me ei osteta omenia* 'we shall not buy any apples').

There is a restricted use of the passive-impersonal voice that corresponds to English passive usage. This is found in statements about an action which is performed intentionally by an inferred but unspecified human agent, e.g. *mies pelastettiin merestä* 'the man was rescued from the sea', i.e. the man was saved by some human intervention. If there had been no information about how the man survived or if his escape had been by his own efforts, Finnish would require the use of an appropriately derived verb in the active voice, e.g. *mies pelastui merestä* 'the man saved himself from the sea'.

3.3 Nominal Morphology and Usage

The morphology of the Finnish noun and adjective provides for the expression of five functions. The noun has five slots in fixed sequence. Slot 1: *stem* (including any embedded derivational suffix). Slot 2: *number* (singular vs. plural). Slot 3: *case suffix*. Slot 4: *personal possessor suffix*. Slot 5: *enclitic suffixes*. Demonstratives and adjectives used attributively precede the noun and there is concord in Slots 2 and 3, but they have no marking in Slot 4. Demonstratives and adjectives may have enclitic suffixes independently of the head word.

In Slots 2, 3, 4 and 5, function is indicated by the opposition zero vs. suffix. In Slot 2 zero marks singular. Grammatical plurality is marked by -*t* in the nominative and accusative cases, by -*t*-, -*i*-, or by both in the genitive case, and by -*i*- in all other cases. If a personal possessor suffix is added to the nominative or accusative plural, the -*t* suffix is not used and plurality is indicated by context or syntax, or both, e.g. *poikani on täällä* 'son-my is here', but *poikani ovat täällä*, where the plural verb *ovat* signifies the plural number of homonymic *poikani*.

3.3.1 The Case System

In Slot 3 a zero suffix indicates nominative singular. All other cases are marked. Back/front variation occurs in the vowel component of certain case suffixes as a result of vowel harmony. In the chart showing the case system the front vowel form follows the stroke in the suffix column; in the partitive, genitive and illative cases, variation in the phonemic structure of the suffix is dependent on the class of word stem (see sections 3.1, 3.1.2). The two examples in the chart, *mies* 'man' and *kirja* 'book' illustrate, in addition to vowel harmony and phonemic structure variation, two stem types: *mies* represents one of the types of word that has a consonant and a vowel stem (e.g. *mies*-, *miehe*-), while *kirja* is typical of words that have only a vowel stem (*kirja*-). Where more than one realisation of a suffix occurs, the form most common in standard usage is given. The accusative case has two suffixes in the singular; -*n* marks the accusative of all nouns and adjectives, -*t* that of the personal pronouns (i.e. *minu-t* 'me', *sinu-t* 'you (familiar)', *häne-t* 'him/her') and the interrogative pronoun *kuka* (accusative *kene-t*) 'who'. In the illative case -V- is identical with the stem vowel subsequent to the marking of number; the bracketed form in the translative is used when a personal possessor suffix follows in Slot 4; the bracketed form in the comitative marks attributive adjectives.

The Case System of *mies* and *kirja*

Case	Suffix	Singular	Plural
Nominative	-Ø; -t	mies; kirja	miehet; kirjat
Accusative	-n (-t); -t	miehen; kirjan	miehet; kirjat
Genitive	-n	miehen; kirjan	miesten; kirjojen
General local cases			
Essive	-na/ä	miehenä; kirjana	miehinä; kirjoina
Partitive	-a/ä; -t/ä; -tta/ä	miestä; kirjaa	miehiä; kirjoja
Translative	-ksi (→-kse-)	mieheksi; kirjaksi	miehiksi; kirjoiksi
Interior local cases			
Inessive	-ssa/ä	miehessä; kirjassa	miehissä, kirjoissa
Elative	-sta/ä	miehestä; kirjasta	miehistä; kirjoista
Illative	-Vn; -hVn; -sVVn	mieheen; kirjaan	miehiin; kirjoihin
Exterior local cases			
Adessive	-lla/ä	miehellä; kirjalla	miehillä; kirjoilla
Ablative	-lta/ä	miehellä; kirjalta	miehiltä; kirjoilta
Allative	-lle	miehelle; kirjalle	miehille; kirjoille
Instructive	-in	miehin; kirjoin	miehin; kirjoin
Comitative	-ineen (-ine)	miehineen; kirjoineen	miehineen; kirjoineen
Abessive	-tta/ä	miehettä; kirjatta	miehittä; kirjoitta

There are marked differences in the productivity of the various cases. Apart from the nominative, the cases in most common use are the accusative, genitive, the three so-called general 'local' cases (essive, partitive, translative) and the six specific 'local' cases, which are subdivided into interior (inessive 'in', elative 'from (outside)', illative 'into') and exterior (adessive 'at or near', ablative 'from (outside)', allative 'to, towards'). Certain cases, such as the instructive (e.g. *hampa-in kyns-in* 'with tooth and nail', *kaik-in voim-in* 'with all one's might') and comitative (e.g. *äiti perhe-ineen* 'the mother accompanied by her family'), are only productive nowadays in very restricted areas of usage. The abessive (e.g. *raha-tta* 'moneyless'), for example, occurs productively mainly in non-finite verbal constructions (see section 5.3); used with nominals it has largely given way to prepositional *ilman* (e.g. *ilman rahaa* 'without money'). In addition to its function as the subject of a sentence the nominative singular stands in certain specific environments as object. The most common of these

environments is in marking nouns and adjectives which are the direct object
in affirmative sentences of monopersonal (i.e. 3rd person singular) verbs of
obligation (e.g. *meidän täytyy ostaa kirja* lit.'us-to it is necessary buy-to the
book'), the 2nd persons and the 1st person plural of the imperative mood
(e.g. *osta kirja!* 'buy the book!'), and verbs in the passive-impersonal voice
(e.g. *me ostetaan kirja* 'we buy the book'). If the object is a personal
pronoun or the interrogative pronoun *kuka*, however, it is marked in all
these forms by the *-t* accusative suffix.

   In modern Finnish the accusative of nouns and adjectives is marked in the
singular by the same suffix as the genitive singular. Historically, however,
they are of different origin (acc. *-n* < *-m*). In affirmative sentences the
accusative denotes the object of a resultative action (e.g. *hän osti kirjan* 'he/
she bought the book') and an object that is in itself definite and total (e.g.
hän joi maidon 'he/she drank (all) the milk', cf. partitive object *maitoa*
denoting that only some of the milk was drunk). In normal usage the
difference in accusative and genitive function of the *-n* suffix is made clear by
the contextual and syntactic environment. In the genitive case nominal items
precede the constituent they govern (e.g. *nuoren tytön musta koira* 'the
young girl's black dog'). The second major area of usage of the genitive case
is in the headwords of postpositions (e.g. *talon takana* 'behind the house',
mäen päällä 'on top of the hill'). In certain constructions the genitive has a
dative function. This is most apparent in fixed expressions such as *Jumalan
kiitos* 'God-to thanks', i.e. 'thanks be to God', and in statements of state or
condition of the kind *minun on jano* 'me-to is thirst', i.e. 'I am thirsty'. The
dative function in the expression of obligation occurs with monopersonal
verbs (e.g. *minun pitää äänestää* 'I must vote') and in various constructions
based on the verb *olla* (e.g. *minun on mentävä* 'I have an obligation to go').

   Comparison with other Finno-Ugric languages and the evidence of certain
historically fixed forms indicate that the components of the general local case
suffixes once denoted various perceptions of location and movement. The
essive case appears to have indicated a stationary location (cf. fixed forms
kaukana 'far away', *ulkona* 'outside'). The partitive marked separation,
movement away from the main body or substance (cf. *kaukaa* 'from afar',
ulkoa 'from outside'). The translative, which historically is much younger
than the essive or partitive, appears to have indicated movement towards an
object, a function still found in such forms as *lähemmäksi* 'coming closer',
rannemmaksi 'moving closer to the shore' (e.g. a boat). While comparable
spatial and kinetic features underlie certain of the present-day functions of
these cases, the specific oppositions of location and movement are expressed
with greater precision by the six interior and exterior local cases, in which
some features of the morphology of the general local cases are embedded.
Adessive *-ssa/-ssä*, for example, is thought to derive from internal location
marker *-s* + *n*V, elative *-sta/-stä* from *-s-* + separation marker *-t*V. Similarly
the *-n*V and *-t*V components have been identified in the adessive *-lla/-llä* and

ablative *-lta/-ltä* with the initial *-l-* thought to derive from an exterior locative.

While retaining certain features of their original spatial and kinetic functions all the general local cases have developed additional temporal, syntactic and adverbial functions. The essive denotes various static positional and temporal states, e.g. *hän on opettajana siellä* 'he/she is (in employment as) a teacher there', cf. *hän on opettaja* 'he/she is a teacher (but may not be employed as such)'; *pidän häntä hyvänä opettajana* 'I consider him/her a good teacher', *hän opetti siellä kolmena vuotena* 'he/she taught there for three years'.

In modern Finnish the main function of the partitive case is the marking of various categories of the direct object. The object of any verb in the negative is always in the partitive. In affirmative statements several categories of verbs govern a partitive object (e.g. those expressing emotional values). In opposition with the accusative object, the partitive denotes an incomplete or continuing action (e.g. *Mikko söi kanaa* (partitive object) 'Mikko ate some chicken' but *Mikko söi kanan* (accusative object) 'Mikko ate all the chicken'). Other functions of the partitive include that of subject and predicative, where an indefinite divisible quantity is denoted (e.g. *maitoa* 'some milk', *tulta* 'some fire'). Of the secondary functions performed by the translative, the three most productive are those denoting change of form (e.g. *poika kasvoi mieheksi* 'the boy grew into a man'), time (e.g. *menin sinne kolmeksi kuukaudeksi* 'I went there for three months'), and the expression of purpose or intention (e.g. *poika aikoo lääkäriksi* 'the boy intends to become a doctor').

Schematically the oppositions of exterior and interior space and direction of movement can be represented in part by the same model as for the corresponding cases in Hungarian (see page 193, table 10.3).

Table 10.4: The Finnish Interior and Exterior Local Cases

	Stationary	Moving Approaching	Departing
Interior		-Vn	
	-ssa/ä	-hVn	-sta/ä
		-sVVn	
Exterior	-lla/ä	-lle	-lta/ä

Lacking from the Finnish scheme, compared to that of Hungarian, is the closer definition of exterior location and movement in terms of the oppositions of surface, proximity and terminus. In Finnish such distinctions are either contextually determined or require the use of specific postpositions or, less commonly, prepositions.

The range of spatial, temporal and syntactic functions performed by the interior and exterior local cases can be illustrated by the example of the adessive. Spatially it refers to static position on the surface of an object, e.g. *pöydällä* 'on the table', *seinällä* 'on the wall'. In denoting geographic location it functions often in opposition with the static interior case, the inessive, e.g. *maa* 'earth; land; countryside': inessive *maassa* 'in the earth' but *maalla* 'out in the country'; *koulu* 'school': *koulussa* 'in school' but *koululla* 'somewhere on the school premises (inside or outside)'. In temporal expression the adessive denotes time when or during which an action takes place, e.g. *kesällä voimme uida meressä* 'in summer we can swim in the sea', *ensi viikolla olen ulkomailla* 'next week I shall be abroad'. A third area of function is instrumental, denoting the means of performing an action, e.g. *kaadoin koivun kirveellä* 'I felled the tree with an axe', *kuljen Helsinkiin autolla* 'I shall go to Helsinki by car'. A major area of usage is the expression of ownership corresponding to that of English 'have', e.g. *isällä on suuri saari* 'father has a large island', *lehmällä on vasikka* 'the cow has a calf ').

3.3.2 Personal Possessor Suffixes
The fourth slot in the morphology of the noun is occupied by the suffix of personal possessor. The item possessed and its attributes can be preceded by the genitive of the personal pronoun in the 1st and 2nd persons if particular emphasis is required; in the 3rd person the preceding pronoun in the genitive is necessary (cf. use of personal pronouns in the verbal system, section 3.2.1):

Personal Possessor Suffixes

Personal pronoun	Possession suffix	Example		
[minun]	-ni	inessive	veneessäni	'in my boat'
[sinun]	-si	elative	kirjoistasi	'about your books'
hänen	-nsa/ä	nominative	talonsa	'his/her house(s)'
	-Vn	ablative	ystäviltään	'from his/her friends'
		allative	sisarelleen	'to his/her sister'
[meidän]	-mme	adessive	kirkollamme	'at our church'
[teidän]	-nne	elative	kirjeestänne	'from your letter'
heidän	-nsa/ä	illative	kotiinsa	'to their home(s)'
	-Vn	adessive	saarellaan	'on their island'

In modern Finnish the use of the 3rd person suffix *-nsa/ä* is mainly used to mark the singular and plural of the nominative and accusative, when it is added to the vowel stem, and of oblique cases which end in a consonant. The *vowel + n* suffix marks possession in oblique cases ending in a vowel; the vowel component is the same as that of the case suffix vowel, thus generating a long vowel. Possession in the oblique cases ending in a vowel may also be marked by the *-nsa/ä* suffix, although this is becoming less frequent.

Where a case suffix ends in a consonant, that consonant is totally assimilated regressively by the adjacent consonant of the person suffix (e.g. *talo* 'house', illative *taloon* → *taloosi* 'into your house', *taloomme* 'into our house'. Assimilation of this kind leads to homonymic conflict: *taloni* can be the singular or plural of the nominative or accusative, or it can be the singular genitive of *talo*; function is defined by context and syntax. This same assimilation process also produces forms in which consonant gradation is expected but does not occur (e.g. *puku* 'suit', nom. plural *puvut*, gen. singular *puvun* produce, for example, *hänen pukunsa* 'his/her suit', *pukumme* 'our suits', *pukunne* 'your suits'). The explanation for this homonymic clash and the absence of consonant gradation rests on a theory of the historical fusion of embedded case and plural markers. Comparison with other Baltic-Finnic languages in which the same feature occurs suggests that, at an ancient period before the fusion of the markers was complete, the strong grade in the personal possessor forms occurred as part of the language's normal morphophonemic variation. As the fusion process produced various realisations, analogy and levelling focused on the present strong grade forms which have remained fixed.

4 Lexicon

The vocabulary of modern Finnish has several sources. A large stock of words for which no loan source can be identified dates from an ancient Finno-Ugric phase and from the subsequent era lasting until the division of the Baltic-Finnic languages into their present groups. For the sake of reference this part of the lexicon may conveniently be called 'indigenous'. Throughout this era and subsequently the vocabulary has been extended both by loans and by the spontaneous and conscious operation of the language's derivation mechanisms on indigenous and loan materials alike. In particular, conscious derivation, compounding and calquing have played an important role in the generation of Finnish since the Reformation; and in the past one hundred and fifty years, with the planned cultivation of Finnish, these mechanisms have enabled the language to handle change and innovation in the modern world.

Examples of words belonging to the oldest Finno-Ugric layers of indigenous vocabulary refer to such categories as parts of the body (*käsi* 'arm, hand', *pää* 'head', *silmä* 'eye'), gender differentiation and kinship (*uros* 'male animal', *naaras* 'female animal', *isä* 'father', *emo* 'mother', *miniä* 'daughter-in-law'), environment and survival (*vesi* 'water', *joki* 'river', *kala* 'fish', *kuu* 'moon', *kota* 'shelter, house', *talvi* 'winter', *jää* 'ice', *lumi* 'snow'), and verbs denoting numerous basic activities (*elä-* 'live', *kuole-* 'die', *kaata-* 'fell', *mene-* 'go', *otta-* 'take', *teke-* 'do, make', *näke-* 'see', *tietä-* 'know').

The oldest layer of loanwords shows the influence of Indo-European languages during the Finno-Ugric period (*mesi* 'honey', *sata* 'hundred') and intermittently thereafter. Vocabulary sheds very little light on the nature of the contacts between the ancestors of the speakers of Finnish during the thousands of years separating the Finno-Ugric period and the earliest documentation of their location in the Baltic-Finnic region in the last centuries BC. Loans dating from the so-called Pre-Finnic and Proto-Finnic periods suggest the existence of contacts concurrently with speakers of Ancient Baltic and Germanic over at least one millennium in various areas north, east and south of the Gulf of Finland. Lexical materials from this phase indicate development in social organisation with some evidence of pastoralism and simple agriculture in addition to improved techniques of food gathering. In each set of examples, words of Ancient Baltic origin are given first, with examples of East or North Germanic origin following the semicolon. The main areas of borrowing represent experience and perception of nature (*meri* 'sea', *routa* 'permafrost'; *aalto* 'wave', *kallio* 'rock, cliff', *turska* 'cod'), parts of the body (*hammas* 'tooth'; *maha* 'stomach', *kalvo* 'membrane'), technology (*aisa* 'harness shaft', *kirves* 'axe', *tuhat* 'thousand'; *airo* 'oar', *satula* 'saddle', *keihäs* 'spear', *rauta* 'iron'), dwellings (*lauta* 'plank', *tarha* 'enclosure'; *ahjo* 'forge', *porras* 'step', *tupa* 'hut, room'), livelihood (*ansa* 'trap', *lohi* 'salmon', *herne* 'pea'; *leipä* 'bread', *sima* 'mead', *seula* 'sieve'), social organisation (*heimo* 'tribe', *seura* 'group', *talkoot* 'group labour'; *kuningas* 'king', *kauppa* 'trade', *hallitse-* 'rule, govern'), belief (*virsi* 'sacred song', *perkele* 'devil'; *pyhä* 'sacred', *runo* 'poem', *vihki-* 'make sacred').

As the ancestors of the Finns became established in the area of present-day Finland and the neighbouring regions, new vocabulary was borrowed from both western and eastern sources. Early Slavonic materials entered by various routes. Certain Slavonic loans appear to have been borrowed by Finnish as early as the fifth or sixth century to denote early Christian concepts (e.g. *pappi* 'priest', *pakana* 'pagan') and various features of domestic life (e.g. *palttina* 'linen', *saapas* 'boot'). During the middle ages and later the largest number of Slavonic and, more specifically, Russian loans was borrowed by Karelians who lived under Russian rule and belonged to the Russian Orthodox Church. Some of these loans entered Finnish much later in the eighteenth and nineteenth centuries as a result of closer contacts between Karelians and speakers of the eastern Finnish dialects, and in the late nineteenth and twentieth centuries as Finnish language reformers combined features of western and eastern dialects in their shaping of Finnish into a language of culture, business, government and administration.

For almost a thousand years, from the early middle ages until the present century, Swedish was the largest source of loans. As Finland evolved into a modern European society, Swedish loans were adapted to the phonological system of Finnish to convey new and more precise concepts of religion, government, domestic and economic life, and culture. Much of the vocabulary acquired in this way was not in itself native Swedish but was transmitted in its Swedish form from other languages, most importantly from Latin, Greek, German and French, but also from Italian, Arabic, Spanish and English. It is only in the present century that English and German on any significant scale began to reach Finnish directly, and it was not until after the Second World War that English rivalled Swedish as an intermediate source of new loans.

A complex system of derivational suffixes has always provided a very productive source of new vocabulary. Nominal and verbal forms are generated from either nominal or verbal base forms: 85 suffixes create nominals from nominal forms, and 21 create verbs from nominals; from verbs, 44 suffixes generate nominals and 34 generate verbs. An example of how nouns and adjectives are generated can be seen in the following illustration: noun *usko* 'belief' → adj. *usko=ll=inen* (stem: *uskollis-*) 'faithful, loyal' → noun *usko=ll=is=uus* 'fidelity, loyalty'; verb *syö-* 'eat' → noun *syö=minen* 'eating'. The great flexibility that exists between the verb and nominal categories in derivation is apparent from the analysis of the Finnish word for 'invincibility', *voi=tta=ma=ttom=uus*, which comprises five components: (1) verb stem *voi-* 'to be able'; (2) causative suffix *-tta-* → 'to beat, conquer'; (3) *-ma-* noun formative → 'beating, conquering'; (4) *-ttom-* negating adjectival suffix → 'non-beaten, non-conquered'; (5) *-uus* abstract noun suffix.

A distinctive feature of Finnish is the productivity of the language's stock of verbal derivational suffixes. With these the main verb can be adapted to perform several specific verbal functions. Although the examples given below are all well established in the language, the pattern of derivation illustrated is commonly used by native speakers to produce new and immediately intelligible items: *seiso-* 'stand' → momentaneous *seis=ahta-* 'halt'; *pure-* 'bite' → momentaneous *pur=aise-* 'take a bite'; *sylke-* 'spit' → frequentative *sylje=ksi-* 'spit habitually'; *ui-* 'swim' → frequentative *ui=skentele-* 'float'; *hake-* 'fetch' → causative *ha=etta-* 'have fetched'; *siirtä-* 'move, shift (causative)' → intransitive *siirt=y* 'move, shift'; *maista-* 'taste' (transitive) → *maist=u-* 'taste of'.

During the past 150 years all the above methods of vocabulary generation have been cultivated by linguists in their development of Finnish as a national language. Nowadays the government funds a language office to advise on the generation of new items and to monitor linguistic usage generally. Yet despite the numerous layers of loans and later creations that make up the lexicon of Finnish, frequency analyses show that some 60–70 per cent of any modern Finnish text is likely to consist of words belonging to the indigenous lexicon or generated from lexical, morphological and derivational items within that lexicon.

5   Syntax

In view of the morphosyntactic character of Finnish, various features of syntax have already been touched upon in the sections on verbal and nominal morphology. The present section will concern itself with four features of Finnish syntax: concord, numerals, non-finite verbal forms and word order.

5.1   Concord

There are no lexical items in Finnish equivalent in function to the English definite or indefinite article, but various degrees of definiteness can be denoted, where this is not already contextually defined, by the use of three degrees of demonstratives (*tämä* 'this', *tuo* 'that', *se* 'further away (either spatially or figuratively)'); similarly, indefiniteness can be marked by two degrees (*eräs* 'a certain', *yksi* 'one').

In noun phrases, there is concord in number and case of demonstratives and adjectives with their head noun. In the standard literary language there will also be concord in number between a nominative subject and the verb (except where the subject is an accumulation of singular items). In normal spoken language, however, the singular form of the 3rd person usually occurs; in sentences where the use of the singular creates ambiguity (e.g. *poikani on täällä* 'my son is here' or 'my sons are here') the speaker will frequently seek periphrastic ways of conveying plurality rather than use the verb in the plural.

5.2   Numerals

In noun phrases containing numerals and certain measure words, concord and government work differently. The numeral *yksi* 'one' functions as an adjective in concord with the head word (e.g. *yksi kirja jäi pöydälle* 'one book remained on the table', *yhdestä kirjasta en pidä* '(there is) one book I do not like', *hän näki yhden kirjan pöydällä* 'he/she saw one book on the table'). All other numerals and most measure words in the nominative and accusative cases (the Ø-marked accusative is used in such occurrences) govern a noun and its attributes in the partitive singular; in all other cases the numeral governs singular number, but there is concord of case between the numeral and head word (e.g. *kaksi nuorta miestä istui huoneessa* 'two young men were sitting in the room', *huomasin kaksi nuorta miestä huoneessa* 'I noticed two young men in the room', but *kahden nuoren miehen avulla maalasin huoneen* 'with the help of two young men I painted the room').

5.3   Non-finite Verbal Forms

Finnish grammarians have traditionally described as infinitives and participles a complex system of forms that 'function as nouns and noun-like words, adjectives, and adverbs with various shades of verbal meaning'

(Holman page 27). Attention will be drawn here to several of these forms that are productive and determine a range of syntactic relations. The first infinitive has a short and long category. The short category, which serves as the verb referent in dictionaries, functions in much the same way as the English verb infinitive as the complement of an auxiliary (e.g. *haluan laula-a* 'I want to sing'); in certain environments the infinitive can also function as a coverb (e.g. *tyttö juosta viipotti* 'the girl ran daintily').

The long form of the first infinitive and the two forms of the second infinitive are close in structure to the short first infinitive but carry case suffixes and in certain circumstances personal possessor suffixes. The long infinitive is in the translative case and person is marked by the nominal personal possessor markers (e.g. short infinitive *tul-la* 'to come', long form *tulla-kse-ni*, *tullaksesi* etc.), and expresses purpose (e.g. *ostin karttakirjan suunnitellakseni automatkan* 'I bought an atlas in order to plan a car journey'). The second infinitive is marked by the inessive and a historically fixed singular form of the instructive (*-en*). The function of the second infinitive is adverbial, indicating simultaneity (inessive) or manner of action (instructive) (e.g. *auringon paistaessa söimme ulkona* 'while the sun was shining we ate outside'; *hän löi lasta kaikkien nähden* 'he/she beat the child as all were watching'). From the examples cited here, it can also be seen that these infinitives govern the object in the same way as finite verb forms.

The most complex of the infinitives is the third. Its base form is marked by *-ma/mä* and the lexicon includes a stock of nouns formed in this way which are no longer perceived by speakers as non-finite verbal forms (e.g. *kuolema* 'death' ← *kuolla* 'to die', *sanoma* 'message' ← *sanoa* 'to say'). An important function of the third infinitive is as 'agential participle' (Holman) (e.g. *isän rakentama talo* lit. 'father's the building house', i.e. 'the house built by father'); where the agent is a personal pronoun, there is suffix concord with the participle (e.g. *minun rakentamani talo* 'the house built by me'). Concord also exists between the categories of singular and plural and case (e.g. *paljon ihmisiä asui isän rakentamissa taloissa* 'many people lived in the houses built by father').

The second area of usage is after a coverb when the third infinitive occurs in the singular illative, inessive, elative, adessive, or abessive cases. In the inessive case the infinitive functions with the coverb *olla* 'to be' to express continuity of action (e.g. *äiti oli lukemassa sanomalehtiä kun saavuin* 'mother was reading the newspapers when I arrived'; *sunnuntaina olen hoitamassa pihaani* 'on Sunday I shall be tending my garden'; *koko perhe oli keittiössä juomassa kahvia* 'the whole family was in the kitchen drinking coffee'). The illative usage, which is also very common, denotes that an action is about to take place (e.g. *hän tuli syömään lounasta* 'he/she came to eat lunch'; *lähdemme nyt juoksemaan* 'we are going to (start) run(ning) now'). The frequency of usage is also to some extent explained by the fact that a large number of verbs, and also adjectives taking a complement, govern this non-finite form of the verb (e.g. *ruveta* 'to begin', *pyytää* 'to ask, request', *oppia* 'to learn'; *halukas* 'keen, willing', *valmis* 'ready'). A similar pattern of development characterises the elative case, which as part of the third infinitive usually conveys separation (e.g. *tulin taloon sisään hoitamasta pihaani* 'I came into the house after tending my garden'; *perhe tuli juomasta kahvia* 'the family came (once they had finished) from drinking coffee'), but is governed as complement by specific verbs (e.g. *lakata* 'to stop, cease', *kieltää* 'to forbid'). In adessive usage it is the instrumental function of the case which is represented, indicating how the action of the finite verb is accomplished (e.g. *lukemalla kirjallisuutta oppisit maailman menosta* 'by reading literature you would learn about the ways of the world'; *maalaamalla talomme itse säästimme paljon rahaa* 'by painting our house ourselves we saved a lot of money'). As mentioned in section 3.3.1 the use of the abessive third infinitive accounts largely for the productive use of this case in the modern language. Its function is to show that an action does not take place (e.g. *työt jäivät tekemättä* 'the jobs remained undone'; *hän asui Helsingissä kaksi vuotta oppimatta suomea* 'he/she lived in Helsinki for two years without learning Finnish').

5.4 Word Order

Word order in a noun phrase constituent is fixed: demonstrative–numeral–adjective(s)–noun. Within the clause the normal order of constituents is subject–verb–object. This order remains in the type of questions that require the addition of a question word at the beginning of the clause (e.g. *sinä odotat meitä kotona* 'you will wait for us at home', but *missä sinä odotat meitä?* 'where will you wait for us?' or *miksi sinä odotat meitä kotona?* 'why are you waiting for us at home?'). Where a question word is not used, as in the clause 'are you waiting for us at home?', Finnish preposes the focus of the question to which the particle *ko/kö* is suffixed: *odotatko sinä meitä kotona?* 'will you wait for us at home?'.

Since the morphosyntactic system usually makes the grammatical, syntactic and semantic functions of each constituent in the clause unambiguous, considerable flexibility is possible within the general SVO framework, allowing shifts of emphasis and focus to be marked by word order variation. When special emphasis or change of focus is required, word order is usually pragmatically determined in order to place the focus as the first constituent of the clause, e.g. *kotona sinä odotat meitä* 'it is at home that you will wait for us (and nowhere else)'; *meitä sinä odotat kotona* 'you will wait for us (and no one else) at home', *kotona sinä meitä odotat* 'it is at home (and nowhere else) that you will wait for us (and no one else)'.

Bibliography

L. Hakulinen (1979) is an extensive survey of the development of Finnish in the context of the other Baltic-Finnic languages and the Finnish dialects; particular attention is paid to derivation and loanwords.

Among grammars of Finnish in English, Atkinson (1977) is a succinct introductory sketch of Finnish morphology and syntax, while Karlsson (1983) is an intelligent presentation of the morphology of Finnish for the adult student, including useful sections on pronunciation and intonation and on the differences between the colloquial and literary languages. Holman (1984) is a concise linguistic analysis of the finite and non-finite categories of the Finnish verb. Denison (1957) is a pioneering work on the form and numerous functions of the partitive case in all the Baltic-Finnic languages. A. Hakulinen and Karlsson (1979) is the best work on Finnish syntax in recent years; the authors rationalise many of the complications of Finnish by the application of modern linguistic methodology.

Tuomi (1972) is an indispensable tool in studying derivation; Saukkonen *et al.* (1979), a frequency dictionary based on the language of the 1960s, is an invaluable analysis of frequency of vocabulary and parts of speech in various registers.

References

Atkinson, J. 1977. *A Finnish Grammar* (Suomalaisen Kirjallisuuden Seura, Helsinki)

Denison, N. 1957. *The Partitive in Finnish* (Finnish Academy of Sciences, Helsinki)

Hakulinen, A. and F. Karlsson. 1979. *Nykysuomen lauseoppia* (Suomalaisen Kirjallisuuden Seura, Jyväskylä)

Hakulinen, L. 1979. *Suomen kielen rakenne ja kehitys* (4th ed.) (Otava, Helsinki). An abridged English version, *The Structure and Development of the Finnish Language* (trans. J. Atkinson), of the 1st edition (1941, 1946) was published in 1961 (Indiana University Press, Bloomington)

Holman, E. 1984. *Handbook of Finnish verbs* (Suomalaisen Kirjallisuuden Seura, Vaasa)

Karlsson, F. 1983. *Finnish Grammar* (Werner Söderström, Juva)

Saukkonen, P., M. Haipus, A. Niemikorpi, H. Sulkala, 1979. *Suomen kielen taajuussanasto* (Werner Söderström, Porvoo)

Tuomi, T. (ed.) 1972. *Suomen kielen käänteissanakirja. Reverse Dictionary of Modern Standard Finnish* (Suomalaisen Kirjallisuuden Seura, Hämeenlinna)

11 TURKISH AND THE TURKIC LANGUAGES

Jaklin Kornfilt

1 General and Historical Background

A strict terminological distinction should be drawn between Turkic, the name of a language family, and Turkish, the name of a language. Although Turkish is by far the largest language (in terms of number of speakers) in the Turkic family, it accounts for only some 40 per cent of the total number of speakers of Turkic languages. The main geographic locations of Turkic languages are: (1) Turkey (Turkish), (2) the USSR and Iran: the Caucasus and northwestern Iran (e.g. Azerbaidjani), Soviet Central Asia, Kazakhstan and southern Siberia (e.g. Uzbek, Kazakh, Turkmenian, Kirghiz) and on the Volga (e.g. Tatar). One Turkic language (Yakut) is spoken in northern Siberia. (More than one Soviet citizen in ten is a native speaker of a Turkic language). In addition, there are substantial Turkic-speaking communities in northwestern China (Uighur and Kazakh).

In terms of linguistic structure, the Turkic languages are very close to one another, and most of the salient features of Turkish described below (e.g. vowel harmony, agglutinative morphology, verb-final word order, nominalised subordinate clauses) are true of nearly all Turkic languages, with only minor modifications. This similarity of structure makes it difficult to determine the precise number of Turkic languages and their boundaries and to sub-classify them, since one typically finds chains of dialects, with adjacent dialects in essence mutually intelligible and mutual intelligibility decreasing as a function of distance, rather than clear language boundaries. Only one Turkic language, Chuvash, spoken on the middle Volga, is radically different from all its relatives.

The external genetic relationships of the Turkic family remain controversial. The most widely accepted affiliation is with the Mongolian languages (in Mongolia, northern China and parts of the USSR) and the Tungusic languages (Siberia and northeastern China), to form the Altaic phylum; the typological similarities among these three families, though striking (e.g. vowel harmony, SOV word order typology) are not proof of genetic relationship, while even the shared vocabulary has been argued to be the result of intensive contact rather than common ancestry. Bolder hypotheses would extend the Altaic phylum eastwards to include Korean, perhaps even Japanese; or northwards to include the Uralic family (to give a Ural-Altaic phylum).

Turkish is the official and dominant language of Turkey (Turkish Republic), where it is the native language of over 90 per cent of the population, i.e. some 45 million people. (The largest linguistic minority in the Turkish Republic is formed by Kurdish speakers, mainly in southeastern Turkey.) Turkish is also a coofficial language (with Greek) in Cyprus, where it is spoken by 19 per cent of the population, or about 120,000 people. But the largest number of Turkish speakers outside Turkey, perhaps one million, is to be found in the Balkans, especially Bulgaria, but also Yugoslavia (especially Macedonia) and Greece.

Although there is no general agreement in Turkological literature on the most adequate geographic grouping of the Turkic languages, we shall go along with those sources that classify the contemporary language spoken in the Turkish Republic within a South-West (or Oγuz) group, together with Gagauz, Azerbaidjani and Turkmenian, the latter forming the eastern component of the group. Within this group, some sources differentiate a subgroup called *Osman* (i.e. Ottoman), which would consist of the following dialects: Rumelian, Anatolian and South Crimean. Modern standard Turkish represents a standardisation of the Istanbul dialect of Anatolian.

The question of the ancestor language of this group is not settled, either. It seems established, however, that the language of the oldest documents (i.e. the Orkhun inscriptions and the Old Uighur manuscripts) is the ancestor of another group, namely of the Central Asiatic Turkic languages; the South-West languages are presumably descendants of the language of the 'Western Türküt' mentioned in the Chinese Annals.

The ancient languages of this group would be Old Anatolian (Selǰuq) and Old Osman. These labels themselves are misleading, however, and have more political and historical justification than linguistic motivation, since there are no clear-cut criteria to distinguish the languages they represent from one another — while there might be more reason to distinguish Old Osman (which is usually claimed to extend until the fifteenth century, ending with the conquest of Constantinople) from Ottoman proper; but, even there, no justification exists for a strict cut-off point.

The first Anatolian Turkish documents date from the thirteenth century and show that the literary tradition of Central Asia was only very tenuously carried over by the Turkish people (who had been converted to Islam earlier) after invading Anatolia from the east in the late eleventh century. It is clear that these tribes were influenced heavily by both Persian and Arabic from the very beginnings of their settling down in Anatolia, given the higher prestige and development of the culture and literature of these neighbouring Muslim nations. The number of works in Turkish written by the Turks of Anatolia (as opposed to those written by them in Arabic and Persian and even Greek) greatly increased in the fourteenth century, together with the Seljuqi period of feudalism in Anatolia. The gap between the eleventh and thirteenth centuries with respect to the lack of written documents can probably be explained by assuming that the Turkish leaders used Arabic and Persian, not finding a local Turkic language in their new surroundings and not having a strong literary tradition to fall back on — given that these Turkish tribes (to a large part belonging to the Oγuz) were not among the culturally more advanced Turkic groups and, moreover, were geographically separated at that time from the Central Asian centres of Turkic literature.

From the very beginning of its Anatolian period, Turkish was written in the Arabic script, until the Latin script was adopted in the course of the so-called 'writing reform' of 1928 (put into force in 1929), one of the various reforms introduced after the founding of the Turkish Republic with the aim of westernising the country. However, the Uighur script was also employed by the Anatolian Turks up to the fifteenth century, which might explain some features of the Arabic script as used by the Turks of that period and which differ from standard Arabic usage, e.g. vowels are written out in Turkish words. This point, incidentally, has often been brought up to motivate the so-called 'writing reform', arguing that the multiple ambiguities that arise in Turkish within a non-vocalised orthography made the Arabic system highly inadequate for Turkish.

The dialect of the earliest Anatolian texts has various features in common with the Oγuz dialect as documented for the eleventh century, before the migration to Anatolia, and with Qïpchaq (an ancient language of the North-western group) and Turkmenian. Some of these are listed below:

(1) *d* for *t* in Old Turkic. (A number of these *d*s became devoiced again through assimilation in the fifteenth century.)

(2) Initial *b* changes to *v*: *bar-* > *var-* 'to go; to arrive'; *ber-* > *ver-* 'to give'

(3) Suffix-initial γ, *g* disappears.

(4) Word-final γ, *g* disappears in polysyllabic words.

(5) Instead of the second person plural imperative ending *-ler, -lar* in Old Turkic, *-nüz, -nuz* is found (and remains until today).

Forms which are limited to Anatolian Turkish are the following:

(1) The suffix *-ecek, -acaq* appears for the first time in the thirteenth century (but is used as a participle and not yet as a finite verb, as is also possible in Modern Turkish).
(2) The suffix *-iser, -ïsar* is the most widely used suffix for the future tense in Anatolian Turkish between the thirteenth and fifteenth centuries and is seen only very infrequently in some Turkmenian and Qïpchaq works.

However, the differences between Old Turkic and early Anatolian Turkish must not have been great and their phonology essentially identical. The vocabulary is also similar to a large extent, although obviously many borrowings from Islamic sources are seen in the realm of religious-mystical concepts.

In the works of the fourteenth century and afterwards, peculiarities of Eastern Turkic, which had crept into Anatolian Turkish because of the Eastern origins of some authors, disappear almost completely, while the component of Arabic and Persian words and forms increases; such Eastern Turkic features include: initial *m* instead of *b* in words containing a nasal: *men* instead of *ben* 'I'; *min-* instead of *bin-* 'to ride'; initial *b*, which, as mentioned above, changed to *v* in Anatolia and neighbouring areas, remained unchanged in Eastern Turkic and is also sporadically found in early Anatolian works: *ber-* instead of *ver-* 'to give'; and, as another example for a different feature, *bol* instead of *ol* 'to be'.

In the literature written for scholarly, administrative and literary purposes, the Persian and Arabic components became so prevalent that 'Ottoman' became a mixed language, having lost some of its characteristic Turkic properties to the point of not being usable as a medium of communication common to all social classes. During the same time, however, there also was a considerable production of mystical literature and folk poetry which was written for the less educated classes, in the language used by those segments of the population, namely Anatolian Turkish as influenced very little by Persian and Arabic. These works are very close to the 'Republican Turkish' of today and can essentially be understood without too much difficulty. Among the authors of the 'court literature' there were, time and again, also some who called for a purification of the language and ultimately, starting in the eighteenth century, there was a general movement towards a language with local (rather than foreign) features.

The culmination of such movements was reached after the turn of the century. In 1909, a 'Turkish Club' (*Türk Derneği*) was founded in Istanbul and started publishing a journal, proclaiming its aims for a simpler Turkish.

Similar movements and journals followed soon and literary works written in a 'purified' Turkish were produced (see, for instance, the works of Ömer Seyfettin and Ziya Gökalp). Conscious and systematic efforts to establish criteria for maintaining the vocabulary as well as the structural properties of Turkish were continued through the 'War of Liberation' (after World War I) into the founding of the Republic and the reform movements. The language reform, which can be said to have started with the 'writing reform', should therefore be viewed within a tradition of a search for a national identity, combined with a general campaign for westernisation. A Turkish Language Academy was founded in Ankara, with the tasks of etymological research and creation of new words, the latter in accordance with the Turkish rules of word formation and using Turkic roots, where the 'purification' of the language from Arabic and Persian vocabulary had created gaps which could not be filled with current synonyms. Although some of these new creations were judged to be just as foreign to the current colloquial language as the borrowed vocabulary and dropped out of usage almost as soon as they were introduced, the work of the Academy can be judged to have been essentially successful in creating a widely understood language with a transparent morphological component and its own, typologically consistent syntax.

2 Phonology and Orthography

The vowel inventory of Turkish is very symmetric. The eight phonemic vowels are grouped into foursomes with respect to the features of height, backness and rounding, as in table 11.1.

Table 11.1: Turkish Vowels

	[−back] [−round]	[+round]	[+back] [−round]	[+round]
[+high]	i	ü	ɨ	u
[−high]	e	ö	a	o

All vowels of the native vocabulary are underlyingly (or, say, phonemically) short. There is, however, vocalic length on the surface, having various sources: (1) borrowings with unpredictably long vowels; e.g. *ha:dise* 'event, happening'; *ma:zi:* 'past'; (2) compensatory lengthening of words of Turkic origin, where an original voiced velar fricative (which is no longer part of the *surface* inventory of segments in modern standard Turkish) used to follow a vowel. There are some arguments that show this segment to be part of the *phonemic* inventory, since it behaves like a consonant in stem-final position with respect to allomorphy choice of following suffixes. For example, the accusative and dative suffixes are: *-I* and *-A* after a consonant, but *-yI* and

-*yA* after a vowel, respectively. (For the notation with capital letters, see page 235.) After a stem-final phonetically long vowel due to 'compensatory lengthening' (but not after an *inherently* long vowel), the allomorph regularly chosen by consonant-final stems appears; e.g. orthographic *dağ* 'mountain', pronounced *da:*, accusative *daɨ*, dative *daa*. Compare these forms with: *araba* 'car', accusative *arabayɨ*, dative *arabaya*, and *bina:* 'building', accusative *bina:yɨ*, dative *bina:ya*. Where that segment (which is, as shown in the examples above, rendered by the sign *ğ* in Turkish orthography and can never occur word-initially — see also the section on the historical background of Turkish) is in either word-final or pre-consonantal (i.e. in syllable-final) position, the preceding vowel is lengthened; e.g. orthographic *çağ* 'era', pronounced *ča:*, locative *çağda*, pronounced *ča:da*.

Another peculiarity of Turkish vowels is that non-high vowels cannot be round, unless they are in a word-initial syllable. While many borrowed stems are exceptional in this respect (e.g. *dekor* 'stage design'; *pilot* 'pilot'), there is only one affix that is exceptional: the progressive suffix -*(I)yor*.

Perhaps the most prominent property of the Turkish vowels is the fact that they undergo vowel harmony with respect to backness and rounding. We shall discuss this issue in more detail later on, when the phonological rule system of the language is investigated.

The consonant inventory of Turkish is given in table 11.2. The consonants *k*, *g* and *l* have two forms: palatal and velar. Their distribution is, in general,

Table 11.2: Turkish Consonants

	Bilabial	Labio-dental	Dental, Alveolar	Palato-alveolar	Palatal	Velar	Glottal
Stop voiceless	p		t	č		k	
voiced	b		d	ǰ		g	
Fricative							
voiceless		f	s	š			
voiced		v	z	ž			
Nasal	m		n				
Lateral							
approximant			l				
Central							
approximant			r		y		h

determined by the backness versus frontness of the tautosyllabic vowel, e.g. *čök̜* 'collapse' versus *čok* 'many; very'; *bel̜* 'waist' versus *bal* 'honey'; *k̜ör* 'blind' versus *kor* 'ember'; *il̜ik̜* 'marrow' versus *ilik* 'luke-warm'. (χ denotes a palatal consonant.) These assimilative changes are not always predictable, however; there are some borrowings where the palatal variant precedes or follows a tautosyllabic back vowel; e.g. *kal̜p* 'heart'; *k̜ar* 'profit'.

The Latin alphabet used for modern standard Turkish is, both in its printed and handwritten versions, the familiar system used in more familiar European languages — as, for example, in English. The diacritics used for less common sounds make some of the signs very similar to some versions of the phonetic script; for instance, the phonetic symbols for vowels given in table 11.1 are also the ones used in Turkish orthography, with one exception: Instead of *i*, the sign used for the high back non-round vowel, we find *ı*, i.e. a dotless *i*. The difference between the two non-round high vowels is signalled in the same way for capital letters: *İ* for the front, *I* for the back, high non-round vowel. As for the consonants, we have commented on the 'silent' *ğ* earlier. Other letters that don't correspond to the familiar phonetic symbols are the following: *c* for [ǰ], *ç* for [č], *ş* for [š], *j* for [ž].

The orthographic conventions correspond roughly to those of a broad phonetic transcription. Predictable alternations (e.g. those due to syllable-final oral stop devoicing, to voicing assimilation or to vowel harmony) are written out, differing in this respect from, say, the German orthography. Other predictable alternations are not signalled, however: since there are no special signs for the palatal versus velar *k*, *g* and *l*, the alternations that these segments undergo remain unexpressed by the orthography. Unpredictable occurrences of the palatal variants of these consonants with back vowels *is* sometimes shown, however, by placing a circumflex on the vowel: *kâr* [ḵyar]. (A front glide is inserted when the consonant in question is a *ḵ*.) Inherent vowel length is not shown by the writing, although it is unpredictable.

With the exception of some learned words and the borrowed vocabulary of native speakers who either have some knowledge of European languages or live in big cities with extensive western influence, Turkish does not allow consonant clusters in initial position. In standard pronunciation (and increasingly also in the orthography) such clusters that enter the language via borrowings are broken up by an epenthesised high vowel, which — in general — harmonises with the following vowel(s) in backness and rounding, e.g. learned *ḵlüp* 'club', colloquial *kulüp*; learned *kral* 'king', colloquial *kiral*.

Turkish is somewhat more tolerant of syllable-final consonant clusters. Three types of clusters are allowed as a coda: (a) sonorant + obstruent: *ḵent* 'city', *harf* 'letter'; (b) voiceless fricative + oral stop: *çift* 'couple', *şevḵ* (pronounced [šefk]) 'fervour'; (c) *k* + *s*: *raks* 'dance', *boks* 'boxing'. Where a stem has a consonant cluster in syllable-final position that does not fall under any of the permissible sets, again a high vowel is epenthesised which undergoes harmony, e.g. 'forehead' accusative *aln+ı*, nominative *alın*; 'nose' accusative *burn+u*, nominative *burun*; 'city' accusative *şehr+i*, nominative *şehir*; 'time' accusative *vakt+i*, nominative *vakit*.

A subcase of underlying syllable-final consonant clusters are geminate consonants. While Turkish does tolerate geminate consonant sequences when their members are heterosyllabic (e.g. *et+te* 'meat+loc.'), it does not allow them to occupy syllable-final position. Rather than breaking up such clusters by epenthesis, however, the language has a rule of degemination, e.g. 'feeling' accusative *hiss+i*, nominative *his*; 'line' accusative *hatt+ı*, nominative *hat*.

In addition to some rules discussed above (i.e. vowel epenthesis, consonant degemination), there are a few other important phonological rules that were mentioned in passing and which will receive further attention below.

Syllable-final oral stop devoicing: similar to the more general obstruent devoicing rule in languages like German and Russian, Turkish has a rule that devoices oral non-continuants (i.e. regular stops as well as affricates) in syllable-final position, e.g. *kitap* 'book', accusative *kitab+ı*, locative *kitap+ta*; *kireç* 'lime', accusative *kirec+i*, locative *kireç+te*.

The *k*/Ø alternation: The final *k* of a polysyllabic word is deleted phonetically in intervocalic position, where the preceding vowel is short. This *k*/Ø alternation is orthographically rendered as a *k*/ğ alternation, e.g. *kabak* 'pumpkin', accusative *kabağı* [kabaï]; *kabuk* 'crust', accusative *kabuğu* [kabuu]. It is possible to view this phenomenon as a subcase of the voiced/voiceless alternation discussed in the previous section. If it is assumed that the alternating *k*s are derived from underlying *g*s as a result of syllable-final stop devoicing and if a rule of intervocalic fricativisation is posited for the voiced velar stop, the data are essentially covered.

Word-final liquid devoicing: another striking phenomenon somewhat related to stop devoicing is the word-final devoicing of liquids, especially common in the Istanbul dialect and in the speech of educated speakers in the other big cities: *kaṛ* 'snow', *bakıṛ* 'copper', *ḳeḷ* 'bald'. It should be noted, however, that this is not a completely unified phenomenon; some speakers devoice only the palatal *l*, while other speakers do not make a distinction between the two variants of the lateral. (The *r* is devoiced by all speakers who observe the liquid devoicing rule.) It should also be pointed out that liquid devoicing differs from oral stop devoicing in applying at word boundary rather than at syllable boundary; e.g. while the underlying stem-final *b* devoices in: *kitap + lık* 'object designated for books; bookshelf', the stem-final *r* remains voiced in a similar environment: *kar + lı* 'with snow; snowy' (and not: *kaṛlı).

Morpheme-initial voicing assimilation: a morpheme-initial obstruent assimilates in voicing to the preceding segment within the word. This rule has to apply after syllable-final stop devoicing has taken place, e.g. (a) *gemi + ci* 'sailor' (cf. *gemi* 'ship'), *iz + ci* 'boy-scout' (cf. *iz* 'track, trace'), *bakır + cı* 'coppersmith' (cf. *bakır* 'copper'); (b) *kitap + çı* (cf. *kitap* 'book', underlying /kitab/), *şarap+çı* 'wine maker, wine seller' (cf. *şarap* 'wine', underlyingly /şarab/).

Vowel harmony: perhaps the most striking property of Turkish phonology is the fact that the distribution of vowels within a word is governed by vowel harmony, i.e. vowels share the specification for the feature [back] and, if they are high, they also share the specification for [round]: *bülbül + ümüz + ün* 'nightingale + 1 pl. + gen.', 'belonging to our nightingale'; *bülbül + ler + imiz + in* 'nightingale + pl. + 1 pl. + gen.', 'belonging to our nightingales'; *kol + umuz + un* 'arm + 1 pl. + gen.', 'belonging to our arm'; *kol + lar + ımız + ın* 'arm + pl. + 1 pl. + gen.', 'belonging to our arms'. Note that the [−high] vowel of the plural morpheme, while undergoing vowel harmony for backness, does not undergo rounding harmony. Moreover, since there is a condition (mentioned earlier in this section) on [−high] vowels to the effect that they have to be [−round] if they are in a non-initial syllable, the negative specification of this vowel for rounding is fully determined. Note also that once a non-round vowel follows a round vowel (as in the second and fourth examples above) all vowels to the right of that non-round vowel will be non-round as well, irrespective of their height.

This situation can be characterised in more general terms: where a vowel does not share the specification for a harmony feature with preceding vowels, it will create its own harmony domain, in the sense that it will determine the specification with respect to that particular feature for the following vowels. This description also characterises the application of vowel harmony where an exceptional vowel occurs. As mentioned before, many stems have exceptional vowels that violate either backness or rounding harmony or both at once; the second vowel of the progressive marker *-(I)yor* is also exceptional in this respect and never alternates. (Capital letters denote archiphonemes whose missing feature values are predictable by rule. In the case of vowels, *I* stands for a [+high], *A* for a [−high] vowel before application of vowel harmony. In the case of consonants, a capital letter stands for a segment which will undergo syllable-final stop devoicing, morpheme-initial voicing assimilation or intervocalic *k*-deletion. Symbols in parentheses denote affix allomorphy in those instances where the segment in question deletes after a 'like' segment (i.e. a vowel after a vowel, a consonant after a consonant).) In such cases, it is the exceptional vowel (or, if there is more than one, the last exceptional vowel) that determines what kind of vowel harmony the following vowels will undergo. Observe the following examples: *dekor + un + u* 'stage design + 3 sg. + acc.', 'his stage design, acc.', *otobüs + ün + ü* 'bus + 3 sg. + acc.', 'his bus, acc.'; *buket + in + i* 'bouquet + 3 sg. + acc.', 'his bouquet, acc.'; *ermeni + stan + ın + ı* 'Armenian + 'country' + 3 sg. + acc.', 'his Armenia, acc.'.

Sometimes, however, a consonant rather than a vowel can determine (backness) harmony. This happens when a palatal consonant unpredictably follows a back vowel in the same syllable and where that consonant is in stem-final position (or a member of a stem-final consonant cluster). In such cases the following vowels will exhibit *front* harmony; i.e. the 'trigger' of vowel harmony will be the exceptional consonant rather than the regular vowel, e.g. *petrol̡* 'petrol, gasoline', accusative *petrol̡ + ü*; *kal̡p* 'heart', accusative *kal̡b+i*; *val̡s* 'waltz', accusative *val̡s + i*.

Labial Attraction: there are a number of stems with a vowel sequence of *a...u* and an intervening labial consonant (the latter can also be part of a consonant cluster). Since the second vowel, being high, should undergo rounding harmony, it should surface as an *ı*. Its rounding has traditionally been ascribed to the preceding labial consonant. Some examples are *karpuz* 'watermelon', *kavun* 'melon'. The status of this observation in terms of a rule (of assimilation) in modern standard Turkish has been challenged more recently. While such an assimilatory process might have been productive in Early Anatolian Turkish (and could even have been a feature common to the Southwestern Turkic group), it seems that it is less general in the contemporary language; there are a number of examples where the sequence *a...ı* shows up in spite of an intervening labial consonant, e.g. *çarmıh* 'cross', *sabır* 'patience', *kapı* 'door'. Furthermore, an even larger number of stems exhibit *a...u* sequences without any intervening labial consonant; e.g. *ka:nun* 'law', *arzu* 'desire', *fasulya* 'bean'.

Turkish has in general word-final stress: *kitáp* 'book'; *gör + ebil + ecek + lerin + í* 'see + abilit. + fut. + 3 pl. + acc.' 'that they will be able to see'. Some suffixes are exceptional, however, in: (a) rejecting stress when in word-final position: *gör + ecék + ti* 'see + fut. + past' 'he was going to see'; (b) dividing the word into stress domains where not word-final: *gör + é + me + yecek + lerin + i* 'see + abilit. + neg. + fut. + 3 pl. + acc.' 'that they will not be able to see'. Under both circumstances, the vowel preceding the exceptional morpheme (or, rather, the exceptional vowel) receives primary stress.

A rule that applies within a phrase to reduce stresses left-to-right is needed independently: *dérs kitab + i* 'course book + compound marker', 'textbook'. This rule can be used to account for the stress in words like *görémeyeceklerinì* which consist of more than one stress domain and exhibit word-final non-primary stress.

Exceptionality with respect to stress is also exhibited by some unsuffixed stems. Such items do not fall into one clearly and independently defined set. Many (but not all) borrowed stems and almost all place names fall under this group, within which there are subregularities: they are stressed on the antepenultimate syllable, if it is the first non-final closed syllable; otherwise, the penultimate syllable is stressed. Some illustrative examples follow: *İstánbul*, *Ánkara*, *İzmir*, *fasúlya* 'bean', *lokánta* 'restaurant'.

3 Morphology

Turkish morphology is agglutinative and suffixing; there are only very few exceptions to the one-to-one relationship between morpheme and function and only one process that is prefixing rather than suffixing, namely reduplication of the first syllable (with an inserted consonant) in intensifying adjectives and adverbs; e.g. *beyaz* 'white', *bembeyaz* 'completely white'; *çabuk* 'fast', *çarçabuk* 'very fast'.

In the following, a brief survey will be given of the most productive suffixes and some restrictions will be stated that govern their occurrence and the ordering among those morphemes that can cooccur; later on, specific categories of special interest will be discussed. Inflectional suffixes will be referred to as 'verbal' or 'nominal' according to the category of the stem they attach to. By 'nominal stems' are meant nouns, adjectives and adverbs. (Participials and gerundives will fall under the 'nominal' group in this respect.)

As to be expected, derivational suffixes precede inflectional ones. Not surprisingly, among those morphemes that derive nominals, those that attach to verbal stems precede those that attach to nominal ones, where the two types cooccur: *ver* + *im* 'give + abstr. n.', 'profit'; *ver* + *im* + *li* 'give + abstr. n. + with (*adj.*)', 'profitable'; *ver* + *im* + *li* + *lik* 'give + abstr. n. + with (adj.) + abstr. n.', 'profitability'. The suffixes exemplified in the last two examples can attach to underived nominals, as well: *balkon* + *lu* 'with a balcony; balconied'; *dürüst* + *lük* 'honest + abstr. n.', 'honesty'. Both groups are productive; two other productive members of the first group are the action/manner suffix *-(y)Iş*, the result/action morpheme *-mA* and the infinitive marker *-mAK*. In the second group, we find *-CI*, deriving nouns meaning 'professional', and *-sIz*, deriving adjectives meaning 'without'.

The first member of a sequence of nominal inflectional suffixes and hence immediately following derivational morphemes, if present, is the plural marker *-lAr*: *gül* + *üş* + *ler* 'laugh + act. n + pl.', 'laughters; manners of laughing'; *at* + *lar* 'horse + pl.', 'horses'.

Next come nominal agreement suffixes. These are often referred to as 'possessive suffixes' in traditional literature, the reason being that the nominal stem they attach to is often, if not always, interpreted as possessed by a noun phrase within the clause or phrase. The reason they are referred to as 'agreement suffixes' here is that they express the person and number features of their 'possessors'. A more detailed account of these suffixes will be offered in the next part of this section which will be devoted to issues of special interest.

Case morphemes occur last, e.g. *üstün* + *lüğ* + *ümüz* + *ü* 'superior + abstr. n. + 1 pl. + acc.' 'our supremacy (accusative)'. The group of agreement morphemes will be discussed in more detail in the second part of this section. It should be mentioned here, however, that not more than one case morpheme can occur within an immediate sequence of suffixes.

There is only one completely productive morpheme that derives verbs from nominals: *-lA*, which has a meaning related to the causative; e.g. *karşı* + *la* + *mak* 'opposite + deriv. morph. + infin.', 'to go to meet; to oppose; reply to'; *kara* + *la* + *mak* 'black + deriv. morph. + infin.', 'to blacken'. This morpheme can then be followed by the various verbal suffixes which we shall briefly discuss according to the sequential order in which they occur within the word.

The leftmost productive class in the string of verbal suffixes is the category often called 'voice' by traditional grammars. This group consists of the middle/reflexive (-*(I)n*), the reciprocal (-*(I)ş*), the passive (-*Il/n*) and the causative (-*DIr/t*). (The -*IL* allomorph of the passive follows consonants, the -*n* allomorph vowels. -*DIr* is the basic allomorph of the causative; -*t* occurs after polysyllabic stems which end in a vowel or in the oral sonorants *r* and *l*.) The middle/reflexive and the reciprocal cannot cooccur; where the passive cooccurs with either one, it has to follow them. In the very few examples where the causative can cooccur with the middle/reflexive and the reciprocal it has to follow them, and, while it can cooccur with the passive, it has to precede it; e.g. *tanı* + *ş* + *tır* + *ıl* + *dı* + *lar* 'know + recip. + caus. + pass. + past + 3 pl.' 'they were caused to know each other; they were introduced to each other'.

Suffixes of this group can be followed by the verbal negation marker -*mA*, which is one of the suffixes that are exceptional from the point of view of word stress in rejecting word-final stress and causing the preceding vowel to be stressed. This suffix, in turn, is followed either by one of the various mood markers or by purely verbal or gerundive/participial forms, the latter expressing tense in varying degrees of differentiation. The mood markers are: the desiderative -*sA*, the necessitative -*mAlI* and the optative -*(y)a*; e.g. *gör* + *üş* + *me* + *meli* + *yiz* 'see + recip. + neg. + necess. + 1 pl.', 'we shouldn't/mustn't see each other'. The suffixes of the mood category are mutually exclusive.

The tenses are: definite past: -*DI*; reported past: -*mIş*; aorist: -*(A)r*; future: -*(y)AcAK*; present progressive: -*(I)yor*. These forms have also aspectual connotations: the past tenses denote accomplished actions and the aorist actions that are either extended or repeated over a period of time. The present progressive is similar to its English equivalent in denoting an action that, roughly speaking, takes place at the time of the utterance. One difference is that stative verbs, unlike those in English, can take the progressive in Turkish:

ev	+	e	git +	mek	isti +	yor	+	um
home	+	dat.	go +	infin.	want +	pres. prog. +		1 sg.

'I want (*am wanting) to go home'

The main participial forms are those used in relative clauses: -*(y)An* and -*DIK*, and they will be discussed in section 4. Also in this group (from the point of view of positional slots within the morphological word) are so-called verbal nouns and converbs (these are terms often used in traditional literature). The verbal nouns consist mainly of the infinitive suffix -*mAK* and the result/action noun marker -*mA* and were also listed among the derivational morphemes that convert verbs into nominals. Converbs (or gerundives, as they are also called) are suffixes that yield adverbial forms. Some examples are the manner suffix -(y)ArAk, the conjunction adverbial -(y)Ip which denotes close successions of actions and the time adverb suffix -(y)IncA. In general, only one of the suffixes in this group can occur at a time. In other words, within the morphological sequence, the various gerundive, participial and nominal markers take the place of the tense or mood markers, whether they have tense connotations themselves or not.

However, two tense markers (as well as a tense and a mood marker) *can* cooccur in immediate succession to form complex tenses; in such examples, it might be appropriate to view the second marker as a copula carrying the main tense or mood and the preceding sequence as a participial:

```
imtihan +   ım   +   a      başlı +   yor   +   du   +   m
exam    +  1 sg. +  dat.    start +  prog. +  past +  1 sg.
'I was starting my exam (when...)'
```

Note that in such sequences, the present progressive marker -(I)yor retains its aspectual meaning.

The reported past marker -mIş is used as a perfective aspect marker in such sequences (i.e. when it is the first member of the sequence):

```
imtihan +   ım   +   a ˙    başla +   mış   +   tı   +  m
exam  ı +  1 sg +  dat.     start +  perf. +  past +  1 sg.
'I had started my exam (when...)'
```

All tense and some mood markers can occur as the first members in these sequences; however, only the two past tense markers and the mood marker for the desiderative (the latter as a conditional) can occur as the second member, i.e. as the main tense or modality marker. However, all the tenses can be used as a main tense or modality within a periphrastic construction with an auxiliary verb. The most widely used auxiliary is the verb *ol-* 'be, become'; e.g.

```
imtihan + ım + a   başlı +   yor       ol +   acağ +   ım
                +   prog.    be +   fut.  +  1 sg.
'I shall be starting my exam...'
imtihan + ım + a   başla +   mış       ol +   acağ +   ım
                +   perf.
'I shall have started my exam'
```

This mixed positional group is followed by agreement markers, wherever such markers are possible. (Among the suffixes that cannot be followed by agreement markers are the infinitive marker *mAK*, the participial marker -An (unless it functions as a verbal noun) and the gerundive marker -(y)Ip.)

Now that we have looked at the most productive morphemes and some regularities of their distribution, let us discuss some typological characteristics of the morphological system.

Gender is neither overtly expressed in nouns (or pronouns), nor does it affect agreement. Agreement itself (by which term we shall mean agreement of the verbal or nominal head of a construction with its subject in terms of the features of person and number) can be either verbal or nominal; in other words, there are two slightly different paradigms, given in table 11.3.

Table 11.3: Agreement Markers

	Verbal	*Nominal*
1 sg.	-Im	-(I)m
2 sg.	-sIn	-(I)n
3 sg.	-Ø	-(s)I(n)
1 pl.	-Iz	-(I)mIz
2 pl.	-sInIz	(I)nIz
3 pl.	-lAr	-lArI(n)

Note: As before, the suffix-initial vowels in parentheses are deleted after a stem-final vowel; the suffix-initial consonant in parentheses is deleted after a stem-final consonant. The suffix-final consonant in parentheses is deleted in word-final position.

The verbal paradigm appears with the predicates of main clauses and of 'direct complements' (for discussion of the latter, see section 4); the nominal paradigm is used on the head nouns of possessive noun phrases as well as on the nominalised verbs of gerundive and participial complements. Some illustrative examples follow:

Verbal agreement used with a main clause predicate verb:

(Ben) bu   makale + yi   yarın   bitir + eceğ + *im*
I   this article + acc. tomorrow finish + fut. + 1 sg.
'I shall finish this article tomorrow'
(Biz) her   akşam   çok   çalış +   ır   + *ız*
we   every evening a lot work +   aor. + 1 pl.
'We work a lot every evening'

Verbal agreement used with a main clause predicate adjective:

(Ben) bugün çok   yorgun + *um*
I   today very tired + 1 sg.
'I am very tired today'
(Siz) çok   güzel + *siniz*
you   very pretty + 2 pl.
'You are very pretty'

Nominal agreement in a possessive noun phrase:

(Biz-im)   heykel + *imiz*
we-gen.   statue + 1 pl.
'our statue'
Ayşe-nin   araba + *sı*
Ayşe-gen.   car   + 3 sg.
'Ayşe's car'

Nominal agreement used in a gerundive complement:

Herkes   [(biz + im)   heykel + i   kır   +   dığ + *ımız*]   + ı
everybody we + gen. statue + acc. break + ger. + 1 pl.   + acc.
                                              bil   + iyor
                                              know   + 3 sg.
'Everybody knows that we broke the statue'
Herkes   [Ayşe + nin   heykel + i   kır + ma + *sın*] + ı   isti + yor
                                         + ger. + 3 sg.   want + 3 sg.
'Everybody wants Ayşe to break the statue'

Another property of Turkish agreement worth remarking on is the lack of it where modifiers are concerned. This means that neither singular/plural properties of a noun nor its case marking will 'spread' onto its adjective modifier(s) or any of its determiners. As a matter of fact, another striking property of Turkish in this respect is the lack of overt plural marking on a noun where its quantifier clearly expresses plurality; this generalisation holds irrespective of the grammatical relation of the noun phrase involved. The following examples will illustrate this point:

Subject noun phrase:

Beş   adam   (*adam + *lar*)   heykel + i   kır + dı
five   man   (man + pl.)   statue + acc. break + past
'Five men broke the statue'

Indirect object noun phrase:

Beş   adam + a   (*adam + *lar* + a)   yardım   et + ti + m
five   man + dat.   (man + pl. + dat.)   help   do + past + 1 sg.
'I helped five men'

Let us now return to subject-head agreement. The two paradigms in table 11.3 might be slightly misleading in that the suffixes for plural subjects are presented as unanalysed morphemes. However, especially the nominal paradigm in table 11.3 can substantiate a possible claim that, at least for the first and second person plural forms, those suffixes consist of two morphemes: 1 sg. *-(I)m*, 2 sg. *-(I)n*, 1 pl. *-(I)m + Iz*, 2 pl. *-(I)n + Iz*. Hence, it would make sense to view the suffix -*Iz* as a plural marker. (This plurality would have to be confined to subject agreement, however, since the general plurality morpheme, *lAr*, is different.)

The same analysis carries over to the verbal paradigm, if it is assumed that the suffix for person is, idiosyncratically, unrealised in the first person plural agreement form: 1 sg. -*Im*, 2 sg. -*sIn*, 1 pl. -Ø + *Iz*, 2 pl. -*sIn* + *Iz*. The agreement suffixes for third person plural subjects do not seem to fall under this generalisation, simply because their shape is rather different from those of the first and second person plural agreement morphemes. However, we would like to claim that there, too, a further analysis into a person morpheme, distinct from a number morpheme, is possible. Once again, we shall start with the nominal paradigm, which is more perspicuous than the verbal paradigm, since all morphemes are overtly realised: 3 sg. -*(s)I(n)*, 3 pl. -*lAr* + *I(n)*. Two factors are worth noticing: in comparison with the agreement forms for first and second person plural subjects, the order between the person and number suffixes is switched around, i.e. the number morpheme precedes the person morpheme. In addition, the number morpheme itself is suppletive. Instead of the form -*Iz*, the agreement morpheme for (plural) number exhibited elsewhere in both paradigms, we see here the general plurality morpheme -*lAr*. (Note, incidentally, that the suffix for third person appears in a perfectly regular shape: we know that the parenthesised initial *s* of that morpheme is deleted after a consonant. Since, within the third person plural agreement form, the third person suffix always follows the plural number suffix — and hence an *r* — that suffix will always surface without that *s*.)

Once again, the analysis carries over to the verbal paradigm. The agreement form for third person plural exhibits the suppletive morpheme -*lAr* for plural number. Since the third person morpheme remains unexpressed in the verbal paradigm, nothing else but the plural -*lAr* is included in the total form of the third person plural morpheme, as the last line of table 11.3 shows.

Yet another peculiarity of the third person plural morpheme is that, under some circumstances, it can be omitted. Essentially, when the subject noun phrase is overtly present (as we shall see in section 4, subjects can be omitted), the plural 'submorpheme' is optional (and, as a matter of fact, its omission is stylistically preferred):

```
Adam + lar    heykel + i     kır + dı (+lar)
man + pl.     statue + acc.  break + past (+3 pl.)
'The men broke the statue'
Hasan [adam + lar + ın    heykel + i         kır + dık + [lar + ın]] -ı /
                          + gen. statue + acc.       break + dık + pl. + 3 pers.-acc./
              kır + dığ + [ın] + ı    bil + iyor
                          + 3 pers.   know + pres. prog.
'Hasan knows that the men broke the statue'
```

None of the other agreement morphemes exhibits this freedom of partial occurrence.

Yet another property that determines the occurrence of the plural 'submorpheme' of third person plural agreement is the animacy of the subject noun phrase. The stylistic preference we mentioned in favour of omitting the morpheme in question strengthens to the point of almost a grammatical prohibition against its occurrence when the subject is inanimate:

Kitap + lar   masa + dan   yer + e   düş + tü   (??/*+ler)
book + pl.   table + abl.   floor + dat.   fall + past   (3 pl.)
'The books fell from the table to the floor'

Let us now turn to the case system in Turkish. It is a matter of some controversy how many cases Turkish has. Traditional Turkish grammars usually assume five cases: nominative: not marked overtly; accusative: *-(y)I*; dative: *-(y)A*; locative: *-DA*; ablative: *-DAn*. Turkish has also a genitive: *-(n)I(n)*, and an instrumental: *-(y)lA*. It is probably because the genitive is not 'governed' by verbs, but is rather a structural property of the subjects of nominal phrases or clauses, that many grammarians were reluctant to recognise it as a regular case. As for the instrumental, it is a cliticised form of a formerly unbound morpheme; from the synchronic point of view, there are two criteria that could argue against viewing it as a case morpheme: (a) it is exceptional from the point of view of stress (as are all other cliticised morphemes), while all other case morphemes (including the genitive) are regular; (b) it follows the genitive when it is suffixed to a personal pronoun and hence behaves like a postposition that governs a case — namely the genitive in this instance — and not like a regular case morpheme, which can never immediately follow another case suffix, as was mentioned earlier. We shall not take a stand here on this issue.

In conjunction with the discussion about the status of the instrumental, it should be mentioned that various postpositions 'govern' certain cases, similarly to verbs. The point of interest within the context of morphology is that regular nouns are treated differently from pronouns in this respect by those postpositions that take objects in the nominative. Specifically, while full nouns appear in the nominative in those contexts, pronouns have to be marked with the genitive: *kadın gibi* 'like a woman', *Ahmet kadar* 'as much as Ahmet'; but: *ben + im gibi* 'like me', *ben + im kadar* 'as much as I'.

4   Syntax

Turkish is a perfect example of a left-branching type of language where governed elements precede their governors, i.e. objects precede the verb, the postpositional object precedes the postposition and the (adjective, genitive) modifier precedes the modified head.

The unmarked word order in sentences is SOV; if there is more than one object, and if one of them is a direct object, the order with the direct object closer to the verb seems less marked than others:

Hasan   çocuğ + a   elma + yı   ver + di
        child + dat.   apple + acc.   give + past
'Hasan gave the apple to the child'

However, other orders are possible, as well. As a matter of fact, Turkish is rather free in its word order. Often (but not always), the divergences from the unmarked order have a pragmatic, discourse-oriented function, in that the position immediately preceding the verb is the focus position and the sentence-initial position is topic position. New information and material stressed for emphasis appear in focus position and, in addition to being syntactically marked in this way, also receive intonational stress. The topic, i.e. the material that the sentence is about, is placed at the beginning of the sentence and is often separated from it — orthographically by a comma and by a slight pause in speech.

Differently from other SOV languages (e.g. Japanese), Turkish is so lenient about non-canonical word orders that it even permits non-verb-final constructions. Such sentences arise when material is added as an afterthought or when the speaker assumes the hearer to know about it: *Hasan çocuğ + a ver + di elma + yı.* For this example to be felicitous, it must be clear within the discourse that something happened to the apple or even that Hasan gave the apple to somebody.

An embedded sentence takes up the same position that the corresponding noun phrase with the same grammatical relation would and can move around within the main clause with the same ease as a regular noun phrase:

Hasan ban + a   [imtihan + ı   geç + tiğ + in] + i   anlat + tı
      I + dat.   exam + acc.   pass + fact. n. + 2 sg. + acc. \ tell + past
'Hasan told me that you passed the exam'
Hasan ban + a   anlat + tı   [imtihan + ı geç + tiğ + in] + i

The constituents of the embedded sentence are somewhat less free in their word order. While they can still successfully violate the canonical SOV order within their own clause, they have to move to the right of the highest sentence when they cross the boundary of their own clause and cannot 'scramble into' higher material; thus, compare the following examples with the last set of examples above:

Ahmet ban + a   [__ geç + tiğ + in] + i   anlat + tı imtihan + ı
*Ahmet ban + a   [__ geç + tiğ + in] + i   imtihan + ı anlat + tı
(The original site of the 'scrambled' constituent is marked with a __)

In possessive noun phrases, the possessor precedes the head noun; in 'regular' noun phrases, modifiers precede the head. Where there is both an adjectival modifier and an article (only the indefinite article is overtly expressed in Turkish), the adjective precedes the article; where there is both a numeral and an adjective, the unmarked order is for the numeral to precede the adjective:

Ahmed	+ in	kitab + ı	
	+ gen.	book + 3 sg.	'Ahmet's book'
ilgi	+ nç	bir kitap	
interest	+ ing	a book	'an interesting book'
üç	ilginç	kitap	
three			'three interesting books'

The genitive-marked possessor can 'scramble' in either direction, while the article and numerals cannot. The adjective is not free to move, either, as far as spoken language and written prose are concerned. In poetry, however, an adjective can occur to the right of its head. Let us also mention, without going into details, that parts of nominal compounds cannot scramble and that postpositions cannot be stranded.

One striking characteristic of Turkish is that a subject can be left unexpressed in finite clauses (i.e. those exhibiting some type of subject-predicate agreement) as well as in possessive noun phrases:

——okul + a   gid +   eceğ + im
    school + dat   go +   fut. + 1 sg.
'I shall go to school'
Ahmet   [——kitab + ım] + ı   kayb + et + miş
              book + 1 sg. + acc.   loss + do + rep. past
'It is said that Ahmet lost my book'

(The sites of the missing constituents are underlined.) This possibility has been traditionally linked to the rich agreement morphology of Turkish, i.e. to the fact that agreement suffixes will uniquely 'identify' the person and number of the subject which is unexpressed.

Although Turkish has no agreement markers for non-subjects, it is also possible to 'drop' such constituents; e.g. *bul + du + m* 'find + past + 1 sg.' 'I found (it)'. Such examples are more restricted, however, than 'subject-drop' examples. They can never start a discourse, while 'subjectless' finite sentences can. Such constructions are felicitous only if the antecedent of the 'dropped' constituent has been mentioned in the discourse or has somehow been made clear by a pragmatic act.

As we saw before, passive is marked by the morpheme *-Il* (with a morphophonemic alternant *-n*) on the verbal stem. From the syntactic point of view, there are two types of passive constructions; they will be referred to as 'transitive passive' and 'intransitive passive'; the former type is derived from transitive verbs, the latter from intransitive ones. By 'transitive verb' we mean verbs that take direct objects (noun phrases that are marked accusative when they are specific), and by 'intransitive' verbs that do not take such objects (i.e. that either lack objects altogether or take only indirect or oblique objects). The two constructions exhibit the following surface differences: the patient of the action (or, in other words, the direct object of the corresponding active sentence) is the subject of the transitive passive construction. This claim is substantiated by the fact that these subjects exhibit syntactic properties typical of subjects in general: they appear in the nominative case, and in an unmarked word order, in sentence-initial position; the verb agrees with them; they can be the accusative-marked subjects of clauses that act as complements to 'believe-type' verbs (see page 247); they can correspond to the understood subjects of infinitivals; and the agent of the action can appear in an agentive phrase. However, the non-accusative objects that an intransitive verb might cooccur with are not surface subjects in an intransitive passive construction (in the sense that they do not exhibit the criteria just enumerated), and agentive phrases are judged to be awkward at best, if not completely ungrammatical. Some illustrative examples for these differences follow:

> (*Biz*)   döv + *ül* + dü + k
> we   hit + pass. + past + 1 pl.
> 'We were hit'
> *Biz* + *e*   yardım   ed + *il* + di
> we + dat.   help   do + pass. + past
> 'We were helped'
> *biz(+e)   yardım ed + *il* + di + k

> (Biz$_i$)   [PRO$_i$ döv + *ül* + *mek*]   iste + mi + yor + uz
> we   hit + pass. + infin.   want + neg. + pres. prog. + 1 pl.
> 'We don't want to be hit'
> *(biz$_i$)   [PRO$_i$ yardım   ed + *il* + *mek*] iste + mi + yor + uz
>   help   do
> 'We don't want to be helped'

Obviously, verbs that do not take any objects at all can also appear in impersonal passive constructions:

> Koş +   *ul*   + du
> run +   pass.   + past
> 'It was run (i.e. running took place)'
> Eğlen +   *il*   + di
> amuse +   pass. + past
> 'Fun was had'

Agentive phrases are completely ungrammatical in such objectless constructions.

It has been claimed in some relevant literature that only verbs with agentive semantics can enter the intransitive passive construction, but that stative verbs cannot. While this generalisation does hold for most cases in Turkish, it is possible to find examples where non-agentive verbs can successfully enter the construction. Such examples are best when combined with a 'tense' that has an aspectual connotation of duration (rather than, say, momentary or completed action):

Böyle bir hava + da   iyi   uyu + *n* + *ur*
such   a   weather + loc.   good   sleep + pass. + aor.
'One sleeps well in such a weather'

Compare this quite acceptable sentence with the following ungrammatical ones:

*Şimdi iyi   uyu + *n* + *uyor*
now   good   sleep + pass. + pres. prog.
'Now it is being slept well (i.e. one is sleeping well now)'
*Dün   bütün gün uyu + *n* + *du*
yesterday   whole day sleep + pass. + past
'Yesterday it was slept the whole day (i.e. one slept the whole day yesterday)'.

Turkish has various *wh*-question particles most of which are morphologically derived from the particle *ne* 'what': *ne* 'what', *neden* 'why', *niçin* 'why', *niye* 'why', *hangi* 'which', *kim* 'who'. These elements are found in two positions in the sentence: In pre-verbal position (which is, as we saw, the focus position) and in sentence-initial position. The first one of the two is strongly preferred:

Çocuğ + a   kitab + ı   *kim*   ver + di
child + dat.   book + acc.   who   give + past
'Who gave the book to the child?'

Yes-no questions are formed by suffixing the particle *-mI* to the constituent questioned; if the whole sentence is questioned, the particle is attached to the verb, preceding the subject agreement markers in simple tense/aspect forms and preceding the copula and its tense and agreement markers in complex forms:

(Sen) çocuğ + a   kitab + ı   ver + di + n + *mi*
you   child + dat.   book + acc.   give + past + 2 sg. + *mI*
'Did you give the book to the child?
(Sen) çocuğ + a   kitab + ı   ver + ecek + *mi* + y + di +n
                                       +fut. + *mI* + cop. + past + 2 sg.
'Were you going to give the book to the child?'

It should be noted that the particle *-mI* exhibits dual behaviour with respect to the phonology of the language: it is exceptional from the point of view of word stress (rejects domain-final stress), but regular with respect to vowel harmony.

A few examples follow where *-mI* takes a constituent into its scope:

Çocuğ + a   kitab + ı   sen + *mi*   ver + di + n
                              you + *mI*   give + past + 2 sg.
'Was it you who gave the book to the child?'
(Sen)   kitab + ı   çocuğa + a + *mı*   ver + di + n
'Was it the child that you gave the book to?'
(Sen)   çocuğ + a   kitab + ı + *mı*   ver + di + n
'Was it the book that you gave to the child?'

The translations show that such constituent questions correspond to clefted questions in English. (Turkish has also a cleft construction which can enter yes-no questions; formally, the construction consists of a relative clause lacking a head noun.) Note that the questioned constituent is located in the focus position.

One general property of embedded sentences in Turkish is that they lack complementisers that introduce (or terminate) clauses, as say the complementisers *that* or *for...to* in English. But a perhaps even more striking characteristic feature of such clauses is exhibited by their predicates: rather than being fully finite in exhibiting the various tense and aspect markers and their combinations as is the case with verbs of main clauses, the predicates of embedded clauses are 'nominalised' with the help of various morphemes (as we saw in the section on morphology). We also saw that the subject agreement markers on these 'nominalised' predicates come from the nominal rather than the verbal paradigm; one additional criterion for calling these clauses 'nominalised' is that their predicates carry overt case markers:

[Ahmed + in ben + i sev + *diğ* + *in*] + i
    + gen. I + acc. love + fact. n. + 3 sg. (nom.) + acc.
bil + iyor + um
know + pres. prog. + 1 sg.
'I know that Ahmet loves me'
[Ahmed + in ben + i sev + *me* + *sin*] +*i*   isti + yor + um
                              + act./res. n. + 3 sg. (nom.) + acc. want +
'I want Ahmet to love me'

The two 'nominalisation' morphemes exhibited above are the forms exhibited by embedded clauses that function as arguments of the verbs of the higher clause. The semantics of that higher verb and the propositional properties of the clause determine which one of the two morphemes will be chosen, as illustrated by the examples above and their translations.

A subset of the verbs that take clauses with the 'action nominal' marker also take clauses that are marked with the infinitive suffix *-mAK*. These are comparable to English infinitivals in that they necessarily lack overt subjects; note also that they do not carry agreement morphology:

Ben   [sev + il + *mek*]   isti + yor + um
      love + pass. + infin.   want + pres. prog. + 1 sg.
'I want to be loved'

Infinitivals can take case markers, too, and are thus shown to be genuine nominalised clauses, as well:

Ahmet [ben + i   sev + *meğ*] + e   başla + dı
      I + acc.   love + infin. + dat.   start + past
'Ahmet has started loving me'

Clauses which are postpositional objects and adverbial clauses are also nominalised; in part, their morphology and syntax are similar to those of argument clauses as illustrated above and in part somewhat different. But to discuss these details would go beyond the scope of this chapter.

A very small subset of embedded clauses exhibits verbal morphology and syntax identical to that of main sentences. Such clauses occur with verbs of belief and are, essentially, interchangeable with corresponding -*DIK* clauses (i.e. factive nominals) which can also be taken by verbs of belief. In some of the few instances where these constructions have been noted, they have been called 'direct complements'. They are of two types: (a) the embedded subject is marked nominative; the embedded verb exhibits regular verbal subject agreement marking:

Herkes   [(ben) üniversite + ye   başla + *yacağ* + ım]   san + ıyor
everybody I   university + dat. start + fut. + 1 sg.   believe + pres. prog.
'Everybody believes that I shall start university'

(b) the embedded subject is marked accusative; the embedded verb exhibits only tense/aspect marking, but no agreement marking:

Herkes [ben + *i* üniversite + ye   başla   + *yacak*] san + ıyor
              + acc.   + fut.
(Same gloss as for the previous example.)

In addition, there are speakers who also accept a hybrid form where the embedded subject is accusative, but where the embedded verb exhibits regular verbal agreement markers:

Herkes [ben   + *i* üniversite + ye başla   + *yacağ* + ım]   san + ıyor
              + acc.   + fut.   + 1 sg.

Like all modifiers in the language, relative clauses in Turkish precede their heads. The verbs of such clauses are nominalised, and just as is the case with all regular embedded clauses, they lack complementisers. There is a gap in the position of the constituent within the clause that corresponds to the head.

The factive nominal marker -*DIK* is the basic type of morphology in these constructions; -*mA*, the 'result action' nominal, never occurs, and neither does the infinitive. -*DIK* is replaced by the morpheme -*An* where the 'relativised' constituent is a subject, part of a subject or a non-subject of a clause that lacks a subject (e.g. of an intransitive passive construction as in the last example below); yet another difference between the two constructions follows from this last property: -*DIK* is, as usual, followed by nominal agreement morphology; -*An* never is:

> [Ahmed   + *in*   git + *tiğ* + *i*]   okul
>   + gen.   go + *DIK* + 3 sg.   school
> 'the school that Ahmet goes to'
> [okul + a   gid + *en*]   çocuk
> school + dat.   go + *An*   child
> 'the child that goes to school'
> [[oğl + u]   okul + a   gid +*en*]   adam
> son + 3 sg.   school + dat.   go + *An*   man
> 'the man whose son goes to school'
> [gid + *il* + *en*]   okul
> go + pass. + *An*   school
> 'the school that is gone to'

Embedded questions have essentially the shape of regular embedded clauses: they are nominalised. Only -*DIK*-clauses can be embedded questions; -*mA*-clauses cannot. (This probably goes together with the fact that -*DIK*-clauses are independent from the main clause with respect to tense and aspect, since they are overtly marked for at least the future/non-future distinction; -*mA*-clauses lack tense completely and are dependent on the main clause for tense and aspect.) This does not mean that *wh*-elements cannot occur within -*mA*-clauses; when they do, however, the main clause is interpreted as a question rather than the embedded clause, while with -*DIK*-clauses either interpretation is possible:

> Ahmet   [okul + a   *kim* + *in*   git + *tiğ* + in] + i   duy + du
>   school + dat.   who + gen.   go + *DIK* + 3 sg. + acc.   hear + past

This has the embedded question reading: 'Ahmet heard who went to school' and the main clause question reading: 'Who did Ahmet hear goes to school?' (i.e. about whom did Ahmet hear whether he goes to school?'). (These two interpretations are distinguished intonationally, with falling intonation on the main clause verb for the former and slightly rising intonation for the

latter.) This ambiguity disappears when the question element occurs with a
-*mA*-clause:

Ahmet   [okul + a   *kim + in*   git   + *me* + sin] + i   isti + yor
                     who + gen.   + *mA* +   want + pres. prog.
'Who does Ahmet want to go to school?'

The embedded question reading is not possible: '*Ahmet wants whom to go
to school?'.

Yes-no questions are also basically similar to regular embedded clauses,
particularly where constituents of the embedded clause are questioned;
however, where the whole embedded clause is questioned, and where
attachment of the question particle -*mI* is expected on the embedded verb, a
periphrastic construction in the shape of a participial coordinate structure is
found instead (sometimes referred to as an 'A-not-A construction'):

Ahmet   [(ben + im) okul + a   gid + *ip*   git + *me* + *diğ* + im] + i
         I + gen.   go + and   go + neg. + *DIK* + 1 sg. + acc.
                                              sor + du
                                              ask + past
'Ahmet asked whether I go/went to school (or not)'

One cannot say, in this meaning,

*Ahmet [(ben + im) okul + a git + tiğ + im + i + mi] sor + du,

although this is grammatical with the interpretation 'is it about my going to
school that Ahmet asked?'.

One more construction with a main/embedded clause asymmetry in the
sense that a given constraint holding of the embedded structure does not
hold of the main clause is verb-gapping in coordinate structures. In main
clause coordinate structures with identical verbs, either the first or the
second conjunct can lack its verb:

Ahmet   balığ + ı   *pişir + di*,   Mehmet   + *te*   ıstakoz + u
         fish + acc. cook + past   + and lobster + acc.
'Ahmet cooked the fish and Mehmet (cooked) the lobster'
Ahmet balığ + ı, Mehmet + *te* ıstakoz + u *pişir + di*
'Ahmet (cooked) the fish, and Mehmet cooked the lobster'

Most SOV languages (e.g. Japanese) do not allow 'forward gapped'
structures like the first one above. Interestingly enough, Turkish itself does
not allow such structures when they are embedded:

(Ben) [Ahmed + in   balığ + ı,   Mehmed + in + *de*   ıstakoz + u
               pişir + diğ + in] + i   bil + iyor + um
'I know that Ahmet (cooked) the fish and Mehmet cooked the lobster'
*(Ben) [Ahmed + in balığ + ı   *pişir + diğ + in + i*,   Mehmed + in + *de*
                   ıstakoz + u]   bil + iyor + um
'I know that Ahmet cooked the fish and Mehmet (cooked) the lobster'

This concludes our overview of the syntax of Turkish.

Bibliography

For the classification of the Turkic languages, reference may be made to the contributions in Deny et al. (1959). The following works are useful for the historical background to Turkish: Karamanlıoğlu (1972) — an overview of some historical literature, offering the author's own views on the development and geographical typology of the Turkic languages, especially those closely related to Turkish, and a discussion of the language reform — Von Gabain (1963) and Mansuroğlu (1954).

Lewis (1967) is a comprehensive and detailed treatment of the grammar with useful quotations from contemporary literature and the press; Underhill (1976) is a semi-pedagogical grammar, written in an informal generative framework.

Turkish phonology (and not only vowel harmony) has proved of continual interest to generative phonologists, starting with Lees' (1961) pioneering treatment, and new solutions to various problems continue to appear regularly in the generative phonological literature.

The fullest account of the pragmatic functions of Turkish word order is Erguvanlı (1984).

References

Deny, J., K. Grønbech, H. Scheel and Z.V. Togan (eds.) 1959. *Philologiae Turcicae Fundamenta*, vol. 1 (Steiner, Munich)

Erguvanlı, E.E. 1984. *The Function of Word Order in Turkish Grammar* (University of California Press, Berkeley, Los Angeles and London)

Karamanlıoğlu, A. 1972. *Türk Dili — Nereden Geliyor, Nereye Gidiyor* (= Hareket Yayınları, no. 46, Istanbul)

Lees, R.B. 1961. *The Phonology of Modern Standard Turkish* (Indiana University Press, Bloomington)

Lewis, G.L. 1967. *Turkish Grammar* (Oxford University Press, Oxford)

Mansuroğlu, M. 1954. 'The Rise and Development of Written Turkish in Anatolia', in *Oriens*, vol. 7, pp. 250–64.

Menges, K.H. 1959. 'Classification of the Turkic Languages, II', in Deny et al. (1959), pp. 5–10.

Underhill, R. 1976. *Turkish Grammar* (MIT Press, Cambridge, Mass.)

Von Gabain, A. 1963. 'Die Südwest-Dialekte des Türkischen', in *Handbuch der Orientalistik*, I. Abt., 5. Band, 1. Abschn. (E.J. Brill, Leiden), pp. 174–80.

Language Index